ARISTOTLE

THE PHYSICS

BOOKS V–VIII

WITH AN ENGLISH TRANSLATION BY

PHILIP H. WICKSTEED

AND

FRANCIS M. CORNFORD

HARVARD UNIVERSITY PRESS
CAMBRIDGE, MASSACHUSETTS
LONDON, ENGLAND

First published 1934
Reprinted 1935, 1952, 1960, 1968, 1980,
1995, 2000

LOEB CLASSICAL LIBRARY® is a registered trademark
of the President and Fellows of Harvard College

ISBN 0-674-99281-4

Printed in Great Britain by St Edmundsbury Press Ltd,
Bury St Edmunds, Suffolk, on acid-free paper.
Bound by Hunter & Foulis Ltd, Edinburgh, Scotland.

CONTENTS

PREFACE   vii

LIST OF ARISTOTLE'S WORKS   ix

THE PHYSICS

Book V
  Introduction   3
  Text and Translation   6

Book VI
  Introduction   86
  Text and Translation   90

Book VII
  Introduction   204
  Text and Translation   206

Book VIII
  Introduction   264
  Text and Translation   266

INDEX   427

PREFACE

In this volume, as in the previous one, I am solely responsible for the Greek text. I have admitted a few conjectures, some of them adopted from the Oxford translation. As Bywater, among others, has shown, more can be done for Aristotle's text by re-punctuation [a] than by emendation, especially where the style makes no pretence to literary form and no limit can be set to the possibilities of inelegance.

In Book VII. the adoption of Prantl's text (Teubner, 1889) made it necessary to rewrite the translation of Chapters 1-3. In revising the translation as a whole, I have treated Books V. and VII. somewhat differently from Books VI. and VIII. Of Book V. Dr. Wicksteed left a draft marked as needing ' severe revision '; and the same might be said of his version of Book VII. Both Books are comparatively ill-written and obscure. Dr. Wicksteed, in instructions dictated to me just before his death, spoke of Book V. as un-authentic and irrelevant to physics ; and he regarded Book VII. as the work of an acute and competent

---

[a] Editors have missed an opportunity at *Metaphysics* 997 b 23 εἰ γὰρ ἔστιν αἰσθητὰ μεταξὺ καὶ αἰσθήσεις, δῆλον ὅτι καὶ ζῷα ἔσονται μεταξὺ αὐτῶν τε καὶ τῶν φθαρτῶν. Alexander's paraphrase shows that, untroubled by commas, he read (as the sense requires) εἰ γὰρ ἔστιν αἰσθητὰ μεταξύ, καὶ αἰσθήσεις (δῆλον ὅτι) καὶ ζῷα, κτλ.

PREFACE

Aristotelian, but as never having been seen by Aristotle himself. He would have been content to relegate both Books to an appendix. Taking this low estimate of their value, he had not spent nearly so much labour on them as on the other two. I have therefore felt free to revise his version drastically. The interpretations of the obscurer passages are more frequently mine than his. The translation of Books VI. and VIII. was much more carefully finished, and I have held my hand accordingly, though, especially towards the end of VIII., I have partly rewritten some paragraphs and I have, of course, made minor corrections throughout.

In working on this volume I have had the advantage of consulting the very accurate version of R. P. Hardie and R. K. Gaye, which has shown me the way through many difficulties.

Miss R. Wicksteed has revised the proofs of the translation with the greatest care. Her knowledge of mathematics and her familiarity with her father's views have enabled her to suggest improvements in many places, to add some notes (which are not distinguished from Dr. Wicksteed's) on mathematical points, and to rewrite some of the arguments to the chapters. She has also prepared the Index. Our thanks are due to Professor Gilbert Murray, Mr. W. D. Ross, Mr. H. W. B. Joseph, and Professor Neville for advice on various points, and to Mr. Walter Lawrence for preparing the diagrams.

We also wish to thank the Editors of the Series for their patience with long delays.

F. M. CORNFORD

THE TRADITIONAL ORDER of the works of
Aristotle as they appear since the edition of
Immanuel Bekker (Berlin, 1831), and their
division into volumes in this edition.

		PAGES
I.	The Categories (Κατηγορίαι)	1-15
	On Interpretation (Περὶ ἑρμηνείας)	16-24
	Prior Analytics, Books I-II ('Αναλυτικὰ πρότερα)	24-70
II.	Posterior Analytics, Books I-II ('Αναλυτικὰ ὕστερα)	71-100
	Topica, Books I-VIII (Τοπικά)	100-164
III.	On Sophistical Refutations (Περὶ σοφιστικῶν ἐλέγχων)	164-184

(The foregoing corpus of six logical
treatises is known also as the *Organon*).

(*For pages 184-313 see volumes IV-VI.*)

		PAGES
	On Coming-to-be and Passing-away (Περὶ γενέσεως καὶ φθορᾶς)	314-338
	On the Cosmos (Περὶ κόσμου)	391-401
IV.	Physics, Books I-IV (Φυσική)	184-224
V.	Physics, Books V-VIII (Φυσική)	224-267
VI.	On the Heavens, Books I-IV (Περὶ οὐρανοῦ)	268-313

(*For pages 314-338 see volume III.*)

		PAGES
VII.	Meteorologica, Books I-IV (Μετεωρολογικά)	338-390

(*For pages 391-401 see volume III.*)

THE TRADITIONAL ORDER

		PAGES
VIII.	On the Soul, Books I-III (Περὶ ψυχῆς)	402-435
	Parva naturalia :	
	On Sense and Sensible Objects (Περὶ αἰσθήσεως)	436-449
	On Memory and Recollection (Περὶ μνημῆς καὶ ἀναμνήσεως)	449-453
	On Sleep and Waking (Περὶ ὕπνου καὶ ἐγρηγόρσεως)	433-458
	On Dreams (Περὶ ἐνυπνίων)	458-462
	On Prophecy in Sleep (Περὶ τῆς καθ' ὕπνον μαντικῆς)	462-464
	On Length and Shortness of Life (Περὶ μακροβιότητος καὶ βραχυβιότητος)	464-467
	On Youth and Old Age. On Life and Death (Περὶ νεότητος καὶ γήρως. Περὶ ζωῆς καὶ θανάτου)	467-470
	On Respiration (Περὶ ἀναπνοῆς)	470-480
	On Breath (Περὶ πνεύματος)	481-486
IX.	Historia Animalium, Books I-III (Περὶ τὰ ζῷα ἱστορίαι)	486-523
X.	Historia Animalium, Books IV-VI (Περὶ τὰ ζῷα ἱστορίαι)	523-581
XI.	Historia Animalium, Books VII-X (Περὶ τὰ ζῷα ἱστορίαι)	581-639
XII.	Parts of Animals, Books I-IV (Περὶ ζῴων μορίων)	639-697
	On Movement of Animals (Περὶ ζῴων κινήσεως)	698-704
	Progression of Animals (Περὶ πορείας ζῴων)	704-714
XIII.	Generation of Animals, Books I-V (Περὶ ζῴων γενέσεως)	715-789
XIV.	Minor Works :	
	On Colours (Περὶ χρωμάτων)	791-799
	On Things Heard (Περὶ ἀκουστῶν)	800-804
	Physiognomics (Φυσιογνωμονικά)	805-814
	On Plants, Books I-II (Περὶ φυτῶν)	815-830

THE TRADITIONAL ORDER

		PAGES
On Marvellous Things Heard (Περὶ θαυμασίων ἀκουσμάτων) .		830-847
Mechanical Problems (Μηχανικά)		847-858
(For pages 859-930 see volume XV.)		
(For pages 930-967 see volume XVI.)		
On Invisible Lines (Περὶ ἀτόμων γραμμῶν) .		968-972
The Situations and Names of Winds (Ἀνέμων θέσεις καὶ προσηγορίαι) .		973
On Melissus, Xenophanes and Gorgias (Περὶ Μελίσσου, Περὶ Ξενοφάνους, Περὶ Γοργίου)		974-980
XV.	Problems, Books I-XXI (Προβλήματα)	859-930
XVI.	Problems, Books XXII-XXXVIII (Προβλήματα) .	930-967
	(For pages 968-980 see volume XIV.)	
	Rhetoric to Alexander (Ῥητορικὴ πρὸς Ἀλέξανδρον) .	1420-1447
XVII.	Metaphysics, Books I-IX (Τὰ μετὰ τὰ φυσικά) .	980-1052
XVIII.	Metaphysics, Books X-XIV (Τὰ μετὰ τὰ φυσικά) .	1052-1093
	Oeconomica, Books I-III (Οἰκονομικά) .	1343-1353
	Magna Moralia, Books I-II (Ἠθικὰ μεγάλα) .	1181-1213
XIX.	Nicomachean Ethics, Books I-X (Ἠθικὰ Νικομάχεια) .	1094-1181
	(For pages 1181-1213 see volume XVIII.)	
XX.	Athenian Constitution (Ἀθηναίων πολιτεία) .	—
	Eudemian Ethics, Books I-VIII (Ἠθικὰ Εὐδήμεια) .	1214-1249
	On Virtues and Vices (Περὶ ἀρετῶν καὶ κακιῶν) .	1249-1251
XXI.	Politics, Books I-VIII (Πολιτικά) .	1252-1342

THE TRADITIONAL ORDER

PAGES

(For pages 1343-1353 see volume XVIII.)

XXII. " Art " of Rhetoric (Τέχνη ῥητορική) . 1354-1420

(For pages 1420-1447 see volume XVI.)

XXIII. Poetics (Περὶ ποιητικῆς) . . . 1447-1462
[Longinus], On the Sublime
[Demetrius], On Style

ARISTOTLE'S PHYSICS

BOOK V

INTRODUCTION

[Simplicius (*De caelo* 226. 19) tells us that Books I.–IV. of the *Physics* were referred to as the books *Concerning the Principles*,[a] while Books V.–VIII.[b] were called *On Movement*. The earlier Books have, in fact, defined the things which are subject to movement (the contents of the physical world) and analysed certain concepts—Time, Place, and so forth—which are involved in the occurrence of movement. Book V. is a further introduction to the detailed analysis of movement in the last three Books. Certain points of importance may be singled out.

Chapter I. draws the distinction between 'change' (*metabolé*) and 'movement' (*kinesis*).[c] 'Change' is the

---

[a] [*e.g.* at Aristot. *De caelo* 274 a 22.—C.]

[b] [Or VI.–VIII. Simplic. *Phys.* 923.—C.]

[c] [There is no word in English that can be used consistently in its natural sense to represent this use of *kinesis*. 'Motion' suggests to the English ear locomotion only, and in the translation it is normally used where Aristotle is thinking chiefly or solely of locomotion. 'Movement' has been adopted as a conventional rendering; but, as we do not speak of 'movements' of quality or quantity, 'change' has frequently been substituted where the strict distinction between 'change' (*metabolé*), and 'movement' (*kinesis*) is not important. Aristotle himself is not always careful to observe the distinction.

In certain passages where the distinction is important, 'motion' is used for going along a certain track at a certain rate (this is the same for a whole train travelling at 60 miles

3

ARISTOTLE

wider term. It includes (1) the sheer ' coming-into-being '
(*genesis*) of what did not exist, and the reverse passage
into non-existence (' perishing '), the sudden replacement
of one condition by another, and also (2) all processes of
' movement ' proper. ' Movement ' means a passing
which occurs between two positive terms—a starting-
point and a goal—which are called ' contraries ' (or
' opposites '), to distinguish them from the ' contradictories ' positive and negative (' being ' and ' not-being '),
which take their place in the case of ' coming-to-be ' and
' perishing.' The contrary terms do not themselves suffer
' movement '; there is always a subject—the thing
moved—which passes from one to the other.

Chapter II. demonstrates that there are three, and only
three, kinds of ' movement ': (*a*) alteration of *quality*,
(*b*) change of *quantity*, namely, growth and shrinkage,
and (*c*) change of *place*, locomotion. The remaining
categories of existence will not admit ' movement.' A
substance cannot undergo change in respect of its essential being ; if that were changed, it would cease to be the
thing it is, so it can only ' perish ' (pass into not-being).
The category of *Relative* terms is dismissed in a manner
startling to the modern reader who is accustomed to
think of Relations as a class of entity distinct from the
predicates or attributes of a subject. For Aristotle
' relative terms ' (τὰ πρός τι) are merely a not specially
important class of ' predicates.' What we think of as space
relations fall under his other category of Place. Time relations are not mentioned at all: time, regarded as the measure
of all movement, is not itself susceptible of change. So
there remain only changes of quality, quantity, and place.

Chapter III. furnishes definitions of certain terms which
will enter with the discussion of continuity at the beginning of Book VI., viz. *in contact, between, successive,
contiguous, continuous.*

---

an hour and for each of the carriages) ; ' movement ' when
the magnitude of the mobile is also taken into account (the
movement of the whole train is greater than that of any one
carriage).—C.]

4

PHYSICS, V. INTRODUCTION

Chapter IV. enumerates the various senses in which a movement may be said to have *unity*.

Chapter V. defines what is meant by one movement being *contrary* to another. One change of quality, quantity, or place is contrary to another, when one is from A towards B, the other from B towards A, A and B being a pair of contraries or opposites, such as ' white and black,' or ' above and below.'

Chapter VI. considers in what sense *rest* in a given place or condition is contrary either to movement away from, or towards, that place or condition, or to rest in the opposite place or condition.

The book is interspersed with ' problems ' or ' difficulties ' (ἀπορίαι). Some are unimportant objections which might occur to the reader, but can be settled out of hand. Others are questions noted in a preliminary way by the author as calling for detailed consideration at a later stage. This procedure is in accordance with Aristotle's practice in his introductory surveys of the field to be explored. Sometimes he states such a question and leaves it open ; sometimes he very briefly indicates a possible line for the solution.—C.]

ΑΡΙΣΤΟΤΕΛΟΥΣ ΦΥΣΙΚΗΣ

E

CHAPTER I

ARGUMENT

*The ' change' attributed to a thing (in the sense of ' progress'
or ' transition' from one state to another) may be (1) incidental to the change of something else with which it is connected, or (2) may be transferred in our parlance from the
part to the whole, or (3) may be attributable in its proper
sense to the thing in its entirety. And when the change can
be thus properly and integrally attributed to the thing, we
must further distinguish between the several kinds of ' transition.' It may, for instance, be not local (a change of place)
but qualitive (a change of quality), and again subvarieties of
qualitive change may be distinguished (224 a 21–30).*

*This all applies to the agent of the change as well as to the
subject that undergoes it (a 30–34).*

*Moreover, in addition to the proper and integral cause and
subject of the change, we must consider the time in which the
change takes place and the conditions from which, and to
which, the thing that experiences the change passes. This
last point is important. If a bar of cold iron is heated, it is
not heat or coldness that changes, but the iron that changes
or passes from cold to hot. And it is after the point to which
it tends, not that from which it recedes, that the change or
transition is named : the bar ' grows hot' or ' tends heat-*

6

ARISTOTLE'S PHYSICS

BOOK V

CHAPTER I

*wards.' We have already examined the nature of 'move-
ment' (in its extended sense, including 'modification' and
'expansion or contraction') and have now to note that
'shape' and 'state' and 'place' are the 'whence' and
'whither' of change, but are immovable in themselves
(a 34–b 16).*

*It is important, however, to note that these immovable
points of starting and arriving are just as subject to the
distinctions of 'incidental,' 'in virtue of a part,' and
'primary and integral,' as the movements are (b 16–22).*

Summary (b 22–26).

*Dismissing the indeterminate incidental cases and con-
fining ourselves to proper and primary 'changes,' we note
that they reside solely in the primary and integral subject
that experiences the change, and must be in the direction
from one opposite to the other, both opposites being declared
in positive (not negative) terms (b 26–35).*

*This last point must be elaborated. To speak of the 'not-
hot' as the primary and integral 'subject' that undergoes
the change would be idle. For 'knowledge,' or 'sound' or
'angularity' are 'not-hot'; and though 'not-hotness'
may incidentally undergo change when any of these things*

7

ARGUMENT (*continued*)

*do, it cannot be the proper and integral subject of the change.
Taking the ' subject,' then, to be a positive and not a negative,
though the predicate may be a negative, we seem to have three
possibilities. The change (for instance) might be from ' hot
to cold,' from ' hot to not-hot,' or from ' not-hot to hot,' or
from ' not-hot to not-cold.' Obviously the last of these falls
out, for it would include such changes as that from ' treble
to triangular ' (b 35–225 a 12).*

*The forms from ' hot to not-hot ' and its inverse are signi-
ficant if the negation in one term is specific, and is confined
to what is posited by the other term, and if the subject is
potentially capable of renouncing or acquiring (as the case
may be) the shape, state, or place, posited by the ' whither '
of the movement. But if the negation were absolute, e.g.*

224 a 21   Μεταβάλλει δὲ τὸ μεταβάλλον πᾶν τὸ μὲν κατὰ
συμβεβηκός, οἷον ὅταν λέγωμεν τὸ μουσικὸν
βαδίζειν, ὅτι ᾧ συμβέβηκε μουσικῷ εἶναι, τοῦτο
βαδίζει· τὸ δὲ τῷ τούτου τι μεταβάλλειν ἁπλῶς
25   λέγεται μεταβάλλειν, οἷον ὅσα λέγεται κατὰ μέρη·
ὑγιάζεται γὰρ τὸ σῶμα, ὅτι ὁ ὀφθαλμὸς ἢ ὁ θώραξ,
ταῦτα δὲ μέρη τοῦ ὅλου σώματος. ἔστι δὲ δή τι
ὃ οὔτε κατὰ συμβεβηκὸς κινεῖται οὔτε τῷ ἄλλο
τι τῶν αὑτοῦ, ἀλλὰ τῷ αὐτὸ κινεῖσθαι πρῶτον·
30   καὶ τοῦτ' ἐστὶ τὸ καθ' αὑτὸ κινητόν. κατ' ἄλλην
δὲ κίνησιν ἕτερον, οἷον ἀλλοιωτόν· καὶ ἀλλοιώσεως
ὑγιαντὸν ἢ θερμαντὸν ἕτερον.

Ἔστι δὲ καὶ ἐπὶ τοῦ κινοῦντος ὡσαύτως· τὸ μὲν
γὰρ κατὰ συμβεβηκὸς κινεῖ, τὸ δὲ κατὰ μέρος (τῷ

ARGUMENT (*continued*)

'*from hot to non-entity*' *or the inverse, we should be in the face of absolute genesis or absolute annulling, neither of which (if there were such things) would be movements at all, since the one would have no '*whence,*' *and the other no '*whither*' (a 12–34).*

*All change, transition, or movement, then, must be between two positively indicated terms each of which is a member of a specific pair of opposites or is intermediate between the pair. But note that '*shortages*' *can be positively, as well as negatively, indicated (a 34–b 5).*

*An examination of the categories will convince us that '*movement,*' *in its extended sense, must be from and to either quality, or quantity, or place (b 5–9).*

WHEN we say that anything moves or changes, (1) it may be that the change mentioned is incidental to some other change or dependent on it ; as we might say ' here comes Culture,' when it is really the apostle of culture who ' comes,' and incidentally brings culture with him. Or (2) it may be that we ascribe to a whole a change that has taken place in some one of its parts ; for ' the body is healed ' when the diseased eye or chest is cured. But (3) there must always be something that moves or changes, neither incidentally nor in the sense that some part of it moves, but in that it is in motion itself and directly. This last is what is *essentially* capable of movement or change. It is different for each kind of change ; for instance, there is that which is capable of qualitive change, and within the field of qualitive change, there is a distinction between ' what can be healed ' and ' what can be warmed.'

Again, the distinctions now drawn apply to that which causes motion, as well as to that which moves ;

9

224 a τῶν τούτου τι), τὸ δὲ καθ' αὑτὸ πρῶτον· οἷον ὁ
μὲν ἰατρὸς ἰᾶται, ἡ δὲ χεὶρ πλήττει.

Ἐπεὶ δ' ἔστι μέν τι τὸ κινοῦν πρῶτον, ἔστι δέ
τι τὸ κινούμενον, ἔτι ἐν ᾧ (ὁ χρόνος), καὶ παρὰ
224 b ταῦτα ἐξ οὗ καὶ εἰς ὅ (πᾶσα γὰρ κίνησις ἔκ τινος
καὶ εἴς τι· ἕτερον γὰρ τὸ πρῶτον κινούμενον κεὶ
εἰς ὃ κινεῖται καὶ ἐξ οὗ, οἷον τὸ ξύλον καὶ τὸ θερμὸν
καὶ τὸ ψυχρόν, τούτων δὲ τὸ μὲν ὅ, τὸ δὲ εἰς ὅ,
τὸ δὲ ἐξ οὗ), ἡ δὴ κίνησις δῆλον ὅτι ἐν τῷ ξύλῳ,
5 οὐκ ἐν τῷ εἴδει· οὔτε γὰρ κινεῖ οὔτε κινεῖται τὸ
εἶδος ἢ ὁ τόπος ἢ τὸ τοσόνδε. ἀλλ' ἔστι κινοῦν
καὶ κινούμενον καὶ εἰς ὃ κινεῖται (μᾶλλον γὰρ εἰς
ὃ ἢ ἐξ οὗ κινεῖται, ὀνομάζεται ἡ μεταβολή· διὸ καὶ
ἡ ϕθορὰ εἰς τὸ μὴ ὂν μεταβολή ἐστιν—καίτοι καὶ
10 ἐξ ὄντος μεταβάλλει τὸ ϕθειρόμενον—καὶ ἡ γένεσις
εἰς ὄν, καίτοι καὶ ἐκ μὴ ὄντος). τί μὲν οὖν ἐστιν
ἡ κίνησις, εἴρηται πρότερον· τὰ δ' εἴδη καὶ τὰ
πάθη καὶ ὁ τόπος, εἰς ἃ κινοῦνται τὰ κινούμενα,
ἀκίνητά ἐστιν, οἷον ἡ ἐπιστήμη καὶ ἡ θερμότης.
15 (καίτοι ἀπορήσειεν ἄν τις εἰ τὰ πάθη κινήσεις, ἡ
δὲ λευκότης πάθος· ἔσται γὰρ εἰς κίνησιν μεταβολή.

---

[a] [This statement (cf. the summary at 224 b 25) contains
the main point of the paragraph : the change occurs *in* the
subject undergoing it, not in the termini (qualities, quanti-
ties, places) from which the change starts and at which it
ends. Cf. Simplic. 804. 18 πρῶτον δείκνυσιν ἐν τίνι ἐστὶν ἡ
κίνησις. That the change occurs in the moved rather than
in the mover has been shown in Book III., chapter iii.—C.]

[b] [This possible difficulty is due solely to the ambiguity
of the Greek word for ' affection ' (πάθος). Aristotle himself sometimes uses it (instead of πάθησις) for the *process* of
being affected (*e.g.* ' whitening ') as well as for the state

for the healer is primarily a physician and incidentally a man ; and the contusion raised by the fist is said to be raised by the man whose fist it is.

Now, if there is always a thing that causes movement directly and a subject that is moved, and there is also a time *in which* the movement takes place, and further a *whence* and a *whither* (for every movement is ' from that to this,' and the thing that *passes* from ' that ' to ' this ' is distinct from both of them ; the kindling log, for instance, is not itself either the 'heat' into which, nor the ' coldness ' out of which, it passes) —all this being so, the movement, or passing, clearly pertains to the log itself and not to the condition of heat or coldness [a] ; for no quality or place or magnitude either causes movement or experiences it. We have, then, a mover and a moved and the ' whither ' of the movement. (I say the ' whither ' rather than the ' whence,' because it is from its ' whither ' that a process of change takes its name. Thus we call a change into non-existence ' perishing,' though the ' whence ' of the change is existence no less truly than its ' whither ' is non-existence ; and we call it ' genesis ' if its ' whither ' is existence, in spite of non-existence being its ' whence.') Thus, to our previous account of movement we may now add that the ' forms ' and ' conditions ' and ' place,' which are all goals of movement, are themselves without movement, as for instance 'knowledge' and 'heat.' (Yet the question might occur whether anything that affects a subject should not be regarded as a movement,[b] and whether ' whiteness ' does not so affect its subject—in which case there would be a move-

(' whiteness ') resulting from the process.   Bonitz, *Index* 556 a.—C.]

224 b ἀλλ' ἴσως οὐχ ἡ λευκότης κίνησις, ἀλλ' ἡ λεύκανσις).

Ἔστι δὲ καὶ ἐν ἐκείνοις καὶ τὸ κατὰ συμβεβηκός,
καὶ τὸ κατὰ μέρος καὶ κατ' ἄλλο, καὶ τὸ πρώτως
καὶ μὴ κατ' ἄλλο[1]· οἷον τὸ λευκαινόμενον εἰς μὲν
τὸ νοούμενον μεταβάλλει κατὰ συμβεβηκός (τῷ
20 γὰρ χρώματι συμβέβηκε νοεῖσθαι), εἰς δὲ χρῶμα
ὅτι μέρος τὸ λευκὸν τοῦ χρώματος, καὶ εἰς τὴν
Εὐρώπην ὅτι μέρος αἱ Ἀθῆναι τῆς Εὐρώπης, εἰς
δὲ τὸ λευκὸν χρῶμα καθ' αὑτό.

Πῶς μὲν οὖν καθ' αὑτὸ κινεῖται, καὶ πῶς κατα
συμβεβηκός, καὶ πῶς κατ' ἄλλο τι, καὶ πῶς τὸ
25 αὐτὸ πρῶτον, καὶ ἐπὶ κινοῦντος καὶ ἐπὶ κινουμένου,
δῆλον, καὶ ὅτι ἡ κίνησις οὐκ ἐν τῷ εἴδει ἀλλ' ἐν
τῷ κινουμένῳ καὶ κινητῷ κατ' ἐνέργειαν.

Ἡ μὲν οὖν κατὰ συμβεβηκὸς μεταβολὴ ἀφείσθω·
ἐν ἅπασί τε γάρ ἐστι καὶ ἀεὶ καὶ πάντων. ἡ δὲ
μὴ κατὰ συμβεβηκὸς οὐκ ἐν ἅπασιν, ἀλλ' ἐν τοῖς

---

[1] [The mss. have τὸ before both κατ' ἄλλο and μὴ κατ' ἄλλο.
It was excised by Bonitz.—C.]

[a] [In such expressions Aristotle sometimes uses the neuter,
though the thing or subject he has in mind may be a person.
This makes the example of 'travelling to Athens' less odd.
Cf. τὸ βαδίζον, 232 a 4.—C.]
[b] [The phrase used above, 224 a 28 τῷ αὐτὸ κινεῖσθαι
πρῶτον.—C.]

ment, the goal or 'whither' of which would itself
be a movement. But, I take it, it is not really the
affection 'whiteness' that is a movement, but the
process of 'whitening.')

Note, further, that in these unmoving goals of
movement also the distinctions hold between incidental and primary and between 'in virtue of a
part other than the whole' and 'in its own entirety.'
Thus, a thing that is turning white [a] may incidentally
pass into being an object of thought (for the 'being
an object of thought' is incidental to its colour); and
it progresses into 'colour' in virtue of the whiteness
it passes into being a 'part' (species) of the genus
'colour' (just as one might say that so and so had
'gone to Europe' if he had gone to Athens); whereas
the primary fact is that the subject has progressed
into 'white colour.'

So now all is clear as to a movement of a subject as
such 'on its own account,' as contrasted with movement that is 'incidental' or 'in virtue of a part'; as
to what is meant by a thing moving or being moved
'itself directly' [b]; and as to the applicability of these
distinctions alike to the cause of movement and the
subject of movement; and further it is clear that
movement takes place not in the form (which is its
'whence' or 'whither') but in the subject itself
which, being potentially movable, is at the time
actually in motion.

Here, then, we may dismiss the 'incidental' change;
because it is always at work in subjects of all sorts and
in respect of any of their properties. But change
which is not incidental is not found in subjects of all
sorts but moves on the line between terms which are

13

224 b 30 ἐναντίοις καὶ τοῖς¹ μεταξὺ καὶ ἐν ἀντιφάσει· τούτου
δὲ πίστις ἐκ τῆς ἐπαγωγῆς. ἐκ δὲ τοῦ μεταξὺ
μεταβάλλει· χρῆται γὰρ αὐτῷ ὡς ἐναντίῳ ὄντι
πρὸς ἑκάτερον· ἔστι γάρ πως τὸ μεταξὺ τὰ ἄκρα.
διὸ καὶ τοῦτο πρὸς ἐκεῖνα κἀκεῖνα πρὸς τοῦτο
λέγεταί πως ἐναντία· οἷον ἡ μέση βαρεῖα πρὸς
τὴν νήτην καὶ ὀξεῖα πρὸς τὴν ὑπάτην, καὶ τὸ φαιὸν
35 λευκὸν πρὸς τὸ μέλαν καὶ μέλαν πρὸς τὸ λευκόν.

225 a ᾿Επεὶ δὲ πᾶσα μεταβολή ἐστιν ἔκ τινος εἴς τι
(δηλοῖ δὲ καὶ τοὔνομα· μετ’ ἄλλο γάρ τι καὶ τὸ
μὲν πρότερον δηλοῖ τὸ δ’ ὕστερον), μεταβάλλοι
ἂν τὸ μεταβάλλον τετραχῶς· ἢ γὰρ ἐξ ὑποκειμένου
εἰς ὑποκείμενον, ἢ ἐξ ὑποκειμένου εἰς μὴ ὑπο-
5 κείμενον, ἢ οὐκ ἐξ ὑποκειμένου εἰς ὑποκείμενον, ἢ
οὐκ ἐξ ὑποκειμένου εἰς μὴ ὑποκείμενον (λέγω δὲ
ὑποκείμενον τὸ καταφάσει δηλούμενον). ὥστε
ἀνάγκη ἐκ τῶν εἰρημένων τρεῖς εἶναι μεταβολάς
—τήν τε ἐξ ὑποκειμένου εἰς ὑποκείμενον καὶ
τὴν ἐξ ὑποκειμένου εἰς μὴ ὑποκείμενον καὶ τὴν ἐκ
10 μὴ ὑποκειμένου εἰς ὑποκείμενον· ἡ γὰρ οὐκ ἐξ
ὑποκειμένου εἰς μὴ ὑποκείμενον οὐκ ἔστι μεταβολὴ
διὰ τὸ μὴ εἶναι κατ’ ἀντίθεσιν· οὔτε γὰρ ἐναντία
οὔτε ἀντίφασίς ἐστιν.

῾Η μὲν οὖν οὐκ ἐξ ὑποκειμένου εἰς ὑποκείμενον
μεταβολὴ κατ’ ἀντίφασιν γένεσίς ἐστιν, ἡ μὲν
15 ἁπλῶς ἁπλῆ, ἡ δὲ τὶς τινός· οἷον ἡ μὲν ἐκ μὴ
λευκοῦ εἰς λευκὸν γένεσις τούτου, ἡ δὲ ἐκ τοῦ μὴ
ὄντος ἁπλῶς εἰς οὐσίαν γένεσις ἁπλῶς, καθ’ ἣν

---

¹ [τοῖς F, Simplic. 811. 3: ἐν τοῖς al.—C.]

ᵃ [Aristotle notes that he is here using ὑποκείμενον,
‘ subject,’ to mean, not ‘ substance,’ but anything (whether
14

either (*a*) contraries (or their intermediates), or (*b*) contradictories ; as is evident by a survey of instances. A change may start from an intermediate between two contraries because for the purposes of change the intermediate can be treated as opposed to either extreme, so that it may be regarded as a kind of contrary to them, and they to it. Thus, baritone may be contrasted with either bass or alto, and grey is light compared to black and dark compared to white.

Well then, since every transition is from something to something else (for the very word ' trans-ition ' implies a ' going across ' from where you were before to where you are afterwards), there seem to be four ways of transit, as follows. Using ' positive '[a] to mean something denoted by an affirmative term, a transition may be (1) from positive (A) to positive (B), or (2) from positive (A) to negative (not-A), or (3) from negative (not-A) to positive (A), or (4) from negative (not-A) to negative (not-B). But since a transition from not-A to not-B would not be a change at all, because there is no opposition (there are no contraries and no contradiction), it drops out with our exclusion of the ' incidental.' This leaves only three transitions or changes to consider.

Of these (3) the transition from not-A to its contra-dictory A is genesis—either an unqualified ' coming into being ' out of the mere negation or a qualified ' coming to be this or that ' from being not this or that. Thus the transition of *x* from ' not-white ' to ' white ' is a coming-to-be *of white* ; whereas the trans-ition of *x* from simple non-existence to existence is an unqualified coming into being : we mean that *x*

substance or attribute) that is denoted by a *positive* name. —C.]

15

225 a ἁπλῶς γίγνεσθαι καὶ οὐ τὶ γίγνεσθαι λέγομεν. ἡ
δὲ ἐξ ὑποκειμένου εἰς οὐχ ὑποκείμενον φθορά,
ἁπλῶς μὲν ἡ ἐκ τῆς οὐσίας εἰς τὸ μὴ εἶναι, τὶς δὲ
ἡ εἰς τὴν ἀντικειμένην ἀπόφασιν, καθάπερ ἐλέχθη
20 καὶ ἐπὶ τῆς γενέσεως.

Εἰ δὴ τὸ μὴ ὂν λέγεται πλεοναχῶς, καὶ μήτε τὸ
κατὰ σύνθεσιν ἢ διαίρεσιν ἐνδέχεται κινεῖσθαι
μήτε τὸ κατὰ δύναμιν τὸ τῷ ἁπλῶς κατ᾽ ἐνέργειαν
ὄντι ἀντικείμενον (τὸ μὲν γὰρ μὴ λευκὸν ἢ μὴ
ἀγαθὸν ὅμως ἐνδέχεται κινεῖσθαι κατὰ συμβεβηκός
25 —εἴη γὰρ ἂν ἄνθρωπος τὸ μὴ λευκόν—τὸ δὲ
ἁπλῶς μὴ τόδε οὐδαμῶς), ἀδύνατον¹ τὸ μὴ ὂν
κινεῖσθαι· εἰ δὲ τοῦτο, καὶ τὴν γένεσιν κίνησιν
εἶναι· γίγνεται γὰρ τὸ μὴ ὂν (εἰ γὰρ καὶ ὅτι
μάλιστα κατὰ συμβεβηκὸς γίγνεται, ἀλλ᾽ ὅμως
ἀληθὲς εἰπεῖν ὅτι ὑπάρχει τὸ μὴ ὂν κατὰ τοῦ
30 γιγνομένου ἁπλῶς). ὁμοίως δὲ καὶ τὸ ἠρεμεῖν.
ταῦτά τε δὴ συμβαίνει δυσχερῆ τῷ κινεῖσθαι τὸ

---

¹ [ἀδύνατον Met. 1067 b 30 (T, Themistius): ἀδύνατον γὰρ
codd.—C.]

ᵃ [More literally : ' Now if " that which is not " has
several senses, and there can be no movement of " that
which is not," whether we take it (1) in the sense of " the
false, whether affirmatively or negatively stated " or (2) in
the sense of " that which has only potential as opposed to
actual existence in the full sense " (for whereas " what is
not-white " or " not-good " can nevertheless be in movement incidentally—e.g. " that which is not-white " might
be a man—what is simply not a particular thing at all
cannot be in movement in any way), then it is impossible
for " that which is not " to be in movement ; and, that being
so, " coming-to-be " cannot be a movement, for " that which
is not " does come to be.' The next sentence, εἰ γὰρ καὶ ὅτι
μάλιστα κατὰ συμβεβηκὸς γίγνεται (sc. τὸ μὴ ὂν =the shortage
or στέρησις) κτλ. justifies the last statement, that there is

16

has simply come into existence, not that it has ' come-to-be (become) this or that.' In like manner (2) the transition from A to not-A is ' perishing '—either un-qualified if it be from existence to simple non-exist-ence or qualified if it be to the negation of some speci-fied thing asserted of the subject, just as in the case of genesis.

[a] And though ' is ' and ' isn't ' have other significa-tions in addition to ' exists ' and ' does not exist,' yet in no case can that which ' is not ' partake of motion. In assertion or negation it is a relation and not a sub-ject of any kind, of which we say that it ' is ' or ' isn't,' and a relation cannot ' move.' Nor again is the poten-tially existent, that ' does not exist ' actually, capable of motion—except indeed incidentally, in the sense that, if the man moves, his non-paleness or non-excellence incidentally moves with him. Lastly, that which is absolutely ' not anything ' can in no sense move. From all this it follows that genesis cannot be a movement, for, if it were, the non-existent in its transit to existence would have to move. So (how-ever much incidental genesis there may be) the case of absolute genesis would imply that the non-existent was already there and moving. But it cannot be in motion, nor, for that matter, at rest either.[b] Besides these obstacles to any movement of ' that which is

---

[a] genesis of what is not. ' For however true it may be that the coming-to-be of what is not (*i.e.* the shortage) is inci-dental (to the matter that accompanies it), it is none the less true that " non-existent " is predicable of whatever comes-to-be in the unqualified sense.'—C.]

[b] [Later, at 230 a 7, it is explained that for abiding in being (or in not-being), the term ' unchangingness ' should be used, not ' rest,' which is properly opposed to ' move-ment.'—C.]

225 a μὴ ὄν, καὶ εἰ πᾶν τὸ κινούμενον ἐν τόπῳ· τὸ δὲ
μὴ ὂν οὐκ ἔστιν ἐν τόπῳ· εἴη γὰρ ἂν πού. οὐδὲ
δὴ ἡ φθορὰ κίνησις· ἐναντίον μὲν γὰρ κινήσει ἢ
κίνησις ἢ ἠρεμία, ἡ δὲ φθορὰ γενέσει ἐναντίον.

Ἐπεὶ δὲ πᾶσα κίνησις μεταβολή τις, μεταβολαὶ
δὲ τρεῖς αἱ εἰρημέναι, τούτων δὲ αἱ κατὰ γένεσιν
225 b καὶ φθορὰν οὐ κινήσεις (αὗται δ᾽ εἰσὶν αἱ κατ᾽
ἀντίφασιν), ἀνάγκη τὴν ἐξ ὑποκειμένου εἰς ὑποκείμενον μεταβολὴν κίνησιν εἶναι μόνην. τὰ δὲ
ὑποκείμενα ἢ ἐναντία ἢ μεταξύ (καὶ γὰρ ἡ στέρησις
κείσθω ἐναντίον, καὶ δηλοῦται καταφάσει—τὸ
5 γυμνὸν καὶ νωδὸν[1] καὶ μέλαν).

Εἰ οὖν αἱ κατηγορίαι διήρηνται οὐσίᾳ καὶ
ποιότητι καὶ τῷ ποῦ καὶ τῷ ποτὲ καὶ τῷ πρός τι
καὶ τῷ ποσῷ καὶ τῷ ποιεῖν ἢ πάσχειν, ἀνάγκη
τρεῖς εἶναι κινήσεις—τήν τε τοῦ ποιοῦ καὶ τὴν τοῦ
ποσοῦ καὶ τὴν κατὰ τόπον.

[1] [νωδὸν Prantl, following some MSS. at *Met.* 1068 a 7.—C.]

CHAPTER II

ARGUMENT

[*The statement that there are only three kinds of 'movement'
—change of quality, of quantity, and of place—is established
by showing that things belonging to the other categories do
not admit of change.*

A substance (*though it can 'come into being'*) cannot
change into its contrary, for it has none (225 b 10–11).

not,' it may be urged, further, that anything that moves must have position, which the non-existent cannot have, since it is not anywhere. Neither can perishing be a movement ; for the opposite of a movement is either movement or rest, whereas the opposite of perishing is genesis.

Since, then, every movement is a transition, and two of the three forms of transition, viz. genesis and perishing (which are transits to and from contradictory opposites) are not movements, it remains that the only transition that is a movement is that from positive to positive. And these positive terms may be either contrary or intermediate ; for we must count shortage (which can often be expressed by a positive term, such as ' naked,' ' toothless,' or ' black') as a contrary.[a]

If, then, the categories are enumerated as substantive existence, quality, whereness, whenness, relation, quantity, action, and being-acted-on, it follows that there are three kinds of movement— qualitive, quantitive, and local.

[a] [This paragraph concludes the argument of the chapter. The next should stand at the beginning of chap. ii., the main thesis of which it announces.—C.]

CHAPTER II

ARGUMENT (continued)

A relative term *cannot change, except incidentally* (b 11–13).

In the category of action or passion (*which would include the active ' moving ' and the passive ' being moved '*) *there can be no change of any sort of change* (*including generation*) (b 13–16). *A series of proofs follows* :

19

ARGUMENT (continued)

(1) (a) *A change is not a subject such as can undergo a change of quality, quantity, or place ; and if* (b) *we merely mean that something other than the change itself passes from one process of change into another process of change, it is this subject that changes from one to the other ; the first process of change does not itself pass into the second process of change. So we have not a change* of *a change* (b 16–33).

(2) *Change of change, and, in particular, generation of generation, would involve an infinite regress* (b 33–226 a 6).

(3) *Generation of generation would involve perishing of generation, which could occur only when generation is coming into being. This is absurd* (a 6–10).

(4) *In a change of change what can serve as the necessary* subject *to undergo the change, and what does it change into ?* (a 10–16).

(5) *Since there are only three kinds of change (of quality,*

225 b 10 Κατ' οὐσίαν δ' οὐκ ἔστι κίνησις, διὰ τὸ μηδὲν εἶναι οὐσίᾳ τῶν ὄντων ἐναντίον.

Οὐδὲ δὴ τοῦ[1] πρός τι· ἐνδέχεται γὰρ θατέρου μεταβάλλοντος ⟨μὴ⟩[2] ἀληθεύεσθαι θάτερον μηδὲν μεταβάλλον, ὥστε κατὰ συμβεβηκὸς ἡ κίνησις αὐτῶν.

Οὐδὲ δὴ ποιοῦντος καὶ πάσχοντος, οὐδὲ παντὸς

---

[1] [τοῦ om. E Simplic. 834. 20 (lemma): τῷ cett. τοῦ is read by Dr. Ross at *Met.* 1868 a 11 with A[b].—C.]

[2] [⟨μὴ⟩ Schwegler (*cf. Met.* 1067 b 19).—C.]

---

[a] [Aristotle's doctrine of substance, with its logical premiss : ' every proposition has a subject and a predicate,' precluded him from recognizing relations as a class of entity distinct from predicates and subsisting *between* subjects without belonging to, or inhering in, them. In his view, a woman loses her relative predicate ' wife ' when her husband dies, her loss being ' incidental ' to the change (perishing) which occurs in the husband ; no change of any

ARGUMENT (continued)

quantity, place) the change which undergoes change as well as the change it undergoes must be of one of these kinds ; which leads to absurdities (a 16–19).

The conclusion is : a change can change only in the incidental sense already dismissed (a 19–23).

There remain, then, only three kinds of ' change ' : (1) of quality, called ' modification,' (2) of quantity, ' increase ' and ' decrease,' and (3) of place, ' locomotion ' (a 23–b 1).

A note, pointing out that ' modification ' includes changes in degree of the same quality, e.g. from ' sweet ' to ' sweeter ' or ' less sweet ' (b 1–8).

The various meanings of ' moveless ' : (1) ' essentially immovable ' ; (2) ' hard to move ' ; (3) ' not moving, though movable.' Only this last can be properly described as ' at rest ' (b 8–16).

Summary (b 16–17).—C.]

THE field on which movement takes place is not that of substantive existence ; for movement is between contraries, and there is nothing contrary to substance.

Nor is it relation ; for, when one of two related subjects changes, the relative term may cease to be true of the other, though that other has not changed at all.[a] All changed relation, then, must be incidental to something else.

Nor is it action and passion, whether in the wide

of the types Aristotle recognizes has occurred in the wife. What we regard as space relations fall under his category of Place. If I move my position, a pillar which was ' on the right ' ceases to be ' on the right,' though the pillar has not moved. Here the change in the relative term from ' on the right ' to ' not on the right ' is *incidental* to a change (*per se*) of place on the part of the other subject. *Cf.* Themistius 170. 21 ; Alex. *ap.* Simplic. 834. 27. At 246 b 11 Aristotle says that ' relative terms ' (τὰ πρός τι) are not subject to coming-into-being or change of any kind.—C.]

25 b 15 κινουμένου καὶ κινοῦντος, ὅτι οὐκ ἔστι κινήσεως κίνησις οὐδὲ γενέσεως γένεσις, οὐδ' ὅλως μεταβολὴ μεταβολῆς.

Πρῶτον μὲν γὰρ διχῶς ἐνδέχεται κινήσεως εἶναι κίνησιν· ἢ ὡς ὑποκειμένου, οἷον ὁ ἄνθρωπος κινεῖται ὅτι ἐκ λευκοῦ εἰς μέλαν μεταβάλλει, ὥστε οὕτω[1] καὶ ἡ κίνησις ἢ θερμαίνεται ἢ ψύχεται ἢ τόπον μεταλλάττει ἢ αὐξάνεται ἢ φθίνει—τοῦτο
20 δὲ ἀδύνατον· οὐ γὰρ τῶν ὑποκειμένων τι ἡ μεταβολή—ἢ τῷ ἕτερόν τι ὑποκείμενον ἐκ μεταβολῆς μεταβάλλειν εἰς ἕτερον εἶδος, οἷον ἄνθρωπος ἐκ νόσου εἰς ὑγίειαν. ἀλλ' οὐδὲ τοῦτο δυνατὸν πλὴν κατὰ συμβεβηκός. αὕτη γὰρ ἡ κίνησις ἐξ ἄλλου

[1] [ὥστε οὕτω *Met.* 1068 a 18: οὕτω EH: ἆρά γε οὕτω cett.—C.]

---

[a] [' Subject ' here means that which *undergoes* change and persists through it. That all change between two contraries involves this third term was proved in Book I. chap. vi. —C.]

[b] [The argument is very obscure. I suggest the following as a more literal rendering. ' Or (*b*) change of change might occur in virtue of some subject, other than the change itself, shifting out of a process of change (towards a certain condition) into a change towards some different condition. For instance, a man passing from sickness to health (might shift into a change towards some other condition). But this (change in the subject's changes) is only possible *incidentally*.' (Aristotle proceeds to prove that it can only be incidental by arguing that the second change, into which the subject passes out of his original change, can only be the reverse of that original change. If he is falling ill, the shift can only be getting well : we can't imagine a process of falling ill turning into any other sort of process.) ' For this latter change (viz. the change towards some different condition) is a change from one condition towards another—this is true of any change, including becoming and perishing,

22

sense of the terms or as they are applied to the
agent and patient of movement ; for there can be
neither movement of movement, nor generation of
generation, nor, in general, change of change.

For (1) in the first place, there can only be two
conceivable senses in which movement of movement
could be understood. (*a*) It might mean that a
movement was itself the subject *a* or mobile, corresponding to the man who changes from fair to dark,
so that in the same way movement is warmed or
chilled, or removes to another place, or expands or
contracts. But this is impossible, for movement is
not a subject at all. *b* Or (*b*) it might mean that
some subject, other than the movement itself, might
pass out of one process of change into another, as a
man may pass from disease to health. But neither is
this possible except incidentally ; for this movement
itself must be along a definite line from one ' form '

though the terms are contradictories in becoming and
perishing, contraries in the case of movement. Our man,
then, is changing simultaneously (1) from health to sickness,
and (2) from this original process of sickening into another
process of change (towards some other condition). It appears,
then, that, after he has begun to fall ill, he is to have changed
into (that other supposed process of change) whatever it may
be—for (logically, though not in the case supposed) it might
be (not another change but) a state of rest—and further that
this other change must, in any case, be not any random change
(but of the appropriate kind), and it must be a change from
some one definite condition to another. It follows that this
change must be actually the reverse change—getting well.
But (falling ill cannot itself change into getting well ; so) the
change occurs incidentally, just as, supposing there is a
change from the process of recollecting to the process of
forgetting, that is only because the subject to whom the
processes belong is changing, now into a state of knowledge,
now into a state of ignorance.'—C.]

225 b εἴδους εἰς ἄλλο ἐστὶ μεταβολή. (καὶ ἡ γένεσις δὲ
25 καὶ ἡ φθορὰ ὡσαύτως, πλὴν αἱ μὲν εἰς ἀντικείμενα
ὡδί, ἡ δὲ ὡδί—ἡ κίνησις.[1]) ἅμα οὖν μεταβάλλει
ἐξ ὑγιείας εἰς νόσον καὶ ἐξ αὐτῆς ταύτης τῆς
μεταβολῆς εἰς ἄλλην. δῆλον δὴ ὅτι ὅταν νοσήσῃ,
μεταβεβληκὸς ἔσται εἰς ὁποιανοῦν (ἐνδέχεται γὰρ
ἠρεμεῖν) καὶ ἔτι εἰς μὴ τὴν τυχοῦσαν ἀεί, κἀκείνη
30 ἔκ τινος εἴς τι ἕτερον· ὥστε καὶ ἡ ἀντικειμένη
ἔσται, ἡ ὑγίανσις. ἀλλὰ τῷ συμβεβηκέναι, οἷον
εἰ ἐξ ἀναμνήσεως εἰς λήθην μεταβάλλει ὅτι ᾧ
ὑπάρχει ἐκεῖνο μεταβάλλει, ὁτὲ μὲν εἰς ἐπιστήμην
ὁτὲ δὲ εἰς ἄγνοιαν.[2]

Ἔτι εἰς ἄπειρον βαδιεῖται, εἰ ἔσται μεταβολῆς
μεταβολὴ καὶ γενέσεως γένεσις. ἀνάγκη δὴ καὶ
35 τὴν προτέραν, εἰ ἡ ὑστέρα ἔσται· οἷον εἰ ἡ ἁπλῆ
226 a γένεσις ἐγίγνετό ποτε, καὶ τὸ γιγνόμενον ἐγίγνετο·
ὥστε οὔπω ἦν γιγνόμενον ἁπλῶς ἀλλά τι γιγνόμενον

---

[1] [ἡ δὲ ὡδί—ἡ κίνησις Simplic. 840. 6, Met. 1068 a 25 A[b]:
ἡ ὡδὶ ἡ κίνησις in lit. E: ἡ δὲ κίνησις H: ἡ δὲ κίνησις οὐχ ὁμοίως
FI.—C.]
[2] [ἄγνοιαν Smith (cf. Ross, Met. 1068 a 33): ὑγίειαν codd.
—C.]

---

[a] [More literally, understanding ἀνάγκη δὴ καὶ τὴν
προτέραν (γένεσιν εἶναι γενέσεως γένεσιν), εἰ ἡ ὑστέρα ἔσται
(γενέσεως γένεσις). ' If there is to be a process of coming-
into-being B, resulting in the (final) coming-into-being A,
that earlier process B must itself result from a still earlier
process C. Thus, if our (final) simple process A was ever in
process of coming-into-being, then that which was coming-
to-be it was itself in process of coming-into-being, so that
we should not yet have arrived at something simply coming-
into-being, but only at something that was already coming-

24

to another. (The same principle applies to genesis
and perishing as well as to movement, only that the
terms in the former case are direct contradictories
and in the latter case not so, though contrasted.)
We are to suppose, then, that the subject changes
from health to sickness and at the same time changes
out of this change into some other. Now it is obvious
enough that when he has actually become sick, he
may start upon any other change or cease to change
at all ; but this is one change *succeeding* (or not)
another, it is not one change *changing into* another.
And each successive change must always be along
a definite line, though it might be along any one of
all the possible lines, including the direct opposite of
the one it succeeds—in this case the change from
sickness to health. But naturally the *subject* of
change may incidentally carry with him his change
of one kind into a change of another kind that he
enters into while the first change is going on ; for
instance, he may shift from the process of recollecting
something and so arriving at knowledge to the process of forgetting it and so arriving at ignorance.

(2) Again, if genesis is to have a genesis, and
there is to be change of change, then we must go
back *ad infinitum*. The consequent necessarily presupposes the antecedent,[a] so that if the ultimate
genesis was once in the course of being generated,
the ultimate generand was at best only in procéss
of being generated there, even though the subject
that was in course of becoming

to-be-something-that-was-coming-to-be. And this again was
at some time coming-into-being, so that even then we
should not yet have something (simply) coming-into-being.'
—C.]

226 a [καὶ]¹ γιγνόμενον ἤδη· καὶ πάλιν τοῦτ' ἐγίγνετό
ποτε, ὥστ' οὐκ ἦν πω τότε γιγνόμενον. ἐπεὶ²
δὲ τῶν ἀπείρων οὐκ ἔστι τι πρῶτον, ὥστ' οὐδὲ τὸ
5 ἐχόμενον. οὔτε γίγνεσθαι οὖν οὔτε κινεῖσθαι οἷόν
τε οὔτε μεταβάλλειν οὐδέν.

Ἔτι τοῦ αὐτοῦ κίνησις ἢ ἐναντία (καὶ ἔτι
ἠρέμησις), καὶ γένεσις καὶ φθορά, ὥστε τὸ γιγνόμενον, ὅταν γένηται³ γιγνόμενον, τότε φθείρεται·
οὔτε γὰρ εὐθὺς γιγνόμενον οὔθ' ὕστερον· εἶναι γὰρ
10 δεῖ τὸ φθειρόμενον.

Ἔτι ὕλην δεῖ ὑπεῖναι καὶ τῷ γιγνομένῳ καὶ τῷ
μεταβάλλοντι. τίς οὖν ἔσται; ὥσπερ τὸ ἀλλοιωτὸν
ἢ σῶμα ἢ ψυχή, οὕτω τί τὸ γιγνόμενον κίνησις
ἢ γένεσις; καὶ πάλιν τί εἰς ὃ κινοῦνται; δεῖ γὰρ

---

¹ [καὶ excised by Bonitz, who also (perhaps rightly) cut
out τι before γιγνόμενον.—C.]

² [ἐπεὶ . . . ἐχόμενον Met. 1068 b 4 Aᵇ. The unfamiliarity
of ὥστε in apodosi (for which cf. 232 a 2 and 13) would lead
to the two obvious attempts to supply a main clause which
appear in the alternative readings: (1) ἐπὶ (for ἐπεὶ) in
Simplicius 846. 24 (with omission of τι, as in E here), and (2)
ἐπεὶ δὲ τῶν ἀπ. οὐκ ἔστι τι πρῶτον, οὐκ ἔσται τὸ πρῶτον, ὥστ' κτλ.,
the reading of most mss. here and at Met. 1068 b 4 (though
F here omits οὐκ ἔστι τι πρῶτον). The superfluity of words
is out of keeping with the style of our passage.—C.]

³ [γένηται EF Met. 1068 b 8: γίγνηται cett. Simplic.
849. 8.—C.]

ᵃ [The Greek is obscure. If a process-of-coming-into-
being (genesis A) could itself be in a process-of-coming-into-
being (genesis B), it must be possible that it should be in
a process-of-perishing. But when? For a thing to perish
it must be 'in being' (εἶναι δεῖ τὸ φθειρόμενον). Hence
our genesis A cannot perish either (1) εὐθὺς γιγνόμενον
(i.e. ἐν ἀρχῇ τοῦ γίγνεσθαι, Simplic.), at the moment when it
enters on the supposed genesis B, for then it was not yet in
being, or (2) ὕστερον, which seems to mean the moment when
genesis B is complete, so that genesis A has come-to-be, and

the generand was. And again, taking the ultimate genesis as itself a generand, *its* genesis was once in process of generation, so that it was not itself yet generated, and so forth. And since there is no first link of our infinitely receding chain, neither is there the next or any following link; so it would be impossible that anything should ever come into existence, or move, or change.

(3) Again, the subject of any specific movement is identically the subject of the contrary movement (and of its cessation in rest) and what is capable of being generated is also capable of being destroyed. If, then, genesis is capable of being generated, it is capable of being destroyed. But when? As it begins? As it ends? No; for to be destroyed a thing must be there to destroy. Genesis, then, would have to be being destroyed while it was being generated; which is impossible.[a]

(4) Again, in a case of genesis, as in all cases of change, there must be a subject which passes from the starting-point to the goal. Thus, in all modifications there must be a body that undergoes the modification, if it be physical, or a mind, if it be mental; but what is the corresponding thing that becomes a movement or a genesis? Besides, what goal can we assign to the genesis of a genesis or the movement of a movement? The goal can only be the move-

all later times. For genesis *A* cannot perish at that moment, since it is the moment when it comes-to-be, or later, because a genesis is not the sort of thing that persists ' in being ' after it has come to be, but is over from that moment. So the only time left for perishing is ὅταν γένηται γιγνόμενον, ' when it has begun to be a thing that is coming-into-being ' and is in the process of genesis *B*. But *during* that process it is coming-into-being and cannot also be in process of perishing.—C.]

226 a εἶναι τὴν τοῦδε ἐκ τοῦδε εἰς τόδε κίνησιν ἢ γένεσιν.[1]
15 ἅμα δὲ πῶς καὶ ἔσται; οὐ γὰρ ἔσται μάθησις ἡ
τῆς μαθήσεως γένεσις, ὥστ᾽ οὐδὲ γενέσεως γένεσις,
οὐδέ τίς τινος.

Ἔτι εἰ τρία εἴδη κινήσεως ἔστι, τούτων τινὰ
ἀνάγκη εἶναι καὶ τὴν ὑποκειμένην φύσιν καὶ εἰς
ἃ κινοῦνται· οἷον τὴν φορὰν ἀλλοιοῦσθαι ἢ φέρεσθαι.

Ὅλως δ᾽, ἐπεὶ κινεῖται τὸ κινούμενον πᾶν
20 τριχῶς, ἢ τῷ κατὰ συμβεβηκὸς ἢ τῷ μέρος τι
ἢ τῷ καθ᾽ αὑτό, κατὰ συμβεβηκὸς μόνον ἂν
ἐνδέχοιτο μεταβάλλειν τὴν μεταβολήν, οἷον εἰ ὁ
ὑγιαζόμενος τρέχοι ἢ μανθάνοι· τὴν δὲ κατὰ
συμβεβηκὸς ἀφεῖμεν πάλαι.

Ἐπεὶ δὲ οὔτε οὐσίας οὔτε τοῦ πρός τι οὔτε τοῦ
ποιεῖν καὶ πάσχειν, λείπεται κατὰ τὸ ποιὸν καὶ τὸ
25 ποσὸν καὶ τὸ ποῦ κίνησιν εἶναι μόνον· ἐν ἑκάστῳ
γάρ ἐστι τούτων ἐναντίωσις. ἡ μὲν οὖν κατὰ τὸ
ποιὸν κίνησις ἀλλοίωσις ἔστω· τοῦτο γὰρ ἐπέζευκ-

---

[1] [δεῖ . . . γένεσιν Simplic. 853. 1 (lemma). The mss.
exhibit various mixtures of this reading with the alternative
reading given in note a.— C.]

---

[a] [The alternative reading δεῖ γὰρ εἶναί τι τὴν τοῦδε ἐκ
τοῦδε εἰς τόδε κίνησιν, καὶ μὴ κίνησιν ἢ γένεσιν would refer
to the first question: what is the subject which undergoes
the becoming or change? The movement itself? No,
for then ' the movement of something from this to that
must be something that is *in being* (and so can undergo the
change and persist through it) and not a movement or
becoming.'—C.]

[b] [Or ' And how can the goal just described ever exist at
all? For the becoming of a process of learning will never
actually *be* the process of learning; so neither will the
becoming of " becoming " (ever actually *be* " becoming ")

28

ment or genesis of something from something to something else.[a] [b] And how could the motion be at the same time the station in which it ceases ? If the generating process were coming to know, the goal would be knowledge, not coming to it. So with all else, and so with genesis : the goal cannot be genesis, but the something generated.

(5) Again, if there are only three kinds of 'movement' in the wide sense, both the movement which is supposed to undergo the change and the movement into which it changes can only be a movement of one of these three kinds ; thus a local movement must undergo a process of qualitative modification or be itself locally moved.

In conclusion, then, since any subject of movement moves in one of three ways—either incidentally, or in virtue of a part, or primarily, it is only in the incidental sense that a change can be changing, as, for instance, when a man who is recovering his health carries his 'recovering' with him as he changes his place in a race or passes from ignorance to knowledge of something. And we have already agreed to dismiss the 'incidental' sense of change from our consideration.[c]

Since, then, movement can ·pertain neither to substantive being nor to relation nor to acting and being acted on, it remains that it pertain exclusively to quality, quantity, and locality, each of which embraces contrasts. Movement in quality is what we call 'modification,' which is a common term applicable to change in either direction between the

nor will the particular becoming of any particular " becoming " (ever *be* that particular " becoming ").'—C.]

  [c] [At 224 b 26.—C.]

226 a ται κοινὸν ὄνομα. λέγω δὲ τὸ ποιὸν οὐ τὸ ἐν τῇ
οὐσίᾳ (καὶ γὰρ ἡ διαφορὰ ποιότης) ἀλλὰ τὸ παθητικόν, καθ' ὃ λέγεται πάσχειν ἢ ἀπαθὲς εἶναι. ἡ
30 δὲ κατὰ τὸ ποσὸν τὸ μὲν κοινὸν ἀνώνυμος,[1] καθ'
ἑκάτερον δ' αὔξησις καὶ φθίσις—ἡ μὲν εἰς τὸ
τέλειον μέγεθος αὔξησις, ἡ δ' ἐκ τούτου φθίσις.
ἡ δὲ κατὰ τόπον καὶ τὸ κοινὸν καὶ τὸ ἴδιον ἀνώνυμος, ἔστω δὲ φορὰ καλουμένη τὸ κοινόν· καίτοι
λέγεταί γε ταῦτα φέρεσθαι μόνα κυρίως, ὅταν μὴ
35 ἐπ' αὐτοῖς ᾖ τὸ στῆναι τοῖς μεταβάλλουσι τὸν
226 b τόπον, καὶ ὅσα μὴ αὐτὰ ἑαυτὰ κινεῖ κατὰ τόπον.

Ἡ δὲ ἐν τῷ αὐτῷ εἴδει μεταβολὴ ἐπὶ τὸ μᾶλλον
καὶ ἧττον ἀλλοίωσίς ἐστιν. ἡ γὰρ ἐξ ἐναντίου
εἰς ἐναντίον κίνησίς ἐστιν ἢ ἁπλῶς ἢ πῇ· ἐπὶ μὲν
γὰρ τὸ ἧττον ἰοῦσα εἰς τοὐναντίον λεχθήσεται
5 μεταβάλλειν, ἐπὶ δὲ τὸ μᾶλλον ὡς ἐκ τοὐναντίου
εἰς αὐτό. διαφέρει γὰρ οὐδὲν πῇ μεταβάλλειν ἢ
ἁπλῶς, πλὴν πῇ δεήσει τἀναντία ὑπάρχειν· τὸ δὲ

---

[1] [ἀνώνυμος E: ἀνώνυμον cett., but ἀνώνυμος (ἀνώνυμοι I) in
l. 33].

---

a [Unlike 'growth' (in quantity), which means only
transition in one direction, from small to large.—C.]

b [τὸ ἐν τῇ οὐσίᾳ πάθος, a quality which constitutes the
differentia of an essence, e.g. 'having no angles,' when
'circle' is defined as 'a figure having no angles' (Met.
1020 a 33). A thing cannot part with such a quality without
ceasing to be the thing it is (being destroyed).—C.]

c [The Greek φέρεσθαι, though it often means 'to move
(voluntarily) from place to place,' is passive in form, and
strictly means 'to be borne (along).' Aristotle eliminates

contraries concerned.[a] By quality I do not mean any quality that is of the essence of the thing that undergoes the change [b] (though its differentia is of course a quality in the general sense of the word), but that passive quality with regard to which it is said to be ' affected ' or to be incapable of being affected. As to quantity, there is no general term that applies equally to changes in either direction between greater and less ; but ' increase ' is used for the movement towards the full size, ' decrease' for movement in the contrary direction. As to motion from place to place, we have neither common nor particular terms, but let ' locomotion ' pass as the common term, though the Greek word [c] in its strict sense applies only to things which, in changing their place, have not the power to stop, and to things that do not move *themselves* from place to place.

The change towards a greater or a less degree of the same quality is a ' modification ' [d] ; for the movement from contrary to contrary may be either complete or partial. If a thing moves towards the lesser degree of one contrary it is said to be changing towards the other, and if towards the greater degree, to be changing from the other. Nor is there any difference between complete and partial change save in the partial persistence of both contraries in

this suggestion from φορά—his regular name for ' locomotion ' generally.—C.]

[d] [The term ' modification ' includes (besides changes from white to black and from black to white) the changes from ' white ' (*i.e.* prevailingly white, *cf.* p. 191) to ' whiter ' or to ' less white.' The change from ' white ' to ' less white ' can be described as a change *towards* the contrary ' black '; that from ' white ' to ' whiter ' as a change *from* the contrary black towards white itself (εἰς αὐτό).—C.]

226 b μᾶλλον καὶ ἧττόν ἐστι τῷ πλέον ἢ ἔλαττον ἐνυπάρχειν τοὐναντίον καὶ μή.

Ὅτι μὲν οὖν αὗται τρεῖς μόναι κινήσεις εἰσίν,
10 ἐκ τούτων δῆλον.

Ἀκίνητον δ' ἐστὶ τό τε ὅλως ἀδύνατον κινηθῆναι
(ὥσπερ ὁ ψόφος ἀόρατος), καὶ τὸ ἐν πολλῷ χρόνῳ
μόλις κινούμενον ἢ τὸ βραδέως ἀρχόμενον (ὃ
λέγεται δυσκίνητον), καὶ τὸ πεφυκὸς μὲν κινεῖσθαι
καὶ δυνάμενον μὴ κινούμενον δὲ τότε ὅτε πέφυκε
15 καὶ οὗ καὶ ὥς, ὅπερ ἠρεμεῖν καλῶ τῶν ἀκινήτων
μόνον· ἐναντίον γὰρ ἠρεμία κινήσει, ὥστε στέρησις
ἂν εἴη τοῦ δεκτικοῦ.

Τί μὲν οὖν ἐστι κίνησις καὶ τί ἠρεμία, καὶ
πόσαι μεταβολαὶ καὶ ποῖαι κινήσεις, φανερὸν ἐκ
τῶν εἰρημένων.

---

[a] [Cf. 229 a 2, ' a lesser degree of something always means an admixture of the contrary.'—C.]

[b] [Cf. Simplic. 865. 11, who instances the fixed stars, whose risings shift only a degree in a hundred years. But Aristotle may mean the popular use of ' immovable ' for ' that which can only be moved by a great effort taking a long time.' This can be described *alternatively* (ἤ) as ' slow to begin ' or ' hard to move.'—C.]

CHAPTER III

ARGUMENT

[*Certain terms which will occur in the analysis of motion, must be defined* (226 b 18–21).

Things are together *in place when they are in the same proper place. Things* touch *when their extremes are in this sense ' together '* (b 21–23). Between *is applicable only to change (of quality, quantity, or place) where the opposite extremes are contraries, not to ' becoming,' where they are contradictories* (227 a 7–10). *A term is* between *two other*

32

the latter ; and the difference of degree means the presence or absence in it of more or less of the other contrary.[a]

The conclusion is now established that the three movements examined are the only ones that there are.

We say a thing is ' moveless ' either because by its nature it is insusceptible of motion (as a sound is invisible) ; or because its movement is so slow as to be hardly perceptible,[b] or because it is ' slow to begin,' [c] which is equivalent to ' inapt to move,' or lastly because, though it could move under given conditions of time, place, and manner, it is not actually moving. And it is only to this last class of ' moveless ' things that I apply the term ' rest.' For rest is the contrary of motion and must therefore be the shortage of that which might by nature be present to the subject in question.

We have now elucidated the questions, what motion is, and what station or rest, and how many kinds of change there are, and how many of motion.

[c] As a man may be ' slow to wrath ' (Themistius).

CHAPTER III

ARGUMENT (continued)

terms, if something that changes continuously reaches it before reaching the extreme or contrary. Meanings of 'continuously changing,' and of ' contrary ' as applied to local movement (226 b 23–34).

A thing is next-in-succession to another, if it comes after the starting-point and has nothing of the same kind between it and that which it succeeds (b 34–227 a 6).

ARISTOTLE

ARGUMENT (continued)

If it is next-in-succession and also touches the other, it is contiguous (a 6–7).

The continuous is a species of the contiguous, found where the extremities of the two things coalesce into one or are bound to be together (a 10–17).

Of these last three terms, ' next-in-succession' is implied

26 b 18 Μετὰ δὲ ταῦτα λέγωμεν τί ἐστι τὸ ἅμα καὶ χωρίς, καὶ τί τὸ ἅπτεσθαι, καὶ τί τὸ μεταξύ, καὶ 20 τί τὸ ἐφεξῆς, καὶ τί τὸ ἐχόμενον καὶ συνεχές, καὶ τοῖς ποίοις ἕκαστον τούτων ὑπάρχειν πέφυκεν.

Ἅμα μὲν οὖν λέγεται ταῦτ' εἶναι κατὰ τόπον, ὅσα ἐν ἑνὶ τόπῳ ἐστὶ πρώτῳ, χωρὶς δὲ ὅσα ἐν ἑτέρῳ·

---

a The term 'together' is somewhat misleading, for it suggests close proximity rather than absolute identity of position. We speak of things being together when we mean that their *common* place includes little besides their several proper places, as sheep in a fold or a concourse of people in a hall or market-place, and in that sense of the term any number of bodies can be together in one common place. Whereas it is impossible for two bodies to be 'together' in the sense in which the term is used by Aristotle: for two bodies cannot occupy the same space, and as the proper place of a thing includes no space except what is in the occupation of that thing, two bodies cannot exist in the same proper place. On the other hand the several qualities (*e.g.* colour, weight, temperature, etc.) of a thing are bound all to exist 'together' in the sense of each permeating the whole of the space filled by the thing they qualify. Consequently the proper place of each is identical with that of each of the others. (See Vol. I. Introd. pp. liv *sq.*, and Bk. IV. Introd., for the connexion and distinction between space and place.)

Again, *points* which occupy no space at all nevertheless have proper places, defined unequivocally by position, and there is no difficulty about any number of points being

34

ARGUMENT (continued)

*in ' contiguous,' contiguous is implied in ' continuous,'
which therefore comes last in order of genesis (a 17–27).
Polemic against the Pythagorean doctrine of separately
existing monads which are both units of number and
points, i.e. units of magnitude having position in space
(a 27–32).*

Summary (a 32–b 2).—C.]

LET us proceed to consider the meaning of the terms
' together,' ' apart,' ' touching,' ' between,' ' next in
succession (but not touching),' ' contiguous,' and
' continuous,' and the question to what each of the
qualifications so described naturally belongs.

Things are said to be ' *together* ' in place when the
immediate and proper place of each is identical with
that of the other,[a] and ' *apart* ' (or ' severed ') when
this is not so.

'together' in the same proper place, for the presence of one
presents no obstacle to the presence of another.   For instance,
the mid-points of the several diameters of a single sphere
are bound to be 'together' at the centre.

Things which are not bound to be together may happen,
under certain conditions, to be so : *e.g.* the mid-points of
the diameters of different spheres will be together if the
spheres happen to be concentric, but they are no more
bound to be so than the spheres are bound to be concentric.

Things 'touch' each other if any point on the boundary
of the one is in the same proper place as any point on the
boundary of the other.   If these points only happen to be
together, the things are said to be 'contiguous,' if they are
'held together' or in other words are bound to be so, they
are said to be 'continuous.'   [The notion of 'contact' is
more carefully analysed in *De gen. et corr.* 322 b 30 ff.,
and it is there explained in what sense contact is possible
between mathematical entities, as conceived by Aristotle.
—C.]

226 b   ἅπτεσθαι δὲ ὧν τὰ ἄκρα ἅμα.

227 a 7   ⟨Ἐπεὶ δὲ πᾶσα μεταβολὴ ἐν τοῖς ἀντικειμένοις,
τὰ δὲ ἀντικείμενα τά τε ἐναντία καὶ τὰ κατὰ
ἀντίφασιν, ἀντιφάσεως δ' οὐδὲν ἀνὰ μέσον,
φανερὸν ὅτι ἐν τοῖς ἐναντίοις ἔσται τὸ μεταξύ.⟩[1]

226 b μεταξὺ δέ, εἰς ὃ πέφυκε πρότερον[2] ἀφικνεῖσθαι
25 τὸ μεταβάλλον ἢ εἰς ὃ ἔσχατον μεταβάλλει κατὰ
φύσιν συνεχῶς μεταβάλλον. ἐν ἐλαχίστοις δ'
ἐστὶν τὸ μεταξὺ τρισίν· ἔσχατον μὲν γάρ ἐστι τῆς
μεταβολῆς τὸ ἐναντίον, συνεχῶς δὲ κινεῖται τὸ
μηθὲν ἢ ὅτι ὀλίγιστον διαλεῖπον τοῦ πράγματος
—μὴ τοῦ χρόνου (οὐδὲν γὰρ κωλύει διαλείποντα,
30 καὶ εὐθὺς δὲ μετὰ τὴν ὑπάτην φθέγξασθαι τὴν
νεάτην) ἀλλὰ τοῦ πράγματος—ἐν ᾧ κινεῖται.
τοῦτο δὲ ἔν τε ταῖς κατὰ τόπον καὶ ἐν ταῖς ἄλλαις
μεταβολαῖς φανερόν. ἐναντίον δὲ κατὰ τόπον τὸ

---

[1] [This sentence stands here in Themistius. It is clearly out of place in the mss. (here and at *Met.* 1069 a 2) after ἅπτηται in 227 a 7. Prantl proposed to place it after φανερόν 226 b 32. The logic would be improved by also transposing the next sentences thus: ἐν ἐλαχίστοις δ' ἐστὶν τὸ μεταξὺ τρισίν· ἔσχατον μὲν γάρ ἐστι τῆς μεταβολῆς τὸ ἐναντίον, μεταξὺ δέ, εἰς ὃ . . . συνεχῶς μεταβάλλον. συνεχῶς δὲ κινεῖται, κτλ. But Themistius does not support this.—C.]

[2] [πρότερον Them. 172. 24, *Met.* 1068 b 28: πρῶτον codd. —C.]

ᵃ [ἔσχατον μὲν γάρ κτλ.. Literally, 'for *extreme* (as used in the above definition) means the contrary, in a process of change.'—C.]

ᵇ Colour, for instance, or pitch, not necessarily 'distance.' The meaning of the qualification 'only the minimum' has perplexed the commentators, but it is shown at 239 a 20 that there is no minimum of anything continuous, and therefore no break (however small) would be the minimum in a continuous thing. So the definition resolves itself into 'no break.'

ᶜ [*Literally*, 'For there is nothing to prevent one from

36

They ' *touch* ' each other when their extremes are in this sense ' together.'

Since all change is between opposites, and opposites are either contraries or contradictories, and there is nothing between contradictories, it is clear that the intermediate or ' between ' can only exist when there are two contraries. B is ' *between* ' A and C if anything passing (locally or otherwise) by a continuous change in accordance with its nature must necessarily come to B before it reaches the extreme C on its way thereto from A. ' Between ' implies at least three terms : the ' whence ' of the passing, the opposite of the whence, namely the ' whither,' and something on the line of passage, nearer to the whence than the whither is [a] ; and the passage is 'continuous' if there is no break or leap in the course—or, if any, only the minimum. I am speaking of a break not in time, but in that with respect to which the changing thing is changing [b] ; for in time the bottom note of the diapason may be followed by the top note (which constitutes the maximum possible break or leap in the scale) just as immediately as any two notes severed by the smallest conceivable interval.[c] All which applies not only to changes of place but the other kinds of change as well. In the local application of the word, one thing is the ' contrary ' of another, if it is farther from it, in a straight line, than any other individual thing leaving a gap (in time, and yet covering the whole course " continuously," *e.g.* a man walking from London to Cambridge may stop a night at Hitchin and yet cover every yard of the road), and, on the other hand, the highest note can be sounded by a player immediately after the lowest ' (but then, though there is no gap in time, he will not have covered the musical interval 'continuously.' So continuity of time does not involve continuity in the change. *Cf.* 264 b 6).—C.]

37

226 b κατ' εὐθεῖαν ἀπέχον πλεῖστον· ἡ γὰρ ἐλαχίστη
πεπέρανται, μέτρον δὲ τὸ πεπερασμένον.

35 Ἐφεξῆς δὲ οὗ μετὰ τὴν ἀρχὴν ὄντος ἢ θέσει ἢ
227 a εἴδει ἢ ἄλλῳ τινὶ οὕτως ἀφορισθέντος μηδὲν μεταξύ
ἐστι τῶν ἐν ταὐτῷ γένει καὶ οὗ ἐφεξῆς ἐστιν (λέγω
δ' οἷον γραμμὴ γραμμῆς ἢ γραμμαί, ἢ μονάδος
μονὰς ἢ μονάδες, ἢ οἰκίας οἰκία· ἄλλο δ' οὐδὲν
κωλύει μεταξὺ εἶναι). τὸ γὰρ ἐφεξῆς τινι[1] ἐφεξῆς,
5 καὶ ὕστερόν τι· οὐ γὰρ τὸ ἓν ἐφεξῆς τῶν δύο, οὐδ'
ἡ νουμηνία τῆς δευτέρας ἐφεξῆς, ἀλλὰ ταῦτ'
ἐκείνων.

Ἐχόμενον δὲ ὃ ἂν ἐφεξῆς ὂν ἅπτηται.

10 Τὸ δὲ συνεχὲς ἔστι μὲν ὅπερ ἐχόμενόν τι· λέγω
δ' εἶναι συνεχὲς ὅταν ταὐτὸ γένηται καὶ ἓν τὸ
ἑκατέρου πέρας οἷς ἅπτονται καὶ (ὥσπερ σημαίνει
τοὔνομα) συνέχηται· τοῦτο δὲ οὐχ οἷόν τε δυοῖν
ὄντοιν εἶναι τοῖν ἐσχάτοιν. τούτου δὲ διωρισμένου
15 φανερὸν ὅτι ἐν τούτοις ἐστὶ τὸ συνεχὲς ἐξ ὧν ἕν
τι πέφυκε γίγνεσθαι κατὰ τὴν σύναψιν. καὶ ὡς

---

[1] [τινὶ all mss. here. At *Met.* 1068 b 35 A[b] has τινὶ, the rest τινὸς.—C.]

---

[a] [The rendering 'contiguous' is justified because 'in no passage other than the present is there any attempt to distinguish ἐχόμενον from ἁπτόμενον,' Ross on *Met.* 1068 b 26-1069 a 14.—C.]

[b] *Cf. continent* = continuous land unparted by sea, a 'continent' person, one who can 'hold himself together.' In Greek and Latin the etymological implication of the phrase is more general and obvious than in English.

of the same order in the field under consideration. The straight line is chosen because, as the shortest, it is the only definite one between any two positions, and a measure or standard must be definite.

One thing is '*next in succession*' to another if it comes after the point you start from in an order determined by position, or 'form,' or whatsoever it may be, and if there is nothing of its own kind between it and that to which it is said to be next in succession. (By 'nothing of its own kind' I mean, for instance, that there must be no other line or lines between one line and the line to which it is next in succession; or no monad or monads, or no house or houses, between the one next in succession and the one it is next in succession to. But there is nothing against a thing being said to be next in succession to another because things of a different kind to themselves intervene between them.) For what is next in succession must succeed *something* and be a thing that comes later; for no one would say that 'one' comes next in succession to 'two,' or the first of the month to the second, but the other way round.

'*Contiguous*'[a] means next in succession and touching.

Lastly, the '*continuous*' is a subdivision of the contiguous; for I mean by one thing being continuous with another that those limiting extremes of the two things in virtue of which they touch each other become one and the same thing, and (as the very name indicates) are 'held together,'[b] which can only be if the two limits do not remain two but become one and the same. From this definition it is evident that continuity is possible in the case of such things as can, in virtue of their natural constitution,

227 a ποτε γίγνεται τὸ συνέχον ἕν, οὕτω καὶ τὸ ὅλον
ἔσται ἕν, οἷον ἢ γόμφῳ ἢ κόλλῃ ἢ ἁφῇ ἢ προσφύσει.

Φανερὸν δὲ καὶ ὅτι πρῶτον τὸ ἐφεξῆς ἐστιν.
τὸ μὲν γὰρ ἁπτόμενον ἐφεξῆς ἀνάγκη εἶναι, τὸ δ᾽
20 ἐφεξῆς οὐ πᾶν ἅπτεσθαι (διὸ καὶ ἐν προτέροις τῷ
λόγῳ τὸ ἐφεξῆς ἐστι, οἷον ἐν ἀριθμοῖς, ἁφὴ δ᾽
οὐκ ἔστιν). καὶ εἰ μὲν συνεχές, ἀνάγκη ἅπτεσθαι,
εἰ δὲ ἅπτεται, οὔπω συνεχές· οὐ γὰρ ἀνάγκη ἕν
εἶναι αὐτῶν τὰ ἄκρα, εἰ ἅμα εἶεν, ἀλλ᾽ εἰ ἕν,
ἀνάγκη καὶ ἅμα. ὥστε ἡ σύμφυσις ὑστάτη κατὰ
25 τὴν γένεσιν· ἀνάγκη γὰρ ἅψασθαι, εἰ συμφύσεται
τὰ ἄκρα· τὰ δὲ ἁπτόμενα οὐ πάντα συμπέφυκεν,
ἐν οἷς δὲ μὴ ἔστιν ἁφή, δῆλον ὅτι οὐκ ἔστιν οὐδὲ
σύμφυσις ἐν τούτοις.

῞Ωστ᾽ εἰ ἔστι στιγμὴ καὶ μονὰς οἵας λέγουσι κεχω-
ρισμένας, οὐχ οἷόν τε εἶναι μονάδα καὶ στιγμὴν τὸ
αὐτό· ταῖς μὲν γὰρ ὑπάρχει τὸ ἅπτεσθαι, ταῖς δὲ
30 μονάσι τὸ ἐφεξῆς. καὶ τῶν μὲν ἐνδέχεται εἶναί τι

---

[a] *Cf.* Vol. I. Introd. p. l. The more general and
abstract has the rational priority, but the more concrete
and particular the experiential priority. Abstract numbers
are 'nexts.' to each other (for in the abstract there is not a
monad between the monad and the dyad, or between the
two monads of the dyad), but abstract numbers must be
spaced and cannot touch one another.

[b] [Aristotle here draws a controversial conclusion against
those Pythagoreans who identified the monads of which
numbers are composed with points, existing in space, of
which bodies are composed, and interpreted 'All things
(bodies) are numbers' in this literal sense. (See *Met.*
1080 b 16 and Ross *ad loc.*)—C.]

[c] [According to Aristotle, two points cannot touch each
other without coinciding; but he may be thinking of the
Pythagorean 'points,' which had (indivisible) magnitude and

40

become one by touching; and the whole will have the same sort of union as that which holds it together, *e.g.* by rivet or glue or contact or organic union.

It is further evident that of these terms—'next-in-succession,' 'contiguous,' 'continuous'—'next in succession' is the first in logical order. For things that touch each other must be nexts-in-succession, but nexts-in-succession need not be touching; and accordingly 'next-in-succession' is a property of things of a higher order of abstraction, such as numbers, where there is no question of contact.[a] And again, if things make a continuous whole, there must be touching; but if they touch, it does not follow that they become continuous; for it does not follow that their extremities become identical if they come together, but they must have come together if they have become identical. Thus, genetically, natural coalescence comes last of all; for if the extremities are to coalesce, they must come into contact; but not all extremities that come into mutual contact therefore become identified, while obviously things incapable of touching each other are also incapable of natural coalescence.

It follows that if, as they say, there were such things as sejunct points and monads,[b] then the point and the monad could not be identical; for two points could touch each other,[c] but two monads can only be next-in-succession to each other. And between any two points there can be found intermediate points, for

position in space. So far, this argument and the next are *ad homines*; but that numbers (and hence the units composing them) cannot touch is common ground. See the next note.—C.]

227 a μεταξύ (πᾶσα γὰρ γραμμὴ μεταξὺ στιγμῶν), τῶν δ'
οὐκ ἀνάγκη· οὐδὲν γὰρ μεταξὺ δυάδος καὶ μονάδος.

Τί μὲν οὖν ἐστι τὸ ἅμα καὶ χωρίς, καὶ τί τὸ
227 b ἅπτεσθαι, καὶ τί τὸ μεταξὺ καὶ τὸ ἐφεξῆς, καὶ τί
τὸ ἐχόμενον καὶ τὸ συνεχές, καὶ τοῖς ποίοις
ἕκαστον τούτων ὑπάρχει, εἴρηται.

---

a What is actually in the text is 'every line lies between
two points.' So too ' there need not be anything between,
etc.' The commentators are agreed as to the meaning, but the
expression as it stands is strange, not to say perverse.
[Aristotle's logic can be saved by translating: Also
there can be something between two points, for every line is
between points ; but it does not follow (that there can be
anything) between the monads (units) composing numbers,
for between 2 and 1 there is nothing at all.' Two Pyth-

CHAPTER IV

ARGUMENT

[*There are various senses in which a movement or change
may be said to have* unity (227 b 3–4).

(1) *All changes are* generically *one, which fall within the
same category, or* summum genus, *of entities* (b 4–6).

(2) *All changes are* specifically *one, which fall within one
indivisible species of entity. There are also the intermediate
cases of the divisible species which lie between the highest
genus and the lowest species* (b 6–14).

*It might be suggested that specific unity could be claimed
for any change that returns to its starting-point. But,
since a point may do this either by vibrating to and fro along
a straight line or by going round a circle, we should then
have to say that vibration and circulation are specifically
identical, which they are not. Also it would mean that
different modes of covering the same track (such as walking
and rolling) would be specifically identical, which they are
not. So our requirement that ' that in which the change*

between every two points there is a line,[a] and in
every line there are points ; but there can be nothing
between two successive numbers, the monad and the
dyad for instance.

So now the meaning of 'together' and 'apart,'
'touching,' 'between' and 'next-in-succession,' 'contiguous' and 'continuous' has been set forth, and also
of what things these several terms can be predicated.

agorean points can indeed (as Aristotle has just said) be in
contact, but they *can* be at the two ends of a line with a row
of contiguous points (constituting the Pythagorean line)
between them. But the numbers of the series 1, 2, 3, etc.
and the units composing these numbers are (according to
the Pythagoreans) separated from one another by 'nothing'
—a 'void' (213 b 28), which cannot be filled by a row of
units connecting the numbers or the units.—C.]

CHAPTER IV

ARGUMENT (*continued*)

*takes place' must be an indivisible species is to be under-
stood as applying both to the track followed and the mode of
progression* (b 14–20).

(3) *A change has* absolute or unqualified unity, *when it
is one in essence and numerically. The conditions to be
satisfied are : (a) that ' in which' the change takes place
must be an indivisible species, (b) the time occupied must be
essentially one and unintermittent, and (c) the thing moved
must be essentially one thing (not merely accidentally one,
like a man and his colour) and numerically one (not merely
specifically one, like two particular instances of the same
sort of change)* (b 20–228 a 3).

*With respect to this last condition difficulties might be
raised. Suppose one and the same individual repeatedly undergoes a change that is specifically the same. Is the change then
one and the same ? Only if we admit that one and the same
thing can exist, cease to exist, and then exist again* (a 3–6).

ARISTOTLE

Another problem : According to the doctrine of Flux, my body (the subject of changes of state and affections) is itself becoming different at every moment. Can its state of health, then, be one and the same from dawn till now ? If so, why not say that my state of health which I had and lost is one and the same as my state of health which I now have ? Here we must distinguish. (a) If we accept the Flux doctrine, all the states of the changing body must be numerically different at different moments ; but (b) if a state (and a fortiori its subject) can remain one and the same for a stretch of time (e.g. from dawn till now), then there can be two numerically different actualities of the same potentiality in the same subject (two actual states of health) separated by an interval, and we need not say that these are one and the same. Or we might say they are one and the same, if it is possible to hold that one and the same thing can exist, cease to exist,

227 b 3   Μία δὲ κίνησις λέγεται πολλαχῶς· τὸ γὰρ ἓν πολλαχῶς λέγομεν.

Γένει μὲν οὖν μία κατὰ τὰ σχήματα τῆς κατη-
5 γορίας ἐστίν· φορὰ μὲν γὰρ πάσῃ φορᾷ τῷ γένει μία, ἀλλοίωσις δὲ φορᾶς ἑτέρα τῷ γένει.

Εἴδει δὲ μία, ὅταν τῷ γένει μία οὖσα καὶ ἐν ἀτόμῳ εἴδει ᾖ. οἷον χρώματος μέν εἰσι διαφοραί·

---

¹ [The clumsiness and repetitions of the following sentences could be remedied by transposing λευκότητος δ' οὐκέτι and reading ἁπλῶς for τῷ (πῶς H : πως Simplic. 882. 22) in l. 11 as follows: οἷον χρώματος μέν εἰσι διαφοραί—τοιγαροῦν ἄλλη τῷ εἴδει μέλανσις καὶ λεύκανσις—⟨λευκότητος δ' οὐκέτι⟩· πᾶσα οὖν λεύκανσις πάσῃ λευκάνσει ἡ αὐτὴ κατ᾽ εἶδος ἔσται, καὶ πᾶσα μέλανσις μελάνσει. διὸ ἁπλῶς εἴδει μία λεύκανσις λευκάνσει πάσῃ, εἰ δ᾽ ἔστιν ἆτθ᾽ κτλ. 'For instance, "colour" has specific differences (*e.g.* black and white)—accordingly, the processes of blackening and whitening are specifically different—but 'whiteness' has not; so every case of whitening or of blackening is specifically the same as every other. Hence *absolute* specific unity will subsist between every whitening

44

and exist again. These difficulties are, however, outside our scope (a 6–20).

In order to be 'one' absolutely, a change must have con-tinuity. This means that there must be no shift from a change of one specific kind to a change of another kind and no intervals of rest in the time occupied (a 20–b 11).

(4) *By the unity of a motion we sometimes mean that it is complete* (b 11–15).

(5) *Another meaning of unity is* uniformity. *Uniformity or its opposite is found in changes of every kind, in respect of their path, time, goal, and manner (quick and slow). Any movement that is one and continuous can be either uniform or not. But a movement composed of two specifically different movements cannot be uniform. Therefore such movements cannot be one and continuous* (b 15–229 a 6). —C.]

'ONE single movement,' or ' change ' is an ambiguous term, because ' oneness ' itself has a variety of mean-ings.

(1) Changes are of one kind *generically* when they fall within the same category of existence ; thus, every kind of local movement, or change as to place, is generically one with every other ; but a change of quality would differ from it generically.

(2) Changes are of one and the same kind *specifi-cally* when they are identical both in the genus and in the *species specialissima* [a] to which they belong. Thus, all changes of colour constitute a species

[a] [*Or* ' indivisible species.' In a Table of Division of a genus into species and subspecies, we arrive finally at a lowest species, which cannot be further subdivided by a ' specific difference,' but is directly predicable of existing individuals, whose ' form ' or ' essence ' it constitutes.—C.]

and every other; but, since certain terms are both genera and species, clearly the changes in such cases will be specifically identical *in a sense*, but not absolutely.—C.]

ARISTOTLE

227 b τοιγαροῦν ἄλλη τῷ εἴδει μέλανσις καὶ λεύκανσις·
πᾶσα δ' οὖν¹ λεύκανσις πάσῃ λευκάνσει ἡ αὐτὴ
10 κατ' εἶδος ἔσται, καὶ πᾶσα μέλανσις μελάνσει.
λευκότητος δ' οὐκέτι· διὸ τῷ εἴδει μία λεύκανσις
λευκάνσει πάσῃ. εἰ δ' ἔστιν ἅτθ' ἃ καὶ γένη ἅμα
καὶ εἴδη ἐστίν, δῆλον ὡς ἔστιν ὡς εἴδει μία ἔσται,
ἁπλῶς δὲ μία εἴδει οὔ· οἷον ἡ μάθησις, εἰ ἡ
ἐπιστήμη εἶδος μὲν ὑπολήψεως γένος δὲ τῶν
ἐπιστημῶν.

15 Ἀπορήσειε δ' ἄν τις εἰ εἴδει μία κίνησις, ὅταν
ἐκ τοῦ αὐτοῦ τὸ αὐτὸ εἰς τὸ αὐτὸ μεταβάλλῃ (οἷον
ἡ μία στιγμὴ ἐκ τοῦδε τοῦ τόπου εἰς τόνδε τὸν
τόπον πάλιν καὶ πάλιν)· εἰ δὲ τοῦτ', ἔσται ἡ
κυκλοφορία τῇ εὐθυφορίᾳ ἡ αὐτή, καὶ ἡ κύλισις
τῇ βαδίσει. ἢ διώρισται, τὸ ἐν ᾧ ἂν ἕτερον ᾖ τῷ
20 εἴδει, ὅτι ἑτέρα κίνησις· τὸ δὲ περιφερὲς τοῦ εὐθέος
ἕτερον τῷ εἴδει.

Γένει μὲν οὖν καὶ εἴδει κίνησις μία οὕτως·

¹ [δ' οὖν EH, οὖν cett.—C.]

ᵃ The others being general opinion or original and personal
sagacity. *Cf. De anim.* 417 a 31, 427 b 25.
ᵇ [This interpretation (given by Themistius) of τὸ ἐν ᾧ
covers the case of the vibrating or circulating point, but not
the difference between walking and rolling (two specifically
different *modes* of traversing the *same* path). Simplicius
(884. 3) observes this and supposes that τὸ ἐν ᾧ means the
mode of movement, not the path. But the earlier statement
referred to can only be 227 b 6 ὅταν . . . ἐν ἀτόμῳ εἴδει ᾖ,
and this covers both the track and the mode.—C.]

46

within the genus of quality, but not a *species specialissima*, for changing towards black and changing towards white differ specifically ; whereas all changes towards black are identical with each other both in genus and *species specialissima*, and so are all changes towards white. Whiteness itself, then, can no longer differentiate classes of motion towards itself ; hence all such motions are specifically one. Of course, if a certain group forms a genus with respect to its own subdivisions and a species with respect to a higher genus that embraces it and others, its members are the same generically and in a certain sense specifically as well, but not in the absolute sense of belonging to one and the same *species specialissima*. Thus ' acquiring knowledge by instruction ' is generic in that many different kinds of knowledge may be gained by instruction, but instruction itself is only one specific way, amongst others,*a* of coming to belief in things.

The question might be asked whether all motions of an identical mobile from a given position to the same position again (as a single point may move from this place to that again and again) are specifically one and the same ; if so, then rectilinear and circular motion, or walking and rolling along, would be specifically one and the same. We should reply : It has been laid down that if the path traversed *b* is specifically of a different kind, as the straight line and the circle are, then the movements are different.

We have now seen what constitutes generic and specific identity of motion.

ARISTOTLE

227 b ἁπλῶς δὲ μία κίνησις ἡ τῇ οὐσίᾳ μία καὶ τῷ
ἀριθμῷ. τίς δ᾽ ἡ τοιαύτη, δῆλον διελομένοις· τρία
γάρ ἐστι τὸν ἀριθμὸν περὶ ἃ λέγομεν τὴν κίνησιν
—ὅ, καὶ ἐν ᾧ, καὶ ὅτε. λέγω δ᾽ ὅτι ἀνάγκη εἶναί
25 τι τὸ κινούμενον, οἷον ἄνθρωπον ἢ χρυσόν,[1] καὶ
ἔν τινι τοῦτο κινεῖσθαι, οἷον ἐν τόπῳ ἢ ἐν πάθει,
καὶ ποτέ, ἐν χρόνῳ γὰρ πᾶν κινεῖται. τούτων δὲ
τὸ μὲν εἶναι τῷ γένει ἢ τῷ εἴδει μίαν ἐστὶν ἐν τῷ
πράγματι ἐν ᾧ κινεῖται,[2] τὸ δὲ ἐχομένην[3] ἐν τῷ
χρόνῳ, τὸ δὲ ἁπλῶς μίαν ἐν ἅπασι τούτοις· καὶ ἐν
30 ᾧ γὰρ ἓν δεῖ εἶναι καὶ ἄτομον (οἷον τὸ εἶδος), καὶ
τὸ ὅτε, οἷον τὸν χρόνον ἕνα καὶ μὴ διαλείπειν, καὶ
τὸ κινούμενον ἓν εἶναι μὴ κατὰ συμβεβηκός (ὥσπερ
τὸ λευκὸν μελαίνεσθαι καὶ Κορίσκον βαδίζειν· ἐν
δὲ Κορίσκος καὶ λευκόν, ἀλλὰ κατὰ συμβεβηκός),
228 a μηδὲ κοινόν (εἴη γὰρ ἂν ἅμα δύο ἀνθρώπους

[1] [χρυσόν is suspicious. Themistius 175. 6 οἷον τὸν ἄνθρωπον ἢ τὸ ἄστρον.—C.]
[2] [The Oxford translation adopts Bonitz's insertion after
κινεῖται of τὸ δὲ τῷ ὑποκειμένῳ μίαν ἐν τῷ πράγματι ὃ κινεῖται,
'it is the thing moved that makes the motion one in
subject.'—C.]
[3] [ἐχομένην Oxford translation (cf. Simplic. 885. 2 ὁ δὲ
συνεχὴς χρόνος καθ᾽ αὑτὸν ἐχομένας ποιεῖ τὰς κινήσεις): ἐχόμενον
ἦν codd.—C.]

[a] [Or, 'the medium (viz. the species) must have the
(absolute specific) unity of the indivisible species,' not merely

(3) But for a change to be *absolutely and individually* ' one,' it must be not only of one and the same specific nature, but essentially and numerically one change. What sort of change satisfies this description will appear on analysis, as follows. There are three things that we speak of as factors of movement : the subject, the track followed, and the ' when ' of the passage. I mean by the ' subject ' (say) the man or the gold that shifts from here to there, and by the ' track followed ' the actual path or the successive gradations of quality over which the progress extends. The ' when ' speaks for itself, for all change takes place in time. Of these three things, the unity of the medium through or over which the track passes determines the generic or specific unity of the change, and the continuity of the time occupied determines its unbrokenness ; so that, if we add the identity of the subject, the oneness will be unqualified. For the medium must be one, not only generically but specifically,[a] and the ' when,' to wit the time of passage, must be unbrokenly one and not intermittent, and that which moves be one essentially and not only incidentally. This last qualification means that if Coriscus, who is pale, is walking and getting bronzed at the same time, though the pallid being who is getting bronzed is also walking yet the identity is only incidental and not essential to either of the two different changes that are taking place. Nor is a movement or progress one and the same (although it be the same in itself and in the time it occupies) if it is made in common by several subjects ; for two men may be

the generic unity of (say) movement in a straight line and movement in a circle.—C.]

228 a ὑγιάζεσθαι τὴν αὐτὴν ὑγίανσιν, οἷον ὀφθαλμίας·
ἀλλ' οὐ μία αὕτη, ἀλλ' εἴδει μία).

Τὸ δὲ Σωκράτη τὴν αὐτὴν μὲν ἀλλοίωσιν
ἀλλοιοῦσθαι τῷ εἴδει, ἐν ἄλλῳ δὲ χρόνῳ καὶ πάλιν
5 ἐν ἄλλῳ, εἰ μὲν ἐνδέχεται τὸ φθαρὲν πάλιν ἓν
γίγνεσθαι τῷ ἀριθμῷ, εἴη ἂν καὶ αὕτη μία· εἰ δὲ
μή, ἡ αὐτὴ μὲν μία δ' οὔ.

Ἔχει δ' ἀπορίαν ταύτῃ παραπλησίαν καὶ πότερον
μία ἡ ὑγίεια καὶ ὅλως αἱ ἕξεις καὶ τὰ πάθη τῇ
οὐσίᾳ εἰσὶν ἐν τοῖς σώμασιν· κινούμενα γὰρ
10 φαίνεται τὰ ἔχοντα καὶ ῥέοντα. εἰ δὴ ἡ αὐτὴ καὶ
μία ἡ ἔωθεν καὶ νῦν ὑγίεια, διὰ τί οὐκ ἂν καὶ ὅταν
διαλιπὼν λάβῃ πάλιν τὴν ὑγίειαν, καὶ αὕτη κἀκείνη
μία τῷ ἀριθμῷ ἂν εἴη; ὁ γὰρ αὐτὸς λόγος. πλὴν
τοσοῦτον διαφέρει, ὅτι εἰ μὲν δύο τὸ αὐτὸ τοῦτο

---

[a] [Perhaps a reference to the Pythagorean doctrine of
recurrence recorded by Eudemus (Simplic. 732. 30) : ' If
one could believe what the Pythagoreans say, that things
numerically one and the same recur, I shall be talking to
you with my staff in my hand and you will be sitting just
as you are now and everything else will be just the same.'
—C.]

in process of being cured of the same disease (say) ophthalmia, and at the same time, yet the cure, or progress to health, though one and the same in kind in both cases, is two cures and not one and the same single cure.

But if Socrates once again passes through the same specific modification that he has passed through before, then, if we consider it possible for that which has perished to come into existence again and be individually and numerically one and the same,[a] we may say that Socrates is making ' one and the same ' recovery, for instance ; but if we do not admit the above-named possibility, we shall say that he is making ' the same ' recovery but not ' one and the same.'

Another question, analogous to this, has been raised : Has health, or any other state or affection that occurs in material bodies, an essential unity, since the bodily seat of them is supposed, by some, to be in a perpetual state of movement and flux ?[b] Now, if my health this morning is one and the same state as my health at this moment, why should not the health I lost and then recovered after an interval of time be likewise one and the same numerically ? The reasoning seems to be the same. There is, however, this much difference : (a) if this same subject is (at the two different moments) two things in

[b] The Heracleitean doctrine. If our bodies themselves and all the things revealed to us by the senses are momentarily mutable, how can there be any enduring identity at all ? [φαίνεται may mean : ' It is an observed fact,' though the statement that it is observed fact may be put in the mouth of those who raise the question, the physicists mentioned at 265 a 2.—C.]

228 a οὕτως τῷ ἀριθμῷ, καὶ τὰς ἕξεις ἀνάγκη[1] (μία γὰρ
15 ἀριθμῷ ἐνέργεια ἑνὸς ἀριθμῷ)· εἰ δ᾽ ἡ ἕξις μία,
ἴσως οὐκ ἄν τῳ δόξειέ πω μία καὶ ἡ ἐνέργεια εἶναι·
ὅταν γὰρ παύσηται βαδίζων οὐκέτι ἔσται ἡ
βάδισις, πάλιν δὲ βαδίζοντος ἔσται. εἰ δ᾽ οὖν
μία καὶ ἡ αὐτή, ἐνδέχοιτ᾽ ἂν τὸ αὐτὸ ἓν καὶ

[1] [Alexander (Simplic. 889. 8) recorded the reading ὅτι εἰ
μὲν δύο οὕτως τῷ ἀριθμῷ, καὶ τὰς ἕξεις ἀνάγκη, understanding
the subject of εἰ μὲν δύο to be τὸ ὑποκείμενον τῇ ἕξει, ὅπερ διὰ
τὴν συνεχῆ ῥύσιν οὐ μένει ἓν τῷ ἀριθμῷ. I believe this is right
substantially, but the necessary subject cannot be supplied
from the context; it must be mentioned. Hence I have
retained τὸ αὐτὸ τοῦτο with MSS. other than EH (which have
δι᾽ for τὸ) and I (which omits τὸ). The objections to supply-
ing αἱ ἕξεις as the subject of εἰ μὲν δύο are: (1) This involves
changing ἕξεις (before ἀνάγκη) to ἐνεργείας and so introducing
a distinction between an *actual state* (ἕξις) of health and
activities (ἐνέργειαι) resulting from that state. There is no
question of such a distinction in the cases mentioned, but
only of states of health which *are* actualities (ἐνέργειαι).
Activities only come in later in the illustration from walking.
(2) The resulting statement does not seem to fulfil the
promise of τοσοῦτον διαφέρει by stating any difference that
distinguishes the cases in question. But the reading and
interpretation must be taken as very uncertain.—C.]

---

[a] [My body is the subject (ὑποκείμενον) which has the
capacity for states (ἕξεις) of health or disease. Any such
ἕξις which is actually realized at any moment is, with respect to that capacity, an 'actuality' (ἐνέργεια). ἐνέργεια here
means in particular an *actually realized state*, though the
statement is true if ἐνέργεια is taken also to include any
'*activity*' arising from such a state. The argument is: If

the sense under consideration, viz. numerically two, then it follows at once that its states must be numerically two, for the numerically different subject must have a numerically different actuality [a] ; whereas (b) if the state is one (over a stretch of time), that may not be considered sufficient ground for saying that the actuality can only be one numerically ; for when a man stops walking that act of walking ceases, but (he retains his power of walking and) when he starts again, there will be a second act of walking.[b] But, apart from that distinction, if we say that my health is one and the same, it may be possible that one and the same thing should cease to be and exist

we accept the flux doctrine, that my body becomes a different thing (numerically) from moment to moment, then of course, its actual states, such as health (whether enjoyed continuously or at intervals), must also be different things numerically from moment to moment. The change of the subject to a numerically different subject must carry with it a similar change of all its capacities, states, affections, activities, etc.—C.]

[b] [Supposition (b) abandons the flux doctrine. Aristotle supposes his own view : that the subject with its δυνάμεις and ἕξεις can remain one and the same over a length of time, and its δυνάμεις and ἕξεις can (as in the illustration from walking) have numerically different actualities (ἐνέργειαι) separated by intervals. We can thus assert that my state of health, considered as the actuality of my capacity for health, can subsist either as one and the same actuality continuously from morning till now, or as a series of numerically different actualities separated by intervals of ill-health ; just as my one power of walking can have many instances of activity separated by intervals of inactivity.—C.]

228 a φθείρεσθαι καὶ εἶναι πολλάκις. αὗται μὲν οὖν
20 εἰσιν αἱ ἀπορίαι ἔξω τῆς νῦν σκέψεως.

Ἐπεὶ δὲ συνεχὴς πᾶσα κίνησις, τήν τε ἁπλῶς
μίαν ἀνάγκη καὶ συνεχῆ εἶναι (εἴπερ πᾶσα διαιρετή),
καὶ εἰ συνεχής, μίαν. οὐ γὰρ πᾶσα γένοιτ' ἂν
συνεχὴς πάσῃ, ὥσπερ οὐδ' ἄλλο οὐδὲν τῷ τυχόντι
τὸ τυχόν, ἀλλὰ ὅσων ἓν τὰ ἔσχατα. ἔσχατα δὲ
25 τῶν μὲν οὐκ ἔστι, τῶν δ' ἐστὶν ἄλλα τῷ εἴδει καὶ
ὁμώνυμα· πῶς γὰρ ἂν ἅψαιτο ἢ ἓν γένοιτο τὸ
ἔσχατον γραμμῆς καὶ βαδίσεως; ἐχόμεναι μὲν
οὖν εἶεν ἂν καὶ αἱ μὴ αὐταὶ τῷ εἴδει μηδὲ τῷ γένει·
δραμὼν γὰρ ἄν τις πυρέξειεν εὐθύς, καὶ οἷον ἡ
λαμπὰς ἐκ διαδοχῆς φορὰ ἐχομένη, συνεχὴς δ' οὔ·
30 κεῖται γὰρ τὸ συνεχές, ὧν τὰ ἔσχατα ἕν. ὥστ'
ἐχόμεναι καὶ ἐφεξῆς εἰσι τῷ τὸν χρόνον εἶναι

---

a [A further suggestion for a line of argument that might
be taken, if we were to pursue this discussion. Even if we
do not take the view put forward in (b), but suppose that
two actual states of health separated by a interval of ill-
health are not numerically two actualities but *one and the
same* actuality, that might be defended on the supposition
suggested above (228 a 5), that one and the same thing
can exist, cease to exist, and come into existence again.
I am responsible for the reading and interpretation of this
paragraph, as I could not construct any text that would
correspond with Dr. Wicksteed's rendering, which may have
been provisional.—C.]

b [*e.g.* the indivisible monad (Simplic.).—C.]

c [λαμπάς was the official name of the torch-race itself.
Simplic. 892. 1 quotes Plato, *Rep.* 328 A λαμπὰς ἔσται . . .
ἀφ' ἵππων τῇ θεῷ.—C.]

d *Cf.* p. 34 note a.

e [Understanding ἐχόμεναι in the sense defined at 227 a 6
(succession and contact). But Aristotle seems here to use
ἐχόμενον loosely, for he has just said that movements which
are not even generically the same can be ἐχόμεναι (conse-

again many times over.[a] However, these problems lie outside our present inquiry.

What constitutes the unity of a movement? Not its indivisibility (for every movement is potentially divisible without limit), but its uninterrupted continuity. Thus if a movement is strictly one, it must be continuous, and if continuous, one. It is impossible for one movement to be so united with any other movement, taken at random, as to make the two one movement ; for continuity is in no case possible between things taken at random, but only between such things as have limiting extremes capable of *identifying* coincidence ; and there are things [b] that have no limiting extremes at all, and others whose limiting extremes, though called by the same name of ' end,' are of differing nature ; for how can the ' end ' of a walking come into contact with the ' end ' of a line and become identical with it ? It is true that movements differing not only in species but in genus may come next-to-each-other-without-interval, for a man might catch a feverish cold at the moment when he stopped running ; and a torch [c] passed from hand to hand might be carried first by one runner and then by another with no interval between. But the ' carryings,' each pertaining to a different ' carrier,' would not be continuous ; for we agreed that things can only be continuous with each other when the end of one and the beginning of the other are *identically unified.*[d] Thus the running and taking fever are ' nexts without contact ' because there is no break of time between them, and on the same ground the two carryings are ' nexts by contact ' [e] with each other,

cutive), but he can hardly mean that they can be in contact. —C.]

228 a συνεχῆ, συνεχὲς δὲ τῷ τὰς κινήσεις· τοῦτο δ',
228 b ὅταν ἓν τὸ ἔσχατον γίγνηται ἀμφοῖν. διὸ ἀνάγκη
τὴν αὐτὴν εἶναι τῷ εἴδει καὶ ἑνὸς καὶ ἐν ἑνὶ χρόνῳ
τὴν ἁπλῶς συνεχῆ κίνησιν καὶ μίαν—τῷ χρόνῳ
μέν, ὅπως μὴ ἀκινησία μεταξὺ ᾖ· ἐν τῷ διαλείποντι
5 γὰρ ἠρεμεῖν ἀνάγκη. πολλαὶ οὖν καὶ οὐ μία ἡ
κίνησις, ὧν ἐστιν ἠρεμία μεταξύ· ὥστε εἴ τις
κίνησις στάσει διαλαμβάνεται, οὐ μία οὐδὲ συνεχής·
διαλαμβάνεται δέ, εἰ μεταξὺ χρόνος. τῆς δὲ τῷ
εἴδει μὴ μιᾶς καὶ εἰ μὴ διαλείπεται ὁ χρόνος, ὁ
μὲν[1] χρόνος εἷς, τῷ εἴδει δ' ἡ κίνησις ἄλλη· τὴν
10 μὲν γὰρ μίαν ἀνάγκη καὶ τῷ εἴδει μίαν εἶναι,
ταύτην δ' ἁπλῶς μίαν οὐκ ἀνάγκη. τίς μὲν οὖν
κίνησις ἁπλῶς μία, εἴρηται.

Ἔτι δὲ λέγεται μία καὶ ἡ τέλειος, ἐάν τε κατὰ
γένος ἐάν τε κατ' εἶδος ᾖ ἐάν τε κατ' οὐσίαν,
ὥσπερ καὶ ἐπὶ τῶν ἄλλων τὸ τέλειον καὶ ὅλον τοῦ
ἑνός. ἔστι δ' ὅτε κἂν ἀτελὴς ᾖ μία λέγεται, ἐὰν
15 ᾖ μόνον συνεχής.

Ἔτι δ' ἄλλως παρὰ τὰς εἰρημένας λέγεται μία

---

[1] [μὲν Bonitz : μὲν γὰρ codd.—C.]

---

[a] *Cf.* p. 34 note *a*.
[b] [More literally, ' Accordingly they (movements falling under different species or genera) are *contiguous* and *next-in-succession* by virtue of the continuity of the time, but *continuity* requires that the movements themselves shall be continuous, *i.e.* both must have an identical extremity.'—C.]
[c] One material entity, one animal, or one man, must be a complete or whole. One mathematical entity, one mathematical figure, one circle.

56

but there is a break in the continuity of the carryings, since the end of the one does not become actually *identical* with the beginning of the other,[a] as in the case of continuous movements.[b] So that for a movement to possess absolute unity and continuity (*a*) the movement must be specifically the same throughout the course, and (*b*) the mobile must retain its numerical identity, and (*c*) the time occupied must be ' one ' in the sense explained above.   The time must be one (*i.e.* continuously occupied by the motion) so that no intervals may break the movement; for if a movement leaves gaps of time, those gaps must needs be occupied by station, and if station is inserted between, the motion is not single but plural.   So if any motion be interrupted by station, it is not one or continuous ; and it is so interrupted if there are gaps in the time. Again, if the movement be not of the same kind, even if the time occupied be continuous, the movement is not, for the time is ' one,' but the movements, since they differ in kind, are not ; for in order to be one, a movement must have identity of kind, though it may have identity of kind without necessarily being one in every sense.   This, then, suffices to define the strict conditions of one-and-the-sameness in movement.

(4) Sometimes we mean to imply, by calling a thing ' one,' that it is *complete* in itself, whether we have the genus or the species or the individual in view.[c] And so with motion, a whole, complete in itself, may be implied by ' oneness.'   Sometimes, however, a motion, even if it be not complete, is called ' one,' provided only that it be continuous.

(5) And in addition to all these meanings, by calling a movement ' one and the same ' we may imply that it is *uniform* throughout its course ; for though we

ARISTOTLE

228 b ἡ ὁμαλής. ἡ γὰρ ἀνώμαλος ἔστιν ὡς οὐ δοκεῖ μία
ἀλλὰ μᾶλλον ἡ ὁμαλής, ὥσπερ ἡ εὐθεῖα· ἡ γὰρ
ἀνώμαλος διαιρετή. ἔοικε δὲ διαφέρειν ὡς τὸ
μᾶλλον καὶ ἧττον. ἔστι δ' ἐν ἁπάσῃ κινήσει τὸ
20 ὁμαλῶς ἢ μή· καὶ γὰρ ἂν ἀλλοιοῖτο ὁμαλῶς, καὶ
φέροιτο ἐφ' ὁμαλοῦ (οἷον κύκλου ἢ εὐθείας), καὶ
περὶ αὔξησιν ὡσαύτως καὶ φθίσιν. ἀνωμαλίας[1]
δ' ἐστὶ διαφορὰ ὅτε μὲν ἐφ' ᾧ κινεῖται—ἀδύνατον
γὰρ ὁμαλὴν εἶναι τὴν κίνησιν μὴ ἐπὶ ὁμαλῷ
μεγέθει, οἷον ἡ τῆς κεκλασμένης κίνησις ἢ ἡ τῆς
25 ἕλικος ἢ ἄλλου μεγέθους ὧν μὴ ἐφαρμόττει τὸ
τυχὸν ἐπὶ τὸ τυχὸν μέρος—ὅτε δὲ οὔτε ἐν τῷ ποῦ
οὔτε ἐν τῷ ποτὲ οὔτε εἰς ὅ, ἀλλ' ἐν τῷ ὥς· ταχυ-
τῆτι γὰρ καὶ βραδυτῆτι ἐνίοτε διώρισται· ἧς μὲν
γὰρ τὸ αὐτὸ τάχος, ὁμαλής, ἧς δὲ μή, ἀνώμαλος.
διὸ οὐκ εἴδη κινήσεως οὐδὲ διαφοραὶ τάχος καὶ
30 βραδυτής, ὅτι πάσαις ἀκολουθεῖ ταῖς διαφόροις
κατ' εἶδος. ὥστ' οὐδὲ βαρύτης καὶ κουφότης ἡ
εἰς τὸ αὐτό, οἷον γῆς πρὸς αὐτὴν ἢ πυρὸς πρὸς

---

[1] [ἀνωμαλία E, Oxford translation.—C.]

---

a [Cf. Themist. 176. 23 μᾶλλον δὲ μία κίνησις καὶ ἡ ὁμαλὴ
τῆς ἀνωμάλου· τὴν γὰρ ἀνώμαλον διαιρεῖν ἐοίκασιν αἱ ἐξαλλαγαί,
and Alex. ap. Simplic. 895. 27. But the sentence may be
rendered : ' But the difference (between uniform and not
uniform) seems to be a difference of degree (rather than
of kind),' and connected with the following statement:
' It occurs in *every* sort of movement.'—C.]
b [' Tapering spiral,' like the convolution (ἑλική) of a
snail-shell. Apollonius of Perga (born about 262 B.C.?)

58

may ascribe a certain unity to a movement that varies
in form over different portions of its course; yet that
which is uniform (the movement on a straight line,
for example) is one in a fuller sense ; for you can
divide what is not uniform into sections not similar
to each other. So that the oneness that includes
uniformity seems to be more one than that which
does not.[a] This distinction between uniformity and
varioformity applies to all forms of passing-here-to-
there ; for a change of quality may be uniform, and a
local passing from here to there may be over a uniform course (for instance, on a circle or a straight
line), and the same with growth or expansion and its
reverse. And it is sometimes in the form of the track
that we find the determinant of varioformity in the
motion, for there can be no uniformity of motion save
over a track of uniform figure, not *e.g.* over a line bent
back at an angle, or a tapering spiral,[b] or any other
figure, parts of which taken at random will not fit
upon each other. But sometimes the variation is
neither in the form of the track, nor in the continuity
or discontinuity of the time occupied, nor in the
maintaining or reversing of the direction, but in a
quality of the motion itself ; for the variation may be
in its quickness or slowness, since a motion uniform in
speed may be called uniform, and varying in speed
varying. It follows that velocity is not special to any
one genus of change. Nor is swift and slow movement identical with heaviness and lightness, for heaviness always works one way, that of earth to earth,
and lightness always the other way, that of fire to

first demonstrated, in his lost book *On the Cochlias,* that one
type of helix—the cylindrical—is a uniform curve. Proclus
in Eucl. p. 105 Friedlein.—C.]

229 a αὐτό. μία μὲν οὖν ἡ ἀνώμαλος τῷ συνεχής (ἧττον δέ, ὅπερ τῇ κεκλασμένῃ συμβαίνει φορᾷ· τὸ δ' ἧττον μίξις ἀεὶ τοῦ ἐναντίου)· εἰ δὲ πᾶσαν τὴν μίαν
5 ἐνδέχεται καὶ ὁμαλὴν εἶναι, οὐκ ἂν εἴησαν αἱ ἐχόμεναι καὶ μὴ κατ' εἶδος αἱ αὐταί[1] μία καὶ συνεχής· πῶς γὰρ ἂν εἴη ὁμαλὴς ἡ ἐξ ἀλλοιώσεως συγκειμένη καὶ φορᾶς; δέοι γὰρ ἂν ἐφαρμόττειν.

[1] [οὐκ ἂν εἴησαν . . . αἱ αὐταὶ: καὶ μή, οὐκ ἂν εἴησαν αἱ (αἱ om. E) μὴ κατ' εἶδος ἐχόμεναι αὐται (ἐχόμεναι καὶ αὐταί I) codd. My reading is based on Themistius 177. 12 εἰ τοίνυν τὴν μὲν συνεχῆ καὶ μίαν κίνησιν ἐνδέχεται καὶ ὁμαλὴν εἶναι, τὴν δὲ ἐκ τῶν εἴδει διαφερουσῶν κινήσεων συγκειμένην ἀδύνατον ὁμαλὴν εἶναι, οὐκ ἄν ποτε γένοιτο ἡ τοιαύτη μία συνεχής, ὅτι μηδ' ὁμαλής. I assume that the καὶ μή, which does not appear after καὶ ὁμαλὴν in Themistius (its presence or absence there does not affect the argument), was part of an attempt to correct αἱ μὴ κατ' εἶδος ἐχόμεναι αὐται. The argument is: any non-uniform movement can be *one* in the sense of being continuous (though it has less unity than the uniform); and since any motion of whatever sort that is one can also be uniform, both uniformity and non-uniformity are always compatible with being one and continuous. It follows that a movement composed of consecutive movements of two different kinds cannot be one and continuous; for uniformity is not compatible with change of kind in the movement (*e.g.* from alteration to locomotion).—C.]

CHAPTER V

ARGUMENT

[*What is meant by one movement being* contrary *to another movement or* (*as considered in the next chapter*) *to rest?* (229 a 7–8).

The possibilities are exhausted by five alternatives. One of these involves only one positive goal, and this is the case of coming-to-be and perishing. The remaining four have two positive goals or opposites (a 8–16).

fire ; but swift and slow are common to both alike.ᵃ A movement that is not uniform, then, may have a certain unity, in virtue of its continuity in time, though a lesser unity than if it were uniform. An instance would be a movement on a line bent back at an angle. This 'lesser,' here as elsewhere, implies an admixture of the contrasted principle. And since any kind of continuous change may be either uniform or not, changes that succeed each other without interval, but are not of like kind, cannot be one and continuous ; for how could a progress compounded of alternate changes of quality and of place be uniform ? If it were, a change of place would be capable of being laid over a change of quality and exactly coinciding with it.

ᵃ [*Or*, ' And so neither does that heaviness, or that lightness, which (causes motion) in the same direction—*e.g.* the heaviness of earth as compared with earth, or the lightness of fire as compared with fire—(constitute a specific difference).' One piece of earth may be heavier than another, but both naturally move downwards. Such differences are not ' specific,' as are the heaviness of *all* earth and the lightness of *all* fire, which cause these elements to move naturally in opposite directions.—C.]

CHAPTER V

ARGUMENT (*continued*)

Two of them may be dismissed, as not yielding actual motions that are in fact contrary, though they may be distinguished conceptually (a 16–27).

Two remain, which are really reducible to one : A ' movement ' (change of quality, quantity, or place) is contrary to another when one is from A towards B, the other from B towards A, A and B being opposites. Examples illustrate

*this. The change with only one positive goal is a ' change '
(viz. coming-to-be or perishing), but not ' movement '
(a 27–b 14).*
Movement from or towards an intermediate between two

229 a 7 Ἔτι δὲ διοριστέον ποία κίνησις ἐναντία κινήσει·
καὶ περὶ μονῆς δὲ τὸν αὐτὸν τρόπον.

Διαιρετέον δὲ πρῶτον πότερον ἐναντία κίνησις
10 ἡ ἐκ τοῦ αὐτοῦ τῇ εἰς τὸ αὐτό (οἷον ἡ ἐξ ὑγιείας
τῇ εἰς ὑγίειαν), οἷον καὶ γένεσις καὶ φθορὰ δοκεῖ,
ἢ ἡ ἐξ ἐναντίων (οἷον ἡ ἐξ ὑγιείας τῇ ἐκ νόσου),
ἢ ἡ εἰς ἐναντία (οἷον ἡ εἰς ὑγίειαν τῇ εἰς νόσον),
ἢ ἡ ἐξ ἐναντίου τῇ εἰς ἐναντίον (οἷον ἡ ἐξ ὑγιείας
τῇ εἰς νόσον), ἢ ἡ ἐξ ἐναντίου εἰς ἐναντίον τῇ
ἐξ ἐναντίου εἰς ἐναντίον (οἷον ἡ ἐξ ὑγιείας εἰς
15 νόσον τῇ ἐκ νόσου εἰς ὑγίειαν). ἀνάγκη γὰρ ἢ
ἕνα τινὰ τούτων εἶναι τῶν τρόπων ἢ πλείους· οὐ
γὰρ ἔστιν ἄλλως ἀντιθεῖναι.

Ἔστι δ' ἡ μὲν ἐξ ἐναντίου τῇ εἰς ἐναντίον οὐκ
ἐναντία (οἷον ἡ ἐξ ὑγιείας τῇ εἰς νόσον), ἡ αὐτὴ γὰρ
καὶ μία· τὸ μέντοι γ' εἶναι οὐ ταὐτὸ αὐταῖς, ὥσπερ

---

[a] [Because in this case there is only one positive goal—
existence—with its contradictory, non-existence. In the
remaining cases there are two contrary positive goals, and
these cases alone are considered in the following context, as
alone relevant to ' movement,' *i.e.* change of quality, quantity, or place. We recur to case (1) at 229 b 10, where it
appears that this is ' change,' but not ' movement.'—C.]

ARGUMENT (*continued*)

*opposites may be regarded as movement from or towards one
of the opposites* (b 14–21).
      The definition of ' contrary movement ' is stated (b 21–22).
—C.]

WE must further determine what change or transition
is contrary to what other, and likewise as to cessation
from change.

To begin with : (1) are two movements contrary
when the one recedes from, the other approaches,
the same thing ? So receding from health and
approaching health would be contrary movements.
This, one would say, holds for coming to be
and ceasing to be.[a] Or (2) should we say that
contrary movements recede from the opposite positions—that receding from health is the contrary of
receding from sickness ? Or (3) is the approaching
one opposite (health) contrary to approaching the
other (sickness) ? Or (4) receding from one opposite
to approaching the other ? That would be ' from
health ' contrary to ' towards sickness.' Or (5)
' from the one opposite towards the other ' contrary
to ' from the other towards the one ' ? That would
be ' from sickness to health ' contrary to ' from
health to sickness.' It must be either one, or more
than one, of these, for they exhaust the possibilities
of contrast.

Now (4) a movement away from the one opposite
and a movement towards the other (*e.g.* from health
and towards sickness) are not contrary, for they are
actually one and the same movement, though conceptually they are different aspects of it and differ
in their definitions (as, for example, losing health is

63

229 a 20 οὐ ταὐτὸ τὸ ἐξ ὑγιείας μεταβάλλειν καὶ τὸ εἰς
νόσον. οὐδ' ἡ ἐξ ἐναντίου τῇ ἐξ ἐναντίου· ἅμα
μὲν γὰρ συμβαίνει ἐξ ἐναντίου καὶ εἰς ἐναντίον (ἢ
μεταξύ· ἀλλὰ περὶ τούτου μὲν ὕστερον ἐροῦμεν),
ἀλλὰ μᾶλλον τὸ εἰς ἐναντίον μεταβάλλειν δόξειεν
ἂν εἶναι αἴτιον τῆς ἐναντώσεως ἢ τὸ ἐξ ἐναντίου.
25 ἡ μὲν γὰρ ἀπαλλαγὴ ἐναντιότητος, ἡ δὲ λῆψις·
καὶ λέγεται δ' ἑκάστη εἰς ὃ μεταβάλλει μᾶλλον ἢ
ἐξ οὗ, οἷον ὑγίανσις ἡ εἰς ὑγίειαν, νόσανσις[1] δ' ἡ
εἰς νόσον.

Λείπεται δὴ ἡ εἰς ἐναντία, καὶ ἡ εἰς ἐναντία ἐξ
ἐναντίων. τάχα μὲν οὖν συμβαίνει τὰς εἰς ἐναντία
καὶ ἐξ ἐναντίων εἶναι, ἀλλὰ τὸ εἶναι ἴσως οὐ ταὐτό
30 (λέγω δὲ τὸ εἰς ὑγίειαν τῷ ἐκ νόσου καὶ τὸ ἐξ
ὑγιείας τῷ εἰς νόσον). ἐπεὶ δὲ διαφέρει μεταβολὴ

----

[1] [νόσανσις FHI.   *Cf.* 230 a 22 : νόσωσις cett.—C.]

----

a A difference that is very sensible when we are leaving
one pleasant company to join another, for instance.
b [That a change towards something intermediate between
two opposites may be regarded as a change towards the
remoter opposite, is explained below, 229 b 14.—C.]
c Both ὑγίανσις and νόσανσις (elsewhere νόσωσις) appear
to be coined words. The translation has the advantage
of the original in so far as it employs one coined word
only.   Aristotle's economy of intellectual or imaginative
effort in finding illustrations is a noteworthy feature of his
style, though when he gives his mind to it he shows himself a master. [The gist of Aristotle's remarks is : Nothing
is gained by distinguishing case (2) from case (3). The
actual movement is the same in both cases, and would
more naturally be described in terms of case (3).—C.]

conceived in reference to health, and approaching
disease in reference to disease).[a] Nor (2) should
contrary movements be defined as receding from the
opposite extremes respectively ; for receding from
either opposite coincides with approaching the other
opposite (or a point between ; but of that more
hereafter),[b] but one would look for the principle of
opposition rather in approach than in receding ; for
the one is of the nature of getting hold of an opposite,
the other in the nature of escaping from it, and movements take their names rather from what they are
changing to than from what they are changing from
—' healthening ' for passing from sickness towards
health, ' sickening ' for passing from health towards
sickness.[c]

This reduces us to (3) the case of the movement
towards one opposite as the contrary of the movement towards the other, and (5) the movement from
opposite A towards opposite B as the contrary of the
movement from B towards A.[d] Now movements
towards one extreme really coincide with movements
away from the other, though they may be distinguished conceptually : ' towards health ' from ' from
disease,' I mean, or ' from health ' from ' towards
disease.' [e] And since ' change ' is a wider term than

[d] [The phrase ἡ εἰς ἐναντία ἐξ ἐναντίων is used as a com-
pendious equivalent for ἡ ἐξ ἐναντίου εἰς ἐναντίον τῇ ἐξ ἐναντίου εἰς ἐναντίον above (l. 13).—C.]
[e] [That is, apart from the (negligible) conceptual difference, case (3) is reducible to case (5), which alone remains.
This result of the whole analysis is stated in the next sentence : One ' movement ' (i.e. change of quality, quantity,
or place)—as distinguished from coming-to-be and perishing,
which are included in the wider term ' change '—is contrary
to another when one is from A towards B, the other from
B towards A, A and B being contraries.—C.]

229 a κινήσεως (ἡ ἔκ τινος γὰρ ὑποκειμένου εἰς τι
ὑποκείμενον μεταβολὴ κίνησίς ἐστιν), ἡ ἐξ ἐναντίου
229 b εἰς ἐναντίον τῇ ἐξ ἐναντίου εἰς ἐναντίον κίνησις
ἐναντία (οἷον ἡ ἐξ ὑγιείας εἰς νόσον τῇ ἐκ νόσου
εἰς ὑγίειαν). δῆλον δὲ καὶ ἐκ τῆς ἐπαγωγῆς,
ὁποῖα δοκεῖ τὰ ἐναντία εἶναι· τὸ νοσάζεσθαι γὰρ
5 τῷ ὑγιάζεσθαι, καὶ τὸ μανθάνειν τῷ ἀπατᾶσθαι
μὴ δι' αὐτοῦ (εἰς ἐναντία γάρ· ὥσπερ γὰρ ἐπιστήμην, ἔστι καὶ ἀπάτην καὶ δι' αὐτοῦ κτᾶσθαι καὶ
δι' ἄλλου), καὶ ἡ ἄνω φορὰ τῇ κάτω (ἐναντία γὰρ
ταῦτα ἐν μήκει), καὶ ἡ εἰς δεξιὰ τῇ εἰς ἀριστερά
(ἐναντία γὰρ ταῦτα ἐν πλάτει), καὶ ἡ εἰς τὸ ἔμ-
10 προσθεν τῇ εἰς τὸ ὄπισθεν (ἐναντία γὰρ καὶ ταῦτα).
ἡ δὲ εἰς ἐναντίον μόνον οὐ κίνησις ἀλλὰ μεταβολή,
οἷον τὸ γίγνεσθαι λευκὸν μὴ ἔκ τινος. καὶ ὅσοις
δὲ μὴ ἔστιν ἐναντίον, ἡ ἐξ αὐτοῦ τῇ εἰς αὐτὸ
μεταβολῇ ἐναντία· διὸ γένεσις φθορᾷ ἐναντία καὶ
ἀποβολὴ λήψει· αὗται δὲ μεταβολαὶ μέν, κινήσεις
δ' οὔ.

---

^a [ὑποκείμενον here means ' something positive,' τὸ κατα-
φάσει δηλούμενον (as explained at 225 a 6), including the
' shortage,' which can be expressed positively (225 b 3).—C.]

^b [Simplic. 904. 1 explains the point of the parenthesis :
' being deceived *by another* ' is the proper antithesis of
learning (from another) ; the antithesis of ' being deceived
on your own account ' would be ' discovery ' (εὕρεσις) on
your own account.—C.]

^c Simplicius justly points out that these directions are
purely anthropocentric, the man's largest dimension ' height '
being taken as ' length,' and the other dimensions being
decided by the structure of the organism. But no one
knew better than Aristotle that such definitions are arbitrary,
and that east, for example, is to the right if you are looking
north and to the left if you are looking south, and that if

66

' movement ' (for only change from something *a* to something else, not change from nothing to something or the reverse, is movement), it follows from what we have said that movements are contrary when one of them is a passing from this opposite to that, and the other from that to this (in our example, one from health towards disease and the other from disease towards health). And if we take a survey of the instances, we shall find that these are exactly what we actually think of as contrary passings ; for example, sickening and gaining health, or being taught to believe the truth and being led into error by someone else (these are opposites, for error, like knowledge, can be acquired by another's agency as well as by one's own *b*), or motion upwards and motion downwards, which are contrary in the direction of length ; or ' to right ' and ' to left,' contrary in the direction of breadth ; or ' forward ' and ' backward,' contrary in the direction of depth.*c* But for one of two opposites to emerge, but not out of or from anything, would be a change from not being there to being there, but not a passing or movement. Such would be the genesis of something white not out of something else defined. And in the case of such things as have no opposites change from a thing is contrary to the change towards that same thing *d* : thus coming into being is contrary to ceasing to be, and losing to gaining ; but such are changes, not movements or passings.

you talk seriously of up and down, right and left, fore and back cosmically, you must define the terms cosmically. *Cf.* Vol. I. Introd. p. lxii.

d [This is case (1) at the beginning of the analysis (229 a 9). It is now seen to be a case of ' *change*,' but not of ' *movement*,' only one positive goal being involved.—C.]

229 b 15 Τὰς δὲ εἰς τὸ μεταξὺ κινήσεις, ὅσοις τῶν
ἐναντίων ἔστι μεταξύ, ὡς εἰς ἐναντία πως θετέον.
ὡς ἐναντίῳ γὰρ χρῆται τῷ μεταξὺ ἡ κίνησις, ἐφ'
ὁπότερα ἂν μεταβάλλῃ, οἷον ἐκ φαιοῦ μὲν εἰς τὸ
λευκὸν ὡς ἐκ μέλανος καὶ ἐκ λευκοῦ εἰς φαιὸν ὡς
εἰς μέλαν, ἐκ δὲ μέλανος εἰς φαιὸν ὡς εἰς λευκὸν
20 τὸ φαιόν· τὸ γὰρ μέσον πρὸς ἑκάτερον λέγεταί πως
τῶν ἄκρων, καθάπερ εἴρηται καὶ πρότερον.

Κίνησις μὲν δὴ κινήσει ἐναντία οὕτως ἡ ἐξ
ἐναντίου εἰς ἐναντίον τῇ ἐξ ἐναντίου εἰς ἐναντίον.

---

^a [At 224 b 31.—C.]

CHAPTER VI

ARGUMENT

[*In what sense is rest contrary to movement? Generally
speaking rest is opposed to movement, as being the ' shortage '
of movement ; and this applies to all species of movement.
But the question must be treated in more detail (229 b 23–27).*

*Every movement involves two opposites A and B. Rest in
A is the contrary of movement from A to B, not of movement from B to A (b 27–31).*

*Rest in A is also opposed to rest in B ; while if we oppose
rest in A to any movement, that movement can only be movement from A to B (b 31–230 a 7).*

Where there are not two opposites, there is no ' movement '

Now movements to something between such opposites as have anything between them are to be regarded in a sense as movements towards one or the other opposite; for the movement either way—from a state between to either opposite, or from either opposite to a state between—makes that state between function as the opposite from which it is receding or towards which it is approaching as the case may be. Thus a thing on the way from grey to white is as though on the way from black, and from white to grey as though to black, and from black to grey as though to white. For, in a sense, that which is between is so called in contrast with either extreme, as we have already noted.[a]

Contrary movements, then, as above defined, are such as pass, the one from this opposite to that, and the other from that to this.

CHAPTER VI

ARGUMENT (continued)

proper, but only ' change ' with one terminal point, viz. the coming-into-being of something or its ceasing-to-be. Here we should not speak of ' rest ' (the proper opposite of ' movement '), but of ' unchangingness.' The thing can be unchangingly in being. What is the opposite of this condition? (1) If the alternative to ' in being ' is sheer non-existence, there is no opposite condition, for there will be nothing at all to be in any opposite condition. But (2) if by ' that which is not ' we merely mean this ' matter ' which has not yet acquired this ' form,' then this matter is something to which we can attribute ' unchangingness in not being ' what it will be when it has acquired the form (a 7–18).

ARGUMENT (*continued*)

In local change, either movement or rest may be natural *or* unnatural. *Does the same antithesis apply to other kinds of movement and to coming-into-being and perishing ? It may be argued that since ' violence' is ' against nature,' violent or enforced changes of all sorts can be called ' unnatural.' So the contrast of ' natural' and ' unnatural' is common to all changes and states of rest. In place, for example, the* natural *motion upwards of fire is contrary* (1) *to the* natural *motion downwards of earth, and* (2) *to its own* unnatural *motion downwards. So with rest : the* unnatural *rest above of earth is contrary* (1) *to its own* natural *motion downwards, and* (2) *to its own* natural *rest below. Thus the*

229 b 23   Ἐπεὶ δὲ κινήσει οὐ μόνον δοκεῖ κίνησις εἶναι
ἐναντία ἀλλὰ καὶ ἠρεμία, τοῦτο διοριστέον. ἁπλῶς
25 μὲν γὰρ ἐναντίον κίνησις κινήσει, ἀντίκειται δὲ
καὶ ἠρεμία (στέρησις γάρ, ἔστι δ' ὡς καὶ ἡ
στέρησις ἐναντία λέγεται), ποιᾷ δὲ ποιά,[1] οἷον τῇ
κατὰ τόπον ἡ κατὰ τόπον.

Ἀλλὰ τοῦτο νῦν λέγεται ἁπλῶς· πότερον γὰρ
τῇ ἐνταυθοῖ[2] μονῇ ἡ ἐκ τούτου ἢ ἡ εἰς τοῦτο
κίνησις ἀντίκειται; δῆλον δὴ ὅτι ἐπεὶ ἐν δυσὶν

---

[1] [ποιᾷ δὲ ποιά. This correction, also adopted by the Oxford translation, is favoured by the οἷον which follows, and by Philoponus's paraphrase (858. 32): ποιᾷ δὲ ποιά, the reading of all mss. and of Themistius 178. 4 and (apparently) Simplicius 906. 20 may be due to wrong punctuation of the preceding clauses.—C.]

[2] [ἐνταυθοῖ. At the other place cited in Bonitz's Index where this form occurs in Aristotle, *De caelo* 295 b 23 οὗ δὲ φέρεται κατὰ φύσιν, καὶ μένει ἐνταυθοῖ, there is the variant ἐνταῦθα, but not here. It is hard to believe that Aristotle would choose to use ἐνταυθοῖ here coupled with a word negating motion (though in the *De caelo* there might be a

ARGUMENT (continued)

*contrast of natural and unnatural holds of states of rest, as
well as of motions (a 18–b 21).*

*Though we recognize unnatural states of rest, we ought
not to speak of them as arising by a process of 'coming to a
standstill.' This term should be reserved for natural movement of a thing to its proper place (b 21–28).*

*A thing in process of change (e.g. from health to sickness)
is partially still 'in health,' partially already 'in sickness.'
Can we, then, say that staying in health is contrary to
'falling sick'? May we say the thing, in so far as it is still
in health, is in a sense at rest? (b 28–231 a 2).*

Conclusion (231 a 2–4).

*Alternative statements of two problems already considered
(231 a 4–17).—C.]*

But since we find a contrast not only between a
given motion and its counter motion but also between
experiencing that motion and being at rest from it,
we must examine this matter also. For, while the
opposite of a motion, in the full and proper sense, is
the motion counter to it, absence of motion is also
contrasted with motion, as being its non-accomplishment (for non-accomplishment is a kind of opposite
to the 'might be'), and this holds in each particular
category, *e.g.* local rest is contrasted with local
motion.

This statement, however, is too general and needs
qualification. Is abiding here opposed to moving
hence or to moving hither? Evidently, since a
movement must be between two terms *A* and *B*,

---

sort of attraction to the notion of 'whither' in οὗ δὲ φέρεται),
while he couples ἐνταῦθα with φέρεσθαι. Perhaps ἐνταυθί
should be read in both places.—C.]

229 b 30 ἡ κίνησις ὑποκειμένοις, τῇ μὲν ἐκ τούτου εἰς τὸ
ἐναντίον ἢ ἐν τούτῳ μονή, τῇ δ' ἐκ τοὐναντίου εἰς
τοῦτο ἢ ἐν τῷ ἐναντίῳ.

Ἅμα δὲ καὶ ἀλλήλαις ἐναντίαι αὗται· καὶ γὰρ
230 a ἄτοπον εἰ κινήσεις μὲν ἐναντίαι εἰσίν, ἠρεμίαι δ'
ἀντικείμεναι οὐκ εἰσίν· εἰσὶ δὲ αἱ ἐν τοῖς ἐναντίοις,
οἷον ἡ ἐν ὑγιείᾳ τῇ ἐν νόσῳ ἠρεμίᾳ. κινήσει δὲ
τῇ ἐξ ὑγιείας εἰς νόσον· τῇ γὰρ ἐκ νόσου εἰς
ὑγίειαν ἄλογον (ἡ γὰρ εἰς αὐτὸ κίνησις ἐν ᾧ
5 ἕστηκεν ἠρέμησις μᾶλλόν ἐστιν, ᾗ συμβαίνει γε
ἅμα γίγνεσθαι τῇ κινήσει), ἀνάγκη δὲ ἢ ταύτην
ἢ ἐκείνην εἶναι· οὐ γὰρ ἥ γ' ἐν λευκότητι ἠρεμία
ἐναντία τῇ ἐν ὑγιείᾳ.

Ὅσοις δὲ μὴ ἔστιν ἐναντία, τούτων μεταβολὴ
μὲν ἔστιν ἀντικειμένη ἡ ἐξ αὐτοῦ τῇ εἰς αὐτό,
κίνησις δ' οὐκ ἔστιν· οἷον ἡ ἐξ ὄντος τῇ εἰς ὄν.
10 καὶ μονὴ μὲν τούτων οὐκ ἔστιν, ἀμεταβλησία δέ.
καὶ εἰ μέν τι εἴη ὑποκείμενον, ἡ ἐν τῷ ὄντι ἀμεταβλησία τῇ ἐν τῷ μὴ ὄντι ἐναντία· εἰ δὲ μὴ ἔστι τι
τὸ μὴ ὄν, ἀπορήσειεν ἄν τις τίνι ἐναντία ἡ ἐν τῷ

---

[a] [Simplic. 908. 21, interprets ὑποκείμενον here as the
'matter' which gains form in 'becoming.' This can have
an existence of its own without the form it may come to
gain ; so there is something to be in a state of changelessness.
But if 'what is not' means the absolutely non-existent,
there is nothing to be in such a state ; so how can there be
such a state for nothing to be in ?—C.]

movement from A to its opposite B will have for its opposite the abiding fixed in A, and movement from B to A will have for its opposite the abiding fixed in B.

At the same time these two fixities are also contrary to one another; for it would be absurd that there should be contrary movements and not also opposite states of rest, and there are such in fact, namely the states of rest in the opposite terms, *e.g.* abiding in health is opposed to abiding in sickness. The movement to which abiding in health is opposed is the movement from health to sickness; for it would be absurd to oppose it to the reverse movement from sickness to health (since movement towards the goal at which the subject is at rest is rather a process of 'coming to rest,' and 'coming to rest' is a process that coincides with the movement towards that goal), and it can only be one or the other of these two movements between health and sickness: no other opposite term can be in question, for that would involve the impossible consequence that rest in (say) 'whiteness' should be opposed to rest in health.

If a term has no opposite, then there can be no 'movement' from it or to it, but there may be a 'change' from its not being there to its being there and *vice versa*. In such a case you cannot say that it 'makes a stay' in being, or in not being, but only that there is *absence of change* from being or not-being. Now if there is some subject [a] that changes from not being this or that into being it, then its not-changing from being that thing is the opposite of its not-changing from not being it. But if that which isn't the thing does not exist at all, one would be at a loss to express the opposite of the thing's being in existence and not changing from it, and one could

73

230 a ὄντι ἀμεταβλησία, καὶ εἰ ἠρεμία ἐστίν. εἰ δὲ
τοῦτο, ἢ οὐ πᾶσα ἠρεμία κινήσει ἐναντία, ἢ ἡ
15 γένεσις καὶ ἡ φθορὰ κίνησις. δῆλον τοίνυν ὅτι
ἠρεμία μὲν οὐ λεκτέα, εἰ μὴ καὶ αὗται κινήσεις,
ὅμοιον δέ τι καὶ ἀμεταβλησία. ἐναντία δὲ ἢ οὐδενὶ
ἢ τῇ ἐν τῷ μὴ ὄντι ἢ τῇ φθορᾷ (αὕτη γὰρ ἐξ αὑτῆς,
ἡ δὲ γένεσις εἰς ἐκείνην).

᾿Απορήσειε δ᾿ ἄν τις διὰ τί ἐν μὲν τῇ κατὰ τόπον
20 μεταβολῇ εἰσὶ καὶ κατὰ φύσιν καὶ παρὰ φύσιν
καὶ μοναὶ καὶ κινήσεις, ἐν δὲ ταῖς ἄλλαις οὔ, οἷον
ἀλλοίωσις ἡ μὲν κατὰ φύσιν ἡ δὲ παρὰ φύσιν·
οὐδὲν γὰρ μᾶλλον ἡ ὑγίανσις ἢ ἡ νόσανσις κατὰ
φύσιν ἢ παρὰ φύσιν, οὐδὲ λεύκανσις ἢ μέλανσις·
ὁμοίως δὲ καὶ ἐπ᾿ αὐξήσεως καὶ φθίσεως (οὔτε
25 γὰρ αὗται ἀλλήλαις ἐναντίαι ὡς φύσει ἢ παρὰ
φύσιν, οὔτε αὔξησις αὐξήσει). καὶ ἐπὶ γενέσεως δὲ
καὶ φθορᾶς ὁ αὐτὸς λόγος· οὔτε γὰρ ἡ μὲν γένεσις
κατὰ φύσιν ἡ δὲ φθορὰ παρὰ φύσιν—ἡ γὰρ γήρανσις
κατὰ φύσιν—οὔτε γένεσιν ὁρῶμεν τὴν μὲν κατὰ
φύσιν τὴν δὲ παρὰ φύσιν. ἢ εἰ ἔστι τὸ βίᾳ παρὰ
30 φύσιν, καὶ φθορὰ ἂν εἴη φθορᾷ ἐναντία ἡ βίαιος
ὡς παρὰ φύσιν οὖσα τῇ κατὰ φύσιν. ἆρ᾿ οὖν καὶ

---

[a] [Ceasing-to-be is a change whose starting-point is the thing's 'unchangingness in being.' This starting-point is also the goal of coming-to-be. So ceasing-to-be is contrary to it in some such way as movement is contrary to rest, while 'unchangingness in not-being' is contrary to it in some such way as rest is contrary to rest.—C.]

[b] [For the doctrine of the natural trend of the elements to their proper regions see Vol. I. Gen. Introd. pp. lxii ff. —C.]

hardly say whether such opposite were or were not a state of rest. If we are to speak of 'rest' in such a case, we must either say that 'rest' is not always opposed to 'movement,' or else that coming-to-be and ceasing-to-be are movements. It is clear, then, that since (as we have seen) these are not movements, we must not speak of rest, but call it something analogous to rest, namely unchangingness. Is there, then, an opposite to 'unchangingness in being'? Not if the non-existence opposed to existence is absolute; but otherwise the non-change of being a thing is opposed either to its non-change in non-existence or to its ceasing-to-be (which is a change from it, whereas genesis is a change to it).[a]

One might naturally ask why there are natural and unnatural [b] movings and abidings in locality, but not in other ways of passing from this to that. For instance, there is no natural or unnatural change of quality, for getting health is no more natural or unnatural than sickening, nor is growing white more or less natural than growing black; and in the same way neither are growth and shrinkage opposed to each other as one natural and the other unnatural, nor is one growth opposed to another in that way. And so again with coming-to-be and perishing, for neither is coming-to-be natural and perishing unnatural (for growing old is natural) nor do we distinguish between natural and unnatural coming-to-be. We may answer that if by 'unnatural' we mean 'enforced'[c] then perishing may be opposed to perishing if the one is natural and the other enforced. Is there,

---

[c] [For the contrast between natural and enforced or unnatural movement see Book IV. chap. viii., 215 a 2.—C.]

230 a γενέσεις εἰσὶν ἔνιαι βίαιοι καὶ οὐχ εἱμαρμέναι, αἷς
230 b ἐναντίαι αἱ κατὰ φύσιν, καὶ αὐξήσεις βίαιοι καὶ
φθίσεις, οἷον αὐξήσεις αἱ τῶν ταχὺ διὰ τρυφὴν
ἡβώντων, καὶ οἱ σῖτοι οἱ ταχὺ ἁδρυνόμενοι καὶ μὴ
πιληθέντες; ἐπὶ δ' ἀλλοιώσεως πῶς; ἢ ὡσαύτως·
εἶεν γὰρ ἄν τινες βίαιοι, αἱ δὲ φυσικαί, οἷον οἱ
5 ἀφιέμενοι μὴ ἐν κρισίμοις ἡμέραις, οἱ δ' ἐν
κρισίμοις· οἱ μὲν οὖν παρὰ φύσιν ἠλλοίωνται οἱ
δὲ κατὰ φύσιν. ἔσονται δὴ[1] ἐναντίαι αἱ φθοραὶ
ἀλλήλαις, οὐ γενέσει. καὶ τί γε κωλύει; ἔστι
γὰρ ὧς· καὶ γὰρ εἰ ἡ μὲν ἡδεῖα ἡ δὲ λυπηρὰ εἴη·
ὥστ' οὐχ ἁπλῶς φθορὰ φθορᾷ ἐναντία, ἀλλ' ᾗ ἡ
10 μὲν τοιαδὶ ἡ δὲ τοιαδὶ αὐτῶν ἐστιν. ὅλως μὲν
οὖν ἐναντίαι κινήσεις καὶ ἠρεμίαι τὸν εἰρημένον
τρόπον εἰσίν· οἷον ἡ ἄνω τῇ κάτω. τόπου γὰρ
ἐναντιώσεις αὗται· φέρεται δὲ τὴν μὲν ἄνω φορὰν
φύσει τὸ πῦρ, τὴν δὲ κάτω ἡ γῆ, καὶ ἐναντίαι
15 αὐτῶν αἱ φοραί· τὸ δὲ πῦρ ἄνω μὲν φύσει, κάτω

---

[1] [δὴ HI Simplic. 911. 24: δ' cett.   In Themistius 179. 6
the MSS. vary.—C.]

---

[a] [Simplicius 911. 13 sees a reference to the 'Gardens of
Adonis.' 'These were baskets or pots filled with earth, in
which wheat, barley, lettuces, fennel, and various kinds of
flowers were sown and tended for eight days, chiefly or

then, such a thing as coming-into-being which is enforced and out of the naturally ordained way, and so contrary to natural coming-into-being, and are there forced growings and shrinkages, such as a youth's rapid growth to maturity due to luxury, or the rapid ripening of corn that is not packed solidly in the mould?[a] And how about qualitive modifications? It is the same with these, we may say : some may be considered forced and some natural; for instance recovery from a fever is a natural alteration if it occurs on a critical day, unnatural if the day is not critical. We shall, then, have perishings contrary in this respect rather to each other than each to an opposite coming-to-be. Why not ? For in a sense there are such, since one might be easy and another grievous, so that, if one way of perishing were not unqualifiedly opposed to another, yet they might be contrasted in so far as they have contrary qualities. It is, then, universally true that movements and states of rest are contrary in the manner just described.[b] Take for instance the contrariety of upward and downward movement and of rest above and rest below. These are contrarieties in respect of place ; and of the movements concerned, the natural movement of fire is upward, of earth downward, and these movements of theirs are contrary ; moreover, for fire upward movement is natural, down-

---

exclusively by women. Fostered by the sun's heat, the plants shot up rapidly, but having no root they withered as rapidly away, and at the end of eight days were carried out with the images of the dead Adonis, and flung with them into the sea or into springs.' Frazer, *Adonis Attis Osiris* (1914), i. 236.—C.]

[b] [*i.e.* the contrast of natural and unnatural occurs (as has just been argued) in *all* types of movement, and also in the opposition of movement to rest.—C.]

ARISTOTLE

230 b δὲ παρὰ φύσιν, καὶ ἐναντία γε ἡ κατὰ φύσιν αὐτοῦ
τῇ παρὰ φύσιν. καὶ μοναὶ δ' ὡσαύτως· ἡ γὰρ
ἄνω μονὴ τῇ ἄνωθεν κάτω κινήσει ἐναντία, γίγνεται δὲ τῇ γῇ ἡ μὲν μονὴ ἐκείνη παρὰ φύσιν,
ἡ δὲ κίνησις αὕτη κατὰ φύσιν. ὥστε [κινήσει]
20 ⟨μονῇ⟩[1] μονὴ ἐναντία ἡ παρὰ φύσιν τῇ κατὰ
φύσιν τοῦ αὐτοῦ (καὶ γὰρ ἡ κίνησις ἡ τοῦ αὐτοῦ
ἐναντία οὕτως)· ἡ μὲν γὰρ κατὰ φύσιν ἔσται
αὐτῶν—ἡ ἄνω ἢ ἡ κάτω—ἡ δὲ παρὰ φύσιν.

Ἔχει δ' ἀπορίαν εἰ ἔστι πάσης ἠρεμίας τῆς μὴ
ἀεὶ γένεσις, καὶ αὕτη τὸ ἵστασθαι. τοῦ δὴ παρὰ
φύσιν μένοντος, οἷον τῆς γῆς ἄνω, εἴη ἂν γένεσις·
25 ὅτε ἄρα ἐφέρετο ἄνω βίᾳ, ἵστατο. ἀλλὰ τὸ μὲν
ἱστάμενον ἀεὶ δοκεῖ φέρεσθαι θᾶττον, τὸ δὲ βίᾳ

---

[1] [I have inserted μονῇ because, if κινήσει is retained, this
sentence is a mere repetition of the previous one, is redundant
in itself, and leaves the argument incomplete. Sense and
symmetry require the statement that the natural rest is
opposed to the unnatural rest of the same element. This
statement was promised above, and is implied in the parallel
passage below, 231 a 13-17. If μονῇ had dropped out, κινήσει
might easily be wrongly supplied.—C.]

---

[a] [Aristotle's answer seems to be that, though any state
of rest which is not permanent must have come to be, the
process by which an *unnatural* state of rest comes to be must
not be identified with 'coming to a standstill'—a term
which should be reserved for the termination of a *natural*
movement.—C.]
[b] [Logic requires us to understand τοῦ παρὰ φύσιν μένοντος
(τῆς ἠρεμίας) γενεσις ἂν εἴη.—C.]
[c] [*e.g.* a stone falls faster and faster in its *natural* movement

78

ward movement unnatural, and its natural movement is certainly contrary to its unnatural movement. Also the same contrast of natural and unnatural applies to the 'staying where it is' of each element. 'Staying above' is contrary to motion from above downwards, and for earth staying above is an unnatural occurrence, while motion from above downwards is natural. And accordingly, one staying will be contrary to another— the unnatural staying contrary to the natural staying of the same thing (just as the unnatural movement was contrary to the natural movement of the same thing); for one of the two stayings—staying above or staying below as the case may be—will be natural, the other unnatural.

The further question arises, whether every state of rest which does not exist at all times has a coming-into-being, and whether this coming-into-being can be identified with 'coming to a standstill.' [a] Now when a thing is in an unnatural state of rest—when earth, for instance, stays aloft—that state of rest [b] must have a coming-into-being; and (if this is identified with 'coming to a standstill') that will mean that the earth in question was 'coming to a standstill' at a time when it was being forced upwards against its nature. But a thing that is coming to a standstill seems always to be moving with a quickening velocity, whereas what is forced against its nature is always losing velocity. [c] So (if we identify the coming-to-be of an unnatural state of rest with 'coming to a standstill,' and an unnatural movement cannot be said to come to a standstill), we shall have a thing which

towards the earth, but loses speed if you throw it up 'violently' into the air.—C.]

230 b τοὐναντίον. οὐ γενόμενον ἄρα ἠρεμοῦν ἔσται
ἠρεμοῦν. ἔτι¹ δοκεῖ τὸ ἵστασθαι² ἢ ὅλως εἶναι
τὸ εἰς τὸν αὐτοῦ τόπον φέρεσθαι ἢ συμβαίνειν
ἅμα.

"Εχει δ' ἀπορίαν εἰ ἐναντία ἡ μονὴ ἡ ἐνταῦθα
τῇ ἐντεῦθεν κινήσει· ὅταν γὰρ κινῆται ἐκ τουδὶ ἢ
30 καὶ ἀποβάλλῃ, ἔτι δοκεῖ ἔχειν τὸ ἀποβαλλόμενον·
ὥστ' εἰ αὕτη ἢ³ ἠρεμία ἐναντία τῇ ἐντεῦθεν εἰς
τοὐναντίον κινήσει, ἅμα ὑπάρξει τἀναντία. ἢ πῇ
ἠρεμεῖ, εἰ ἔτι μένει; ὅλως δὲ τοῦ κινουμένου τὸ
231 a μὲν ἐκεῖ, τὸ δὲ εἰς ὃ μεταβάλλει· διὸ καὶ μᾶλλον
κίνησις κινήσει ἐναντίον ἢ ἠρέμησις.

¹ [Prantl reads εἰ for ἔτι (τι E), with a comma before
it.—C.]
² [H, incorporating here the statement which Aristotle
implies and ought to have made explicitly (viz. that ' coming
to a stand ' should be strictly reserved for natural movements), reads : ἔτι δοκεῖ τὸ ἵστασθαι κυρίως λέγεσθαι ἐπὶ τοῦ
κατὰ φύσιν εἰς τὸν οἰκεῖον τόπον ἰόντος, ἀλλ' οὐκ ἐπὶ τοῦ παρὰ
φύσιν, ἢ ὅλως, κτλ. This (omitting ἀλλ') was also read by
Simplicius (914. 15). Dr. Wicksteed adopted this reading,
but regarded it as doubtful, adding a note : ' Aristotle may
be taken to mean that a lump of earth which "stays up,"
however it got there, is not really " at rest " there, because it
would go down if not forcibly held up. Therefore the
violent movement that brought it there cannot properly be
said to have been " bringing it to a state of rest." ' The
meaning of ' coming to a standstill ' and its relation to
motion and rest are discussed in Book VI. chap. viii. The
string of ἀπορίαι, of which this is the first, are so carelessly
jotted down that it is no good trying to restore a complete
and logical sense by emendation.—C.]
³ [αὕτη ἡ: αὐτὴ ἡ I: ἡ αὐτὴ FH: ambiguo E: αὐτὴ cett.
—C.]

will *be* in a state of rest without ever having *come to be* in a state of rest—an absurd conclusion. Besides it is generally recognized that 'coming to a standstill' is either identical with a thing's moving to its proper place or a concomitant of that motion.[a]

Again it may be questioned whether 'staying in a place' is really the contrary of 'moving out of it'[b]; for when a thing starts moving out of its place or parting with some condition, it seems still to possess the condition it is losing, so that if the very being in it is the contrary of moving out of it towards the opposite, it combines two contraries. Or can it still be said to be at rest in some sort as long as any of it is left there? At any rate, whenever anything is in process of shifting, some of it is in the state it occupied and is leaving, and some of it in the state it is changing into. So one counter movement is more perfectly contrary to the other than is the 'staying in place' which it abolishes.[c]

---

[a] [*Cf.* 230 a 4.—C.]

[b] [This was asserted at 229 b 29, where the example was 'staying in health' and 'movement from health to sickness.' In such cases, rather than in locomotion, the change seems gradual and the changing thing 'appears still to possess (in some degree) the condition that is being lost.' Probably Aristotle has such changes chiefly in mind here; the word 'place' does not occur. The whole question is more carefully considered in Book VI. chap. v.—C.]

[c] [Themistius paraphrases ἠρέμησις by μονή, but ἠρέμησις might mean the process of coming to rest. The sentence may be an afterthought, meaning: A thing in process of change is partly in the state it is leaving, partly in the state it is changing into (and in which it will come to rest); and that is another reason for saying that the contrary of a movement is a movement (in the reverse direction) rather than a coming to rest (which coincides with the movement and has the same goal).—C.]

231 a Καὶ περὶ μὲν κινήσεως καὶ ἠρεμίας, καὶ πῶς
ἑκατέρα μία, καὶ τίνες ἐναντίαι τίσιν, εἴρηται.

5 Ἀπορήσειε δ' ἄν τις καὶ περὶ τοῦ ἵστασθαι,
εἰ καὶ ὅσαι παρὰ φύσιν κινήσεις, ταύταις ἔστιν
ἠρεμία ἀντικειμένη. εἰ μὲν οὖν μὴ ἔσται, ἄτοπον·
μένει γάρ. βίᾳ δέ· ὥστ' ἠρεμοῦν τι ἔσται οὐκ
ἀεὶ ἄνευ τοῦ γενέσθαι. ἀλλὰ δῆλον ὅτι ἔσται·
ὥσπερ γὰρ κινεῖται παρὰ φύσιν, καὶ ἠρεμοῖ ἄν τι
10 παρὰ φύσιν.
Ἐπεὶ δ' ἔστιν ἐνίοις κίνησις κατὰ φύσιν καὶ
παρὰ φύσιν, οἷον πυρὶ ἡ ἄνω κατὰ φύσιν ἡ δὲ
κάτω παρὰ φύσιν, πότερον αὕτη ἐναντία ἢ ἡ τῆς
γῆς (αὕτη γὰρ φέρεται κατὰ φύσιν κάτω); ἢ δῆλον
ὅτι ἄμφω, ἀλλ' οὐχ ὡσαύτως, ἀλλ' ἡ μὲν[1] κατὰ
15 φύσιν, ὡς κατὰ φύσιν οὔσης τῆς αὑτοῦ· ἡ δ' ἄνω
τοῦ πυρὸς τῇ κάτω ὡς ἡ κατὰ φύσιν οὖσα τῇ παρὰ

---

[1] [ἀλλ' ἡ μὲν . . . ἄνω, Oxford translation: ἀλλ' ἡ μὲν κατὰ
φύσιν ὡς κατὰ φύσιν οὔσης τῆσδ' αὑτοῦ· ἡ ἄνω Bekker: ἀλλ' ἡ
μὲν ὡς κατὰ φύσιν κατὰ φύσιν οὖσα τῆσδ' αὑτοῦ· ἡ ἄνω F: ἡ
(before ἄνω) om. E: Simplic. (paraphr.) 919. 23 ἀλλ' ἡ μὲν
τῆς γῆς κατὰ φύσιν τῇ τοῦ πυρὸς κατὰ φύσιν ὡς κατὰ φύσιν ἄμφω,
ἡ δὲ τοῦ πυρὸς παρὰ φύσιν τῇ κατὰ φύσιν αὑτοῦ ὡς ἡ παρὰ φύσιν
τῇ κατὰ φύσιν.
I have adopted the Oxford translator's reading as the
easiest correction of Bekker's text, but should not construe
it : 'the natural motion of earth is contrary inasmuch as the
motion of fire is also natural.' I should understand ἀλλ' ἡ
μὲν (sc. τῆς γῆς κατὰ φύσιν κίνησις) κατὰ φύσιν (ἐναντία ἐστὶν)
ὡς, κτλ. 'But the one (last mentioned, viz., the natural
downward movement of earth) is a natural contrary, the
motion of fire (to which it is opposed) being (also) a natural
motion.' Possibly the original text was something like :
ἀλλ' ἡ μὲν (sc. τῆς γῆς κάτω) ὡς κατὰ φύσιν ⟨οὖσα τῇ κατὰ φύσιν⟩
οὔσῃ· ἡ δὲ αὑτοῦ ἄνω [τοῦ πυρὸς] τῇ κάτω, ὡς κτλ.—C.]

Let this suffice for movement and staying still, and in what the unity of each consists, and which are contrary to which.[a]

Yet another question occurs concerning the coming of things to a stand : Is there a state of rest opposed to such movements as are against nature and enforced? It would be absurd that there should not be ; for the thing does stay where it is. On the other hand, this is the result of 'violence'; so we shall have something that *is* in a non-permanent state of rest without ever having *come to be* in that state.[b] But clearly there must be such a state of rest ; for just as things are moved against their nature, so a thing can be at rest against its nature.

[c] Also since some things move both in accordance with their nature and against it, as fire goes up by nature and down by force, is its own down-going or that of the earth the contrary of its up-going (for it is earth that goes down by nature) ? Obviously both its own down-going and that of earth are contrary to it, but not in the same sense. For one is a natural opposition of direction between things whose nature it is to go one this way and the other that. The other is an opposition between the natural up and the un-

---

[a] [The last sentence of the Book. The following paragraphs were omitted in some MSS. known to Simplicius (918. 11), as in some of ours, and passed over by Porphyry and Themistius. They may be alternative drafts of the corresponding paragraphs above.—C.]

[b] [This conclusion is as obscure as the similar statement in the earlier paragraph (b 21 ff.), of which this seems to be a doublet. The suppressed premiss is : there is no coming-to-a-stand in the case of violent or unnatural motion.—C.]

[c] [This paragraph states again a question answered at 230 b 10 ff.—C.]

231 a φύσιν οὔσῃ. ὁμοίως δὲ καὶ ταῖς μοναῖς· ἴσως δ᾽ ἠρεμίᾳ κίνησίς πῃ ἀντικεῖται.

ᵃ [i.e. the *natural* abiding of fire aloft is opposed (a) to the natural abiding of earth below and (b) to its own unnatural abiding below. But in another sense (as stated in the previous paragraph) we must recognize as the opposite

natural down of the same body. There is a similar
opposition between abidings in position of the two
bodies, though it may be said that, in a sense, a state
of rest has for its opposite (not an opposite state of
rest, but) a motion.[a]

of an unnatural state of rest the corresponding unnatural
motion.—C.]

BOOK VI

INTRODUCTION

THE aim of this book is (1) to demonstrate the continuity of Magnitude, Time, and Change, involving their illimitable divisibility by indivisible boundaries ; and (2) to expose the fallacies which result from the denial of this.

The first three Chapters deal with the conceptions of 'a continuum,' 'indivisibles,' 'illimitable divisibility,' 'continuity,' and the relation between time and movement.

In Chapter i. Aristotle defines and distinguishes the terms 'continuous,' 'contiguous,' and 'next-in-succession,' and shows that indivisibles cannot constitute a continuum.

In Chapter ii. he distinguishes between illimitable extension and unlimited divisibility. This gives the clue to the provisional refutation of Zeno's First and Second Dilemmas. Then comes a demonstration that a limited time cannot suffice for illimitable movement, nor can a limited movement occupy illimitable time. It appears to rest on the false assumption that anything less than an illimitable must be limited. Only uniform movement is considered here.

In Chapter iii. he proves that there can be neither rest nor motion in the indivisible 'now.'

The next five Chapters deal with Change and Movement and the relations between the 'factors' of Change.

Chapter iv. treats of the divisibility of 'movement'—embracing change of quality, quantity, and position. It begins with an examination of the condition of a thing which is in the act of changing ; and goes on to the

PHYSICS, VI. INTRODUCTION

analysis of movement into factors, with a demonstration that each factor is divisible, and that its divisibility involves a corresponding divisibility of the movement. This is elaborated in Bk. VIII. chaps. vii. and viii., where it is shown that a break in the continuity of *any* factor breaks that of the movement. So that a movement is continuous only when all its factors are so (see also Bk. V. chap. iii. p. 37 and note *c* on p. 36). This demonstration is an essential step in the discussion of the nature of eternal movement.

In Chapter v. he shows that the 'end' or consummation of a process of change is not a (divisible) *part*, but the final (indivisible) *limit*, of the process, and that the primary time at which the process is finished is an (indivisible) 'now.' Whereas the 'beginning' is a (divisible) part of the process: for the process has not yet begun at its initial limit, and is already in progress before any subsequent point on its course; so there is no indivisible instant at which the process is beginning, and no irreducible 'beginning' to the process, and the primary time when the process is beginning is a divisible period; and it is a divisible part of the subject which first accomplishes a change. He points out the distinction between direct and indirect divisibility.

In Chapter vi. he defines the 'proper time' of a change as the time during any part of which change is occurring. From this definition and the illimitable divisibility of time it follows that any change occupying time must be divisible. (Note that the indivisible unit of numerical change occurs all at once.) The proposition cannot be demonstrated directly (because, until the whole change is accomplished, the mutabile never reaches a stable condition, and is therefore never found *at*, but always approaching or receding from any intermediate point on its course.) He therefore introduces a second mutabile, which changes at the same rate as the first, but for only part of the time, at the end of which it reaches a stable condition and is found (according to the definition of proper time) to have accomplished a corresponding part of the change; the original mutabile changing at equal speed must have

87

ARISTOTLE

accomplished an equal part of the change in an equal time. This reasoning applies to any part of the change and of the time it occupies ; so that

> anything which is in process of changing must have been changing previously ;
> anything which has accomplished a change must have accomplished some change previously ;
> anything which is in process of changing must have accomplished some change previously ;
> anything which has accomplished a change must have been changing previously.

He gives change of magnitude as a particularly obvious example, and notes that the above demonstration also applies to genesis and perishing of continuous and divisible things.

In Chapter vii. he gives a demonstration that (i) a limited movement, whether uniform or not, cannot occupy unlimited time, and (ii) there could not be an unlimited movement in a limited time. His proof follows the same line of argument as the demonstration in Chapter ii. (see p. 112 note *b*). The same reasoning is applied to genesis and extinction.

There is no ' primary,' *i.e.* smallest-possible or irreducible first component of time, or of dimension, or of anything that is continuous.

Chapter viii. Both coming to rest and being at rest (*a*) occupy divisible periods of time ; (*b*) are going on during any part of that proper time ; and (*c*) have no irreducible earliest stage within that proper time. A moving thing never exactly ' covers ' any definite stationary object during any part of the proper time of its movement, but at any indivisible instant it must necessarily do so.

In Chapter ix. he discusses Zeno's four dilemmas and two others, all designed to prove that belief in the reality of motion leads to impossible consequences. He refutes Zeno's 1st and 2nd dilemmas (provisionally) by pointing out the complete parallelism between time and distance

88

with respect to extension and divisibility. In his final refutation in Bk. VIII. he recognizes that this does not dispose of the deeper underlying problem of the reality, not only of motion, but of time and space themselves and of any continuum whatever. He refutes Zeno's 3rd and 4th dilemmas by denying the assumptions on which they rest. The contention that if change is possible a thing could be *e.g.* both white and not white simultaneously, is refuted by pointing out that the supposed proof depends on the equivocal use of terms. The same criticism applies to the contention that a rotating sphere is both in motion and at rest simultaneously.

Chapter x. Proof that an indivisible cannot move (or change) on its own account, but only concomitantly ; and that no change can be unlimited except rotary locomotion.

Z

CHAPTER I

ARGUMENT

*The terms ' continuity,' ' contiguity ' (or touching), and
' next - in - succession ' defined and distinguished. These
definitions suffice to show that a continuum (such as length,
time, movement) cannot be constituted by indivisibles (points,
' nows,' stations) or be resolved into them. Nor can two
points (nows, stations) be continuous or contiguous one with
another (231 a 21–29).*

*Further demonstration that points cannot by contiguity
form a continuum ; for indivisibles must either be in the
same proper place (i.e. be positionally identical) or else be
entirely isolated (they cannot occupy different places without
having intervals between them), whereas the successive parts
of a continuum occupy different places but have nothing
between them (a 29–b 6).*

*A line cannot be constituted by a succession of points
which are ' next without contact ' ; for between ' nexts '
there is nothing of their own category, and what lies between
any two points is linear extension which is divisible at
intermediate points (see above). So that points lie between
any two points, and no point is next to any other (b 6–18).*

*A formal proof that the argument holds equally for
spatial magnitude, time, and motion, and that all three
hang together. It rests on two axioms :*

The first : *That when motion is taking place, something
is moving from here to there and* vice versa.

The second : *That the mobile or subject which experiences the motion cannot simultaneously be* in the act of
moving towards *a given position and* in the state of being
already at it.

BOOK VI

CHAPTER I

ARGUMENT (*continued*)

The steps of the argument are : (1) *If L, a component of motion, is itself a motion, then (by axiom* ii) *after L has started and before it has finished, P (the mobile) is (by axiom* i) *past the start and short of the finish of A (the distance). Therefore A is divisible in correspondence with L ; and so likewise are B and C with M and N.* (2) *If it were still maintained that A, etc., need not be (divisible) distances but might be (indivisible) ' terms' in the distance, it would involve one or other of the following impossibilities :* (a) *If L, etc., were motions, P would be in motion (while L was in progress) without moving from A ; and so with M and N, and B and C.* (b) *If L, etc., were not motions, P would never be in motion but would accomplish the motion without moving. Therefore both distance and motion must be divisible* (b 18–232 a 18).

Time is divisible if distance and motion are, and vice versa, *for if the whole of the length A is traversed in time T, a part of it would be traversed (at equal speed) in less than T. Or if the whole time T were occupied in traversing the distance A, then in part of the time less than A would be traversed* (a 18–22).

Note.—The absence of method in the system of lettering in the Greek text makes the discussion in this and the following chapter unnecessarily difficult to follow. Therefore an entirely independent system of lettering has been adopted in the translation. But for purposes of comparison duplicate diagrams are given showing the two systems of lettering side by side. Where there is no diagram the Greek letters are given in brackets after the English.

231 a 21   Εἰ δ' ἐστὶ συνεχὲς καὶ ἁπτόμενον καὶ ἐφεξῆς ὡς
διώρισται πρότερον—συνεχῆ μὲν ὧν τὰ ἔσχατα ἕν,
ἁπτόμενον δὲ ὧν ἅμα, ἐφεξῆς δὲ ὧν μηδὲν μεταξὺ
συγγενές—ἀδύνατον ἐξ ἀδιαιρέτων εἶναί τι συνεχές,
25 οἷον γραμμὴ ἐκ στιγμῶν, εἴπερ ἡ γραμμὴ μὲν
συνεχὲς ἡ στιγμὴ δ' ἀδιαίρετον. οὔτε γὰρ ἓν τὰ
ἔσχατα τῶν στιγμῶν (οὐ γάρ ἐστι τὸ μὲν ἔσχατον
τὸ δ' ἄλλο τι μόριον τοῦ ἀδιαιρέτου), οὔθ' ἅμα τὰ
ἔσχατα (οὐ γάρ ἔστιν ἔσχατον τοῦ ἀμεροῦς οὐδέν,
ἕτερον γὰρ τὸ ἔσχατον καὶ οὗ ἔσχατον).
30   Ἔτι δὲ ἀνάγκη ἤτοι συνεχεῖς εἶναι τὰς στιγμὰς
ἢ ἁπτομένας ἀλλήλων, ἐξ ὧν ἐστι τὸ συνεχές· ὁ
231 b δ' αὐτὸς λόγος καὶ ἐπὶ πάντων τῶν ἀδιαιρέτων.
συνεχεῖς μὲν δὴ οὐκ ἂν εἶεν διὰ τὸν εἰρημένον
λόγον· ἅπτεται δ' ἅπαν ἢ ὅλον ὅλου ἢ μέρος
μέρους ἢ ὅλου μέρος. ἐπεὶ δ' ἀμερὲς τὸ ἀδιαίρετον,
5 ανάγκη ὅλον ὅλου ἅπτεσθαι. ὅλον δ' ὅλου ἁπτόμενον οὐκ ἔσται συνεχές· τὸ γὰρ συνεχὲς ἔχει
τὸ μὲν ἄλλο τὸ δ' ἄλλο μέρος, καὶ διαιρεῖται εἰς
οὕτως ἕτερα καὶ τόπῳ κεχωρισμένα.

---

^a That is to say if their limits are not only ' together ' but
united, or in other words bound to be together.

^b These definitions are given in Bk. V., 226 b 18 *sqq.*, and
constitute the only portion of that Book which is relevant to
the context.   That some such exposition of the terms did occur
elsewhere in Aristotle's work and probably occupied a place
between Bks. IV. and VI. may be taken for granted.   But this
by no means implies that it was the whole of this Book, or
even this relevant portion of it in the form in which we
have it, that originally furnished the previous definition here
referred to.

^c The Greek does not imply that a limit is itself a part of
that which it limits.   See Vol. I. Introd. pp. lxxxiii ff. and
Vol. II., List of Corrigenda.

THE terms ' continuous,' ' contiguous,' and ' next-in-succession ' have been defined above as follows : things are ' continuous ' if (while they are themselves distinct in the sense of occupying different places) their limits are one,[a] ' contiguous ' if their limits are together, ' next-in-succession ' if they have nothing of the same nature as themselves between them.[b] If these definitions are accepted, it follows that no continuum can be made up of indivisibles, as for instance a line out of points, granting that the line is continuous and the point indivisible. For two points cannot have identical limits, since in an indivisible there can be no distinction of a limit from some part other than the limit[c] ; and (for the same reason) neither can the limits be together, for a thing that has no parts has no limit, since a limit must be distinct from what it limits.

Yet the points would have to be either *continuous* or *contiguous* if they were to make a continuum. And the same is true of any indivisible. As to the impossibility of their being continuous, the proof just given will suffice ; but we will consider the alternative of contiguity further. If A is contiguous with B, either A in its entirety must touch B in its entirety, or a part of one must touch a part of the other, or a part of one the other in its entirety. But since the indivisible has no parts, if two indivisibles touched each other at all it must be in their entirety. But if they were touching in their entirety, they could not make a continuum, for a continuum is divisible into parts which are distinguishable from each other in the sense of being in different places.[d]

[d] See 232 b 25.

231 b Ἀλλὰ μὴν οὐδ' ἐφεξῆς ἔσται στιγμὴ στιγμῆς,
ἢ τὸ νῦν τοῦ νῦν, ὥστ' ἐκ τούτων εἶναι τὸ μῆκος
ἢ τὸν χρόνον· ἐφεξῆς μὲν γάρ ἐστιν ὧν μηθέν ἐστι
μεταξὺ συγγενές, στιγμῶν δ' ἀεὶ τὸ μεταξὺ γραμμή,
10 καὶ τῶν νῦν χρόνος. ἔτι διαιροῖτ' ἂν εἰς ἀδιαίρετα,
εἴπερ ἐξ ὧν ἐστιν ἑκάτερον, εἰς ταῦτα διαιρεῖται.
ἀλλ' οὐθὲν ἦν τῶν συνεχῶν εἰς ἀμερῆ διαιρετόν.
ἄλλο δὲ γένος οὐχ οἷόν τ' εἶναι μεταξὺ τῶν
στιγμῶν καὶ τῶν νῦν οὐθέν. εἰ γὰρ ἔσται, δῆλον
ὡς ἤτοι ἀδιαίρετον ἔσται ἢ διαιρετόν· καὶ εἰ

---

a [I have partly re-written this paragraph on the assumption that it contains a series of arguments against the thesis that a *continuous* linear magnitude or stretch of time could be made up of a row of *successive* points or moments.—C.]

b [At 231 a 24 ff.—C.]

c [Successive points (nows) which cannot touch must have something between them. It has been asserted above that what does lie between them is something of the *same* kind (συγγενές)—a line (time). Aristotle now forestalls the objection that what lies between might be something of a *different* kind, *e.g.* a 'void' such as some Pythagoreans (213 b 24) supposed to separate the distinct points composing a line. Such a 'void' was not a line, and did not itself contain points. On that view our continuous line is to be composed of points that will be 'successive' (with nothing of *the same kind* between them), each point being separated from the next by a stretch of 'void.' Against this Aristotle argues as follows. This void stretch must be either (a) indivisible, or (b) divisible either (α) into indivisible parts or (β) infinitely. If (β) it is infinitely divisible, 'then it is a continuous magnitude,' τοῦτο δὲ συνεχές (it is, in fact, a linear magnitude, such as we said did lie between points, and the alleged 'successive' points are not successive, for they have something of the *same* kind between them). (And it *must* be infinitely divisible. Alternatives (a) and (α) can be dismissed; for this 'void' is a constituent part of our line, which is *ex hypothesi* to be a continuum), 'and it is manifest that any continuum (like our line) is divisible infinitely, for if there

94

Again,[a] one point, so far from being continuous or
contiguous with another point, cannot even be the
next-in-succession to it, or one 'now' to another 'now,'
in such a way as to make up a length or a space of
time; for things are 'next' to each other when
there is nothing of their own sort between them,
and two points have always a line (divisible at
intermediate points) between them, and two
'nows' a space of time (divisible at intermediate
'nows'). Moreover, if a succession of indivisibles
could make up a continuum either of magnitude or
time, that continuum could be resolved into its
indivisible constituents. But, as we have seen,[b]
no continuum can be resolved into elements which
have no parts. Further, there cannot be anything of
a *different kind* between the points or the 'nows.'[c]
For if there could be such a thing, clearly it must
be either (*a*) something indivisible or (*b*) something

were indivisible parts they would have to touch one another'
(in order to make up a continuum; and that we have seen
to be impossible, 231 b 2 ff.); 'for the extremities of continuous things meet and become *one*.' The last statement is
explicable if it is remembered that ἅπτεσθαι was, from Euclid
onwards, the technical term in geometry for the 'meeting'
of two lines, ἐφάπτεσθαι being used for the 'touching' of two
circles (Heath, *Thirteen Books of Euclid*, ii. 2). Two lines
laid end to end 'meet' in such a way that their end-points
coalesce, and the two lines unite into one continuous line.
It was stated at 227 a 24 that 'the extremities must meet
(ἅψασθαι), if they are to coalesce.' Similarly when a line is
divided, the ends of the two sections are not two distinct
points in contact with, or successive to, one another. If,
however, two lines meet at an angle, the end point of the one
and the beginning point of the other are the same point,
but the lines do not unite into a continuous line. This is
important in view of the argument (Bk. VIII. chapters vi.–viii.)
on continuity of movement. The conclusion here established
is used at 234 a 6 ff.—C.]

231 b 15 διαιρετόν, ἢ εἰς ἀδιαίρετα ἢ εἰς ἀεὶ διαιρετά.
τοῦτο δὲ συνεχές. φανερὸν δὲ καὶ ὅτι πᾶν συνεχὲς
διαιρετὸν εἰς ἀεὶ διαιρετά (εἰ γὰρ εἰς ἀδιαίρετα,
ἔσται ἀδιαίρετον ἀδιαιρέτου ἁπτόμενον)· ἓν γὰρ
τὸ ἔσχατον καὶ ἅπτεται τῶν συνεχῶν.

Τοῦ δὲ αὐτοῦ λόγου καὶ μέγεθος καὶ χρόνον καὶ
20 κίνησιν ἐξ ἀδιαιρέτων συγκεῖσθαι καὶ διαιρεῖσθαι
εἰς ἀδιαίρετα, ἢ μηθέν. δῆλον δὲ ἐκ τῶνδε. εἰ
γὰρ τὸ μέγεθος ἐξ ἀδιαιρέτων σύγκειται, καὶ ἡ
κίνησις ἡ τούτου ἐξ ἴσων κινήσεων ἔσται ἀδιαι-
ρέτων· οἷον εἰ τὸ ΑΒΓ ἐκ τῶν Α, Β, Γ ἐστὶν
ἀδιαιρέτων, ἡ κίνησις ἐφ' ἧς ΔΕΖ, ἣν ἐκινήθη τὸ
25 Ω ἐπὶ τῆς ΑΒΓ, ἕκαστον τὸ μέρος ἔχει ἀδιαίρετον.

$$\underline{\text{Α} \quad \text{Β} \quad \text{Γ}}$$

$$\underline{\text{Δ} \quad \text{Ε} \quad \text{Ζ}}$$

εἰ δὴ παρούσης κινήσεως ἀνάγκη κινεῖσθαί τι
καὶ εἰ κινεῖταί τι, παρεῖναι κίνησιν, καὶ τὸ κινεῖσθαι
ἔσται ἐξ ἀδιαιρέτων. τὸ μὲν δὴ Α ἐκινήθη τὸ Ω
τὴν τὸ Δ κινούμενον κίνησιν, τὸ δὲ Β τὴν τὸ Ε,
καὶ τὸ Γ ὡσαύτως τὴν τὸ Ζ. εἰ δὴ ἀνάγκη
τὸ κινούμενόν ποθέν ποι μὴ ἅμα κινεῖσθαι καὶ

divisible ; and if divisible, divisible either (a) into indivisibles or (β) into divisibles that are divisible without limit. But in the latter case it is a continuum. And it is manifest that any continuum is divisible into parts that are divisible without limit—for if the parts were indivisible, we should have one indivisible touching another—since the extremities of things that are continuous meet and become *one*.

Now the same argument applies to spatial magnitude and time and motion, so that if it can be shown that any one of them cannot be so built up and broken down, it follows that none of them can. The following proof will make this clear. If a distance is composed of indivisibles, the motion through it must be composed of an equal number of indivisible motions. Let **ABC** be the distance traversed by **P**

distance   <u>A   B   C</u>

movement   <u>L   M   N</u>

in course of the movement **LMN**. Then if **ABC** is composed of the indivisibles **A**, **B**, and **C**, the motion of **P** will be, throughout, composed of indivisible motions. And if you grant that while the movement is taking place, there must be something in motion, and that if there is something in motion there must be a movement in progress, then (on the hypothesis) the whole movement of the moving thing must be composed of indivisibles. So **P** was in passage over **A** when experiencing the motion **L**, and so for **B** and **M**, and for **C** and **N**. Now, when anything moves from here to there it cannot have

97

231 b 30 κεκινῆσθαι οὗ ἐκινεῖτο ὅτε ἐκινεῖτο (οἷον εἰ
Θήβαζέ τις βαδίζει, ἀδύνατον ἅμα βαδίζειν Θήβαζε
232 a καὶ βεβαδικέναι Θήβαζε), τὴν δὲ τὸ Α τὴν ἀμερῆ
ἐκινεῖτο τὸ Ω, ᾗ ἡ τὸ Δ κίνησις παρῆν, ὥστ᾽[1] εἰ
μὲν ὕστερον διῆλθεν ἢ διῄει, διαιρετὴ ἂν εἴη (ὅτε
γὰρ διῄει, οὔτε ἠρέμει οὔτε διεληλύθει ἀλλὰ
μεταξὺ ἦν)· εἰ δ᾽ ἅμα διέρχεται καὶ διελήλυθε, τὸ
5 βαδίζον ὅτε βαδίζει βεβαδικὸς ἐκεῖ ἔσται, καὶ
κεκινημένον οὗ κινεῖται.

Εἰ δὲ τὴν μὲν ὅλην τὴν ΑΒΓ κινεῖταί τι, καὶ ἡ
κίνησις ἣν κινεῖται τὰ Δ, Ε, Ζ ἐστί, τὴν δ᾽ ἀμερῆ
τὴν Α οὐθὲν κινεῖται ἀλλὰ κεκίνηται, εἴη ἂν ἡ
κίνησις οὐκ ἐκ κινήσεων ἀλλ᾽ ἐκ κινημάτων, καὶ
10 τὸ[2] κεκινῆσθαί τι μὴ κινούμενον (τὴν γὰρ Α διελήλυθεν οὐ διεξιόν)· ὥστε ἔσται τι βεβαδικέναι
μηδέποτε βαδίζον· ταύτην γὰρ βεβάδικεν οὐ βαδίζον
ταύτην. εἰ οὖν ἀνάγκη ἢ ἠρεμεῖν ἢ κινεῖσθαι πᾶν,
ἠρεμεῖ δὲ καθ᾽ ἕκαστον τῶν Α, Β, Γ, ὥστ᾽ ἔσται
τι συνεχῶς ἠρεμοῦν ἅμα καὶ κινούμενον· τὴν γὰρ

---

[1] [ὥστε in apodosi, as below, l. 13.—C.]
[2] [τὸ om. FHI : τῷ Oxf. Trans. Either of the MS. readings is possible with εἴη ἂν meaning (with τὸ) 'we should
have' or (without τὸ) 'it would be possible.'—C.]

---

[a] [A distinct argument, refuting the hypothesis that a
movement can consist of a series of indivisible components
occupying atoms of time and complete as soon as begun.
Epicurus later upheld this view. (Bailey, *Greek Atomists*,
p. 316).—C.]
[b] [Literally, 'and if P is not *in motion* at all over the
section A (which has no parts) but *has moved*.'—C.]

already *got there* while still *moving thither* (for instance, the man who is walking to Thebes cannot have already got to Thebes and be there at the same time as he is still walking to Thebes). But P was moving over the indivisible A exactly while its motion L was in progress. Accordingly if (i) P had not completed the movement while experiencing it, but only when it had ceased, then A must be divisible; because while P was moving, it was neither at rest (since it had already started to cover A) nor had it covered A (for it was still in the act of covering it). But if (ii) when P were moving, at one and the same time it both had accomplished and was accomplishing the movement, it would both have arrived at the term of the motion and be moving towards it: the walker, while still walking, would have finished his walk and be at his destination.

a Again, if anything moved over the whole distance ABC and the motions were L, M, and N, and if the indivisible A did not mark a distance moved over, but a (potential) term of movement,*b* (and so with B and C,) then the whole corresponding motion LMN would consist not in experiencing motions, but in having experienced them, and that which never was in motion would have accomplished the movement; for without ever passing through A, it would have passed through it. It would then be possible for our walker to have finished his walk without ever taking it: he would have walked this distance without walking *over* it. So if we grant that every mobile must be either actually moving or at rest, and if P is at rest in each of the components of ABC, we shall have P both resting and moving at one and the same time continuously;

ARISTOTLE

232 a 15 ΑΒΓ ὅλην ἐκινεῖτο καὶ ἠρέμει ὁτιοῦν μέρος, ὥστε
καὶ πᾶσαν. καὶ εἰ μὲν τὰ ἀδιαίρετα τῆς ΔΕΖ
κινήσεις, κινήσεως παρούσης ἐνδέχοιτ᾽ ἂν μὴ
κινεῖσθαι ἀλλ᾽ ἠρεμεῖν· εἰ δὲ μὴ κινήσεις, τὴν
κίνησιν μὴ ἐκ κινήσεων εἶναι.

'Ομοίως δ᾽ ἀνάγκη τῷ μήκει καὶ τῇ κινήσει
ἀδιαίρετον εἶναι τὸν χρόνον καὶ συγκεῖσθαι ἐκ τῶν
20 νῦν ὄντων ἀδιαιρέτων. εἰ γὰρ πᾶσα[1] διαιρετός,
ἐν τῷ ἐλάττονι δὲ τὸ ἰσοταχὲς δίεισιν ἔλαττον,
διαιρετὸς ἔσται καὶ ὁ χρόνος· εἰ δὲ ὁ χρόνος
διαιρετὸς ἐν ᾧ φέρεταί τι τὴν Α, καὶ ἡ τὸ Α ἔσται
διαιρετή.

[1] [πᾶσα: Themistius (184. 30) apparently read ἅπας (sc.
χρόνος), with copies known to Alexander (Simplic. 936. 22):
πᾶς ἀδιαίρετος is recorded by Aspasius. Simplicius doubted
whether γραμμή should be supplied with πᾶσα, or (with less
'violence') κίνησις, in which case the argument is from
motion to time, and from time to distance. Did Aristotle
write πᾶσ᾽ ἡ Α—'If A is divisible throughout'? Cf. Alex. ap.
Simpl. (936. 25) δείξας ὅτι ἂν τὸ μέγεθος πάντῃ διαιρετὸν ᾖ, καὶ ὁ
χρόνος ἔσται διαιρετός.—C.]

CHAPTER II

ARGUMENT

*Development of the implications of the continuous nature
of linear magnitudes, of time, and of motion, established
in the last chapter. If P is moving at a higher velocity than
Q, then not only does P (i) cover a greater distance in a given
time, and (ii) cover a given distance in a lesser time, but also
(iii) covers a greater distance in a lesser time (232 a 23–b 20).*

*Every motion occupies time, and any period of time
can be occupied by motion; and the motion occupying
any period (however short) may be quicker or slower. It
follows that time must be continuous. This is proved by*
100

since it was at once moving over the whole **ABC** and at rest in each several component, and therefore in the whole, of **ABC**. Further, if the indivisible components of the motion **LMN** were to be considered as motions, we should have to say that a thing, while in motion, might be not moving but at rest; whereas if they were not motions, we should have to say that a movement might be made of components that were not movements but stations.

Again, from indivisible components of distance and motion would follow indivisible components of time, which would, on that hypothesis, be made up of indivisible ' nows.' But if on the other hand we admit that every distance or motion is divisible, so must the corresponding periods of time be, since a thing moving at a uniform velocity will cover a part of any distance in less time than the whole. And conversely if the time in which the distance **A** is covered is divisible, so must **A** be.

CHAPTER II

ARGUMENT (*continued*)

taking two bodies moving at different speeds. However short a time the slower takes to cover a given distance, the quicker will always take still less time, and in that lesser time the slower will always cover a still shorter distance ; in this way both the time and the distance may be reduced without limit ; therefore the continuity of time follows from the continuity of magnitude and vice versa. This conclusion agrees with popular belief (b 20–233 a 17).

Further, if either time or linear magnitude is illimitable in extension or divisible without limit, so must the other be (a 17–21).

ARISTOTLE

ARGUMENT (*continued*)

The distinction between illimitable extension and unlimited divisibility gives the clue to the fallacy of Zeno's argument against the possibility of motion ' because it would involve that a moving body would have to pass an illimitable number of points and thus establish illimitable contacts in a limited time.' For both the distance and the time are limited in extent but unlimited in divisibility, and the contacts do not occupy time any more than they occupy space, but are established by divisibility (a 21–31).

Two proofs that an illimitable time cannot be required to

232 a 23 Ἐπεὶ δὲ πᾶν μέγεθος εἰς μεγέθη διαιρετόν (δέδεικται γὰρ ὅτι ἀδύνατον ἐξ ἀτόμων εἶναί τι
25 συνεχές, μέγεθος δ' ἐστὶν ἅπαν συνεχές), ἀνάγκη τὸ θᾶττον ἐν τῷ ἴσῳ χρόνῳ μεῖζον καὶ ἐν τῷ ἐλάττονι ἴσον καὶ ἐν τῷ ἐλάττονι πλεῖον κινεῖσθαι, καθάπερ ὁρίζονταί τινες τὸ θᾶττον.

Ἔστω γὰρ τὸ ἐφ' ᾧ Α τοῦ ἐφ' ᾧ Β θᾶττον. ἐπεὶ τοίνυν θᾶττόν ἐστι τὸ πρότερον μεταβάλλον, ἐν ᾧ χρόνῳ τὸ Α μεταβέβληκεν ἀπὸ τοῦ Γ εἰς τὸ
30 Δ (οἷον τῷ ΖΗ), ἐν τούτῳ τὸ Β οὔπω ἔσται πρὸς τῷ Δ ἀλλ' ἀπολείψει· ὥστε ἐν τῷ ἴσῳ χρόνῳ πλεῖον δίεισι τὸ θᾶττον.

Ἀλλὰ μὴν καὶ ἐν τῷ ἐλάττονι πλεῖον. ἐν ᾧ

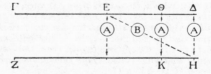

γὰρ τὸ Α γεγένηται πρὸς τῷ Δ, τὸ Β ἔστω πρὸς

ᵃ Though not so much greater as in case (i). *Vide infra.*

ARGUMENT (*continued*)

traverse any limited distance. Both depend on there being
some distance for which a limited time suffices. In the
first this is taken for granted (233 a 32 ff.); in the second
mentioned as a necessary condition (223 b 8). Then follows
a proof that such distances do exist (see p. 112 note b).
The same line of argument shows that illimitable distance
cannot be traversed in a limited time (a 31–b 15).

Further proof that there is no continuum which cannot be
divided (b 15–32).

Since any magnitude can be divided into magnitudes
(for it has been shown that nothing continuous can
be composed of atomic constituents, and all magnitude
is continuous), it follows that if P is quicker than Q it
will (i) cover a greater distance in the same time;
(ii) cover the same distance in a lesser time; (iii)
cover a greater distance in a lesser time.[a] 'Quicker'
has been defined in this way.

For (i) since P is quicker than Q and therefore
is in advance of it, in the time OT which it has taken
P to change from A to D, Q will not have reached D
but will still be short of it. So in the same time
the quicker will cover a greater distance than the
slower.

But (iii) we may go further and say that the

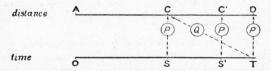

quicker will cover a greater distance in less time.
For in the time it has taken P to reach D, let Q have

ARISTOTLE

232 b τῷ Ε τὸ βραδύτερον ὄν. οὐκοῦν ἐπεὶ τὸ Α πρὸς
τῷ Δ γεγένηται ἐν ἅπαντι τῷ ΖΗ χρόνῳ, πρὸς
τῷ Θ ἔσται ἐν ἐλάττονι τούτου· καὶ ἔστω ἐν τῷ
ΖΚ. τὸ μὲν οὖν ΓΘ, ὃ διελήλυθε τὸ Α, μεῖζόν
5 ἐστι τοῦ ΓΕ, ὁ δὲ χρόνος ὁ ΖΚ ἐλάττων τοῦ
παντὸς τοῦ ΖΗ· ὥστε ἐν ἐλάττονι μεῖζον δίεισιν.

Φανερὸν δὲ ἐκ τούτων καὶ ὅτι τὸ θᾶττον ἐν
ἐλάττονι χρόνῳ δίεισι τὸ ἴσον. ἐπεὶ γὰρ τὴν

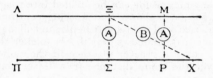

μεῖζω ἐν ἐλάττονι διέρχεται τοῦ βραδυτέρου, αὐτὸ
δὲ καθ᾽ αὑτὸ λαμβανόμενον ἐν πλείονι χρόνῳ τὴν
10 μείζω τῆς ἐλάττονος (οἷον τὴν ΛΜ τῆς ΛΞ),
πλείων ἂν εἴη ὁ χρόνος ὁ ΠΡ ἐν ᾧ τὴν ΛΜ διέρχεται ἢ ὁ ΠΣ ἐν ᾧ τὴν ΛΞ. ὥστε εἰ ὁ ΠΡ χρόνος
ἐλάττων ἐστὶ τοῦ ΠΧ ἐν ᾧ τὸ βραδύτερον διέρχεται τὴν ΛΞ, καὶ ὁ ΠΣ ἐλάττων ἔσται τοῦ ἐφ᾽
ᾧ ΠΧ· τοῦ γὰρ ΠΡ ἐλάττων, τὸ δὲ τοῦ ἐλάττονος
ἔλαττον καὶ αὐτὸ ἔλαττον. ὥστε ἐν ἐλάττονι
15 κινήσεται τὸ ἴσον.

Ἔτι δ᾽ εἰ πᾶν ἀνάγκη ἢ ἐν ἴσῳ χρόνῳ ἢ ἐν
ἐλάττονι ἢ ἐν πλείονι κινεῖσθαι, καὶ τὸ μὲν ἐν
πλείονι βραδύτερον τὸ δ᾽ ἐν ἴσῳ ἰσοταχὲς τὸ δὲ
θᾶττον οὔτε ἰσοταχὲς οὔτε βραδύτερον, οὔτ᾽ ἂν ἐν
ἴσῳ οὔτ᾽ ἐν πλείονι κινοῖτο τὸ θᾶττον. λείπεται
104

reached **C**. Now since **P** takes the whole time **OT** to reach **D**, it will have reached **C′** (any point between **C** and **D**) in a shorter time, say **OS′**. Then the distance **AC′**, which **P** has covered, is greater than **AC**; while the time **OS′** is less than the whole time **OT** (which **Q** takes to reach **C**). Accordingly, **P** will cover the greater distance in the lesser time.

From these conclusions it follows directly that (ii) **P** covers an equal distance **AC** in less time than **Q**.

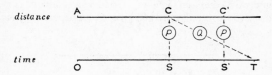

For since (as we have just seen) **P** covers a greater distance **AC′** in less time than **Q** takes to cover the lesser distance **AC**, and since **P** regarded by itself takes a longer time **OS′** to cover a greater distance **AC′** than to cover the lesser distance **AC**, consequently **P**'s time (**OS**) for covering **AC** is less than something (**OS′**) which is itself less than **Q**'s time (**OT**) for covering **AC**. Thus the quicker covers the same distance in less time than the slower.

Again, since when two mobiles both cover the same distance, their respective motions (while covering that distance) must occupy either an equal time or a longer or a shorter time, and if one takes more time than the other it is slower, if it takes the same time it is of equal speed, and if it is quicker it is neither of equal speed nor slower, the quicker cannot take either an equal or a longer time. So it can only

105

232 b οὖν ἐν ἐλάττονι· ὥστ' ἀνάγκη καὶ τὸ ἴσον μέγεθος
20 ἐν ἐλάττονι χρόνῳ διιέναι τὸ θᾶττον.

Ἐπεὶ δὲ πᾶσα μὲν κίνησις ἐν χρόνῳ καὶ ἐν
ἅπαντι χρόνῳ δυνατὸν κινηθῆναι, πᾶν δὲ τὸ κινούμενον ἐνδέχεται καὶ θᾶττον κινεῖσθαι καὶ βραδύτερον, ἐν ἅπαντι χρόνῳ ἔσται τὸ θᾶττον κινεῖσθαι
καὶ βραδύτερον· τούτων δ' ὄντων ἀνάγκη καὶ τὸν
25 χρόνον συνεχὲς εἶναι. λέγω δὲ συνεχὲς τὸ διαιρετὸν
εἰς ἀεὶ διαιρετά· τούτου γὰρ ὑποκειμένου τοῦ
συνεχοῦς, ἀνάγκη συνεχῆ εἶναι τὸν χρόνον. ἐπεὶ
γὰρ δέδεικται ὅτι τὸ θᾶττον ἐν ἐλάττονι χρόνῳ

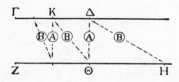

διίεισι τὸ ἴσον, ἔστω τὸ μὲν ἐφ' ᾧ Α θᾶττον τὸ δ'
ἐφ' ᾧ Β βραδύτερον, καὶ κεκινήσθω τὸ βραδύτερον
30 τὸ ἐφ' ᾧ ΓΔ μέγεθος ἐν τῷ ΖΗ χρόνῳ. δῆλον
τοίνυν ὅτι τὸ θᾶττον ἐν ἐλάττονι τούτου κινήσεται
τὸ αὐτὸ μέγεθος· καὶ κεκινήσθω ἐν τῷ ΖΘ. πάλιν
δ' ἐπεὶ τὸ θᾶττον ἐν τῷ ΖΘ διελήλυθε τὴν ὅλην τὴν
ΓΔ, τὸ βραδύτερον ἐν τῷ αὐτῷ χρόνῳ τὴν ἐλάττω
233 a διίεισιν· ἔστω οὖν ἐφ' ἧς ΓΚ. ἐπεὶ δὲ τὸ βραδύτερον τὸ Β ἐν τῷ ΖΘ χρόνῳ τὴν ΓΚ διελήλυθε,
τὸ θᾶττον ἐν ἐλάττονι διίεισιν, ὥστε πάλιν διαιρεθήσεται ὁ ΖΘ χρόνος. τούτου δὲ διαιρουμένου

ᵃ In the figure the unit of distance and the unit of time are take a shorter time. Consequently the quicker must cover the same distance in a shorter time.

Again, since every movement takes place in time, and in any period of time movement can take place, and everything that moves can move at a greater or lesser velocity, quicker or slower movements may take place within any period of time however small ; whence it follows that time must be continuous. I mean by continuous ' capable of being divided into parts that can in their turn be divided again, and so on without limit ' ; and on this definition I say that time is of necessity continuous.

It has been shown that the quicker will cover

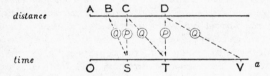

the same distance in a lesser time. Let P be the quicker, Q the slower, and let Q have moved over the distance AD in the time OV. It is clear then that the quicker P will cover that same distance in a shorter time ; let this time be OT. Again, since the quicker P has covered the whole distance AD in the time OT, the slower Q in that same time covers a shorter distance, say AC. And since the slower Q has covered AC in the time OT, P will cover that same distance in less than OT, so that the time will be divided again (at S). And the time being so

supposed to be represented by equal lines, and the velocity of P is plotted as twice that of Q. The proof would hold on any other convention or hypothesis.

233 a καὶ τὸ ΓΚ μέγεθος διαιρεθήσεται κατὰ τὸν αὐτὸν
5 λόγον. εἰ δὲ τὸ μέγεθος, καὶ ὁ χρόνος. καὶ ἀεὶ
τοῦτ' ἔσται μεταλαμβάνουσιν ἀπὸ τοῦ θάττονος
τὸ βραδύτερον καὶ ἀπὸ τοῦ βραδυτέρου τὸ θᾶττον,
καὶ τῷ ἀποδεδειγμένῳ χρωμένοις· διαιρήσει γὰρ
τὸ μὲν θᾶττον τὸν χρόνον, τὸ δὲ βραδύτερον τὸ
μῆκος. εἰ οὖν ἀεὶ μὲν ἀντιστρέφειν ἀληθές, ἀντι-
10 στρεφομένου δὲ ἀεὶ γίγνεται διαίρεσις, φανερὸν
ὅτι πᾶς χρόνος ἔσται συνεχής.

Ἅμα δὲ δῆλον καὶ ὅτι μέγεθος ἅπαν ἐστὶ
συνεχές· τὰς αὐτὰς γὰρ καὶ τὰς ἴσας διαιρέσεις
ὁ χρόνος διαιρεῖται καὶ τὸ μέγεθος. ἔτι δὲ καὶ ἐκ
τῶν εἰωθότων λόγων λέγεσθαι φανερὸν ὡς εἴπερ
ὁ χρόνος ἐστὶ συνεχής, ὅτι καὶ τὸ μέγεθος, εἴπερ
15 ἐν τῷ ἡμίσει χρόνῳ ἥμισυ διέρχεται καὶ ἁπλῶς
ἐν τῷ ἐλάττονι ἔλαττον· αἱ γὰρ αὐταὶ διαιρέσεις
ἔσονται τοῦ χρόνου καὶ τοῦ μεγέθους.

Καὶ εἰ ὁποτερονοῦν ἄπειρον, καὶ θάτερον, καὶ
ὡς θάτερον, καὶ θάτερον· οἷον εἰ μὲν τοῖς ἐσχάτοις
ἄπειρος ὁ χρόνος, καὶ τὸ μῆκος τοῖς ἐσχάτοις, εἰ
20 δὲ τῇ διαιρέσει, τῇ διαιρέσει καὶ τὸ μῆκος, εἰ δὲ
ἀμφοῖν ὁ χρόνος, ἀμφοῖν καὶ τὸ μέγεθος.

ᵃ Length and distance are used indifferently in this section
according to convenience to represent μῆκος.

ᵇ If Aristotle here uses ' magnitude ' as a variant for
' length,' he means by ' any ' magnitude ' any however
small.' If he means to distinguish between ' length ' (or
' distance ') and ' area,' ' volume ' or ' weight ' or any other
' measurable ' (in which sense, ' time,' ' temperature,'
' pressure,' etc., are all ' magnitudes '), then he assumes that
his reader understands that a ratio between two lengths, for
instance, can be identical with, greater, or less than, a ratio
between two areas etc., so that what is proved of time and
distance is proved of time and any other magnitude, viz. that

divided, the distance AC will also be divided in the same proportion. And if the distance is divided, the time is correspondingly divided. And this process may be carried on without limit, if you determine the lesser time P takes to cover a given distance as compared with Q, and then determine the lesser distance that Q covers in that lesser time as compared with P. For in comparison with Q, P will always curtail the *time*, and in comparison with P, Q will always curtail the *distance*. But if this conversion always holds, however many divisions have been made, and every conversion leads to a further division, it is evident that (if length is continuous) so is time.[a]

Thus the continuity of time follows on that of magnitude and also the continuity of magnitude [b] on that of time, for divisions and subdivisions of the given time and the given magnitude can always be made to keep pace in number and in ratio without limit. Moreover our ordinary way of talking assumes that the continuity of time carries with it that of magnitude, for we do not hesitate to say that half the time suffices to cover half the distance, or generally the lesser time the lesser distance ; for the divisions of the distance can always be made in the same ratio as the divisions of the time.

Likewise, if either time or magnitude is unlimited in any respect, so is the other in the same respect. For instance, if the time extends in both directions without limit, so will the distance ; and if time is divisible without limit, so will distance be ; and if time is both extended without limit and divisible without limit, so will distance be.

the one is divisible, without limit, in the same ratio as the other.

ARISTOTLE

233 a   Διὸ καὶ ὁ Ζήνωνος λόγος ψεῦδος λαμβάνει τὸ
μὴ ἐνδέχεσθαι τὰ ἄπειρα διελθεῖν ἢ ἅψασθαι τῶν
ἀπείρων καθ᾽ ἕκαστον ἐν πεπερασμένῳ χρόνῳ.
διχῶς γὰρ λέγεται καὶ τὸ μῆκος καὶ ὁ χρόνος
25 ἄπειρον, καὶ ὅλως πᾶν τὸ συνεχές—ἤτοι κατὰ
διαίρεσιν ἢ τοῖς ἐσχάτοις. τῶν μὲν οὖν κατὰ
ποσὸν ἀπείρων οὐκ ἐνδέχεται ἅψασθαι ἐν πεπερασμένῳ χρόνῳ, τῶν δὲ κατὰ διαίρεσιν ἐνδέχεται· καὶ
γὰρ αὐτὸς ὁ χρόνος οὕτως ἄπειρος. ὥστε ἐν τῷ
30 ἀπείρῳ καὶ οὐκ ἐν τῷ πεπερασμένῳ συμβαίνει
διιέναι τὸ ἄπειρον, καὶ ἅπτεσθαι τῶν ἀπείρων τοῖς
ἀπείροις, οὐ τοῖς πεπερασμένοις.

   Οὔτε δὴ τὸ ἄπειρον οἷόν τε ἐν πεπερασμένῳ
χρόνῳ διελθεῖν, οὔτ᾽ ἐν ἀπείρῳ τὸ πεπερασμένον·

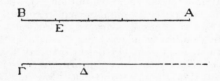

ἀλλ᾽ ἐάν τε ὁ χρόνος ἄπειρος ᾖ, καὶ τὸ μέγεθος
ἔσται ἄπειρον, ἐάν τε τὸ μέγεθος, καὶ ὁ χρόνος.

---

   [a] Zeno makes it appear as though the number of the contacts to be established accord in the case of the distance with
its *divisibility* (which is unlimited), but in the case of time
with its *extension* (which is limited).   So that the set of contingents would be illimitable on one side and limited on the
other.   Whereas, in reality it accords with *divisibility* (which
is unlimited) in both cases.   So that the contingents are
illimitable on both sides.
   [b] A definite distance and a definite period of time are

110

Hence Zeno's argument makes a false assumption in asserting that it is impossible for a thing to traverse or severally come in contact with illimitable things in a limited time. For there are two senses in which a distance or a period of time (or indeed any continuum) may be regarded as illimitable, viz., in respect to its divisibility or in respect to its extension.[a] Now it is not possible to come in contact with quantitively illimitable things in a limited time, but it is possible to traverse what is illimitable in its divisibility ; for in this respect time itself is also illimitable. Accordingly, a distance which is (in this sense) illimitable is traversed in a time which is (in this sense) not limited but illimitable ; and the contacts with the illimitable (points) are made at ' nows ' which are not limited but illimitable in number.[b]

Thus it is impossible for an illimitable distance to be covered in a limited time, or for an illimitable time to be occupied in covering a limited distance ; if the

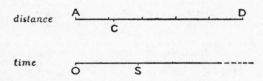

time is illimitable so must the distance be, and if the distance, the time. To prove this, let the line AD

divisible in exactly the same way : the distance *at* points *into* shorter distances, the time *at* nows *into* shorter periods. A point marks off a stage in the journey, and the corresponding now marks off the time taken to accomplish that stage. Neither the points nor the nows are limitable.

233 a 35 ἔστω γὰρ πεπερασμένον μέγεθος ἐφ' οὗ ΑΒ,
χρόνος δὲ ἄπειρος ἐφ' ᾧ Γ· εἰλήφθω δέ τι τοῦ
233 b χρόνου πεπερασμένον, ἐφ' ᾧ ΓΔ. ἐν τούτῳ οὖν
δίεισί τι τοῦ μεγέθους, καὶ ἔστω διεληλυθὸς ἐφ' ᾧ
ΒΕ. (τοῦτο δὲ ἢ καταμετρήσει τὸ ἐφ' ᾧ ΑΒ ἢ
ἐλλείψει ἢ ὑπερβαλεῖ· διαφέρει γὰρ οὐθέν). εἰ γὰρ
5 ἀεὶ τὸ ἴσον τῷ ΒΕ μέγεθος ἐν ἴσῳ χρόνῳ δίεισι
(τοῦτο δὲ καταμετρεῖ τὸ ὅλον), πεπερασμένος ἔσται
ὁ πᾶς χρόνος ἐν ᾧ διῆλθεν· εἰς ἴσα γὰρ διαιρεθήσεται καὶ[1] τὸ μέγεθος. ἔτι δὲ εἰ μὴ πᾶν μέγεθος
ἐν ἀπείρῳ χρόνῳ δίεισιν, ἀλλ' ἐνδέχεταί τι καὶ ἐν
πεπερασμένῳ διελθεῖν, οἷον τὸ ΒΕ (τοῦτο δὲ κατα-
10 μετρήσει τὸ πᾶν), καὶ τὸ ἴσον ἐν ἴσῳ δίεισιν, ὥστε
πεπερασμένος ἔσται καὶ ὁ χρόνος. ὅτι δὲ οὐκ
ἐν ἀπείρῳ δίεισι τὸ ΒΕ, φανερόν, εἰ ληφθείη ἐπὶ

[1] [καὶ Ε and Alexander, Aspasius, and Themistius
(Simplic. 950. 3): ὡς καὶ cett.—C.]

---

[a] For in any case a limited multiple of AC will equal or
exceed AD ; and the same limited multiple of the time OS
must equal or exceed the time occupied in traversing AD.
This time itself, therefore, must be limited.

[b] The argument that a time must be finite if it is less than
infinite time is unsound, and inconsistent with the definition
of infinity in Bk. III. chs. v., vi. and vii. (see especially 207 a
7 *sq.*). For being less than infinite does not preclude it from
exceeding any *definite* time whatever, and therefore imposes
no limit on its duration. One infinite can have any ratio
(finite or infinite) to another, as is recognized in the proof
that the universe is limited in *De caelo*, i. 3, 271 b 27 *sqq.*
But the argument is not only unsound but unnecessary, for
to deny that there is *any* distance which can be traversed in
a limited time is to deny that any movement at all can ever
be completed, and this is to deny the reality of motion, which
is axiomatic to Aristotle (see Bk. VIII. chap. i. p. 269 and iii.

represent the limited distance, and the line from O
an illimitable time. Take S anywhere on the line
from O. Then in the limited time OS the mobile
will traverse a certain part of the (limited) distance;
let that part be represented by AC. (AC will
either be an exact measure of AD or be less or
greater than some exact measure of it, and it
doesn't matter which it is.[a]) For since a distance
equal to AC will always be traversed in an equal
time, then (taking the case in which AC is an exact
measure of AD) the whole time occupied in covering
AD will be limited; for it will be divided into the
same (limited) number of parts that the distance AD
has been divided into. Again, if it be granted that
it does not require an illimitable time to cover any
distance whatever, but that there are distances for
which a limited time suffices, such as AC (which we
will suppose to be an exact measure of AD), then,
if equal distances are traversed in equal times, it
follows that the time taken in traversing AD must,
like the distance AD itself, be finite. That a limited
time *does* suffice for AC is evident,[b] for if we take as
one limit of the time the instant at which the mobile

p. 293). The reader who has only an elementary acquaintance
with mathematics is recommended to consult De Morgan's
Algebra, Chapter vi, where he discusses the meaning of the
term ' infinite ' and its application to limits and series.

At 238 a 8 *sq.* the same argument is applied to motion
whose velocity is not uniform. It is assumed, however, that
the velocity varies within limits or rather that it could not
fall below any assignable limit whatever, for otherwise the
length of time that would suffice for the final stage of the
journey might rise above any assignable limit (notwith-
standing that it would require less time than the whole distance requires). And if there is any part of the distance for
which no limited time suffices, it follows that no limited time
will suffice for the whole.

233 b θάτερα πεπερασμένος ὁ χρόνος· εἰ γὰρ ἐν ἐλάττονι
τὸ μέρος δίεισι, τοῦτο ἀνάγκη πεπεράνθαι, θατέρου
γε πέρατος ὑπάρχοντος. ἡ αὐτὴ δ' ἀπόδειξις καὶ
15 εἰ τὸ μὲν μῆκος ἄπειρον ὁ δὲ χρόνος πεπερασμένος.

Φανερὸν οὖν ἐκ τῶν εἰρημένων ὡς οὔτε γραμμὴ
οὔτε ἐπίπεδον οὔτε ὅλως τῶν συνεχῶν οὐθὲν ἔσται
ἄτομον, οὐ μόνον διὰ τὸ νῦν λεχθὲν ἀλλὰ καὶ ὅτι
συμβήσεται διαιρεῖσθαι τὸ ἄτομον. ἐπεὶ γὰρ ἐν
20 ἅπαντι χρόνῳ τὸ θᾶττον καὶ βραδύτερόν ἐστι, τὸ
δὲ θᾶττον πλεῖον διέρχεται ἐν τῷ ἴσῳ χρόνῳ,
ἐνδέχεται καὶ διπλάσιον καὶ ἡμιόλιον διιέναι μῆκος·
εἴη γὰρ ἂν οὗτος ὁ λόγος τοῦ τάχους. ἐνηνέχθω

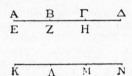

οὖν τὸ θᾶττον ἡμιόλιον ἐν τῷ αὐτῷ χρόνῳ, καὶ
διῃρήσθω τὰ μεγέθη τὸ[1] μὲν τοῦ θάττονος ἐφ' ᾧ
25 ΑΒΓΔ εἰς τρία ἄτομα, τὸ δὲ τοῦ βραδυτέρου εἰς
δύο ἐφ' ὧν ΕΖ, ΖΗ. οὐκοῦν καὶ ὁ χρόνος διαιρεθήσεται εἰς τρία ἄτομα· τὸ γὰρ ἴσον ἐν τῷ ἴσῳ χρόνῳ
δίεισιν. διῃρήσθω οὖν ὁ χρόνος εἰς τὰ ΚΛ, ΛΜ,
ΜΝ. πάλιν δ' ἐπεὶ τὸ βραδύτερον ἐνήνεκται τὴν

[1] [τὸ Oxf. Trans. *Cf.* Simplic. 954. 1.—C.]

---

[a] [Literally, ' For since in any and every time (occupied by
movement) there can be a distinction of faster and slower.'
—C.]

is at the point **A**, then, since by hypothesis time without the other limit suffices for the transit of **AD** in its totality, something less than that time (*i.e.* a period which *has* its other limit) will suffice for the lesser **AC**. The same proof applies to the case of an unlimited distance and limited time.

Evidently, then, neither length nor surface nor any continuum whatever can be indivisible, since (in addition to what has been said already) the contrary supposition would involve a division of the indivisible. For since there may be a faster or slower transit over any distance whatever,[a] and the mobile at the greater velocity covers more distance in an equal time, then according to the ratio of the velocities, the one mobile may cover twice or once and a half the distance covered by the other in the same time.

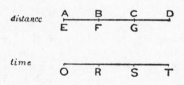

Let it be once and a half, and let **AD**, which the faster covers in the given time, consist of the three indivisibles **AB**, **BC**, **CD**. Then the distance covered in the same time by the slower will be two indivisibles, **EF** and **FG**. Now to the three atomic distances **AB**, **BC**, **CD**, there would correspond three atoms of time **OR**, **RS**, **ST**, making up the whole time taken by the swifter to cover **AD**. But this same time would be what the slower takes to cover **EF** and **FG**. It follows that half that distance (say

233 b ΕΖ, ΖΗ, καὶ ὁ χρόνος τμηθήσεται δίχα. διαιρε-
30 θήσεται ἄρα τὸ ἄτομον, καὶ τὸ ἀμερὲς οὐκ ἐν
ἀτόμῳ δίεισιν ἀλλ᾿ ἐν πλείονι. φανερὸν οὖν ὅτι
οὐδέν ἐστι τῶν συνεχῶν ἀμερές.

CHAPTER III

ARGUMENT

*The present or 'now' which divides the past from the
future must be indivisible. For the final limit of the past
and the initial limit of the future cannot be 'next,' but must
either be (i) at the same instant, or (ii) be separated by a
(divisible) period of time. If 'now' were a period of time,
it would not be the authentic limit between the past and the
future, but a period of time embracing that limit; for it
would itself be divisible into past and future, and no part
of it could definitely be said to be either past or future, for*

33 Ἀνάγκη δὲ καὶ τὸ νῦν τὸ μὴ καθ᾿ ἕτερον ἀλλὰ
καθ᾿ αὐτὸ καὶ πρῶτον λεγόμενον ἀδιαίρετον εἶναι,
35 καὶ ἐν ἅπαντι τὸ τοιοῦτο χρόνῳ ἐνυπάρχειν. ἔστι
234 a γὰρ ἔσχατόν τι τοῦ γεγονότος, οὗ ἐπὶ τάδε οὐθέν
ἐστι τοῦ μέλλοντος, καὶ πάλιν τοῦ μέλλοντος, οὗ
ἐπὶ τάδε οὐθέν ἐστι τοῦ γεγονότος· ὃ δὴ ἔφαμεν
ἀμφοῖν εἶναι πέρας. τοῦτο δὲ ἂν δειχθῇ ὅτι
τοιοῦτόν ἐστι καθ᾿ αὑτὸ καὶ ταυτόν, ἅμα φανερὸν
5 ἔσται καὶ ὅτι ἀδιαίρετον.

Ἀνάγκη δὴ τὸ αὐτὸ εἶναι τὸ νῦν τὸ ἔσχατον
ἀμφοτέρων τῶν χρόνων· εἰ γὰρ ἕτερον, ἐφεξῆς μὲν
οὐκ ἂν εἴη θάτερον θατέρῳ διὰ τὸ μὴ εἶναι συνεχὲς

---

a i.e. not as we speak of ' this present year,' in virtue of the
actual ' now ' being included in that period.

b [Λt 222 a 12.—C.]

EF) would take the slower half the time OT. But
that will involve bisecting the atom of time RS, and
the mobile will take not an atom of time but more
(an atom and a half) to cover its atomic distance EF.
There is then no continuum that cannot be divided
into parts.

CHAPTER III

ARGUMENT (*continued*)

*the authentic limit would be indeterminate as it might come
at any point within the period* (233 b 33–234 a 24).

*Why nothing can be either in motion or at rest in a 'now,'
but all movement and rest must occupy time* (a 24–b 9).

FURTHER, what we call 'now' or 'the present' (not
in any derivative sense,[a] but primarily and on its
own account) must be indivisible, and there must be
such a 'now' embraced in any defined period of time
whatever. For the 'now' may be regarded as the
limit up to which the past has run, none of the future
being this side of it, and also as the limit from which
the future runs, none of the past being that side
of it. And accordingly we have defined it [b] as the
limit alike of the past on one side and of the future
on the other. If, then, we can make good that it is
really one and the same thing, namely the authentic
'now,' that limits the past and future, it will be clear
also that it is indivisible.

Granting that the 'present now' is what divides
the past and future, the limits of the past and future
as determined above must be the same as each other
and as the present ; for if they were different from
each other, they could not be next-in-succession to
each other, for it has been shown that two limits can-

117

234 a ἐξ ἀμερῶν, εἰ δὲ χωρὶς ἑκάτερον, μεταξὺ ἔσται
χρόνος· πᾶν γὰρ τὸ συνεχὲς τοιοῦτον ὥστ᾽ εἶναί
10 τι συνώνυμον μεταξύ τῶν περάτων. ἀλλὰ μὴν εἰ
χρόνος τὸ μεταξύ, διαιρετὸν ἔσται (πᾶς γὰρ χρόνος
δέδεικται ὅτι διαιρετός)· ὥστε διαιρετὸν τὸ νῦν.
εἰ δὲ διαιρετὸν τὸ νῦν, ἔσται τι τοῦ γεγονότος ἐν
τῷ μέλλοντι καὶ τοῦ μέλλοντος ἐν τῷ γεγονότι·
καθ᾽ ὃ γὰρ ἂν διαιρεθῇ, τοῦτο διοριεῖ τὸν παρ-
15 ήκοντα καὶ τὸν μέλλοντα χρόνον. ἅμα δὲ καὶ οὐκ
ἂν καθ᾽ αὑτὸ εἴη τὸ νῦν, ἀλλὰ καθ᾽ ἕτερον· ἡ γὰρ
διαίρεσις οὐ καθ᾽ αὑτό. πρὸς δὲ τούτοις τοῦ νῦν
τὸ μέν τι γεγονὸς ἔσται τὸ δὲ μέλλον, καὶ οὐκ ἀεὶ
τὸ αὐτὸ γεγονὸς ἢ μέλλον. οὐδὲ δὴ τὸ νῦν τὸ

ᵃ [Literally, ' because a continuum (such as time has been
shown to be) cannot be composed of indivisibles ' (which
might be ' successive '), as we saw in chap. i.—C.]

ᵇ [καθ᾽ ὃ γὰρ κτλ. ' For at whatever point (this extended
' now ') is actually divided, that point will be the boundary
between past and future.' Accordingly, Aristotle argues,
that segment of the extended now which lies before the actual
point of division is really a part of the past, but it will be ' in
the future,' since it is part of the supposed extended present,
which, as it is the present, must be after the past and so in
the future.—C.]

ᶜ [Literally, ' for the division (which carves out this extended now) is not a division in the proper sense ' (viz. an
indivisible boundary).—C.]

ᵈ Aristotle is not now speaking of the present as something
which is always moving with the passage of time, so that
what *was* future becomes past—but as something which is
regarded as a period of time, divisible at any point into past
and future. Let RT be the divisible present, then it could be
divided at *any* point into past and future. If it were divided
at S_1, then RS_1 would be past and S_1T would be future. But
it might equally well be divided at S_2, in which case RS_2
would be past and S_2T would be future; so that S_1S_2 might
equally well be claimed as past or as future. Thus there

not be 'nexts' to each other [a] ; and if the two limits
of time were separated, there must lie between them
something of the denomination of the continuum they
limit, which in this case is time. The ' now ' that
separates the past from the future would in that case
itself be a period of time, and as such it would be
divisible. Thus the ' now ' that separates past and
future would be divisible, and so would contain past
and future. But all that was beyond the past was
declared to be future with no past in it, whereas this
supposed extended ' now ' lies beyond the limit of
the past and is therefore future, but it *has* some past
in it. And by analogous reasoning, being this side
of the future, it is past, but has some of the future in

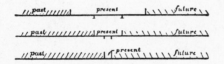

it.[b] Again, such a ' now ' would not be the proper
but the derivative ' now,' for it would not be the
limit but only the segment of a continuum within
which the limit occurs.[c] Besides, a portion of this
' now ' would be past and another portion future, and
it would not in every case be the same portion that
was past or future.[d] In fact the ' now ' itself would

would be nothing to determine which part of the ' present '
was past and which future.

ARISTOTLE

234 a αὐτό· πολλαχῇ γὰρ διαιρετὸς ὁ χρόνος. ὥστ᾽ εἰ
20 ταῦτα ἀδύνατον ὑπάρχειν τῷ νῦν, ἀνάγκη τὸ αὐτὸ
εἶναι τὸ ἐν ἑκατέρῳ νῦν. ἀλλὰ μὴν εἰ ταὐτό,
φανερὸν ὅτι καὶ ἀδιαίρετον· εἰ γὰρ διαιρετόν, πάλιν
ταὐτὰ συμβήσεται ἃ καὶ ἐν τῷ πρότερον. ὅτι μὲν
τοίνυν ἐστί τι ἐν τῷ χρόνῳ ἀδιαίρετον ὃ φαμεν
εἶναι τὸ νῦν, δῆλόν ἐστιν ἐκ τῶν εἰρημένων.

"Οτι δ᾽ οὐδὲν ἐν τῷ νῦν κινεῖται, ἐκ τῶνδε
25 φανερόν ἐστιν. εἰ γάρ, ἐνδέχεται καὶ θᾶττον
κινεῖσθαι ἐν αὐτῷ καὶ βραδύτερον. ἔστω δὴ τὸ
νῦν ἐφ᾽ ᾧ Ν, κεκινήσθω δ᾽ ἐν αὐτῷ τὸ θᾶττον τὴν

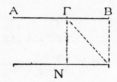

ΑΒ. οὐκοῦν τὸ βραδύτερον ἐν τῷ αὐτῷ ἐλάττω
τῆς ΑΒ κινηθήσεται, οἷον τὴν ΑΓ. ἐπεὶ δὲ τὸ
βραδύτερον ἐν ὅλῳ τῷ νῦν κεκίνηται τὴν ΑΓ, τὸ
30 θᾶττον ἐν ἐλάττονι τούτου κινηθήσεται· ὥστε
διαιρεθήσεται τὸ νῦν. ἀλλ᾽ ἦν ἀδιαίρετον. οὐκ
ἄρα ἔστι κινεῖσθαι ἐν τῷ νῦν.

᾽Αλλὰ μὴν οὐδ᾽ ἠρεμεῖν. ἠρεμεῖν γὰρ ἐλέγομεν
τὸ πεφυκὸς κινεῖσθαι μὴ κινούμενον ὅτε πέφυκε

---

a [At 226 b 12.—C.]

not be identical with itself, because the time of
which it consisted could be divided at many poincs.
Thus, if all these contradictions follow from the hypothesis that the limit to which the past reaches is other
than the limit from which the future starts, it follows
that the two definitions of 'now' define one and the
same 'now.' And if that be so, obviously the present
'now' is indivisible ; for if it were divisible, we should
be back again in the same impossibilities. Thus we
have shown that there is a something pertaining to
time which is indivisible, and this something is what
we mean by the 'present' or 'now.'

That nothing can move in the 'present now,' the
following considerations will show. If it is possible
for there to be motion in the 'now,' then there can
be faster or slower motion in it. Let **N** be the

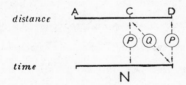

' now,' and let the faster movement cover **AD** in **N**.
Then the slower will cover something less, say **AC**,
in **N**. But since the slower covers **AC** in the whole
of **N**, the faster will cover it in less than **N**. But
this means dividing the 'now,' which we have found
to be indivisible. Motion in the 'now' is therefore
impossible.

And neither is rest or 'station' possible in the
'now.' For, as we were saying,[a] a thing is ' at rest '
only if it is naturally capable of such and such motion,

121

234 a καὶ οὗ καὶ ὥς· ὥστ᾽, ἐπεὶ ἐν τῷ νῦν οὐδὲν πέφυκε

κινεῖσθαι, δῆλον ὡς οὐδ᾽ ἠρεμεῖν.

35 Ἔτι δ᾽, εἰ τὸ αὐτὸ μέν ἐστι τὸ νῦν ἐν ἀμφοῖν τοῖν

234 b χρόνοιν, ἐνδέχεται δὲ τὸν μὲν κινεῖσθαι τὸν δ᾽

ἠρεμεῖν ὅλον, τὸ δ᾽ ὅλον κινούμενον τὸν χρόνον ἐν

ὁτῳοῦν κινηθήσεται τῶν τούτου καθ᾽ ὃ πέφυκε

κινεῖσθαι, καὶ τὸ ἠρεμοῦν ὡσαύτως ἠρεμήσει,

συμβήσεται τὸ αὐτὸ ἅμα ἠρεμεῖν καὶ κινεῖσθαι· τὸ

5 γὰρ αὐτὸ ἔσχατον τῶν χρόνων ἀμφοτέρων, τὸ νῦν.

Ἔτι δ᾽ ἠρεμεῖν μὲν λέγομεν τὸ ὁμοίως ἔχον καὶ

αὐτὸ καὶ τὰ μέρη νῦν καὶ πρότερον· ἐν δὲ τῷ νῦν

οὐκ ἔστι τὸ πρότερον, ὥστε οὐδ᾽ ἠρεμεῖν.

Ἀνάγκη ἄρα καὶ κινεῖσθαι τὸ κινούμενον ἐν

χρόνῳ καὶ ἠρεμεῖν τὸ ἠρεμοῦν.

---

[a] ' Beginning ' here means the initial limit, not (as at 236 a 15) the first part.

[b] *i.e.* they cannot be instantaneous.

but at this specified time and this specified place (though still retaining its natural capacity for such motion) it is not actually moving. So that if (as just proved) nothing has a natural capacity of moving in the 'now,' nothing can be said to be at rest 'in it.'

Moreover, if a stretch of time be divided by a 'now' into two periods, we have seen that this 'now' *qua* end of the first period and *qua* beginning[a] of the second is the same. Now suppose a mobile to be in motion in the whole of the first period and at rest in the whole of the second. Being in motion in the whole of the first period, it will be in motion in any of it which is naturally capable of being moved in; so that if its end were capable of being moved in, it would be moving in that. And, by parity of reasoning, if the beginning of the second period were capable of being rested in, it would be at rest in the beginning of that. But the end of one and the beginning of the other are the same 'now': therefore if a 'now' were capable of being moved in and rested in, the same mobile would be at once moving in it *qua* end of one section and at rest in it *qua* beginning of the other.

Yet again, we say a thing is at rest when it has not changed its position, either in respect to its totality or in respect to its parts, between now and then: but there is no 'then' in 'now'; so there is no being at rest.

Both motion and rest, then, must necessarily occupy time.[b]

ARISTOTLE

CHAPTER IV

INTRODUCTORY NOTE

The demonstration that anything that changes must be divisible begins with an examination of the condition of a thing ' in motion ' which includes changing in quality, quantity or position.

There are four logical alternatives :

(1) to be *both* entirely in one contrary *and* entirely in the other,

(2) to be *either* entirely in one contrary *or* entirely in the other,

(3) *not* to be in either *at all*,

(4) to be *partially* in one and *partially* in the other.

Of these the first is not possible under any circumstances ; the second is not possible when the subject is actually ' in motion ' ; the third is not possible when the motion is between these contraries only. There remains the fourth—the only one possible when the thing is in the act of changing from the one contrary to the other.

There is no relevant distinction between the various processes of change, but their incidental differences must be taken into account when applying the general argument. To make this clear we may vary the illustration

ARGUMENT

[*Everything that can be in a process of change must be divisible into parts, for it must, while changing, be partially in the one condition, partially in the other* (234 b 10–20).

A movement is divisible both (i) *in respect of the time it occupies and* (ii) *according to the movements of the parts of the thing moved.* (ii) *Three proofs that the movement of the whole is equivalent to the sum of the movements of the parts* (b 20–235 a 10). (i) *The divisibility of movement in respect of time* (a 10–13).

CHAPTER IV

INTRODUCTORY NOTE (*continued*)

given in the text, and suppose the contraries to be light and darkness The change from the one to the other of these may occur in either of two ways.

1st way : A black shadow may gradually invade a bright surface and eventually eclipse it entirely ; in this case the immediate subject of change is the area of the shadow. Now when any part of the surface comes under shadow it remains so, and for it the change is over. Similarly the change has not yet begun for any part that is still in the light ; but during any period of the change the shadow progresses over some part of the surface, and any such progress is divisible because any part of the surface is divisible.

2nd way : the light may gradually fade from the whole surface simultaneously ; in this case the immediate subject of change is the brightness. As the shadow deepens the whole surface passes simultaneously from lighter to darker and the progress of the change is measured by the degree in which it does so. Any such progress is divisible because any degree is divisible.

Change of position is measured by linear distance, and is divisible because any distance is so. Similarly increase and decrease of magnitude is divisible because any magnitude is so.

ARGUMENT (*continued*)

The movement, the time it occupies, the actual ' being in motion,' and the field in which the movement occurs are all susceptible of being divided correspondingly with the thing moved (a 13–18). This is established in detail. (i) The divisions of movement and time correspond (a 18–24). (ii) The ' being in motion ' (i.e. the condition of the thing moved in so far as it is actually being moved) can be

ARISTOTLE

*divided into parts in the same way as the movement ; as a
whole it is, like the movement, continuous* (a 25–34). *(iii)
Whatever forms a field of change (e.g. distance, quantity,
quality) is correspondingly divisible, though a* quale *is*

234 b 10   Τὸ δὲ μεταβάλλον ἅπαν ἀνάγκη διαιρετὸν εἶναι.
ἐπεὶ γὰρ ἔκ τινος εἴς τι πᾶσα μεταβολή, καὶ ὅταν
μὲν ᾖ ἐν τούτῳ εἰς ὃ μετέβαλλεν, οὐκέτι μεταβάλλει, ὅταν δὲ ἐξ οὗ μετέβαλλε, καὶ αὐτὸ καὶ τὰ
15 μέρη πάντα, οὐ μεταβάλλει (τὸ γὰρ ὡσαύτως ἔχον
καὶ αὐτὸ καὶ τὰ μέρη οὐ μεταβάλλει)· ἀνάγκη οὖν
τὸ μέν τι ἐν τούτῳ εἶναι τὸ δὲ ἐν θατέρῳ τοῦ μετα-
βάλλοντος· οὔτε γὰρ ἐν ἀμφοτέροις οὔτ᾽ ἐν μηδετέρῳ
ὅλον δυνατόν. (λέγω δὲ εἰς ὃ μεταβάλλει τὸ
πρῶτον κατὰ τὴν μεταβολήν, οἷον ἐκ τοῦ λευκοῦ
τὸ φαιόν, οὐ τὸ μέλαν· οὐ γὰρ ἀνάγκη τὸ μεταβάλλον
20 ἐν ὁποτερῳοῦν εἶναι τῶν ἄκρων.) φανερὸν οὖν ὅτι
πᾶν τὸ μεταβάλλον ἔσται διαιρετόν.

Κίνησις δ᾽ ἐστὶ διαιρετὴ διχῶς, ἕνα μὲν τρόπον
τῷ χρόνῳ, ἄλλον δὲ κατὰ τὰς τῶν μερῶν τοῦ κινουμένου κινήσεις· οἷον, εἰ τὸ ΑΓ κινεῖται ὅλον, καὶ
τὸ ΑΒ κινηθήσεται καὶ τὸ ΒΓ. ἔστω δὴ τοῦ μὲν
25 ΑΒ ἡ ΔΕ, τοῦ δὲ ΒΓ ἡ ΕΖ, κίνησις τῶν μερῶν.
ἀνάγκη δὴ τὴν ὅλην, ἐφ᾽ ἧς ΔΖ, τοῦ ΑΓ εἶναι
κίνησιν· κινήσεται γὰρ κατὰ ταύτην, ἐπείπερ

ᵃ See p. 81 note *b.*

divisible only accidentally (a 34–37). *All these entities also go together in respect of being limited or unlimited, the attributes ' divisible ' and ' unlimited ' belonging primarily to the thing that changes* (a 37–b 5).—C.]

ANYTHING that changes must be divisible (with respect to that which is primarily affected by the change). For every change moves along a definite line from this condition to that ; and when the mobile has already reached the ' condition to which ' then the change is no longer in progress ; and as long as it remains, as a whole and in all its parts, in the ' condition from which' so long the change is not yet in progress (for such is the definition of the static as opposed to the changing state). It follows, then, that during the whole progress of the change it must be partly under one condition and partly under the other, for it cannot be entirely under both or under neither. (I am speaking, of course, not of the extreme, but of a proximate degree of change—from white to grey, for instance, not from white to black—for it would not follow that it must be under one or other of the extreme conditions.) It is clear therefore that anything that changes must be divisible into parts.[a]

A movement is divisible in two ways : according to the time it occupies ; according to the movements of the several parts of the moving thing. Thus, if AC moves as a whole there will be a movement of AB and also of BC.

Let LM represent the movement of the part AB, and MN the movement of the part BC. Then the whole LN must necessarily represent the movement of the whole AC. LN will constitute its movement,

127

234 b ἑκάτερον τῶν μερῶν κινεῖται καθ᾽ ἑκατέραν, οὐδὲν

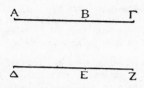

δὲ κινεῖται κατὰ τὴν ἄλλου κίνησιν· ὥστε ἡ ὅλη κίνησις τοῦ ὅλου ἐστὶ μεγέθους κίνησις.

30 Ἔτι δ᾽ εἰ πᾶσα μὲν κίνησις τινός, ἡ δ᾽ ὅλη κίνησις ἡ ἐφ᾽ ἧς ΔΖ μήτε τῶν μερῶν ἐστι μηδ- ετέρου (μέρους γὰρ ἑκατέρα) μήτε ἄλλου μηδενός (οὗ γὰρ ἡ ὅλη ὅλου, καὶ τὰ μέρη τῶν μερῶν· τὰ δὲ μέρη τοῦ ΔΖ τῶν ΑΒ, ΒΓ καὶ οὐδένων ἄλλων· πλειόνων γὰρ οὐκ ἦν μία κίνησις), κἂν ἡ ὅλη κίνησις εἴη ἂν τοῦ ΑΒΓ μεγέθους.

235 a Ἔτι δ᾽ εἰ μὲν ἔστιν ἄλλη τοῦ ὅλου κίνησις, οἷον ἐφ᾽ ἧς ΘΙ, ἀφαιρεθήσεται ἀπ᾽ αὐτῆς ἡ ἑκατέρων τῶν μερῶν κίνησις· αὗται δ᾽ ἴσαι ἔσονται ταῖς ΔΕ,

---

[a] The corresponding parts of the movement and of the mobile are here represented by the same length for the sake of simplicity ; but all that is necessary is that the ratio of a part of the mobile to the whole of the mobile shall be the same as the ratio of the movement of that part to the movement of the whole.

[b] But to change along some other line—*i.e.* in some other category. [Literally, ' for, as we have seen (at 228 b 1 ff.), a movement that is single, cannot be the movement of more than one thing.'—C.]

since **LM** and **MN** respectively constitute the movements of each of its parts, and a thing's movement

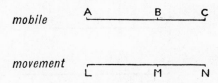

cannot be constituted by the movement of anything else. Accordingly the whole movement is the movement of the whole magnitude.[a]

Besides, every movement is the movement of some mobile. Now the whole movement represented by **LN** is not the movement of either of the parts taken by itself, for each part of **LN** is the movement of one part of **AC**. Neither is it the movement of anything else than the sum of the parts ; for that same whole whose movement constitutes the whole movement is made up of those parts whose movements constitute the parts of the movement. That is to say, the parts of the movement which make up **LN** are the movements of the parts **AB**, **BC**, and of nothing else ; for if there were any other movement, not thus accounted for, it would not pertain to the movement along the single path that we are considering.[b] So the movement represented by the sum of **LM** and **MN** is the movement of the mobile **ABC**.

Besides, if there is a movement of the whole **AC** other than that represented by **LN**, let it be represented by **GK**. Now subtract from **GK** successively the movements of the several parts ; these will be equal to **LM** and **MN**, for one thing must have one

235 a ΕΖ· μία γὰρ ἑνὸς κίνησις. ὥστ' εἰ μὲν ὅλη διαιρεθήσεται ἡ ΘΙ εἰς τὰς τῶν μερῶν κινήσεις, ἴση

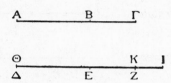

ἔσται ἡ ΘΙ τῇ ΔΖ· εἰ δ' ἀπολείπει τι, οἷον τὸ ΚΙ,
5 αὕτη οὐδενὸς ἔσται κίνησις· οὔτε γὰρ τοῦ ὅλου
οὔτε τῶν μερῶν (διὰ τὸ μίαν εἶναι τοῦ ἑνός), οὔτε
ἄλλου οὐθενός· ἡ γὰρ συνεχὴς κίνησίς ἐστι συνεχῶν
τινῶν· ὡσαύτως δὲ καὶ εἰ ὑπερβάλλει κατὰ τὴν
διαίρεσιν. ὥστ' εἰ τοῦτο ἀδύνατον, ἀνάγκη τὴν
αὐτὴν εἶναι καὶ ἴσην.

Αὕτη μὲν οὖν ἡ διαίρεσις κατὰ τὰς τῶν μερῶν
10 κινήσεις ἐστίν, καὶ ἀνάγκη παντὸς εἶναι τοῦ μερι-
στοῦ αὐτήν.

Ἄλλη δὲ κατὰ τὸν χρόνον· ἐπεὶ γὰρ ἅπασα
κίνησις ἐν χρόνῳ, χρόνος δὲ πᾶς διαιρετός, ἐν δὲ
τῷ ἐλάττονι ἐλάττων ἡ κίνησις, ἀνάγκη πᾶσαν
κίνησιν διαιρεῖσθαι κατὰ τὸν χρόνον.

Ἐπεὶ δὲ πᾶν τὸ κινούμενον ἔν τινι κινεῖται καὶ
15 χρόνον τινά, καὶ παντὸς ἔστι κίνησις, ἀνάγκη τὰς

---

^a *i.e.* any other subject, or of the given subject on any
other part of the given line, or on any other line of change.

movement. Now if by this process **GK** has been exactly resolved into parts, then it is equal to **LN**

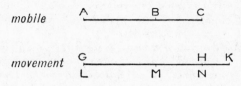

which is also so resolved. But if, after the subtraction, there were any remainder **HK** it would be a movement with no mobile, for it could not be the movement either of the whole **AC** or of the two parts that make it up, since one thing has one movement. But it cannot be the movement of anything else,[a] for by hypothesis we are considering a finite and continuous movement, and therefore the movement of a finite and continuous mobile, on a finite and continuous path. And by parity of reasoning the successive subtractions cannot cover more than **GK**. Since then **GK** is neither more nor less than **LN**, it must be equal to it.

Such then is the division of a movement according to the movements of the several parts of the mobile, and it applies of necessity to everything that is divisible.

Movement can be divided in another way : by time ; for since every movement occurs in time, and time (however short) is always divisible, and in less time the movement is less, it follows that any movement can be divided in correspondence with divisions of time.

And again since anything that moves, moves along a definite line and during a certain time, and has a

235 a αὐτὰς εἶναι διαιρέσεις τοῦ τε χρόνου καὶ τῆς κινήσεως καὶ τοῦ κινεῖσθαι καὶ τοῦ κινουμένου καὶ ἐν
ᾧ ἡ κίνησις (πλὴν οὐ πάντων ὁμοίως, ἐν οἷς ἡ
κίνησις, ἀλλὰ τοῦ μὲν ποσοῦ καθ᾽ αὐτό, τοῦ δὲ
ποιοῦ κατὰ συμβεβηκός).

Εἰλήφθω γὰρ ὁ χρόνος ἐν ᾧ κινεῖται ἐφ᾽ ᾧ Α,
20 καὶ ἡ κίνησις ἐφ᾽ ᾧ Β. εἰ οὖν τὴν ὅλην ἐν τῷ παντὶ
χρόνῳ κεκίνηται, ἐν τῷ ἡμίσει ἐλάττω, καὶ πάλιν
τούτου διαιρεθέντος ἐλάττω ταύτης, καὶ ἀεὶ οὕτως.
ὁμοίως δὲ καὶ ἡ κίνησις διαιρετὴ καὶ ὁ χρόνος
διαιρετός· εἰ γὰρ τὴν ὅλην ἐν τῷ παντί, τὴν
ἡμίσειαν ἐν τῷ ἡμίσει, καὶ πάλιν τὴν ἐλάττω ἐν
τῷ ἐλάττονι.

25 Τὸν αὐτὸν δὲ τρόπον καὶ τὸ κινεῖσθαι διαιρεθήσεται. ἔστω γὰρ ἐφ᾽ ᾧ Γ τὸ κινεῖσθαι· κατὰ
δὴ τὴν ἡμίσειαν κίνησιν ἔλαττον ἔσται τοῦ ὅλου,
καὶ πάλιν κατὰ τὴν τῆς ἡμισείας ἡμίσειαν, καὶ ἀεὶ
οὕτως. ἔστι δὲ καὶ ἐκθέμενον τὸ καθ᾽ ἑκατέραν
τῶν κινήσεων κινεῖσθαι, οἷον κατά τε τὴν ΔΓ καὶ
30 τὴν ΓΕ, λέγειν ὅτι τὸ ὅλον ἔσται κατὰ τὴν ὅλην
(εἰ γὰρ ἄλλο, πλείω ἔσται κινεῖσθαι κατὰ τὴν
αὐτὴν κίνησιν), ὥσπερ ἐδείξαμεν καὶ τὴν κίνησιν
διαιρετὴν εἰς τὰς τῶν μερῶν κινήσεις οὖσαν·
ληφθέντος γὰρ τοῦ κινεῖσθαι καθ᾽ ἑκατέραν, συνεχὲς
ἔσται τὸ ὅλον.

Ὡσαύτως δὲ δειχθήσεται καὶ τὸ μῆκος δι-

---

[a] Aristotle is here thinking, not of the continuous modification of the quality itself (from white to black, for instance),
but of the division, *e.g.* of a blue area, which does not divide
the blueness except in the sense of making it the blueness of
two areas. See Introd. Note.

certain motion, it must be possible to make corresponding divisions: of the time and of the movement,
of the actual being-in-motion and of the mobile, and
of that in respect to which it moves (the line along
which the movement occurs), though not in the same
way in all cases, for a quantum is divisible primarily
and directly, but a quale by concomitance only.[a]

For let the time occupied be represented by
A and the movement by B. Then if the whole
movement has occupied the whole time, less than
the whole movement occupied half the time, and less
again a subdivision of that half, and so on without
limit. And conversely the divisibility of time follows
upon the divisibility of movement; for if the whole
time is long enough for the whole movement, half
the time will suffice for half of it, and a shorter time
still for still less change.

And so too with divisions of the actual being-
in-motion. Let C represent the whole of the being-
in-motion. Then something short of the whole
will correspond to half the movement, and so with
the corresponding quarter of the being-in-motion
and quarter of the movement and so on. And if we
set out the being-in-motion corresponding to each of
the two movements, DC and CE, we may argue that
the whole of the being-in-motion would correspond
with the whole movement (for otherwise there would
be a being-in-motion without any corresponding
movement) just as we showed a total movement
to be divisible into the movements of its parts; for if
the being-in-motion corresponds divisionally with the
divisions of movement which is continuous, it is itself
continuous, and there is no interval between its parts.

And in like manner it can be shown that the

133

235 a 35 αἱρετόν, καὶ ὅλως πᾶν ἐν ᾧ ἐστιν ἡ μεταβολὴ
(πλὴν ἔνια κατὰ συμβεβηκός, ὅτι τὸ μεταβάλλον
ἐστὶ διαιρετόν)·[1] ἑνὸς γὰρ διαιρουμένου πάντα διαιρεθήσεται.

235 b Καὶ ἐπὶ τοῦ πεπερασμένα εἶναι ἢ ἄπειρα ὁμοίως
ἕξει κατὰ πάντων. ἠκολούθηκε δὲ μάλιστα τὸ
διαιρεῖσθαι πάντα καὶ ἄπειρα εἶναι ἀπὸ τοῦ μετα-
βάλλοντος· εὐθὺς γὰρ ἐνυπάρχει τῷ μεταβάλλοντι
τὸ διαιρετὸν καὶ τὸ ἄπειρον. τὸ μὲν οὖν διαιρετὸν
5 δέδεικται πρότερον, τὸ δ᾽ ἄπειρον ἐν τοῖς ἑπομένοις
ἔσται δῆλον.

---

[1] [Punctuation corrected, as in the Oxf. Trans.—C.]

CHAPTER V

ARGUMENT

*In this chapter Aristotle begins by examining the end
(i.e. the completion) of a change, and shows that this is a
limit and is therefore indivisible, and occurs at an indivisible
instant. He gives two independent proofs, one referring
specially to contradictory changes, but also applicable to other
kinds, and one referring specially to changes of place and
quality (235 b 6–30).*

*He shows that if the completion were not the (indivisible)
limit but a (divisible) part of the change, the change would
arrive at completion while it was still going on, which is
impossible (b 30–236 a 7).*

*He then turns to the 'beginning,' and shows that neither
(a) the initial limit nor any subsequent (b) instant or (c)
period can be the primary 'when' of the beginning of a*

6 Ἐπεὶ δὲ πᾶν τὸ μεταβάλλον ἔκ τινος εἴς τι μεταβάλλει, ἀνάγκη τὸ μεταβεβληκός, ὅτε πρῶτον μετα-

distance is divisible, and generally anything in respect
to which a thing changes (with the reservation that
the division is sometimes concomitant, depending
on the fact that the subject that changes is itself
divisible) : for if any one of the connected group we
are examining is divisible, so are all the others.

And they all go together as to being limited or
without limit ; and it is best to consider them all as
following the changing subject itself in these respects,
for divisibility and the absence of limitation primarily
appertain to the subject that changes. As to divisibility, then, our examination is finished, but as to
the absence of limitation it lies before us.

CHAPTER V

ARGUMENT (*continued*)

change. For (a) *at the initial limit the subject is still
unchanged ; (b) no instant follows immediately on the
initial limit (for two indivisibles cannot touch) ; and* (c) *any
period is divisible, and the whole of a divisible period cannot
be the primary 'when' of the beginning* (a 7–27).

*Nor is there any primary part of the subject affected, for
everything that changes is divisible* (a 27–26).

*This argument applies without qualification to change of
quantity, for anything which is directly divisible has no
primary (or least possible) part. In change of quality,
however, there may be a factor not directly divisible, but, as
even this is indirectly divisible, there is no exception to the
rule of divisibility in the factors of change* (236 b 1–18).

Now since everything that changes, changes out of
something into something else, it follows that the

235 b βέβληκεν, εἶναι ἐν ᾧ μεταβέβληκεν. τὸ γὰρ
μεταβάλλον ἐξ οὗ μεταβάλλει ἐξίσταται ἢ ἀπο-
10 λείπει αὐτό· καὶ ἤτοι ταὐτόν ἐστι τὸ μεταβάλλειν
καὶ τὸ ἀπολείπειν, ἢ ἀκολουθεῖ τῷ μεταβάλλειν τὸ
ἀπολείπειν· εἰ δὲ τῷ μεταβάλλειν τὸ ἀπολείπειν,
τῷ μεταβεβληκέναι τὸ ἀπολελοιπέναι· ὁμοίως γὰρ
ἑκάτερον ἔχει πρὸς ἑκάτερον.

Ἐπεὶ οὖν μία τῶν μεταβολῶν ἡ κατ' ἀντίφασιν,
ὅτε μεταβέβληκεν ἐκ τοῦ μὴ ὄντος εἰς τὸ ὄν,
15 ἀπολέλοιπε τὸ μὴ ὄν. ἔσται ἄρα ἐν τῷ ὄντι· πᾶν
γὰρ ἀνάγκη ἢ εἶναι ἢ μὴ εἶναι. φανερὸν οὖν ὅτι
ἐν τῇ κατ' ἀντίφασιν μεταβολῇ τὸ μεταβεβληκὸς
ἔσται ἐν ᾧ μεταβέβληκεν. εἰ δ' ἐν ταύτῃ, καὶ
ἐν ταῖς ἄλλαις· ὁμοίως γὰρ ἐπὶ μιᾶς καὶ τῶν
ἄλλων.

Ἔτι δὲ καθ' ἑκάστην λαμβάνουσι φανερόν, εἴπερ
20 ἀνάγκη τὸ μεταβεβληκὸς εἶναί που ἢ ἔν τινι. ἐπεὶ
γὰρ ἐξ οὗ μεταβέβληκεν ἀπολέλοιπεν, ἀνάγκη δ'
εἶναί που, ἢ ἐν τούτῳ ἢ ἐν ἄλλῳ ἔσται. εἰ μὲν οὖν
ἐν ἄλλῳ, οἷον ἐν τῷ Γ, τὸ εἰς τὸ Β μεταβεβληκός,
πάλιν ἐκ τοῦ Γ μεταβάλλει εἰς τὸ Β (οὐ γὰρ ἦν
25 ἐχόμενον τῷ Β· ἡ γὰρ μεταβολὴ συνεχής). ὥστε

---

a ' Quitting ' here means ' getting free from,' ' to have entirely
quitted,' ' to be entirely free from '; thus ' to have
entirely quitted whiteness ' would mean ' to be entirely free
from any trace of whiteness.'

b [Since the whole passage from A to D is continuous, any
intermediate point C must not be regarded as ' next-without-
an-interval ' to D (cf. 231 b 15 sq., and the definition of ἐχόμενον
227 a 6), so that the change from C to D might occur all at

136

instant it has finished changing, it already is that which it has been changing into. For that which is in the process of changing is coming out of or quitting that which it is changing from, so that if 'quitting' is not the same thing as 'changing from,' at any rate it follows from it ; and if ' to be quitting ' is involved in ' to be changing from,' then ' to have completely quitted' is involved in 'to have completed the change from,' for the relation is identical in either case.[a]

And since one sort of change is the change from one state to the flatly contradictory state, it follows that if a thing has passed out of non-existence into existence it has quitted non-existence. So it will have passed into existence, for everything must either exist or not exist. It is clear then that in the case of contradictory states the thing that has finished changing must already be in the state it was changing into. And if this is true in this particular case of change, it must be true in the other cases too, for there is no pertinent difference between them.

It is easy, moreover, to demonstrate the proposition directly for changes of place or quality, if we admit that everything which has finished changing must be somewhere or in some state. For since it has passed out of where it was and must be somewhere, that somewhere must be either the goal of the change or some other 'where.' If it be another, let the thing which has finished changing to D(B) be now at C(Γ). In that case, once more, it is changing from C to D (for the point C is not ' next ' to D, since the change is continuous).[b] So the thing that had finished

once; but the thing must be in *process* of changing all the way till D is reached.—C.]

235 b τὸ μεταβεβληκός, ὅτε μεταβέβληκε, μεταβάλλει εἰς
ὃ μεταβέβληκεν. τοῦτο δ' ἀδύνατον· ἀνάγκη ἄρα
τὸ μεταβεβληκὸς εἶναι ἐν τούτῳ εἰς ὃ μεταβέβληκεν.
φανερὸν οὖν ὅτι καὶ τὸ γεγονός, ὅτε γέγονεν, ἔσται,
καὶ τὸ ἐφθαρμένον οὐκ ἔσται· καθόλου τε γὰρ
30 εἴρηται περὶ πάσης μεταβολῆς, καὶ μάλιστα δῆλον
ἐν τῇ κατὰ ἀντίφασιν.

Ὅτι μὲν τοίνυν τὸ μεταβεβληκός, ὅτε μεταβέβληκε πρῶτον, ἐν ἐκείνῳ ἐστί, δῆλον· ἐν ᾧ δὲ
πρώτῳ μεταβέβληκε τὸ μεταβεβληκός, ἀνάγκη
ἄτομον εἶναι. (λέγω δὲ πρῶτον ὃ μὴ τῷ ἕτερόν
τι αὐτοῦ εἶναι πρῶτον τοιοῦτόν ἐστιν.) ἔστω γὰρ
35 διαιρετὸν τὸ ΑΓ, καὶ διῃρήσθω κατὰ τὸ Β. εἰ μὲν
οὖν ἐν τῷ ΑΒ μεταβέβληκεν ἢ πάλιν ἐν τῷ ΒΓ,
οὐκ ἂν ἐν πρώτῳ τῷ ΑΓ μεταβεβληκὸς εἴη. εἰ
236 a δ' ἐν ἑκατέρῳ μετέβαλλεν (ἀνάγκη γὰρ ἢ μεταβεβληκέναι ἢ μεταβάλλειν ἐν ἑκατέρῳ), κἂν ἐν τῷ
ὅλῳ μεταβάλλοι· ἀλλ' ἦν μεταβεβληκός. ὁ αὐτὸς
δὲ λόγος καὶ εἰ ἐν τῷ μὲν μεταβάλλει, ἐν δὲ τῷ
μεταβέβληκεν· ἔσται γάρ τι τοῦ πρώτου πρότερον·

ᵃ [Cf. Ross, *Aristotle* (1923), p. 92 : ' An event is in a
nest of times as a body is in a nest of places ; the death of
Caesar took place in March B.C. 44, and also in B.C. 44, and
also in the first century B.C. The " first " time of an event is
the time it precisely occupies, its exact or commensurate
time. There is in this respect a close analogy between
Aristotle's treatment of time and his treatment of place.'—C.]

changing would at the instant at which it finished changing be in process of approaching the 'where', at which it had already arrived. But this is impossible. So the thing that has finished changing must already be in the state into which it has changed. So also it is clear that that which has come into existence at the instant when it has come into existence, exists, and that which has gone out of existence does not exist. The principle which has been laid down as applying to every kind of change is especially obvious in the case of the contradiction between existence and non-existence.

It is evident, then, that the thing that has changed, at the very instant 'at which' it has completed the change, is in the state 'into which.' But we must further note that the time 'at' which, in the primary sense, the change is completed is atomic, *i.e.* indivisible. (I mean by ' in the primary sense ' that it must be directly and primarily the time ' at ' which, not some period that includes that precise instant.) [a] For if we take a divisible OT(AΓ) to represent the time, let it be divided at S(B). Then, if the change came to its completion either in OS(AB) or in ST(BΓ), in neither case can it be primarily located at OT(AΓ). If, on the other hand, the subject were in process of change in both parts (and it must have been either in process of change or in the state of having completed the change in each of them), it would be in process of change in the whole OT(AΓ), which is contrary to the hypothesis that the change reached its completion ' at' the time OT(AΓ). And the argument may be repeated if it be said that the change was in progress during OS(AB), but was completed ' at' ST(BΓ); for then OT(AΓ), the supposed

ARISTOTLE

236 a 5 ὥστε οὐκ ἂν εἴη διαιρετὸν ἐν ᾧ μεταβέβληκεν.
φανερὸν οὖν ὅτι καὶ τὸ ἐφθαρμένον καὶ τὸ
γεγονὸς ἐν ἀτόμῳ τὸ μὲν ἔφθαρται τὸ δὲ γέγονεν.
Λέγεται δὲ τὸ ἐν ᾧ πρώτῳ μεταβέβληκε διχῶς—
τὸ μὲν ἐν ᾧ πρώτῳ ἐπετελέσθη ἡ μεταβολή (τότε
γὰρ ἀληθὲς εἰπεῖν ὅτι μεταβέβληκε), τὸ δὲ ἐν ᾧ
10 πρώτῳ ἤρξατο μεταβάλλειν. τὸ μὲν οὖν κατὰ τὸ
τέλος τῆς μεταβολῆς πρῶτον λεγόμενον ὑπάρχει
τε καὶ ἔστιν· ἐνδέχεται γὰρ ἐπιτελεσθῆναι μεταβολήν, καὶ ἔστι μεταβολῆς τέλος· ὃ δὴ καὶ δέδεικται
ἀδιαίρετον ὂν διὰ τὸ πέρας εἶναι. τὸ δὲ κατὰ τὴν
ἀρχὴν ὅλως οὐκ ἔστιν· οὐ γὰρ ἔστιν ἀρχὴ μετα-
15 βολῆς, οὐδ᾽ ἐν ᾧ πρώτῳ τοῦ χρόνου μετέβαλλεν.
ἔστω γὰρ πρῶτον ἐφ᾽ ᾧ τὸ ΑΔ. τοῦτο δὴ ἀ-

Γ＿＿＿＿＿Α＿Δ

διαίρετον μὲν οὐκ ἔστιν· συμβήσεται γὰρ ἐχόμενα
εἶναι τὰ νῦν. ἔτι δ᾽ εἰ ἐν τῷ ΓΑ χρόνῳ παντὶ

---

a [Aristotle does not mean that a process of change has not
an anterior (as well as a posterior) *limit.* ' Beginning ' here
means ' initial *part*,' falling within the limits (πρώτη κίνησις
rather than ἀρχὴ (=πέρας) κινήσεως, Them. 195. 20). Such
a part would necessarily be infinitely divisible into earlier
and earlier parts and occupy a divisible time.—C.]

b [Literally, ' Then OT cannot be indivisible; for, if it were,
(the?) " nows " would be consecutive ' (which is impossible).
What ' nows '? τὰ νῦν is ambiguous. (1) It may mean ' the
moments,' as in the interpretation adopted by the Oxf.
Trans.: ' the moment immediately preceding the change
and the moment in which the change begins would be consecutive (and moments cannot be consecutive).' But how
does this consequence follow from the indivisibility of OT?
(2) τὰ νῦν may mean moments generally (as at 237 a 25 οὐ
140

' at ' in the primary sense, would only be such in virtue of containing the more primary ST(ΒΓ), and so on indefinitely. Thus the ' time at which ' a change is completed cannot be divisible. It is also clear that that which passes out of existence or comes into existence must do so ' at ' an indivisible moment.

But there is still an ambiguity to clear up. We can speak of the primary ' when ' ' at ' which the change has been completed (for at that instant it is true to say that the change has been accomplished) ; but can we speak of the primary ' when ' in which it began changing ? As to what we call the primary ' when ' in reference to the end or completed change, we may safely assert that there really is such a thing ; for a change can actually be completed and there is such a thing as its end, and we have shown that end to be indivisible, because it is a limit. But with reference to the beginning the phrase has no meaning, for there is no beginning of a process of change,[a] and no primary ' when ' in which the change was (first) in progress. For if there be, let OT re-

time $\quad \overline{\text{K} \qquad \text{O} \qquad \text{T}}$

present that ' when.' Then OT cannot be indivisible, because it must be continuous with the initial limit (and indivisibles cannot be continuous).[b] Or again,

γὰρ ἦν ἐχόμενα τὰ νῦν). The argument may then be: OT is supposed to be an *earliest time* occupied by an *initial part* of the process of change. We cannot regard OT as indivisible without falling back on the false view that the time occupied by a motion can be an atom of time corresponding to an atomic component of motion, and that all stretches of time are made up of such consecutive atoms.—C.]

236 a ἠρεμεῖ (κείσθω γὰρ ἠρεμοῦν), καὶ ἐν τῷ Α ἠρεμεῖ,
ὥστε εἰ ἀμερές ἐστι τὸ ΑΔ, ἅμα ἠρεμήσει καὶ
20 μεταβεβληκὸς ἔσται· ἐν μὲν γὰρ τῷ Α ἠρεμεῖ, ἐν
δὲ τῷ Δ μεταβέβληκεν. ἐπεὶ δ' οὐκ ἔστιν ἀμερές,
ἀνάγκη διαιρετὸν εἶναι καὶ ἐν ὁτῳοῦν τῶν τούτου
μεταβεβληκέναι (διαιρεθέντος γὰρ τοῦ ΑΔ, εἰ μὲν
ἐν μηδετέρῳ μεταβέβληκεν, οὐδ' ἐν τῷ ὅλῳ· εἰ δ' ἐν
ἀμφοῖν μεταβάλλει, καὶ ἐν τῷ παντί· εἰ δ' ἐν
25 θατέρῳ μεταβέβληκεν, οὐκ ἐν τῷ ὅλῳ πρώτῳ.
ὥστε ἀνάγκη ἐν ὁτῳοῦν μεταβεβληκέναι). φανερὸν τοίνυν ὅτι οὐκ ἔστιν ἐν ᾧ πρώτῳ μετα-
βέβληκεν· ἄπειροι γὰρ αἱ διαιρέσεις.

Οὐδὲ δὴ τοῦ μεταβεβληκότος ἔστι τι πρῶτον ὃ
μεταβέβληκεν. ἔστω γὰρ τὸ ΔΖ πρῶτον μετα-
30 βεβληκὸς τοῦ ΔΕ (πᾶν γὰρ δέδεικται διαιρετὸν τὸ
μεταβάλλον)· ὁ δὲ χρόνος ἐν ᾧ τὸ ΔΖ μεταβέβληκεν
ἔστω ἐφ' ᾧ ΘΙ. εἰ οὖν ἐν τῷ παντὶ τὸ ΔΖ μεταβέβληκεν, ἐν τῷ ἡμίσει ἔλαττον ἔσται τι[1] μετα-

---

[1] [τι Oxf. Trans. *Cf.* Simplic. 987. 24: om. EH: τὸ cett.
—C.]

---

[a] If OT is indivisible there is nothing between O and T,
that is to say they are ' in the same place,' Bk. V., chap. iii.
226 b 20, 227 a 10, *i.e.* they are the same instant. If no
part of the change had occurred before O, the thing would
still be unchanged at O. And if some part of it were already
accomplished at T, the thing would simultaneously not have
begun to change and have changed at O = T.

[b] This argument is easily followed with respect to changes
in which the affection itself does not change but gradually
' invades ' the subject ; it is also applicable, *mutatis mutandis*,
to changes in which the affection is simultaneously intensified throughout the entire subject. See Introduction
to chapter iv.

since it is during OT that the change is first taking place, let KO be a static period immediately preceding the change. Then the subject is at rest during the whole period KO, and is therefore unchanged at O,[a] so that if OT is not separable into parts, the subject will simultaneously not have begun its change and have changed, for at O it will not have begun to change, and at T it will have changed. Since, then, the time OT is not inseparable into parts, it is divisible, and in each of its divisions some change must have taken place (for suppose we divide it into two : then, if (1) no change has been accomplished in either of its divisions, neither has any been accomplished in the whole of it ; while if (2) the change is in progress throughout each of them, it is in progress throughout the whole ; and if (3) a change has been accomplished in one or other of them, the ' time,' in the primary sense, of that accomplishment is not the whole of OT. So some change must have taken place during any part of the time OT, however short). It is clear, then, that there cannot be any irreducible period of time which in its entirety is the 'first' period of the change, since there is no limit to the divisions of a period, and so you can always show that the change was already taking place before the whole of any period, however minute, had passed.

Nor is there any segment of the subject of change that is the first to have changed.[b] For if there were, let it be represented by AC, a segment of AD, (for everything that changes has been shown to be divisible). Then let the time which AC has taken to change be represented by OS. If then the whole of AC has changed in the whole of OS, something less than the whole AC will have changed before

143

236 a βεβληκὸς καὶ πρότερον τοῦ ΔΖ, καὶ πάλιν τούτου
ἄλλο, κἀκείνου ἕτερον, καὶ ἀεὶ οὕτως. ὥστε

οὐθὲν ἔσται πρῶτον τοῦ μεταβάλλοντος ὃ μετα-
35 βέβληκεν.

Ὅτι μὲν οὖν οὔτε τοῦ μεταβάλλοντος οὔτε ἐν
ᾧ μεταβάλλει χρόνῳ πρῶτον οὐθέν ἐστι, φανερὸν
ἐκ τῶν εἰρημένων.

236 b Αὐτὸ δὲ ὃ μεταβάλλει ἢ καθ' ὃ μεταβάλλει
οὐκέθ' ὁμοίως ἕξει. τρία γάρ ἐστιν ἃ λέγεται κατὰ
τὴν μεταβολήν—τό τε μεταβάλλον καὶ ἐν ᾧ καὶ ὃ
μεταβάλλει· οἷον ὁ ἄνθρωπος καὶ ὁ χρόνος καὶ τὸ
5 λευκόν. ὁ μὲν οὖν ἄνθρωπος καὶ ὁ χρόνος διαιρε-
τοί, περὶ δὲ τοῦ λευκοῦ ἄλλος λόγος (πλὴν κατὰ
συμβεβηκός γε πάντα διαιρετά· ᾧ γὰρ συμβέβηκε
τὸ λευκὸν ἢ τὸ ποιόν, ἐκεῖνο διαιρετόν ἐστιν).[1]
ἐπεὶ ὅσα γε καθ' αὑτὰ λέγεται διαιρετὰ καὶ μὴ
κατὰ συμβεβηκός, οὐδ' ἐν τούτοις ἔσται τὸ πρῶτον·

---

[1] [Punctuation corrected as in Oxf. Trans. The next
sentence, ἐπεὶ κτλ., explains why ' it is otherwise with that
in respect of which the change takes place,' viz. place or
quality or quantity, in that a distinction is needed between
changes of quality and other changes.—C.]

---

[a] [As Simplic. 988. 9 explains, ὃ μεταβάλλει here has the

the period **OS** is completed, and again still less in less, and less again in less without limit. So that

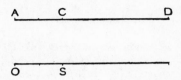

there will be no part of the subject of the change which has in its entirety been the very first part that has changed.

We have now shown that in the subject of change there is no (irreducible) part that can be the *first* to have completed the change, and in the time occupied by the change no (irreducible) *earliest* part in which change has been effected.

But the case is different with that in [a] which, or with respect to which, the actual change takes place. For there are three things which are concerned whenever change is spoken of : (1) the subject of the change ; (2) the duration of it ; and (3) that in respect of which it changes : for instance, (1) the man, (2) the time, and (3) the pallor. Now the man (as a bulk) and the time are divisible, but it is another thing with the pallor (though they are all, it is true, incidentally divisible, for the subject in which the pallor or other quality inheres is divisible). For when that with respect to which the thing changes is not incidentally but primarily divisible, it, too, has

same meaning as τὸ καθ' ὃ μεταβάλλει—the place, quality (*e.g.* pallor), or quantity, in respect of which the subject of change suffers change.—C.]

236 b 10 οἷον ἐν τοῖς μεγέθεσιν. ἔστω γὰρ τὸ ἐφ' ᾧ ΑΒ
μέγεθος, κεκινήσθω δ' ἐκ τοῦ Β εἰς τὸ Γ πρῶτον.

A   B   Γ

οὐκοῦν εἰ μὲν ἀδιαίρετον ἔσται τὸ ΒΓ, ἀμερὲς
ἀμεροῦς ἔσται ἐχόμενον· εἰ δὲ διαιρετόν, ἔσται τι
τοῦ Γ πρότερον εἰς ὃ μεταβέβληκε, κἀκείνου πάλιν
15 ἄλλο, καὶ ἀεὶ οὕτω διὰ τὸ μηδέποτε ὑπολείπειν τὴν
διαίρεσιν. ὥστε οὐκ ἔσται πρῶτον εἰς ὃ μεταβέβληκεν. ὁμοίως δὲ καὶ ἐπὶ τῆς τοῦ ποσοῦ μετα-
βολῆς· καὶ γὰρ αὕτη ἐν συνεχεῖ ἐστι. φανερὸν οὖν
ὅτι ἐν μόνῃ τῶν κινήσεων τῇ κατὰ τὸ ποιὸν
ἐνδέχεται ἀδιαίρετον καθ' αὑτὸ εἶναι.

---

[a] See Introduction to chapter iv.
[b] [AB is a part of space occupied by a 'magnitude' (τὸ
κινούμενον μέγεθος, Simplic.), also called AB; BC is the extension
of this space, over which the motion is to take place.—C.]
[c] [Cf. the argument at 236 a 15. Here the objection is to
thinking of space as capable of being filled by a row of successive atomic magnitudes, and to regarding motion as

CHAPTER VI

ARGUMENT

*If by the 'proper time' of a change we mean the period
which exactly coincides with its duration, then the change
must be going on throughout any part, however small, of the
proper time of the whole change (236 b 19–32).*

*From this it follows that (1) that which is found to be
changing must have been changing previously, (2) that*

no primary part.[a] Take the case of magnitudes.[b]
Let **AB** represent a magnitude, and let it have
changed from **B** to a 'primary' position **C**. Now if

BC is to be indivisible, we shall have two things without parts contiguous to one another (which is impossible)[c]; while if it is divisible, there will be some
position, coming before **C**, into which the thing has
changed, and yet another before that, and so on
without limit, since the divisibility is never exhausted.
So there is no first point that has been reached.
And this argument applies also to change of quantity,
since this change too is in something continuous.
It is manifest, then, that change in respect of quality
is the only change in which there can be a factor not
directly[d] divisible.

occurring all at once from one atomic place to the 'next.'—
C.]
   [d] 'Directly,' for even in a quale there must be incidental
divisibility.

CHAPTER VI

ARGUMENT (continued)

*which has accomplished a change must have accomplished
some lesser change previously, (3) that which is found to be
changing must have previously accomplished some change
(b 32–237 a 17), and (4) that which has accomplished a
change must previously have been changing (a 17–28).*
   It is obvious that all this is true in the case of change of

ARISTOTLE

ARGUMENT (*continued*)

*magnitude, for as magnitude is divisible without limit, there
can be no least possible change of magnitude* (a 28–b 9).
  *The same reasoning may be extended to the becoming and
perishing of all continuous and divisible things, i.e. to the*

236 b 19   Ἐπεὶ δὲ τὸ μεταβάλλον ἅπαν ἐν χρόνῳ μετα-
20 βάλλει, λέγεται δ' ἐν χρόνῳ μεταβάλλειν καὶ ὡς ἐν
πρώτῳ καὶ ὡς καθ' ἕτερον (οἷον ἐν τῷ ἐνιαυτῷ,
ὅτι ἐν τῇ ἡμέρᾳ μεταβάλλει), ἐν ᾧ πρώτῳ χρόνῳ
μεταβάλλει τὸ μεταβάλλον, ἐν ὁτῳοῦν ἀνάγκη
τούτου μεταβάλλειν. δῆλον μὲν οὖν καὶ ἐκ τοῦ ὁρισμοῦ—τὸ γὰρ πρῶτον οὕτως ἐλέγομεν—οὐ μὴν ἀλλὰ
25 καὶ ἐκ τῶνδε φανερόν. ἔστω γὰρ ἐν ᾧ πρώτῳ
κινεῖται τὸ κινούμενον ἐφ' ᾧ ΧΡ, καὶ διῃρήσθω
κατὰ τὸ Κ (πᾶς γὰρ χρόνος διαιρετός). ἐν δὴ τῷ
ΧΚ χρόνῳ ἤτοι κινεῖται ἢ οὐ κινεῖται, καὶ πάλιν
ἐν τῷ ΚΡ ὡσαύτως. εἰ μὲν οὖν ἐν μηδετέρῳ

X   K   P

κινεῖται, ἠρεμοίη ἂν ἐν τῷ παντί· κινεῖσθαι γὰρ ἐν
30 μηθενὶ τῶν τούτου κινούμενον ἀδύνατον. εἰ δ' ἐν
θατέρῳ μόνῳ κινεῖται, οὐκ ἂν ἐν πρώτῳ κινοῖτο
τῷ ΧΡ· καθ' ἕτερον γὰρ ἡ κίνησις. ἀνάγκη ἄρα
ἐν ὁτῳοῦν τοῦ ΧΡ κεκινῆσθαι.
148

consummations of all continuous changes; and also to all temporal changes of any kind. So there is no smallest possible, and no irreducible first stage of either change or becoming (b 9–22).

ALL that changes changes 'in time'; but when we speak of the time 'in' which a change occurs, we may mean either the 'primary' or proper time coinciding with the change or a longer period including the proper time (for instance it may have happened ' in ' such and such a year, because that year includes the day occupied by the change). That being so, the change must be taking place during every part of the proper time which the whole change occupies. This follows from our definition (for this is what we have taken ' the proper time ' to mean), but it can also be demonstrated as follows. Let the proper time of the movement be represented by OT, and let OT be divided at S (for every space of time is divisible). Then in the period OS the mobile is either moving or not; and the same with ST. If it is moving in neither of these periods it is at rest throughout

O————————S————————T

OT, for it is impossible for it to move in OT if it moves in neither of its parts. If it is moving in one only of the two parts, then OT is not the proper time of its movement, for it pertains to the whole OT only in virtue of pertaining to a part distinguishable from that whole. It must then have been moving in any part of OT if OT is to be the proper time of the movement.

236 b Δεδειγμένου δὲ τούτου, φανερὸν ὅτι πᾶν τὸ κινούμενον ἀνάγκη κεκινῆσθαι πρότερον. εἰ γὰρ

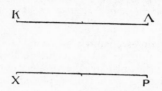

85 ἐν τῷ ΧΡ πρώτῳ χρόνῳ τὸ ΚΛ κεκίνηται μέγεθος, ἐν τῷ ἡμίσει τὸ ὁμοταχῶς κινούμενον καὶ ἅμα
237 a ἀρξάμενον τὸ ἥμισυ ἔσται κεκινημένον. εἰ δὲ τὸ ὁμοταχὲς ἐν τῷ αὐτῷ χρόνῳ κεκίνηταί τι, καὶ θάτερον ἀνάγκη ταὐτὸ κεκινῆσθαι μέγεθος· ὥστε κεκινημένον ἔσται τὸ κινούμενον. ἔτι δὲ εἰ ἐν τῷ παντὶ χρόνῳ τῷ ΧΡ κεκινῆσθαι λέγομεν, ἢ ὅλως
5 ἐν ὁτῳοῦν χρόνῳ, τῷ λαβεῖν τὸ ἔσχατον αὐτοῦ νῦν (τοῦτο γάρ ἐστι τὸ ὁρίζον, καὶ τὸ μεταξὺ τῶν νῦν χρόνος), κἂν ἐν τοῖς ἄλλοις ὁμοίως λέγοιτο κεκινῆσθαι. τοῦ δ' ἡμίσεος ἔσχατον ἡ διαίρεσις· ὥστε καὶ ἐν τῷ ἡμίσει κεκινημένον ἔσται, καὶ ὅλως ἐν ὁτῳοῦν τῶν μερῶν· ἀεὶ γὰρ ἅμα τῇ τομῇ
10 χρόνος ἐστὶν ὡρισμένος ὑπὸ τῶν νῦν. εἰ οὖν ἅπας

---

a Even if our observations are confined to noting what has occurred by the end of a time, we shall see that something has occurred by the end of half the time.

150

On the strength of this we can show that anything found to be moving must have been moving before.

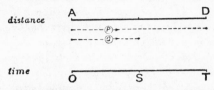

For (1) if P has covered the distance AD in the proper time OT, then Q starting at the same time and moving with equal velocity will cover half the distance in half the time. And of two moving things that move at the same pace, if one accomplishes a given distance in a given time the other must do the same. (Therefore P will have already covered a certain distance in the time OS, and so was moving in a certain period less than OT, which accordingly was not the actual first assignable period during which the mobile was in motion.) So that which is found to be moving must have been moving before.

Again, (2) if what enables us to say that movement *has* taken place in the whole time OT—or generally in any period you please—is that we have taken the terminal 'now' (for the terminal 'now' is what defines a period, a period being what lies between two 'nows'), then movement may equally be said to have taken place in the other periods (OS and ST). But the half (of OT) has its terminal point (S) in our division; accordingly movement will have taken place in the half or, generally, in any part you please; for wherever we divide the period, it will be limited by a 'now' coinciding with that division.[a] And since any period of time is divis-

237 a μὲν χρόνος διαιρετός, τὸ δὲ μεταξὺ τῶν νῦν χρόνος, ἅπαν τὸ μεταβάλλον ἄπειρα ἔσται μεταβεβληκός. ἔτι δ᾽ εἰ τὸ συνεχῶς μεταβάλλον καὶ μὴ φθαρὲν μηδὲ πεπαυμένον τῆς μεταβολῆς ἢ μεταβάλλειν ἢ μεταβεβληκέναι ἀναγκαῖον ἐν ὁτῳοῦν,
15 ἐν δὲ τῷ νῦν οὐκ ἔστι μεταβάλλειν, ἀνάγκη μεταβεβληκέναι καθ᾽ ἕκαστον τῶν νῦν· ὥστ᾽ εἰ τὰ νῦν ἄπειρα, πᾶν τὸ μεταβάλλον ἄπειρα ἔσται μεταβεβληκός.

Οὐ μόνον δὲ τὸ μεταβάλλον ἀνάγκη μεταβεβληκέναι, ἀλλὰ καὶ τὸ μεταβεβληκὸς ἀνάγκη μεταβάλλειν πρότερον. ἅπαν γὰρ τὸ ἔκ τινος εἴς τι
20 μεταβεβληκὸς ἐν χρόνῳ μεταβέβληκεν. ἔστω γὰρ ἐν τῷ νῦν ἐκ τοῦ Α εἰς τὸ Β μεταβεβληκός. οὐκοῦν ἐν μὲν τῷ αὐτῷ νῦν ἐν ᾧ ἐστιν ἐν τῷ Α, οὐ μεταβέβληκεν (ἅμα γὰρ ἂν εἴη ἐν τῷ Α καὶ τῷ Β)· τὸ γὰρ μεταβεβληκός, ὅτε μεταβέβληκεν, ὅτι οὐκ ἔστιν ἐν τούτῳ,[1] δέδεικται πρότερον. εἰ δ᾽ ἐν
25 ἄλλῳ, μεταξὺ ἔσται χρόνος· οὐ γὰρ ἦν ἐχόμενα τὰ νῦν. ἐπεὶ οὖν ἐν χρόνῳ μεταβέβληκε, χρόνος δ᾽ ἅπας διαιρετός, ἐν τῷ ἡμίσει ἄλλο ἔσται μεταβεβληκός, καὶ πάλιν ἐν τῷ ἐκείνου ἡμίσει ἄλλο, καὶ ἀεὶ οὕτως· ὥστε μεταβάλλοι ἂν πρότερον.

Ἔτι δ᾽ ἐπὶ τοῦ μεγέθους φανερώτερον τὸ λεχθέν,

---

[1] [τούτῳ codd. : Simplic. 994. 30 has ταὐτῷ (ACM) or ἐνταῦθα (aF). If τούτῳ is sound, perhaps we should read ὅτε μεταβέβληκεν, ⟨ἐξ οὗ μεταβέβληκεν⟩, ὅτι . . .—C.]

---

ible, and what lies between the two ' nows ' is time, it follows that anything that changes at all has already completed an unlimited succession of changes. Again (3) anything that is continuously changing and has neither perished nor ceased from changing, must at any point either be changing or have changed, and since we have proved that there is no such thing as changing at a ' now,' it follows that at any ' now ' the changing thing must ' have changed,' so that if the nows are without limit, the mobile will have accomplished unlimited changes.

And not only must that which is in process of change have previously accomplished changes, but that which has accomplished a change must previously have been in the process of changing. For if a thing has changed from this to that, it has occupied time in doing so. For suppose a thing has accomplished the change from A to B at an instant. Then the instant at which it has accomplished the change is not the same as that at which it was in A (otherwise it would be in A and B at the same time); for it has already been proved[a] that when a thing has changed, it is not where it was before it had changed. But if the ' now' of A and the ' now' of B are not the same, there must be a space of time between them, for one ' now ' is not contiguous with another one. Since, then, the change has occupied time and time is always divisible, in half the time occupied by the whole change a certain other change will have been accomplished, and again another in the half of that, and so on without limit. The subject, then, has been changing before it has changed.

Moreover, it is helpful to note that all this is more obvious in the case of magnitude, because the

237 a 30 διὰ τὸ συνεχὲς εἶναι τὸ μέγεθος ἐν ᾧ μεταβάλλει
τὸ μεταβάλλον. ἔστω γάρ τι μεταβεβληκὸς ἐκ
τοῦ Γ εἰς τὸ Δ. οὐκοῦν εἰ μὲν ἀδιαίρετόν ἐστι τὸ
ΓΔ, ἀμερὲς ἀμεροῦς ἔσται ἐχόμενον. ἐπεὶ δὲ τοῦτο
ἀδύνατον, ἀνάγκη μέγεθος εἶναι τὸ μεταξὺ καὶ
εἰς ἄπειρα διαιρετόν· ὥστ' εἰς ἐκεῖνα μεταβάλλει
35 πρότερον. ἀνάγκη ἄρα πᾶν τὸ μεταβεβληκὸς
μεταβάλλειν πρότερον· ἡ γὰρ αὐτὴ ἀπόδειξις καὶ
237 b ἐν τοῖς μὴ συνεχέσιν, οἷον ἔν τε τοῖς ἐναντίοις καὶ
ἐν ἀντιφάσει· ληψόμεθα γὰρ τὸν χρόνον ἐν ᾧ
μεταβέβληκε, καὶ πάλιν ταῦτα ἐροῦμεν.

Ὥστε ἀνάγκη τὸ μεταβεβληκὸς μεταβάλλειν καὶ
5 τὸ μεταβάλλον μεταβεβληκέναι, καὶ ἔστι τοῦ μὲν
μεταβάλλειν τὸ μεταβεβληκέναι πρότερον, τοῦ δὲ
μεταβεβληκέναι τὸ μεταβάλλειν· καὶ οὐδέποτε
ληφθήσεται τὸ πρῶτον. αἴτιον δὲ τούτου τὸ μὴ
εἶναι ἀμερὲς ἀμεροῦς ἐχόμενον· ἐπ' ἄπειρον γὰρ
ἡ διαίρεσις, καθάπερ ἐπὶ τῶν αὐξανομένων καὶ
καθαιρουμένων γραμμῶν.

10 Φανερὸν οὖν ὅτι καὶ τὸ γεγονὸς ἀνάγκη γίγνεσθαι
πρότερον καὶ τὸ γιγνόμενον γεγονέναι, ὅσα διαιρετὰ
καὶ συνεχῆ—οὐ μέντοι ἀεὶ ὃ γίγνεται, ἀλλ' ἄλλο

———

a *i.e.* the distance from A has extended from C to D.

b [*Literally*, 'divisible into an unlimited number of parts.
So the thing is in process of changing into those (innumerable parts) before (it completes its change at D).'—C.]

c The continuity of contradictory changes such as coming
into and out of existence is explained below, 237 b 13 *sqq.*

d [Simplicius 996. 19 explains the process meant: Bisect a
line and keep one half undivided; bisect the other half and
add one of its halves to your original undivided half, and so
on.—C.]

e [Aristotle has already said at a 35 that the same reasoning
applies to changes between contraries and between contra-

154

magnitude over which the change takes place is continuous. For suppose a thing has changed from C to D.[a] Then if CD were indivisible, two things which have no parts would be consecutive, and since this is impossible the space between must be a magnitude and therefore divisible without limit. So the subject effects innumerable changes before it has effected any given change.[b] So anything that has changed must previously have been changing, for the same proof holds for changes with respect to what is not continuous,[c] namely changes between contraries and between contradictories. For if we consider the time which the accomplished change has occupied, we may apply the same reasoning whatever the nature of the change.

So then that which has changed must have been changing, and that which is changing must have changed; there is a 'having changed' that comes before 'changing' and a 'changing' before 'having changed,' and we shall never find a stage which is the (irreducible) first stage; the reason being that two indivisibles can never be contiguous, but the interspace can be subdivided without limit, as a line may be divided without limit in such a way that one part is always increasing and the other decreasing.[d]

It is further clear [e] that in the case of all divisible and continuous things, whatever has come to be must previously have been coming to be and whatever is coming to be must previously have come to be, (but not all things are continuous and so what

dictories (*i.e.* becoming and perishing) if you consider the factor of *time*. He now adds that the argument from the infinite divisibility of *magnitude* also applies to becoming and perishing of such things as are continuous and divisible magnitudes.—C.]

155

37 b ἐνίοτε, οἷον τῶν ἐκείνου τι, ὥσπερ τῆς οἰκίας τὸν
θεμέλιον—ὁμοίως δὲ καὶ ἐπὶ τοῦ φθειρομένου καὶ
ἐφθαρμένου. εὐθὺς γὰρ ἐνυπάρχει τῷ γιγνομένῳ
15 καὶ τῷ φθειρομένῳ ἄπειρόν τι, συνεχεῖ γε ὄντι, καὶ
οὐκ ἔστιν οὔτε γίγνεσθαι μὴ γεγονός τι οὔτε γεγονέναι μὴ γιγνόμενόν τι. ὁμοίως δὲ καὶ ἐπὶ τοῦ
φθείρεσθαι καὶ ἐπὶ τοῦ ἐφθάρθαι· ἀεὶ γὰρ ἔσται
τοῦ μὲν φθείρεσθαι τὸ ἐφθάρθαι πρότερον, τοῦ δὲ
ἐφθάρθαι τὸ φθείρεσθαι. φανερὸν οὖν ὅτι καὶ τὸ
20 γεγονὸς ἀνάγκη γίγνεσθαι πρότερον καὶ τὸ γιγνόμενον γεγονέναι· πᾶν γὰρ μέγεθος καὶ πᾶς χρόνος
ἀεὶ διαιρετά· ὥστ' ἐν ᾧ ἂν ᾖ, οὐκ ἂν εἴη ὡς πρώτῳ.

---

a [Viz. bodies, which are necessarily continuous and infinitely divisible.—C.]
b That is : must have accomplished some stage of its
becoming.

CHAPTER VII

ARGUMENT

*The aim of this chapter is to show (1) that a limited change
or ' motion' could not occupy unlimited time ; and as a
definite process of ' coming to rest' or of ' becoming' or of
' perishing' is a limited change, none of these could occupy
unlimited time ; and (2) that in a limited time there could
not be unlimited ' motion.'*

*The only kind of motion which is directly dealt with in
this chapter is locomotion, for every kind of change can be
represented by this kind of movement.*

*Prop. (1). If the motion is uniform it can be divided
into a limited number of equal parts, and each of these parts
will correspond to an equal period of time ; so that the
whole time can be divided into the same number of equal*

has already come to be may be other than that
which is coming to be ; it may be some independent
part of it, as when the foundation has come but the
house is still coming to be,) and it is the same with
passing away and having passed away. For both
what is coming-into-being and what is passing-away
contain, in so far as they are continuous things,[a] an
element of unlimitedness ; and it is impossible for
anything to be in process of coming to be unless it
has already come to be something or to have come
to be unless it has previously been in process of
becoming something ; and it is the same with passing away and having passed away, for passing away
must always have been preceded by having passed
away, and having passed away by passing. It is
clear therefore in the case of coming to be, no less
than in other changes, that what has come to be
must previously have been in process of coming to
be, and that what is coming to be must have come
to be[b] previously, for every magnitude and every
period of time is divisible without limit. Consequently whatever stage the thing may have reached,
that stage can never be the irreducible first stage in
the process.

<h1 style="text-align:center">CHAPTER VII</h1>

ARGUMENT (continued)

parts. On the assumption that these periods of time are
limited in duration as well as in number, it follows that
the whole time will be limited in duration (237 b 23–34). The
proposition is next demonstrated for motion that is not
uniform (in this demonstration it is assumed that the
velocity cannot fall below any assignable limit whatever

ARISTOTLE

(b 34–238 a 19)). *Prop.* (2) *is demonstrated in a similar manner. An 'unlimited motion' may be either* (a) *that which is limited traversing that which is unlimited, or*

237 b 23 Ἐπεὶ δὲ πᾶν τὸ κινούμενον ἐν χρόνῳ κινεῖται, καὶ ἐν τῷ πλείονι μεῖζον μέγεθος, ἐν τῷ ἀπείρῳ
25 χρόνῳ ἀδύνατόν ἐστι πεπερασμένην κινεῖσθαι—μὴ τὴν αὐτὴν ἀεὶ καὶ τῶν ἐκείνης τι κινούμενον, ἀλλ᾽ ἐν ἅπαντι ἅπασαν.

Ὅτι μὲν οὖν εἴ τι ἰσοταχῶς κινοῖτο, ἀνάγκη τὸ πεπερασμένον ἐν πεπερασμένῳ κινεῖσθαι, δῆλον. ληφθέντος γὰρ μορίου ὃ καταμετρήσει τὴν ὅλην,
30 ἐν ἴσοις χρόνοις τοσούτοις ὅσα τὰ μόριά ἐστι, τὴν ὅλην κεκίνηται. ὥστ᾽ ἐπεὶ ταῦτα πεπέρανται καὶ τῷ πόσον ἕκαστον καὶ τῷ ποσάκις ἅπαντα, καὶ ὁ χρόνος ἂν εἴη πεπερασμένος· τοσαυτάκις γὰρ ἔσται τοσοῦτος ὅσος ὁ τοῦ μορίου χρόνος πολλαπλασιασθεὶς τῷ πλήθει τῶν μορίων.

---

a [μὴ τὴν αὐτὴν κτλ. seems intended to exclude perpetual rotation ; ' for the heavenly bodies, for instance, can continually revolve over a finite distance during an unlimited time ' (Philop. 812. 22). In such rotation a body is (1) ' moving continually with the same motion (*i.e.* along a circular track) and (continually) executing some part of that motion.' The last words are somewhat obscure. They might mean (1) that the body is not to be supposed to execute one revolution and then stop, but to be always moving in some region of the track ; but the following words suggest that the meaning is rather (2) that the body is executing one revolution after another, each revolution being regarded as a limited *part* of the unlimited perpetual motion. Aristotle means that he is not denying that a body can revolve for an unlimited time on a limited track, but is denying that it takes 'all' unlimited time to execute 'all' a limited motion.—C.]

b [Literally, ' Consequently, since these fractions are finite, both in the sense that each is a finite quantity, and in the

(b) *that which is unlimited clearing that which is limited,*
or (c) *that which is unlimited clearing that which is un-*
limited (a 19–b 22).

SINCE every thing that moves occupies time in moving,
and moves further in a longer time, it is impossible
for a limited motion to occupy unlimited time.
I am not speaking of a locally recurrent or re-
entrant motion in which the same limited track
may be traversed an unlimited number of times,[a] but
of the whole distance covered in the whole time.

Now it is clear enough that if the motion is of
uniform velocity, a limited distance must be traversed
in a limited time. For if we take any fraction of
the motion the whole-motion will be some multiple
of that fraction and the time-occupied-by-the-whole-
motion will be the *same* multiple of the time-occupied-
by - the - fraction - of - the - motion. Consequently,
since these fractions are finite both in magnitude and
in number, the time also will be finite; for it will
be a multiple of the time-occupied-by-the-fractional-
motion, and will be equal to that period of time
multiplied by the number of fractional-motions.[b]

sense that their sum is a finite multiple of one of them,
the time also will be finite; for it will be a multiple of
the fractional period (occupied by the fractional motion),
equal to such a period multiplied by the number of the
fractional movements.'—C.] Let $\frac{x}{m}$ be a given fraction of the
motion; then $m \frac{x}{m}$ will be the whole motion, then if t is the
time occupied by the fractional motion mt will be the time
occupied by the whole motion. Now m and x are both by
hypothesis limited, therefore Aristotle's conclusion depends
on the unproved assumption that t is also limited. See
p. 112 note *b*.

ARISTOTLE

237 b Ἀλλὰ δὴ κἂν μὴ ἰσοταχῶς, διαφέρει οὐθέν.
35 ἔστω γὰρ ἐφ' ἧς τὸ ΑΒ¹ διάστημα πεπερασμένον ὃ
238 a κεκίνηται ἐν τῷ ἀπείρῳ, καὶ ὁ χρόνος ἄπειρος ἐφ'
οὗ τὸ ΓΔ. εἰ δὴ ἀνάγκη πρότερον ἕτερον ἑτέρου
κεκινῆσθαι—τοῦτο δὲ δῆλον, ὅτι τοῦ χρόνου ἐν
τῷ προτέρῳ καὶ ὑστέρῳ ἕτερον κεκίνηται· ἀεὶ γὰρ
ἐν τῷ πλείονι ἕτερον ἔσται κεκινημένον, ἐάν τε
5 ἰσοταχῶς ἐάν τε μὴ ἰσοταχῶς μεταβάλλῃ, καὶ ἐάν
τε ἐπιτείνῃ ἡ κίνησις, ἐάν τε ἀνίῃ, ἐάν τε μένῃ,
οὐθὲν ἧττον—εἰλήφθω δή τι τοῦ ΑΒ διαστήματος,

A   E   B

τὸ ΑΕ, ὃ καταμετρήσει τὴν ΑΒ. τοῦτο δὴ τοῦ
ἀπείρου ἔν τινι ἐγένετο χρόνῳ· ἐν ἀπείρῳ γὰρ οὐχ
10 οἷόν τε, τὸ γὰρ ἅπαν ἐν ἀπείρῳ. καὶ πάλιν ἕτερον
δὴ ἐὰν λάβω ὅσον τὸ ΑΕ, ἀνάγκη ἐν πεπερασμένῳ
χρόνῳ· τὸ γὰρ ἅπαν ἐν ἀπείρῳ. καὶ οὕτω δὴ
λαμβάνων, ἐπειδὴ τοῦ μὲν ἀπείρου οὐθέν ἐστι μόριον ὃ καταμετρήσει (ἀδύνατον γὰρ τὸ ἄπειρον
εἶναι ἐκ πεπερασμένων καὶ ἴσων καὶ ἀνίσων, διὰ
τὸ καταμετρηθήσεσθαι τὰ πεπερασμένα πλήθει
15 καὶ μεγέθει ὑπό τινος ἑνός, ἐάν τε ἴσα ᾖ ἐάν τε

----

¹ [τὸ ΑΒ Bonitz, cf. Simplic. 1000. 19 : τὸ Α καὶ τὸ Β codd.
—C.]

ᵃ Unlimited time would be better represented by ' the
line from O,' without giving T as the other limit of what is
by hypothesis unlimited.
ᵇ Assuming that the velocity cannot fall below any assignable limit whatever.
ᶜ i.e. less than the unlimited time which it takes to traverse

But if the motion were not of uniform velocity it would make no difference. For let the limited distance supposed to be covered in an unlimited time be represented by **AD** and the unlimited time by **OT**.[a] Then one part of the distance must have been traversed before another part (this is clear because the distance traversed in the earlier part of the time is different from the distance traversed in the later, for with every increase in the time occupied a different amount of the distance will have been traversed, no matter whether the velocity be uniform or not, and none the less though the rate of motion be intensified or relaxed [b] or constant). That being so, take a part **AC** of the whole distance **AD** and

let **AC** be an exact measure of **AD**. Then this part of the motion will occupy a limited stretch of the supposed unlimited time, for since the whole **AD** does but occupy an unlimited time, a fraction of it must occupy less.[c] But again, if I take another part of **AD** equal to **AC** that too must for the same reason occupy a limited time. And if I go on doing this, since there are no definite periods of time which, added together, will make up an unlimited time (for the unlimited cannot be made up of limited items, whether these items are equal to one another or not, because there will always be some unit which will be an exact measure of a limited aggregate of magnitudes, no matter whether they be equal to each other or not, so long as they

the whole distance (because it cannot take as long to traverse a part as it does to traverse the whole). See p. 112 note *b*.

161

238 a ἄνισα, ὡρισμένα δὲ τῷ μεγέθει, οὐθὲν ἧττον), τὸ
δὲ διάστημα τὸ πεπερασμένον ποσοῖς τοῖς ΑΕ
μετρεῖται, ἐν πεπερασμένῳ ἂν χρόνῳ τὸ ΑΒ
κινοῖτο. ὡσαύτως δὲ καὶ ἐπὶ ἠρεμήσεως.
Ὥστε οὔτε γίγνεσθαι οὔτε φθείρεσθαι οἷόν τε
ἀεί τι τὸ αὐτὸ καὶ ἕν.

20 Ὁ αὐτὸς δὲ λόγος καὶ ὅτι οὐδ' ἐν πεπερασμένῳ
χρόνῳ ἄπειρον οἷόν τε κινεῖσθαι οὐδ' ἠρεμίζεσθαι
οὔθ' ὁμαλῶς κινούμενον οὔτ' ἀνωμάλως. ληφθέντος γάρ τινος μέρους ὃ ἀναμετρήσει τὸν ὅλον
χρόνον, ἐν τούτῳ ποσόν τι διέξεισι τοῦ μεγέθους
καὶ οὐχ ὅλον (ἐν γὰρ τῷ παντὶ τὸ ὅλον), καὶ πάλιν ἐν
25 τῷ ἴσῳ ἄλλο, καὶ ἐν ἑκάστῳ ὁμοίως, εἴτε ἴσον εἴτε
ἄνισον τῷ ἐξ ἀρχῆς· διαφέρει γὰρ οὐδέν, εἰ μόνον
πεπερασμένον τι ἕκαστον· δῆλον γὰρ ὡς ἀναιρου-
μένου τοῦ χρόνου τὸ ἄπειρον οὐκ ἀναιρεθήσεται,
πεπερασμένης τῆς ἀφαιρέσεως γιγνομένης καὶ τῷ
ποσῷ καὶ τῷ ποσάκις. ὥστ' οὐ δίεισιν ἐν πεπε-
30 ρασμένῳ χρόνῳ τὸ ἄπειρον. οὐδέν τε διαφέρει τὸ
μέγεθος ἐπὶ θάτερα ἢ ἐπ' ἀμφότερα εἶναι ἄπειρον·
ὁ γὰρ αὐτὸς ἔσται λόγος.

Ἀποδεδειγμένων δὲ τούτων, φανερὸν ὅτι οὐδὲ
τὸ πεπερασμένον μέγεθος τὸ ἄπειρον ἐνδέχεται διελθεῖν ἐν πεπερασμένῳ χρόνῳ, διὰ τὴν αὐτὴν
35 αἰτίαν· ἐν γὰρ τῷ μορίῳ τοῦ χρόνου πεπερασμένον

---

[a] [Defined at 230 a 4 as 'the motion to the goal at which
the thing is at a standstill.'—C.]
[b] [As usual, Aristotle adds the application of the principle,
established in the case of change, to the case of coming-into-
being and perishing : ' One and the same thing (being finite)
cannot be in process of coming into being, or in process of
perishing, for ever.'—C.] The creation or annihilation of a

are finite in magnitude) and since, on the other hand, a certain multiple of AC will cover the whole limited distance AD, it follows that AD will be traversed in a limited period of time. And the case is the same with the process of being brought to rest.[a]

As a consequence [b] one and the same definite process of coming into being or passing out of it cannot possibly occupy an unlimited time.

By the same reasoning it follows conversely that, whether the motion be uniform or no, an illimitable process of moving or of coming to rest cannot be accomplished in a limited time. For if we take a definite fraction of the whole time, that fraction will allow a certain definite stretch, but not the whole, of the magnitude to be traversed (for it is only in the whole time that the whole magnitude is covered), and again in another equal fraction of the time, another definite stretch of the magnitude, and so on. Whether each successive stretch is equal to the first or not makes no difference, so long as each one is limited ; for it is evident that when the limited time is exhausted the unlimited magnitude will not be, for the subtractions from it are limited both in the how much and in the how many. Consequently the unlimited magnitude will not be traversed in a limited time. Nor does it matter whether the magnitude is unlimited in one direction only or in both, for the reasoning holds for either.

And from what has now been proved it follows that a limited magnitude could not traverse an unlimited magnitude in a limited time. And this for the same reason as before. For in a fraction of the

definite thing is a limited change and therefore the above reasoning would apply here also.

238 a δίεισι, καὶ ἐν ἑκάστῳ ὡσαύτως· ὥστ᾽ ἐν τῷ παντὶ
πεπερασμένον.

Ἐπεὶ δὲ τὸ πεπερασμένον οὐ δίεισι τὸ ἄπειρον
238 b ἐν πεπερασμένῳ χρόνῳ, δῆλον ὡς οὐδὲ τὸ ἄπειρον
τὸ πεπερασμένον. εἰ γὰρ τὸ ἄπειρον τὸ πεπερασμένον, ἀνάγκη καὶ τὸ πεπερασμένον διέναι τὸ
ἄπειρον. οὐδὲν γὰρ διαφέρει ὁποτερονοῦν εἶναι τὸ
5 κινούμενον· ἀμφοτέρως γὰρ τὸ πεπερασμένον δίεισι

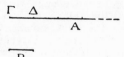

τὸ ἄπειρον. ὅταν γὰρ κινῆται τὸ ἄπειρον ἐφ᾽ ᾧ
τὸ Α, ἔσται τι αὐτοῦ κατὰ τὸ Β πεπερασμένον,
οἷον τὸ ΓΔ, καὶ πάλιν ἄλλο καὶ ἄλλο, καὶ ἀεὶ
οὕτως. ὥστε ἅμα συμβήσεται τὸ ἄπειρον κεκινῆσθαι τὸ πεπερασμένον καὶ τὸ πεπερασμένον
10 διεληλυθέναι τὸ ἄπειρον· οὐδὲ γὰρ ἴσως δυνατὸν
ἄλλως τὸ ἄπειρον κινηθῆναι τὸ πεπερασμένον ἢ
τῷ τὸ πεπερασμένον διέναι τὸ ἄπειρον, ἢ φερό-

---

[a] Cannot ' clear ' it (διελθεῖν), that is to say, cannot have
all got past it, so that *none* of it is on the same side of the
limited stationary magnitude as *all* of it was to begin with.
The importance of the διελθεῖν is significant in relation to
the misunderstanding in Book VII. chapter i.

[b] [Imagine an army forming a column marching past a
saluting-base occupied by a general and his staff. Then
imagine it is the saluting-base that moves carrying the
general and his staff along the extent of the stationary column.

time it would traverse only a limited magnitude, and so too in each successive fractional stretch of the time, and so only a limited magnitude in the whole time.

And since (as we have just seen) a limited magnitude could not traverse an unlimited in a limited time, evidently neither could an *unlimited* magnitude clear [a] a *limited* in a limited time. For if the unlimited could clear the limited, the limited could traverse the unlimited ; for it makes no difference which of the two we think of as moving, for either case involves the traversing of the unlimited by the

limited. Let the line *a* represent an unlimited and the line *b* a limited magnitude. Then when *a* is moving, there will be a limited stretch of it, CD, over against the limited magnitude *b* and then another and another and so on for ever. Consequently the two ways of regarding the process will come to the same thing : we may think either of the unlimited clearing the limited, or the limited traversing the unlimited in the opposite direction.[b] For we may say that the unlimited could not move over the limited in any other way than by the limited traversing the unlimited, that is either travelling along it or measuring it off into parts each equal to its own

These are merely two different ways of obtaining one and the same result.—C.]

ARISTOTLE

238 b μενον ἢ ἀναμετροῦν. ὥστ᾽ ἐπεὶ τοῦτ᾽ ἀδύνατον, οὐκ ἂν δίοι τὸ ἄπειρον τὸ πεπερασμένον.

Ἀλλὰ μὴν οὐδὲ τὸ ἄπειρον ἐν πεπερασμένῳ χρόνῳ τὸ ἄπειρον δίεισιν. εἰ γὰρ τὸ ἄπειρον, καὶ
15 τὸ πεπερασμένον· ἐνυπάρχει γὰρ τῷ ἀπείρῳ τὸ πεπερασμένον. ἔτι δὲ καὶ τοῦ χρόνου ληφθέντος ἡ αὐτὴ ἔσται ἀπόδειξις.

Ἐπεὶ δ᾽ οὔτε τὸ πεπερασμένον τὸ ἄπειρον δίεισιν οὔτε τὸ ἄπειρον τὸ πεπερασμένον οὔτε τὸ ἄπειρον τὸ ἄπειρον[1] ἐν πεπερασμένῳ χρόνῳ κινεῖται, φανερὸν ὅτι οὐδὲ κίνησις ἔσται ἄπειρος ἐν πεπε-
20 ρασμένῳ χρόνῳ. τί γὰρ διαφέρει τὴν κίνησιν ἢ τὸ μέγεθος ποιεῖν ἄπειρον; ἀνάγκη γάρ, εἰ ὁποτερονοῦν, καὶ θάτερον εἶναι ἄπειρον· πᾶσα γὰρ φορὰ ἐν τόπῳ.

[1] [The second τὸ ἄπειρον is omitted in E. This may be due to an easy slip of the pen or the writer of E may have understood the construction to be: ' Since in a limited time neither can the limited traverse an unlimited space nor does the unlimited move over either a limited or an unlimited space . . .' The (unfortunately corrupt) paraphrase of Philoponus 871. 21 suggests that he took the passage so and read ἐπεὶ δ᾽ οὔτε τὸ πεπερασμένον τὸ ἄπειρον δίεισιν, οὔτε τὸ ἄπειρον οὔτε (τὸ?) πεπερασμένον οὔτε (τὸ?) ἄπειρον ἐν πεπερασμένῳ χρόνῳ. In any case the meaning is unaffected.—C.]

[a] [In our illustration we might imagine either the general and his staff riding along the column, or the length of the saluting-base being used as a measure of the column's length.—C.]

166

length.[a] And since this is impossible it is impossible that the unlimited should clear the limited.

Nor is it possible in a limited time for an unlimited magnitude to clear an unlimited one ; for if it were, then *a fortiori* it would be possible for it to clear a limited one, since unlimited magnitude would include limited magnitude. By like reasoning it can be shown that a limited mobile cannot occupy an unlimited time in measuring up a limited distance.[b]

Since then it is impossible that in a limited time either the limited should traverse the unlimited, or the unlimited clear the limited, or the unlimited move over the unlimited,[c] it is evident that in a limited time there could not be unlimited motion : for what difference does it make whether we suppose the movement or the distance to be unlimited, for if either of the two is unlimited so must the other be, for all locomotion is in space ? [d]

[b] [Or, ' the same point (just stated) can be proved if we take the time ' (and argue, on the same lines as at 238 a 20 ff, by dividing the time—rather than the magnitude — into a finite number of parts).—C.]

[c] This does not mean that a limited mobile could not come to be over against different stretches of an illimitable distance, or that different stretches of an illimitable mobile could not come to be over against the same limited object, in a limited time.

[d] [Throughout this chapter Aristotle has really been thinking and speaking of locomotion only, and in any case he regards locomotion as the fundamental kind of change involved in the other kinds.—C.]

ARISTOTLE

CHAPTER VIII

ARGUMENT

[*Since what is coming to a stand must still be in motion, it follows that conclusions already established about things in motion apply to things that are coming to a stand* (238 b 23–26) :

(1) *Coming to a stand must occupy a period of time* (b 26–30),

(2) *It must be happening in any part, however small, of the proper time occupied by the whole process* (b 30–36) ; and hence,

(3) *Within the limits of the proper time occupied by the whole process, there is no portion of time, however small, which can mark an irreducible earliest stage of the process* (b 36–239 a 10).

238 b 23 Ἐπεὶ δὲ πᾶν ἢ κινεῖται ἢ ἠρεμεῖ τὸ πεφυκὸς ὅτε πέφυκε καὶ οὗ καὶ ὥς, ἀνάγκη τὸ ἱστάμενον ὅτε
25 ἵσταται κινεῖσθαι· εἰ γὰρ μὴ κινεῖται, ἠρεμήσει· ἀλλ' οὐκ ἐνδέχεται ἠρεμίζεσθαι τὸ ἠρεμοῦν.

Τούτου δ' ἀποδεδειγμένου, φανερὸν ὅτι καὶ ἐν χρόνῳ ἵστασθαι ἀνάγκη. τὸ γὰρ κινούμενον ἐν χρόνῳ κινεῖται, τὸ δ' ἱστάμενον δέδεικται κινούμενον· ὥστε ἀνάγκη ἐν χρόνῳ ἵστασθαι. ἔτι δὲ[1]
30 τὸ μὲν θᾶττον καὶ βραδύτερον ἐν χρόνῳ λέγομεν, ἵστασθαι δ' ἔστι θᾶττον καὶ βραδύτερον.

Ἐν ᾧ δὲ χρόνῳ πρώτῳ τὸ ἱστάμενον ἵσταται, ἐν ὁτῳοῦν ἀνάγκη τούτου ἵστασθαι. διαιρεθέντος

---

[1] [ἔτι δὲ E: ἔτι δ' εἰ cett. As Themistius (198. 7) and Simplicius (1007. 11) saw, this sentence contains a further proof that coming to rest takes time. It has no connexion with the next.—C.]

---

[a] [*Cf.* 230 a 4.—C.]

[b] [*i.e.* the ' proper time ' of the process as defined chapter vi. *init.*—C.]

CHAPTER VIII

ARGUMENT (*continued*)

Similarly there is no irreducible earliest stage in a period of 'being at rest' (a 10–23).

Finally, if we take the period of time properly occupied by a movement, the moving thing cannot, during any part of that period, be situated so as exactly to 'cover' any stationary object. It can, and must, be so situated at any indivisible instant ; but an indivisible instant, as we have seen, is not a period of time, and neither rest nor motion can occur except during a period of time (a 23–b 4).

This last conclusion is established specially with a view to the refutation of Zeno's argument at the beginning of the next chapter.—C.]

Now since anything which is naturally capable of being in motion or at rest can only move or rest when and where and how its nature allows, it follows that when a mobile is being brought to rest it must be in motion [a] ; for if it is not in motion it will be at rest, and that which is at rest cannot be in process of being brought to rest.

This being so, it is evident that being brought to rest is an experience that occupies time ; for anything in motion is moving in time, and what is being brought to rest, as has been shown, is in motion and therefore its being brought to rest occupies time. Again the terms 'faster' and 'slower' are applied exclusively to what occupies time, and we do apply them to the process of being brought to rest.

If we say that such and such a period is, as such, the period during which the mobile is being brought to rest,[b] it must be in process of being brought to rest during any and every part of that period. For

238 b γὰρ τοῦ χρόνου, εἰ μὲν ἐν μηδετέρῳ τῶν μερῶν
ἵσταται, οὐδὲ ἐν τῷ ὅλῳ, ὥστ' οὐκ ἂν ἵσταιτο τὸ
ἱστάμενον· εἰ δ' ἐν θατέρῳ, οὐκ ἂν ἐν πρώτῳ ὅλῳ
35 ἵσταιτο, καθ' ἕτερον γὰρ ἐν τούτῳ ἵσταται· καθάπερ ἐλέχθη καὶ ἐπὶ τοῦ κινουμένου πρότερον.

239 a   Ὥσπερ δὲ τὸ κινούμενον οὐκ ἔστιν ἐν ᾧ πρώτῳ
κινεῖται, οὕτως οὐδ' ἐν ᾧ ἵσταται τὸ ἱστάμενον·
οὔτε γὰρ τοῦ κινεῖσθαι οὔτε τοῦ ἵστασθαι ἔστι τι
πρῶτον. ἔστω γὰρ ἐν ᾧ πρώτῳ ἵσταται ἐφ' ᾧ
τὸ ΑΒ. τοῦτο δὴ ἀμερὲς μὲν οὐκ ἐνδέχεται εἶναι·
5 κίνησις γὰρ οὐκ ἔστιν ἐν τῷ ἀμερεῖ, διὰ τὸ κεκινῆσθαί τι αὐτοῦ· τὸ δ' ἱστάμενον δέδεικται κινούμενον.
ἀλλὰ μὴν εἰ διαιρετόν ἐστιν, ἐν ὁτῳοῦν αὐτοῦ τῶν
μερῶν ἵσταται· τοῦτο γὰρ δέδεικται πρότερον, ὅτι
ἐν ᾧ πρώτῳ ἵσταται, ἐν ὁτῳοῦν τῶν ἐκείνου ἵσταται. ἐπεὶ οὖν χρόνος ἐστὶν ἐν ᾧ πρώτῳ ἵσταται,
10 καὶ οὐκ ἄτομον, ἅπας δὲ χρόνος εἰς ἄπειρα μεριστός,
οὐκ ἔσται ἐν ᾧ πρώτῳ ἵσταται.

---

[a] [καθ' ἕτερον, as opposed to ἐν πρώτῳ, was used at 236 b 21
of a longer period of which the proper time is only a part,
here of a shorter period which is part of the proper time.
The last words refer to the argument at 236 b 23-32.—C.]
[b] [As shown in chapter vi., 236 b 32 ff. ἐν ᾧ πρώτῳ here
means no *earliest* part within the limits of the proper time
(ἐν ᾧ πρώτῳ) as used in the last paragraph.—C.]
[c] [Literally, ' because of its having accomplished motion
over some part of it,' *i.e.* whatever distance we take, a thing
in motion over that distance has always moved over some
part of it.   But if the distance has parts, it is not indivisible.
The reading of E, διὰ τὸ κεκινῆσθαι ἄν τι αὐτοῦ, would yield
the same sense.—C.]

if we divide this period into two parts, then if the mobile is not in process of being brought to rest in either of them, neither is it so in both together, and therefore it would not be (as by hypothesis it is) in process of being brought to rest at all. Whereas if it were being brought to rest during one only of the parts the whole period would not be the *proper* time of the process, which would take place ' in ' that period only in virtue of its taking place during one part of it, as has already been shown in the case of moving things in general.[a]

And just as there is no first (irreducible) period during which a moving thing can be said to be in motion,[b] so likewise there is no first (irreducible) period during which a thing that is being brought to rest can be said to be undergoing the process ; for there is no irreducible earliest stage of the process in either case. For if there were such a period, let it be OT. Then OT cannot be indivisible ; for no motion can occur in an indivisible instant, since it is always possible for a part of the motion to take place in a part of the time,[c] and we have shown that what is being brought to rest is in motion. If, on the other hand, OT is divisible, the process of arresting must be in progress in every part of it, for we have just shown that the process of arresting must be going on in every part of the proper time of that process. Since, then, the proper time occupied by a process of coming to rest is a stretch of time, not an indivisible instant, and any stretch of time is divisible without limit, there will be no assignable period of time (such as OT) which can mark an irreducible ' earliest stage ' of the process.

239 a Οὐδὲ δὴ τὸ ἠρεμοῦν ὅτε πρῶτον ἠρέμησεν ἔστιν.
ἐν ἀμερεῖ μὲν γὰρ οὐκ ἠρέμησε, διὰ τὸ μὴ εἶναι
κίνησιν ἐν ἀτόμῳ· ἐν ᾧ δὲ τὸ ἠρεμεῖν, καὶ τὸ
κινεῖσθαι· τότε γὰρ ἔφαμεν ἠρεμεῖν, ὅτε καὶ ἐν ᾧ
πεφυκὸς κινεῖσθαι μὴ κινεῖται τὸ πεφυκός. ἔτι δὲ
15 καὶ τότε λέγομεν ἠρεμεῖν, ὅταν ὁμοίως ἔχῃ νῦν
καὶ πρότερον, ὡς οὐχ ἑνί τινι κρίνοντες ἀλλὰ δυοῖν
τοῖν ἐλαχίστοιν· ὥστ᾽ οὐκ ἔσται ἐν ᾧ ἠρεμεῖ ἀμερές.
εἰ δὲ μεριστόν, χρόνος ἂν εἴη, καὶ ἐν ὁτῳοῦν αὐτοῦ
τῶν μερῶν ἠρεμήσει· τὸν αὐτὸν γὰρ τρόπον δει-
20 χθήσεται ὃν καὶ ἐπὶ τῶν πρότερον. ὥστ᾽ οὐδὲν
ἔσται πρῶτον· τούτου δ᾽ αἴτιον ὅτι ἠρεμεῖ μὲν καὶ
κινεῖται πᾶν ἐν χρόνῳ, χρόνος δ᾽ οὐκ ἔστι πρῶτος
οὐδὲ μέγεθος οὐδ᾽ ὅλως συνεχὲς οὐδέν· ἅπαν γὰρ
εἰς ἄπειρα μεριστόν.

Ἐπεὶ δὲ πᾶν τὸ κινούμενον ἐν χρόνῳ κινεῖται
καὶ ἔκ τινος εἴς τι μεταβάλλει, ἐν ᾧ χρόνῳ κινεῖται

---

a [Or ἐν ᾧ may be taken, as by the Oxford Trans., as the
equivalent to ὅτε 'added simply for the sake of introducing
the exact expression used immediately before.'—C.]

b Philoponus (815. 20) is certainly right in taking ἐλάχιστον
as equivalent to πέρας. [I think Philoponus is certainly
wrong. The phrase means ' by two as the minimum '; cf.
1131 a 15, ἔστι δὲ τὸ ἴσον ἐν ἐλαχίστοις δυσίν. 'We mark off
(determine, distinguish) a condition of rest, not by any single
point but by not less than two.'—C.]

c [κατά τι here (as in κατὰ τὸ B at 238 b 6) means being
situated over against some definite stationary object or
measure of distance. πρῶτον (as in the phrase ἐν ᾧ πρώτῳ
χρόνῳ) means the exact correspondence with this object or
distance as opposed to the loose sense of being over against
some part of the object. Aristotle is thinking of his moving
thing as moving past something which would exactly define
its position at a given instant—e.g. the piece of road exactly
occupied by an army. If the army occupies that place for
172

In like manner there is no irreducible first period during which the thing at rest has been resting. For on the one hand it could not be resting in an indivisible instant, because it could not be moving in an indivisible instant, and motion must be possible in any time in which rest is possible ; for we defined the state of rest as the state of a subject which is naturally capable of motion and exists in a time and medium in which [a] motion is naturally possible, but which is not moving. Moreover, we say that a thing is at rest when it has not changed its state between now and some previous instant ; so that we do not judge rest by reference to one limit,[b] but by reference to two. So there can be no indivisible instant in which it is at rest. On the other hand, if what we are speaking of is divisible, it must be a period of time, and in every part of that period the mobile is in a state of ' being at rest,' as demonstrated above. Consequently there can be no period whatever, of which (and of no shorter one) it can be said that in it the mobile was first at rest. The rationale of all this is that all motion and rest occurs in time, and there is no smallest or irreducible first .component of time or of dimension or of anything that is continuous, for all such are divisible without limit.

And since whatever is in motion moves in a period of time and changes from one position to another, it is impossible that the mobile should in its entirety be exactly over against any definite (stationary) thing [c] during the period occupied by its motion—

any period of time, however short, during that period it is at rest, not moving, but at any indivisible instant it must be over against some such place.—C.]

239 a 25 καθ' αὐτὸ καὶ μὴ τῷ ἐν ἐκείνου τινί,[1] ἀδύνατον
τότε κατά τι εἶναι πρῶτον τὸ κινούμενον. τὸ γὰρ
ἠρεμεῖν ἐστι τὸ ἐν τῷ αὐτῷ εἶναι χρόνον τινὰ καὶ
αὐτὸ καὶ τῶν μερῶν ἕκαστον· οὕτω γὰρ λέγομεν
ἠρεμεῖν, ὅταν ἐν ἄλλῳ καὶ ἄλλῳ τῶν νῦν ἀληθὲς
ᾖ εἰπεῖν ὅτι ἐν τῷ αὐτῷ καὶ αὐτὸ καὶ τὰ μέρη. εἰ
30 δὲ τοῦτ' ἔστι τὸ ἠρεμεῖν, οὐκ ἐνδέχεται τὸ μεταβάλλον κατά τι εἶναι ὅλον κατὰ τὸν πρῶτον χρόνον·
ὁ γὰρ χρόνος διαιρετὸς ἅπας, ὥστε ἐν ἄλλῳ καὶ
ἄλλῳ αὐτοῦ μέρει ἀληθὲς ἔσται εἰπεῖν ὅτι ἐν ταὐτῷ
ἐστι καὶ αὐτὸ καὶ τὰ μέρη. εἰ γὰρ μὴ οὕτως
ἀλλ' ἐν ἑνὶ μόνῳ τῶν νῦν, οὐκ ἔσται χρόνον οὐθένα
35 κατά τι, ἀλλὰ κατὰ τὸ πέρας τοῦ χρόνου. ἐν δὲ
239 b τῷ νῦν ἔστι μὲν ἀεὶ κατά τι μένον, οὐ μέντοι
ἠρεμεῖ—οὔτε γὰρ κινεῖσθαι οὔτε ἠρεμεῖν ἔστιν ἐν
τῷ νῦν—ἀλλὰ μὴ κινεῖσθαι μὲν ἀληθὲς ἐν τῷ νῦν
καὶ εἶναι κατά τι, ἐν χρόνῳ δ' οὐκ ἐνδέχεται εἶναι
κατὰ τὸ ἠρεμοῦν· συμβαίνει γὰρ τὸ φερόμενον
ἠρεμεῖν.

---

[1] [τῷ ἐν ἐκείνου τινί EHI, Simplic. 1010. 2 and 27 (lemma):
τῶν ἐν ἐκείνου τινί cett. Cf. Simplic. 1009. 29 (paraphr.) τῷ
ἔν τινι τῶν ἐκείνου, which suggests that, as the Oxf. Trans.
conjectures, the original text had τῷ ἐν τῶν ἐκείνου τινί.—C.]

---

[a] [i.e. the ' proper time ' as already defined.—C.]
[b] That is to say that the mobile and the stationary object
shall exactly fit, so that no part of either is left ' uncovered '
by the other.

occupied, that is to say, in the proper sense, not in the sense that the motion falls within some part of the period in question.[a] For if a mobile is, in its entirety and all its parts, in the same place during a certain period of time, it is then at rest and not in motion; for the definition of being at rest is that it is true to say of the resting thing that from one 'now' to another both it and all its parts remain where they were. So if this is what being at rest means, it is impossible that a thing which is moving shall in its entirety exactly 'cover'[b] a definite stationary thing during any part of the time properly occupied by its motion. For since time is divisible without limit and during *every* part of the proper time of the motion the mobile must be in motion, if it could be stationary in *any* part of it, however small, it could be stationary in such parts successively and so in the whole period. If the assertion refers not to an interval between two 'nows' but to one single 'now,' then the moving thing will not be so situated during any period of time at all but only at a limit of such a period. Now it is true that at any particular instant the moving thing is always situated over against some stationary thing, but it is not 'at rest,' for in the indivisible instant there is neither rest nor motion. Rather, while it is true to say of the moving thing that *at the indivisible instant* it 'does not move' and is over against some definite thing, it cannot *during any period of time* be over against something that is at rest; for if it were it would be both moving and resting.

CHAPTER IX

ZENO'S four celebrated Dilemmas, and two others, are dealt with in this chapter. The forms in which they are given here are presumably those which were currently accepted in Aristotle's time, and his refutations are satisfactory as far as they go.

Zeno's arguments are designed to prove that whether the divisibility of time and distance is limitable or not, motion is alike impossible.

The 1st and 2nd are dilemmas on the supposition that there is no limit to the divisibility of time and distance, the 3rd and 4th on the supposition that they are divisible into indivisible atoms.

The 1st of the other two dilemmas attempts to show that change of quality, and the 2nd that rotation, is impossible.

They all depend on the equivocal use of terms. Different (and sometimes wholly unconnected) meanings are given to the same term in the course of the argument, and conclusions established for one meaning (and excluded from the other) are then transferred to that other. This is done so elusively that it easily escapes detection. If the same term were always used in the same sense, there would be no dilemma. As soon as it is clear how the terms are used in each case the problems raised present no great difficulty.

Aristotle's criticisms are readily followed, except that of Zeno's 4th dilemma, the significance of which may be easily overlooked. The argument appears to be this : if motion, time, and distance consist of indivisible atoms, it will always require an equal time to traverse an equal distance and there can be no differences of velocity, as one atom of time and one atom of distance must always correspond to one atom of motion ; for if either corresponded to more than one, it (the atom of time or distance) would be divisible, because one atom of motion would

CHAPTER IX

ɪɴᴛʀᴏᴅᴜᴄᴛᴏʀʏ ɴᴏᴛᴇ (*continued*)

correspond to less than an atom of time or distance ; and if one atom of motion corresponded to more than one of time or distance, then the atom of motion would be divisible for the same reason.

Now suppose that two sets of equal bodies (B's and C's) move past a set of equal stationary bodies (A's) with equal speed but in opposite directions ; it is evident that in the same time a B will pass one A and two C's. But on our hypothesis (1) if it takes one unit of time for a B to pass one A it will take one unit for it to pass one C. (2) If it takes one unit to pass one C it will take two units to pass two C's and (3) it always takes an equal time to pass an equal number of C's. But we have just seen a B pass one A and two C's in one and the same unit, so that (by 1) it takes one unit, and (by 2) two units of time to pass two C's, and (by 3) these two periods must be equal. Thus if we accept the hypotheses, we must accept the conclusion that one unit of time is equal to two, which is absurd.

Aristotle's criticism does not attack the method of deduction but the hypothesis itself, which precludes the possibility of passing different objects at different speeds, ' for,' he says, ' the assumption that a moving object takes the same time in passing another object whether that other is stationary or in motion, is false.'

But there are deeper problems underlying Zeno's paradoxes which challenge belief in the reality, not only of motion, but of time, distance, or any continuum, and it is these which have chiefly engaged the attention of modern writers (see M. Noël's article " Le mouvement et les arguments de Zénon d'Élée," in the *Revue de Métaphysique et de Morale*, i. pp. 107-125). With the problems underlying the 3rd and 4th dilemmas Aristotle is not here concerned, for he rejects the assumptions on which they rest, and after saying this he gives them no further consideration.

ARISTOTLE

But it is his business to deal with any problem involved in assumptions which he accepts, *e.g.* the Dichotomy, and his final answer to this is not given till Bk. VIII. chap. viii. What he says is briefly this : that indivisible boundaries as such present no obstruction, and make no difference to the possibility of reaching the end of a limited continuum, so that it makes no difference how many there may be. But if they have to be counted, or in any other way require individual attention, they do cause obstruction, and the more of them there are the greater the obstruction.

Now the illimitable set of potential boundaries by which a continuum is inherently divisible cannot in their totality

ARGUMENT

Zeno's contention that ' the flying arrow is not moving' depends on the assumption that the time of its flight is made up of indivisible instants in each of which it is at rest. This assumption has been shown to be false (239 b 5-9).

Zeno's four arguments against motion being a reality, are each in turn examined and refuted.

(1) The Dichotomy.—*That a moving object will never reach any given point, because however near it may be, it must always first accomplish a half-way stage, and then the half-way stage of what is left and so on, and this series has no end. Therefore, the object can never reach the end of any given distance. This has already been refuted* (b 9-14).

(2) The Achilles.—*That the swiftest racer can never overtake the slowest, if the slowest is given any start at all ; because the slowest will have passed beyond his starting-point when the swiftest reaches it, and beyond the point he has then reached when the swiftest reaches it and so on* ad infin. *This rests on the same fallacy as* (1) (b 14-30).

178

PHYSICS, VI. ix.

INTRODUCTORY NOTE (continued)

demand individual attention, for they are only defined
generically and have not reached final and complete actualization as unique individuals, each distinguishable from
any other member of its set. But the boundaries which
are actually made by the dichotomy do reach final and
complete actualization, and must be recognized as such;
their number, however, depends on the amount of dichotomy which is actually completed, and as illimitable
dichotomy can never be completed, the boundaries which
are ever actually made by it cannot be illimitable; and as
there is no impossibility in dealing with any limited number
however great, there is no impossibility of reaching the
end of a limited continuum.

ARGUMENT (continued)

(3) The Flying Arrow.—*That it is impossible for a thing
to be moving during a period of time, because it is impossible
for it to be moving at an indivisible instant. This assumes
that a period of time is made up of indivisible instants,
which cannot be granted* (b 30–33).

(4) The Stadium.—*That half a given period of time is
equal to the whole of it; because equal motions must
occupy equal times, and yet the time occupied in passing
the same number of equal objects varies according as the
objects are moving or stationary. The fallacy lies in the
assumption that a moving body passes moving and stationary
objects with equal velocity* (b 33–240 a 18).

Two further fallacies about movement are refuted:

*It is sometimes argued that a change between contradictory
conditions (e.g. from not-white to white) is impossible because a thing must always be either white or not-white, and
during the process of changing from one to the other it would
be neither white nor not-white. This assumes that ' white '*

179

ARISTOTLE

means ' pure white ' and ' not-white '' means ' without any trace of white,' which is not the customary use of the terms (a 19–29).

239 b 5   Ζήνων δὲ παραλογίζεται· εἰ γὰρ ἀεί, φησίν, ἠρεμεῖ πᾶν ὅταν[1] ᾖ κατὰ τὸ ἴσον, ἔστι δ' ἀεὶ τὸ φερόμενον ἐν τῷ νῦν,[2] ἀκίνητον τὴν φερομένην εἶναι ὀιστόν. τοῦτο δ' ἐστὶ ψεῦδος· οὐ γὰρ σύγκειται ὁ χρόνος ἐκ τῶν νῦν τῶν ἀδιαιρέτων, ὥσπερ οὐδ' ἄλλο μέγεθος οὐδέν.

10   Τέτταρες δ' εἰσὶ λόγοι περὶ κινήσεως Ζήνωνος οἱ παρέχοντες τὰς δυσκολίας τοῖς λύουσι—πρῶτος μὲν ὁ περὶ τοῦ μὴ κινεῖσθαι διὰ τὸ πρότερον εἰς τὸ ἥμισυ δεῖν ἀφικέσθαι τὸ φερόμενον ἢ πρὸς τὸ τέλος, περὶ οὗ διείλομεν ἐν τοῖς πρότερον λόγοις.

   Δεύτερος δὲ ὁ καλούμενος Ἀχιλλεύς. ἔστι δ'

---

[1] [ἠρεμεῖ πᾶν ἢ κινεῖται ὅταν codd.; Philop. 816. 30; Simpl. 1011. 27. Zeller ejected ἢ κινεῖται on the ground that Zeno's premiss was the definition of rest. This is supported by Themistius's paraphrase (199. 4) εἰ γὰρ ἠρεμεῖ, φησίν, ἅπαντα ὅταν ᾖ κατὰ τὸ ἴσον αὐτῷ διάστημα. A possible reading would be : εἰ γὰρ ἀεί, φησίν, ἠρεμεῖ πᾶν ἢ κινεῖται ⟨καὶ μὴ κινεῖται⟩ ὅταν κτλ. 'If everything is either at rest or in motion and is not in motion when it is over against something of equal dimensions, while a moving thing is always so (*i.e.* κατὰ τὸ ἴσον) at the moment, the flying arrow is motionless.'—C.]

[2] [ἐν τῷ νῦν τῷ κατὰ τὸ ἴσον rcF, *i.e.* ' at every moment the moving thing is occupying the moment (of the time occupied by its whole movement) which corresponds to the space equal to its own dimensions.' The time is supposed to be made up of a row of successive indivisible moments corresponding, one to one, with the row of successive positions occupied by the body. τῷ κατὰ τὸ ἴσον was probably added in this ms. to make it clear that ἐν τῷ νῦν means this. *Cf.* Philop. 817. 6, who says that after ἔστι δὲ τὸ φερόμενον ἐν τῷ νῦν we must

180

ARGUMENT (*continued*)

It has been argued that a revolving circle or sphere is not moving, because it is not changing its position. This ignores the difference between change of linear and of rotational position (a 29–b 7).

THE fallacy in Zeno's argument is now obvious ; for he says that since a thing is at rest when it has not shifted in any degree out of a place equal to its own dimensions, and since at any given instant during the whole of its supposed motion the supposed moving thing is in the place it occupies at that instant, the arrow is not moving at *any time* during its flight. But this is a false conclusion ; for time is not made up of atomic ' nows,' any more than any other magnitude is made up of atomic elements.[a]

Of Zeno's arguments about motion, there are four which give trouble to those who try to solve the problems they raise. The first is the one which declares movement to be impossible because, however near the mobile is to any given point, it will always have to cover the half, and then the half of that, and so on without limit before it gets there. And this we have already taken to pieces.[b]

The second is what is known as ' the Achilles,'

---

[a] [This first paragraph ought to be attached to the last paragraph of the preceding chapter, which explained that, while at any indivisible instant a moving object is ' over against ' a stationary object, so as to exactly ' cover ' it, it is not either moving or at rest ' *at* that instant ' (ἐν τῷ νῦν). This chapter should open with the review of Zeno's four arguments which follows.—C.]

[b] [At 233 a 21.—C.]

---

supply the suppressed statement πᾶν δὲ τὸ ἐν τῷ νῦν ἐν τῷ ἴσῳ ἑαυτοῦ ὑπάρχει τόπῳ.—C.]

239 b 15 οὗτος ὅτι τὸ βραδύτατον¹ οὐδέποτε καταληφθήσεται
θέον ὑπὸ τοῦ ταχίστου· ἔμπροσθεν γὰρ ἀναγκαῖον
ἐλθεῖν τὸ διῶκον ὅθεν ὥρμησε τὸ φεῦγον, ὥστ᾽
ἀεί τι προέχειν ἀναγκαῖον τὸ βραδύτερον. ἔστι
20 δὲ καὶ οὗτος ὁ αὐτὸς λόγος τῷ διχοτομεῖν, διαφέρει
δὲ ἐν τῷ διαιρεῖν μὴ δίχα τὸ προσλαμβανόμενον
μέγεθος. τὸ μὲν οὖν μὴ καταλαμβάνεσθαι τὸ
βραδύτερον συμβέβηκεν ἐκ τοῦ λόγου, γίγνεται
δὲ παρὰ ταὐτὸ τῇ διχοτομίᾳ—ἐν ἀμφοτέροις γὰρ
συμβαίνει μὴ ἀφικνεῖσθαι πρὸς τὸ πέρας διαιρουμένου πως τοῦ μεγέθους· ἀλλὰ πρόσκειται ἐν τούτῳ
25 ὅτι οὐδὲ τὸ τάχιστον τετραγῳδημένον ἐν τῷ
διώκειν τὸ βραδύτατον²—ὥστ᾽ ἀνάγκη καὶ τὴν
λύσιν εἶναι τὴν αὐτήν. τὸ δ᾽ ἀξιοῦν ὅτι τὸ προ-
έχον οὐ καταλαμβάνεται, ψεῦδος· ὅτε γὰρ προέχει
οὐ καταλαμβάνεται, ἀλλ᾽ ὅμως καταλαμβάνεται,
εἴπερ δώσει διεξιέναι τὴν πεπερασμένην. οὗτοι
30 μὲν οὖν οἱ δύο λόγοι.

Τρίτος δὲ ὁ νῦν ῥηθείς, ὅτι ἡ οἰστὸς φερομένη
ἔστηκεν. συμβαίνει δὲ παρὰ τὸ λαμβάνειν τὸν

¹ [βραδύτατον. Cf. b 25; Them. 199. 25; Philop. 817. 15
εἰπὼν ὅτι τὸ τάχιστον οὐ καταλήψεται τὸ βραδύτατον; Simpl.
1014. 1; Oxf. Trans.: βραδύτερον codd.—C.]
² [βραδύτατον EI: βραδύτερον FHK.—C.]

ᵃ The distance from the starting-point to the point at
which the slower is overtaken by the swifter is easily calcu-
lated, if the start allowed and the respective velocities are
182

which purports to show that the slowest will never be overtaken in its course by the swiftest, inasmuch as, reckoning from any given instant, the pursuer, before he can catch the pursued, must reach the point from which the pursued started at that instant, and so the slower will always be some distance in advance of the swifter. But this argument is the same as the former one which depends on bisection, with the difference that the division of the magnitudes we successively take is not a division into halves (but according to any ratio we like to assume between the two speeds). The conclusion of the argument is that the slower cannot be overtaken by the swifter, but it is reached by following the same lines as the ' bisection ' argument of the first thesis ; for the reason why neither supposed process lands us at the limit, is that the method of division is expressly so designed as not to get us there, only in this second thesis a declamatory intensification is introduced by representing the swiftest racer as unable to overtake the slowest. The solution then must be identical in both cases, and the claim that the thing that is ahead is not overtaken is false. It is not overtaken *while* it is ahead, but none the less it *is* overtaken if Zeno will allow it to traverse to the end its finite distance.[a] So much for these two theses.

The third thesis is the one just mentioned, namely that the arrow is stationary while on its flight. The demonstration rests on the assumption that time is

given. This then is the definite line or distance ($\dot{\eta} \ \pi\epsilon\pi\epsilon\rho\alpha\sigma\mu\dot{\epsilon}\nu\eta$) which has to be covered, and if it is granted that the racers ever reach this point, it follows that the slower will be overtaken by the swifter. So that the problem is reduced to the question whether the racers can ever reach this particular point on their course. See Book VIII. chapter viii., 263 a 4 ff.

239 b χρόνον συγκεῖσθαι ἐκ τῶν νῦν· μὴ διδομένου γὰρ

τούτου οὐκ ἔσται ὁ συλλογισμός.

Τέταρτος δ᾽ ὁ περὶ τῶν ἐν τῷ σταδίῳ κινουμένων

ἐξ ἐναντίας ἴσων ὄγκων παρ᾽ ἴσους, τῶν μὲν

35 ἀπὸ τέλους τοῦ σταδίου τῶν δὲ ἀπὸ μέσου, ἴσῳ

240 a τάχει, ἐν ᾧ συμβαίνειν οἴεται ἴσον εἶναι χρόνον

τῷ διπλασίῳ τὸν ἥμισυν. ἔστι δ᾽ ὁ παραλογισμὸς

ἐν τῷ τὸ μὲν παρὰ κινούμενον τὸ δὲ παρ᾽ ἠρεμοῦν

τὸ ἴσον μέγεθος ἀξιοῦν τῷ ἴσῳ τάχει τὸν ἴσον

φέρεσθαι χρόνον· τοῦτο δ᾽ ἐστὶ ψεῦδος. οἷον

5 ἔστωσαν οἱ ἑστῶτες ἴσοι ὄγκοι ἐφ᾽ ὧν τὰ ΑΑ, οἱ

δ᾽ ἐφ᾽ ὧν τὰ ΒΒ ἀρχόμενοι ἀπὸ τοῦ μέσου τῶν

Α,[1] ἴσοι τὸν ἀριθμὸν τούτοις ὄντες καὶ τὸ μέγεθος,

οἱ δ᾽ ἐφ᾽ ὧν τὰ ΓΓ ἀπὸ τοῦ ἐσχάτου, ἴσοι τὸν

ἀριθμὸν ὄντες τούτοις καὶ τὸ μέγεθος, καὶ ἰσοταχεῖς

τοῖς Β. συμβαίνει δὴ τὸ πρῶτον Β ἅμα ἐπὶ τῷ

---

[1] [τῶν Α om. EHI, Ross (cf. p. 188 note a).—C.]

184

made up of ' nows,' and if this be not granted the inference fails.

The fourth thesis supposes a number of objects all equal with each other in dimensions, forming two equal trains and arranged so that one train stretches from one end of a racecourse to the middle of it, and the other from the middle to the other end. Then if you let the two trains, moving in opposite directions but at the same rate, pass each other, Zeno undertakes to show that half of the time they occupy in passing each other is equal to the whole of it. The fallacy lies in his assuming that a moving object takes an equal time in passing another object equal in dimensions to itself, whether that other object is stationary or in motion; which assumption is false. For this is his demonstration. Let there be a number of objects **AAAA**, equal in number and bulk to those that compose the two trains but stationary in the middle of the stadium. Then let the objects **BBBB**, in number and dimension equal to the **A**'s, form one of the trains stretching from the middle of the **A**'s in one direction; and from the inner end of the **B**'s let **CCCC** stretch in the opposite direction, being equal in number, dimension, and rate of movement to the **B**'s.

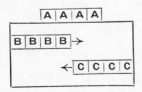

Then when they cross, the first **B** and the first **C** will

240 a 10 ἐσχάτῳ εἶναι καὶ τὸ πρῶτον Γ, παρ' ἄλληλα

κινουμένων. συμβαίνει δὲ[1] τὸ Γ παρὰ πάντα τὰ

B[2] διεξεληλυθέναι, τὸ δὲ Β παρὰ τὰ ἡμίση· ὥστε

ἥμισυν εἶναι τὸν χρόνον· ἴσον γὰρ ἑκάτερόν ἐστι

παρ' ἕκαστον. ἅμα δὲ συμβαίνει τὸ πρῶτον Β[3] παρὰ

πάντα τὰ Γ παρεληλυθέναι (ἅμα γὰρ ἔσται τὸ

15 πρῶτον Γ καὶ τὸ πρῶτον Β ἐπὶ τοῖς ἐναντίοις ἐσχά-

τοις), ἴσον χρόνον παρ' ἕκαστον γιγνόμενον τῶν

Γ[4] ὅσονπερ τῶν Α (ὥς φησι), διὰ τὸ ἀμφότερα

ἴσον χρόνον κατὰ τὰ Α[5] γίγνεσθαι. ὁ μὲν οὖν

---

[1] [δὲ E¹FHK, Simplic. 1017. 29, Alex. (Simpl. 1019. 27),
Oxf. Trans.: δὴ cett.—C.]

[2] [τὰ Β, E¹HI: τὰ Α, FKE², Simplic. 1018. 1, Alex.
(Simpl. 1019. 28), Oxf. Trans. The argument can be
reconstructed with either reading.—C.]

[3] [τὸ πρῶτον Β, written τὸ αβ E: τὰ Β cett.—C.]

[4] [τῶν Γ: τῶν Β codd. The readings and punctuation
adopted provide γιγνόμενον with a subject to agree with
(τὸ Β); it can hardly agree with either τὸ πρῶτον Γ or τὸ
πρῶτον Β to the exclusion of the other. The change of τῶν Β
to τῶν Γ is consequential. Mr. Ross would eject ἴσον χρόνον
. . ὥς φησι (see p. 188 note a).—C.]

[5] [κατὰ τὰ Α: κατὰ τὸ Α Alex. ap. Simplic. 1019. 32: παρὰ
τὰ Α codd.—C.]

simultaneously reach the extreme A's in contrary directions.

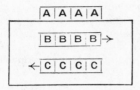

Now during this process the first C has passed all the B's, whereas the first B has only passed half the A's, and therefore only taken half the time; for it takes an equal time (the minimal time) for the C to pass one B as for the B to pass one A. But during this same half-time the first B has also passed all the C's [a] (though the first B takes as long, says Zeno, to pass a C as an A) because measured by their progress through the A's the B's and C's have had the same time in which to cross each other.[b] Such is

[a] [The translation here omits the parenthesis in the Greek: '(for the first C and the first B arrive at the opposite ends simultaneously).' This has already been stated above; it is repeated to justify the statement just made: that 'the first B has passed all the C's *in the same time*' as the first C has passed all the B's (as stated in the previous sentence).—C.]

[b] The first C crosses all the B's while the first B crosses half the A's. Therefore while the first C crosses half the A's it will have time to cross all the B's (as it actually does, by the conditions of the problem). But it takes as long to pass an A as a B or C. Therefore half the time is as long as the whole time.

ARISTOTLE

240 a λόγος οὗτός ἐστιν, συμβαίνει δὲ παρὰ τὸ εἰρημένον
ψεῦδος.

Οὐδὲ δὴ κατὰ τὴν ἐν τῇ ἀντιφάσει μεταβολὴν
20 οὐδὲν ἡμῖν ἔσται ἀδύνατον, οἷον εἰ ἐκ τοῦ μὴ λευκοῦ
εἰς τὸ λευκὸν μεταβάλλει καὶ ἐν μηδετέρῳ ἐστίν,
ὡς ἄρα οὔτε λευκὸν ἔσται οὔτε οὐ λευκόν. οὐ γὰρ
εἰ μὴ ὅλον ἐν ὁποτερῳοῦν ἐστιν, οὐ λεχθήσεται
λευκὸν ἢ οὐ λευκόν· λευκὸν γὰρ λέγομεν ἢ οὐ
λευκὸν οὐ τῷ ὅλον εἶναι τοιοῦτον ἀλλὰ τῷ τὰ

---

[a] [I have printed Dr. Wicksteed's translation of this paragraph as it stands, with some verbal corrections, and given
the text it implies. Mr. W. D. Ross has kindly allowed me
to make use of an unpublished paper giving his interpretation
of the Stadium and the readings he would adopt. I have
made the following literal translation in accordance with his
readings, adding a diagram which varies from the traditional
one only in placing the stationary A's outside the course in
the position of the spectators.

'The fourth is the one about the equal bodies moving in
the stadium past equal bodies in the opposite direction at
equal speed, some (moving) from the end of the stadium,
some from the *midway point* (*i.e.* the turning-point in the
double course). This, he thinks, involves the conclusion that
the half-time is equal to *its double* (*the whole time*). The
fallacy lies in the assumption that a body, moving with equal
speed, takes an equal time in passing a moving body and a
body of the same size that is at rest. This is false.

For instance let the equal stationary bodies be AA, and let
BB, *starting from the mid-point* [omit τῶν A, with EHI], be

his argument, but the result depends on the fallacy above mentioned.[a]

Nor need we be troubled by any attack on the possibility of change based on the axiom that a thing ' must either be or not be ' but cannot ' both be and not be ' this or that at the same time. For, it is argued, if a thing is changing, for instance, from being not-white to being white and is on its way from one to the other, you can truly assert at the same time that it is neither white nor not-white. But this is not true, for we sometimes call a thing ' white ' even if it is not entirely white, and we sometimes call a thing ' not-white ' even if there is some trace of white in it ; we speak of it according to its prevailing con-

equal to them (the A's) in number and size, and let the CC *starting from the end (of the stadium)* be equal to them in number and size and equal to the B's in speed.

' Then it follows that the front B is opposite the (right-hand) end A (and the rear C) at the same time as the front C is opposite the (left-hand) end A (and the rear B), when they move past one another.

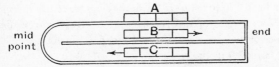

' And it follows that the (front) C has passed all the *B's*, while the (front) B has passed *half that number (of bodies,* viz. *the A's),* so that the (B's) time is half (the C's time); for either takes the same time in passing each (body).

' And it follows that at the same moment the (front) B has passed all the C's ; for the front C and the front B will arrive at the opposite end A's simultaneously. [Omit ἴσον χρόνον . . . ὥς φησι: a gloss on l. 12 ἴσον γὰρ ἑκάτερόν ἐστι παρ' ἕκαστον], because both the B's and the C's take the same time in passing the A's (παρὰ τὰ A).'—C.]

ARISTOTLE

240 a 25 πλεῖστα ἢ τὰ κυριώτατα μέρη· οὐ ταὐτὸ δ' ἐστὶ
μὴ εἶναί τε ἐν τούτῳ καὶ μὴ εἶναι ἐν τούτῳ ὅλον.
ὁμοίως δὲ καὶ ἐπὶ τοῦ ὄντος καὶ ἐπὶ τοῦ μὴ ὄντος[1]
καὶ τῶν ἄλλων τῶν κατ' ἀντίφασιν· ἔσται μὲν γὰρ
ἐξ ἀνάγκης ἐν θατέρῳ τῶν ἀντικειμένων, ἐν οὐδ-
ετέρῳ δ' ὅλον ἀεί.

30 Πάλιν ἐπὶ τοῦ κύκλου καὶ ἐπὶ τῆς σφαίρας καὶ
ὅλως τῶν ἐν αὑτοῖς κινουμένων, ὅτι συμβήσεται
αὐτὰ ἠρεμεῖν· ἐν γὰρ τῷ αὐτῷ τόπῳ χρόνον τινὰ
ἔσται καὶ αὐτὰ καὶ τὰ μέρη, ὥστε ἠρεμήσει ἅμα
καὶ κινήσεται. πρῶτον μὲν γὰρ τὰ μέρη οὐκ ἔστιν
240 b ἐν τῷ αὐτῷ οὐθένα χρόνον, εἶτα καὶ τὸ ὅλον μεταβάλλει ἀεὶ εἰς ἕτερον· οὐ γὰρ ἡ αὐτή ἐστιν ἡ ἀπὸ
τοῦ Α λαμβανομένη περιφέρεια καὶ ἡ ἀπὸ τοῦ Β
καὶ τοῦ Γ καὶ τῶν ἄλλων ἑκάστου σημείων, πλὴν
ὡς ὁ μουσικὸς ἄνθρωπος καὶ ἄνθρωπος, ὅτι συμ-
5 βέβηκεν. ὥστε μεταβάλλει ἀεὶ ἡ ἑτέρα εἰς τὴν
ἑτέραν, καὶ οὐδέποτε ἠρεμήσει. τὸν αὐτὸν δὲ
τρόπον καὶ ἐπὶ τῆς σφαίρας καὶ ἐπὶ τῶν ἄλλων τῶν
ἐν αὑτοῖς κινουμένων.

1 [Perhaps we should read, with Simplic. 1021. 22 ὁμοίως
δὲ καὶ ἐπὶ τοῦ ὄντος καὶ μὴ ὄντος. The mss. and Philop. 818. 10
betray some confusion.—C.]

dition or the conditions of its most significant parts or aspects. For to say that a thing is not in a certain condition ' at all ' and to say that it is not ' altogether,' in it are two different things. And so, too, in the case of being or not being or any other pair of contradictory opposites. For during the whole process of changing it must be prevailingly one or the other and can never be exclusively either.[a]

Again it is said that a rotating circle or sphere or anything else that moves within its own dimensions is stationary because in itself and all its parts it will remain in the same place for the given time : so it will be in motion and at rest at the same time. But in the first place its parts are not in the same place during any space of time, and in the second place the whole is also continuously changing to a different (rotational) position[b]; for the circumference measured round from A to A again is not identical with the circumference as measured from B to B or from C to C or any other point, except by accidental concomitance, as the cultivated person is a man. Thus one circumference is ever succeeding another and it will never be at rest. So, too, with the sphere, and any other body that moves within fixed dimensions.

[a] It is more proper to say that during the change, it is ' always partially both but never wholly either than to say that it is " always neither." '—Themistius.
[b] See Book IV., chapter v., Introduction and text, also chapter iv., especially note a, Vol. I. p. 211.

ARISTOTLE

CHAPTER X

ARGUMENT

An indivisible (in the sense of that which is without parts) can only be in motion incidentally, that is to say by being situated in something which is in motion, as things which are in a boat move when the boat moves; but the motion of the whole does not necessarily produce equal motions in every part; it cannot therefore be called a single motion (240 b 8–17). Several proofs are given:

(1) An indivisible cannot on its own account be in process of changing, for while a thing is in the act of changing it must be partially what it is changing to, and partially what it is changing from; but an indivisible cannot be partially this and partially that, and when anything is wholly this or that it is not changing (b 17–30). So that only if time were made up of ' nows' and the mobile could be in a wholly different condition in each, could it change without ever being in the act of changing. This supposition has already been dismissed (b 30–241 a 6).

(2) Before a thing can move through a distance greater than itself, it must move through a distance equal to or less than itself; there is nothing less than an indivisible;

240 b 8 Ἀποδεδειγμένων δὲ τούτων, λέγομεν ὅτι τὸ ἀμερὲς οὐκ ἐνδέχεται κινεῖσθαι πλὴν κατὰ συμ-
10 βεβηκός, οἷον κινουμένου τοῦ σώματος ἢ τοῦ μεγέθους τῷ ἐνυπάρχειν,[1] καθάπερ ἂν εἰ τὸ ἐν τῷ πλοίῳ κινοῖτο ὑπὸ τῆς τοῦ πλοίου φορᾶς ἢ τὸ μέρος τῇ τοῦ ὅλου κινήσει. (ἀμερὲς δὲ λέγω τὸ κατὰ ποσὸν ἀδιαίρετον· καὶ γὰρ αἱ τῶν μερῶν κινήσεις ἕτεραί εἰσι κατ' αὐτά τε τὰ μέρη καὶ κατὰ

[1] [τῷ ἐνυπάρχειν Simplic. 1025. 3 (*cf.* Them. 202. 8), Gottschlich, Prantl: τῶν ἐνυπάρχειν E: τοῦ (τὸ H) ἐν ᾧ ὑπάρχει cett.—C.]

192

CHAPTER X

therefore a point could only measure up a distance by moving through a succession of 'things equal to itself,' i.e. points, and this would only be possible if distance were made up of points, which is not the case (a 6–14).

(3) A similar proof based on the illimitable divisibility of time (a 15–26).

No change between contraries can be unlimited: (a) genesis and extinction are limited by the opposite extremes of existence and non-existence. (b) Changes of quality by the extremes of contrasted qualities. (c) Growth and shrinkage by the limits of magnitude fixed by the nature of the subject. Locomotion is not necessarily between contraries and is not therefore necessarily limited in this way, but any actual change of position must be from an actual ' here ' to an actual 'there,' and movement through illimitable distance would be changing to a 'there' which does not exist ; therefore things cannot actually move all through illimitable distance. The only kind of change which is not limited in this way is rotary locomotion. This then can be going on through illimitable time (a 26–b 12).

WE are now in a position to show that that which has no parts cannot be in motion on its own account but only by its implication with something else, such as a moving body or changing magnitude, in which it exists, just as the movement of what the boat contains is involved in the motion of the boat, or that of a part in the movement of the whole of which it is a part. (By ' that which has no parts ' I mean the quantitively indivisible. For the parts may have movements of their own distinct from the movement

193

240 b 15 τὴν τοῦ ὅλου κίνησιν. ἴδοι δ᾽ ἄν τις ἐπὶ τῆς
σφαίρας μάλιστα τὴν διαφοράν· οὐ γὰρ ταὐτὸν
τάχος ἐστὶ τῶν τε πρὸς τῷ κέντρῳ καὶ τῶν ἐκτὸς
καὶ τῆς ὅλης, ὡς οὐ μιᾶς οὔσης κινήσεως).

Καθάπερ οὖν εἴπομεν, οὕτω μὲν ἐνδέχεται κινεῖσθαι τὸ ἀμερὲς ὡς ὁ ἐν τῷ πλοίῳ καθήμενος τοῦ
20 πλοίου θέοντος· καθ᾽ αὑτὸ δ᾽ οὐκ ἐνδέχεται. μετα-
βαλλέτω γὰρ ἐκ τοῦ ΑΒ εἰς τὸ ΒΓ—εἴτ᾽ ἐκ μεγέθους εἰς μέγεθος εἴτ᾽ ἐξ εἴδους εἰς εἶδος εἴτε κατ᾽
ἀντίφασιν—ὁ δὲ χρόνος ἔστω ἐν ᾧ πρώτῳ μεταβάλλει ἐφ᾽ οὗ Δ. οὐκοῦν ἀνάγκη αὐτὸ καθ᾽ ὃν
μεταβάλλει χρόνον ἢ ἐν τῷ ΑΒ εἶναι ἢ ἐν τῷ ΒΓ
25 ἢ τὸ μέν τι αὐτοῦ ἐν τούτῳ τὸ δ᾽ ἐν θατέρῳ· πᾶν
γὰρ τὸ μεταβάλλον οὕτως εἶχεν. ἐν ἑκατέρῳ μὲν
οὖν οὐκ ἔσται τι αὐτοῦ· μεριστὸν γὰρ ἂν εἴη. ἀλλὰ

---

[a] [The connexion of thought (γάρ) seems to be: 'I am
speaking of what has no distinction of parts at all; *for*, if a
thing has distinguishable parts, these may have movements
of their own distinguishable from the motion of the whole,
even though they all move together in a rigid whole. This
cannot be so if a thing has no parts at all, and it is of such
things that I will show that they can have only incidental
motion.' Aristotle is still thinking of the false assumptions
underlying the Zenonian dilemmas, viz. that there are
minimal (atomic = 'indivisible') times, spaces, movements,
and bodies. In the Stadium, for instance, the moving bodies
(B's and C's) were thought of as minimal bodies (ὄγκοι or
'points' conceived as having *indivisible magnitude*) making
minimal movements over minimal spaces in minimal times.
Aristotle has already disposed of minimal spaces, times, and
movements. It remains to attack the notion of a minimal
(indivisible) body that can move. There is no such thing,
for every body is infinitely divisible. What is strictly
indivisible is such a thing as the point, which really has no

194

of the whole.[a] This difference is most readily seen in the case of a rotating sphere, for the velocity of the parts varies according as they are nearer to the middle or further from it; and this difference amongst the parts is in each case distinguishable from the general motion of the whole, so that the movement of the whole collectively cannot be regarded as a single movement.)

So, as already said, an indivisible may move incidentally after the manner of the man sitting in the boat, but not primarily on its own account. For suppose a thing to change from AB to BC (whether the change concern magnitude or characteristic quality or the coming into being and passing out of it); and let the proper time during which the change is actually and continuously occurring be represented by $T(\triangle)$. Then it follows that during the whole of this period it must either be in the place or condition AB or the place or condition BC or partially in one and partially in the other, for these, as we saw,[b] are the only alternatives possible to anything that is in process of changing. But it (*i.e.* an indivisible) cannot be partly in each, for then it would be divisible.[c] Nor can it be

magnitude or parts at all (ἀμερές). It is now shown that the strictly indivisible thing cannot move except incidentally.—C.]

[b] [At 234 b 15, where it was stated that only the third logical alternative is really possible.—C.]

[c] To make this argument generally applicable (as it is obviously meant to be) it must be taken to mean that all the time the thing is changing it must preserve something—but not all—of what distinguishes that-out-of-which-it-is-coming from that-into-which-it-is-going, while something is being introduced of what distinguishes that-into-which-it-is-going from that-out-of-which-it-is-coming; and this cannot be the case with an indivisible, which is an unanalysable unity. [See note *b* on p. 81.]

240 b μὴν οὐδ' ἐν τῷ ΒΓ· μεταβεβληκὸς γὰρ ἔσται, ὑπόκειται δὲ μεταβάλλειν. λείπεται δὴ αὐτὸ ἐν τῷ
ΑΒ εἶναι καθ' ὃν μεταβάλλει χρόνον· ἠρεμήσει ἄρα,
30 τὸ γὰρ ἐν τῷ αὐτῷ εἶναι χρόνον τινὰ ἠρεμεῖν ἦν.

"Ωστ' οὐκ ἐνδέχεται τὸ ἀμερὲς κινεῖσθαι οὐδ'
ὅλως μεταβάλλειν.   μοναχῶς γὰρ ἂν οὕτως ἦν
αὐτοῦ κίνησις, εἰ ὁ χρόνος ἦν ἐκ τῶν νῦν· ἀεὶ γὰρ
241 a ἐν τῷ νῦν κεκινημένον ἂν ἦν καὶ μεταβεβληκός,
ὥστε κινεῖσθαι μὲν μηδέποτε κεκινῆσθαι δ' ἀεί.
τοῦτο δ' ὅτι ἀδύνατον, δέδεικται καὶ πρότερον·
οὔτε γὰρ ὁ χρόνος ἐκ τῶν νῦν, οὔθ' ἡ γραμμὴ ἐκ
στιγμῶν, οὔθ' ἡ κίνησις ἐκ κινημάτων· οὐθὲν γὰρ
5 ἄλλο ποιεῖ ὁ τοῦτο λέγων ἢ τὴν κίνησιν ἐξ ἀμερῶν,
καθάπερ ἂν εἰ τὸν χρόνον ἐκ τῶν νῦν ἢ τὸ μέγεθος
ἐκ στιγμῶν.

"Ετι δὲ καὶ ἐκ τῶνδε φανερὸν ὅτι οὔτε στιγμὴν
οὔτ' ἄλλο ἀδιαίρετον οὐθὲν ἐνδέχεται κινεῖσθαι.
ἅπαν γὰρ τὸ κινούμενον ἀδύνατον πρότερον μεῖζον
κινηθῆναι αὐτοῦ, πρὶν ἂν ἢ ἴσον ἢ ἔλαττον. εἰ δὴ
10 τοῦτο, φανερὸν ὅτι καὶ ἡ στιγμὴ ἔλαττον ἢ ἴσον
κινηθήσεται πρῶτον· ἐπεὶ δ' ἀδιαίρετος, ἀδύνατον
ἔλαττον κινηθῆναι πρότερον· ἴσην ἄρα ἑαυτῇ. ὥστε
ἔσται ἡ γραμμὴ ἐκ στιγμῶν· ἀεὶ γὰρ ἴσην κινουμένη τὴν πᾶσαν γραμμὴν στιγμὴ καταμετρήσει.

ᵃ [At 239 a 27.—C.]
ᵇ [At 231 b 18 ff., where (232 a 8) the passive form κίνημα,
'a having-been-moved' was contrasted with the usual
(active) form κίνησις and explained by Simplicius as meaning
the term (πέρας) of a motion.—C.]
ᶜ That is to say, its 'movement' would consist in measuring up the line by being over against a succession of contiguous indivisibles.   But the *conceptually* indivisible cannot
be contiguous one with another and make up a line.

in BC, for so it would have completed the change, whereas by hypothesis it is still in process of change. It remains, then, that it is in AB during the period in which it is changing. So it must be at rest, for, as we saw,[a] to remain in the same place or state during a period of time is to be at rest.

So it is not possible for the indivisible to move, or, more generally, to change in any way. For the only hypothesis on which it could be supposed to have any motion while never moving during any period of time would be the hypothesis that time is made up of 'nows,' for then in every 'now' it might be supposed to have moved or to have changed, in such a way as never to be in the process of moving but always in the state of having moved. Now this has already been shown[b] to be impossible; for neither is time made up of 'nows,' nor a line of points, nor motion of ' having-movednesses.' For this is what the assertion of motion being composed of atomic motions amounts to, just as though time could be built up out of 'nows,' or magnitude out of points.

Again, the following is another proof that neither a point nor any other indivisible can move. It is impossible that anything should move through a distance greater than itself without having first moved through a space equal to or less than itself. And this being so, it is evident that neither can a point move through any distance without having first moved through a distance less than itself or equal to it ; and since it is indivisible, the distance it has moved through cannot be less than itself, and must therefore be equal to it. So the line would be made up of points ; for the point, by having moved through a succession of things equal to itself, would have measured up the line[c] ; and if this

197

241 a εἰ δὲ τοῦτο ἀδύνατον, καὶ τὸ κινεῖσθαι τὸ ἀδιαίρετον ἀδύνατον.

15 Ἔτι δ᾽ εἰ ἅπαν ἐν χρόνῳ κινεῖται, ἐν δὲ τῷ νῦν
μηθέν, ἅπας δὲ χρόνος διαιρετός, εἴη ἄν τις χρόνος
ἐλάττων ὁτῳοῦν τῶν κινουμένων ἢ ἐν ᾧ κινεῖται
ὅσον αὐτό (οὗτος μὲν γὰρ ἔσται χρόνος ἐν ᾧ
κινεῖται, διὰ τὸ πᾶν ἐν χρόνῳ κινεῖσθαι, χρόνος δὲ
20 πᾶς διαιρετὸς δέδεικται πρότερον). εἰ ἄρα στιγμὴ
κινεῖται, ἔσται τις χρόνος ἐλάττων ἢ ἐν ᾧ αὐτὴ
ἐκινήθη. ἀλλ᾽ ἀδύνατον· ἐν γὰρ τῷ ἐλάττονι ἔλαττον ἀνάγκη κινεῖσθαι, ὥστε ἔσται διαιρετὸν τὸ
ἀδιαίρετον εἰς τὸ ἔλαττον, ὥσπερ καὶ ὁ χρόνος εἰς
τὸν χρόνον· μοναχῶς γὰρ ἂν κινοῖτο τὸ ἀμερὲς καὶ
25 ἀδιαίρετον, εἰ ἦν ἐν τῷ νῦν κινεῖσθαι δυνατὸν τῷ
ἀτόμῳ· τοῦ γὰρ αὐτοῦ λόγου ἐν τῷ νῦν κινεῖσθαι
καὶ ἀδιαίρετόν τι κινεῖσθαι.

Μεταβολὴ δ᾽ οὐκ ἔστιν οὐδεμία ἄπειρος. ἅπασα
γὰρ ἦν ἔκ τινος εἴς τι καὶ ἡ ἐν ἀντιφάσει καὶ ἡ ἐν
ἐναντίοις· ὥστε τῶν μὲν κατ᾽ ἀντίφασιν ἡ φάσις
καὶ ἡ ἀπόφασις πέρας, οἷον γενέσεως μὲν τὸ
30 ὂν φθορᾶς δὲ τὸ μὴ ὄν, τῶν δὲ ἐν τοῖς ἐναντίοις τὰ
ἐναντία (ταῦτα γὰρ ἄκρα τῆς μεταβολῆς), ὥστε
καὶ ἀλλοιώσεως πάσης[1] ἐξ ἐναντίων γάρ τινων ἡ
ἀλλοίωσις. ὁμοίως δὲ καὶ αὐξήσεως καὶ φθίσεως·

---

[1] [I have punctuated so as to indicate that ἀλλοιώσεως
πάσης is governed by πέρας ἐστὶ τὰ ἐναντία (not ἄκρα) understood.—C.]

---

[a] The argument seems to be that movement would be
possible to an indivisible only if an indivisible transit were
possible, and this could only occur in an indivisible 'now.'
But no motion can occur in a 'now.' Hence no transit can

is impossible, so is the movement of anything that is indivisible.

Again, since a thing must occupy a certain period of time in moving (and cannot move in a 'now') and every period of time is divisible, there could be a time shorter than the time that any mobile requires to pass through a space equal to itself in dimension (for this shorter time will always be a *period* of time in which motion takes place—not an indivisible instant—because any motion occupies a period of time, and we have proved above that any period of time is divisible). If, then, a point moves, there must be a time shorter than that in which it completes a transit equalling it dimensionally. But that is impossible ; for in that shorter time it would move a part of the space equal to itself. So the indivisible space would be divided so as to be smaller, in correspondence with the shorter time ; for that which has no parts and is indivisible could only move if movement were possible in atomic time, for moving in the ' now ' is equivalent to making an indivisible movement.[a]

Nor can any change be without limit ; for we have agreed that every change is from this to that, whether the ' this ' and ' that ' are contrasted or contradictory. Thus the limits of changes between the contradictories are the positive and the negative, *e.g.* existence as the limit of genesis and non-existence of extinction; and in the case of contrasts the contrasted qualities in question, for such are the extreme points of the change. This applies to every form of modification, for modification must be from one quality to another contrasted with it. And it is the same with growth and

be indivisible, and consequently no indivisible can move except accidentally.

199

241 b αὐξήσεως μὲν γὰρ τὸ πέρας τοῦ[1] κατὰ τὴν οἰκείαν
φύσιν τελείου μεγέθους, φθίσεως δὲ ἡ τούτου
ἔκστασις. ἡ δὲ φορὰ οὕτω μὲν οὐκ ἔσται πεπε-
ρασμένη· οὐ γὰρ πᾶσα ἐν ἐναντίοις. ἀλλ' ἐπειδὴ
5 τὸ ἀδύνατον τμηθῆναι οὕτω, τῷ μὴ ἐνδέχεσθαι
τμηθῆναι (πλεοναχῶς γὰρ λέγεται τὸ ἀδύνατον), οὐκ
ἐνδέχεται [τὸ οὕτως ἀδύνατον][2] τέμνεσθαι, οὐδ'
ὅλως τὸ ἀδύνατον γενέσθαι γίγνεσθαι, οὐδὲ τὸ μεταβαλεῖν ἀδύνατον ἐνδέχοιτ' ἂν μεταβάλλειν εἰς ὃ
ἀδύνατον μεταβαλεῖν. εἰ οὖν τὸ φερόμενον μεταβάλλοι εἴς τι, καὶ δυνατὸν ἔσται μεταβαλεῖν. ὥστε
10 οὐκ ἄπειρος ἡ κίνησις, οὐδ' οἰσθήσεται τὴν ἄπειρον·
ἀδύνατον γὰρ διελθεῖν αὐτήν. ὅτι μὲν οὖν οὕτως

---

[1] [τὸ πέρας τοῦ: πέρας τὸ τοῦ Prantl.—C.]

[2] [The sentence down to τέμνεσθαι looks like a mixture of
two constructions: (1) ἐπειδὴ τὸ ἀδύνατον τμηθῆναι οὕτω
⟨λέγεται⟩, τῷ μὴ ἐνδέχεσθαι τμηθῆναι (πλεοναχῶς . . . ἀδύνατον),
οὐκ ἐνδέχεται τὸ οὕτως ἀδύνατον before τέμνεσθαι, where the last
clause is apodosis, and τὸ οὕτως ἀδύνατον is needed and in
place. The sentence might be so understood by one who
did not see that the apodosis really begins with οὐδὲ τὸ
μεταβαλεῖν ἀδύνατον. (2) ἐπειδὴ τὸ οὕτως ἀδύνατον τμηθῆναι,
τῷ μὴ ἐνδέχεσθαι τμηθῆναι (πλεοναχῶς . . . ἀδύνατον), οὐκ
ἐνδέχεται τέμνεσθαι. This is the construction required, but
in it τὸ οὕτως ἀδύνατον before τέμνεσθαι is superfluous and
misplaced. Simplicius's paraphrase (1030. 24): καὶ λέγει
ὅτι τὸ οὕτως ἀδύνατον τμηθῆναι, ὡς μὴ ἐνδέχεσθαι τμηθῆναι,
οὐκ ἐνδέχεται τέμνεσθαι, would be the most satisfactory
reading, with τῷ (or possibly ὥστε, cf. οὕτως . . . ὥστε below,
ll. 10-11 and 13) for Simplicius's ὡς. I assume that τὸ
οὕτως ἀδύνατον either was inserted in order to obtain construction (1), or arises from an attempt to correct τὸ ἀδύνατον
τμηθῆναι οὕτω (where F omits τὸ and E omits οὕτω) to τὸ οὕτως
ἀδύνατον τμηθῆναι.—C.]

---

[a] [For ἔκστασις cf. De caelo 286 a 18 ὕστερον δὲ τὸ παρὰ
φύσιν τοῦ κατὰ φύσιν καὶ ἔκστασίς τίς ἐστιν ἐν τῇ γενέσει τὸ

shrinkage, for growth finds a limit in the full size admitted by the special nature of the subject concerned, and shrinkage in the furthest removal from that size which that nature admits.[a] The limits of local motion do not come under the same principle, for they are not all between contrasted limits.[b] But since that which cannot be divided in the sense that it is conceptually indivisible [c] (for ' cannot ' has more senses than one) cannot be in process of being divided, and more generally it is impossible that that which is incapable of happening [d] should be in process of happening, so neither is it conceivable that a thing incapable of a certain change should be in process of undergoing the change to that which it cannot change to. If, then, the moving body is in process of changing to some place, it must be possible for it to change to that place. So the motion cannot be unlimited, nor can the mobile travel all the way through an unlimited space, for it would have to complete up to the limit that which has no limit. It is clear, then,

---

παρὰ φύσιν τοῦ κατὰ φύσιν. Mr. Stocks (Oxf. Trans.) there translates ἔκστασις by ' derangement.' At 246 b 2 the natural excellences of things are called τελειώσεις (perfections, fulfilments), their defects ἐκστάσεις.—C.]

[b] In the physical universe the centre and circumference may be contrasted as the limits of movement up and down ; but the re-entrant movement of a revolving sphere seems to have no limits. The commentators add the movement of animals as another instance.

[c] [The illustration from ' that which cannot be cut ' is probably taken from the atom of Leucippus and Democritus, which they declared to be *physically* incapable of being cut, being perfectly solid, but not like the mathematical point which is *conceptually* indivisible, having no parts.—C.]

[d] [Here γενέσθαι means ' happen,' ' come to pass ' ; hence ὅλως, which would be inappropriate if *genesis* were meant. —C.]

241 b οὐκ ἔστιν ἄπειρος μεταβολὴ ὥστε μὴ ὡρίσθαι
πέρασι, φανερόν.

'Αλλ' εἰ οὕτως ἐνδέχεται ὥστε τῷ χρόνῳ εἶναι
ἄπειρον τὴν αὐτὴν οὖσαν καὶ μίαν, σκεπτέον. μὴ
15 μιᾶς μὲν γὰρ γιγνομένης, οὐθὲν ἴσως κωλύει, οἷον
εἰ μετὰ τὴν φορὰν ἀλλοίωσις εἴη, καὶ μετὰ τὴν
ἀλλοίωσιν αὔξησις, καὶ πάλιν γένεσις· οὕτω γὰρ
ἀεὶ μὲν ἔσται τῷ χρόνῳ κίνησις, ἀλλ' οὐ μία διὰ
τὸ μὴ εἶναι μίαν ἐξ ἁπασῶν. ὥστε δὲ γίγνεσθαι
μίαν, οὐκ ἐνδέχεται ἄπειρον εἶναι τῷ χρόνῳ, πλὴν
20 μιᾶς· αὕτη δ' ἐστὶν ἡ κύκλῳ φορά.

that there can be no unlimited change in the sense of an accomplished change that has no limits.

It remains, however, to inquire whether any change, remaining one and the same in its nature, can go on without any limit in time. I take it that if you allow the nature of the change to alter, there will be no difficulty in assuming it to go on without any limit, for instance if a local movement should be followed by a change of quality, and that by an expansion, and that by a genetic change ; for thus movement (in the large sense) would always be going on in time, but would not be one movement, since there would be no unity in the successive kinds of movement.[a] But if it is to remain one and the same in kind, there is no movement that can go on without limit in time save one, namely rotary locomotion.[b]

[a] See Book VIII. chapter viii.   [b] See *De caelo*, i. 5.

BOOK VII

INTRODUCTION

[SIMPLICIUS, in his Introduction to this Book, remarks that the more important and relevant of the problems treated in it are discussed in more detail in Book VIII. Some ancient critics accordingly regarded Book VII. as superfluous, and Eudemus passed it over. Themistius treats it in summary fashion. Simplicius himself conjectures that Aristotle wrote Book VII. at some earlier time and, when he had dealt with some of its topics more fully in Book VIII., allowed it to stand as a sort of introductory study.

Chapter I. argues that whatever is in motion must be kept in motion by something, and that if there is a series of things, each member of which moves the next, the series cannot be infinite but must terminate in a First Mover.

Chapter II. The initiating cause of movement or change must be in direct touch with the thing moved or changed. This is true of locomotion, all forms of which can be reduced to varieties of pulling and pushing, where direct contact is clearly necessary. It is also true of alteration of quality (including such alterations as are accompanied by sensation in animate beings) and also of change of quantity. Alteration of quality is further studied in Chapter III. and distinguished from other processes which involve, but are not identical with, changes of quality. Such are the shaping of material into form, and the formation or loss of physical, moral, or intellectual excellences and defects.

Chapter IV. contains a long dialectical inquiry into the question, what conditions must be satisfied if two changes

or motions are to be comparable—such that they can be
called equal to, or greater or less than, one another. It
appears that if two things are to be comparable in respect
of any attribute, the attribute itself and the subject which
has it must both belong to indivisible species. This
requirement will cover the case of the incomparability
of rectilinear motion and rotatory motion; for there is a
specific difference between rectilinear distance and circular
distance which carries with it a specific difference in the
locomotion. (See Vol. I. p. 319, par. 4).

Chapter V. states some simple principles of mechanics.
—C.]

H

CHAPTER I

ARGUMENT

⌜*If a thing is in motion, there must be something that keeps it in motion. This is obvious where the thing is moved by a second thing ; but it is also true, if its source of motion is in itself. (The argument in support of this conclusion is obscure and puzzled the early commentators. The subject is differently treated in Book VIII., chapter iv.) (241 b 24–242 a 16).*

If there is a series of things, each moving its successor and being moved by its predecessor, the series cannot be unlimited but must end in a first mover, which is not itself moved by anything. Two proofs are given. (1) The members of the series will all have distinct motions which occur simultaneously in the finite time occupied by one of them. Then, supposing the motions to be all equal or to increase as we advance

241 b 24   Ἅπαν τὸ κινούμενον ὑπό τινος ἀνάγκη κινεῖσθαι.
25   εἰ μὲν γὰρ ἐν ἑαυτῷ μὴ ἔχει τὴν ἀρχὴν τῆς κινήσεως,
φανερὸν ὅτι ὑφ' ἑτέρου κινεῖται (ἄλλο γὰρ ἔσται
τὸ κινοῦν)· εἰ δὲ ἐν αὑτῷ, ἔστω τὸ εἰλημμένον ἐφ'
οὗ τὸ ΑΒ ὃ κινεῖται καθ' αὑτὸ ἀλλὰ μὴ τῷ τῶν
τούτου τι κινεῖσθαι.   πρῶτον μὲν οὖν τὸ ὑπολαμ-
30   βάνειν τὸ ΑΒ ὑφ' ἑαυτοῦ κινεῖσθαι διὰ τὸ ὅλον τε
κινεῖσθαι καὶ ὑπὸ οὐδενὸς τῶν ἔξωθεν ὅμοιόν ἐστιν

206

BOOK VII

CHAPTER I

ARGUMENT (*continued*)

along the series, their sum would be infinite—an infinite motion in a finite time : which is impossible (242 a 16–b 19). *But this argument is not conclusive, because an unlimited number of motions of different things can occur simultaneously in a finite time. But* (2) *if we take such an unlimited series of things moving in space, they must be either continuous or each in contact with its successor, and so form a unit with a single unlimited motion ; and this unlimited motion could not occupy a finite time. The conclusion is that there must be a first member in our series of moved movers* (b 19–243 a 3).—C.]

If a thing is in motion it is, of necessity, being kept in motion by something. If it has not the source of its motion within itself, then it is clear enough that it is being moved by something else, for what moves it will be a second thing. If on the other hand its source of motion is in itself, let AB represent something that is in motion, not accidentally by virtue of some part of it being in motion, but primarily and in itself. Now in the first place to suppose that AB is being moved by itself because it is in motion as a whole and is not being moved by anything external to itself is like saying

241 b ὥσπερ εἰ τοῦ ΚΛ κινοῦντος τὸ ΛΜ καὶ αὐτοῦ
κινουμένου εἰ μὴ φάσκοι τις τὸ ΚΜ κινεῖσθαι ὑπό
τινος, διὰ τὸ μὴ φανερὸν εἶναι πότερον τὸ κινοῦν
καὶ πότερον τὸ κινούμενον. εἶτα τὸ μὴ ὑπό τινος
242 a κινούμενον οὐκ ἀνάγκη παύσασθαι κινούμενον τῷ
ἄλλο ἠρεμεῖν· ἀλλ' εἴ τι ἠρεμεῖ τῷ ἄλλο πεπαῦσθαι
κινούμενον, ἀνάγκη ὑπό τινος αὐτὸ κινεῖσθαι. τού-
5 του γὰρ εἰλημμένου πᾶν τὸ κινούμενον κινήσεται
ὑπό τινος. ἐπεὶ γὰρ εἴληπται τὸ κινούμενον ἐφ'
ᾧ τὸ ΑΒ, ἀνάγκη διαιρετὸν αὐτὸ εἶναι· πᾶν γὰρ τὸ
κινούμενον διαιρετόν. διῃρήσθω δὴ κατὰ τὸ Γ.
τοῦ δὴ ΓΒ μὴ κινουμένου οὐ κινηθήσεται τὸ ΑΒ·
εἰ γὰρ κινήσεται, δῆλον ὅτι τὸ ΑΓ κινοῖτ' ἂν τοῦ
10 ΒΓ ἠρεμοῦντος, ὥστε οὐ καθ' αὑτὸ κινηθήσεται
καὶ πρῶτον. ἀλλ' ὑπέκειτο καθ' αὑτὸ κινεῖσθαι
καὶ πρῶτον. ἀνάγκη ἄρα τοῦ ΓΒ μὴ κινουμένου
ἠρεμεῖν τὸ ΑΒ. ὃ δὲ ἠρεμεῖ μὴ κινουμένου τινός,
ὡμολόγηται ὑπό τινος κινεῖσθαι. ὥστε πᾶν ἀνάγκη
15 τὸ κινούμενον ὑπό τινος κινεῖσθαι· ἀεὶ γὰρ ἔσται
τὸ κινούμενον διαιρετόν, τοῦ δὲ μέρους μὴ κινουμένου ἀνάγκη καὶ τὸ ὅλον ἠρεμεῖν.

that, if KL is moving LM and is itself in motion, KM

is not being moved by anything, merely because we cannot see which part is being moved by the other—KL by LM or LM by KL. In the second place, if a thing is in motion without being moved by anything, the fact that something else is at rest is no reason why its motion should cease : but if its motion does cease because something else has stopped moving, its own motion must have been caused by that other thing. If this principle is accepted, it can be shown that anything whatever that is in motion is being kept in motion by something. For we have taken AB to represent the thing in motion ; it must then be divisible, for we have seen that every mobile is divisible. Let AB, then, be divided at C. Now if

CB is not in motion, then the whole AB will be not in motion ; for if it were, clearly AC would be in motion although CB is at rest, and thus AB would not be in motion primarily and in itself, which contradicts the hypothesis. Thus when CB is not in motion AB must be at rest. But we have agreed that if a thing is at rest because something else is not in motion, it must have been kept in motion by that other thing. The conclusion is that anything whatever that is in motion must be kept in motion by something ; for whatever is in motion must always be divisible, and if the part is not in motion the whole, likewise, must be at rest.

242 a Ἐπεὶ δὲ πᾶν τὸ κινούμενον ἀνάγκη κινεῖσθαι
ὑπό τινος, ἐάν γέ τι κινῆται τὴν ἐν τόπῳ κίνησιν
ὑπ' ἄλλου κινουμένου, καὶ πάλιν τὸ κινοῦν ὑπ'
20 ἄλλου κινουμένου κινῆται κἀκεῖνο ὑφ' ἑτέρου καὶ
ἀεὶ οὕτως, ἀνάγκη εἶναί τι τὸ πρῶτον κινοῦν καὶ
μὴ βαδίζειν εἰς ἄπειρον. μὴ γὰρ ἔστω, ἀλλὰ
γενέσθω ἄπειρον. κινείσθω δὴ τὸ μὲν Α ὑπὸ τοῦ
Β, τὸ δὲ Β ὑπὸ τοῦ Γ, τὸ δὲ Γ ὑπὸ τοῦ Δ, καὶ
ἀεὶ τὸ ἐχόμενον ὑπὸ τοῦ ἐχομένου. ἐπεὶ οὖν
ὑπόκειται τὸ κινοῦν κινούμενον κινεῖν, ἀνάγκη δ'
ἅμα γίγνεσθαι τὴν τοῦ κινουμένου καὶ τὴν τοῦ
κινοῦντος κίνησιν (ἅμα γὰρ κινεῖ τὸ κινοῦν καὶ
25 κινεῖται τὸ κινούμενον), φανερὸν ὅτι ἅμα ἔσται τοῦ
Α καὶ τοῦ Β καὶ τοῦ Γ καὶ ἑκάστου τῶν κινούντων
καὶ κινουμένων ἡ κίνησις. εἰλήφθω οὖν ἡ ἑκάστου
κίνησις, καὶ ἔστω τοῦ μὲν Α ἐφ' ἧς Ε, τοῦ δὲ Β
ἐφ' ἧς Ζ, τῶν δὲ Γ, Δ ἐφ' ὧν Η, Θ· εἰ γὰρ ἀεὶ
30 κινεῖται ἕκαστον ὑφ' ἑκάστου, ὅμως ἔσται λαβεῖν
μίαν ἑκάστου κίνησιν τῷ ἀριθμῷ· πᾶσα γὰρ κίνησις
ἔκ τινος εἴς τι καὶ οὐκ ἄπειρος τοῖς ἐσχάτοις.
(λέγω δὴ ἀριθμῷ μίαν κίνησιν τὴν ἐκ τοῦ αὐτοῦ
εἰς τὸ αὐτὸ τῷ ἀριθμῷ ἐν τῷ αὐτῷ χρόνῳ τῷ
ἀριθμῷ γιγνομένην. ἔστι γὰρ κίνησις καὶ γένει
35 καὶ εἴδει καὶ ἀριθμῷ ἡ αὐτή—γένει μὲν ἡ τῆς

---

[a] [Aristotle has in view the concentric celestial spheres,
each influenced by those outside it and influencing those
within it. There must be an outermost sphere or ' first
mover which is also moved ' (242 b 35) and beyond that an
unmoved mover.—C.]

[b] [i.e. each member of the series being both a mover (τὸ
κινοῦν) and a moved (τὸ κινούμενον), simultaneously imparts
motion qua mover and suffers motion qua moved.—C.]

[c] [' In extent ' or towards the extremes, but this does
not exclude unlimited divisibility.—C.]

Now since anything that is in motion is, of necessity, being moved by something, suppose a thing is being moved locally by another thing that is in motion, and that again by another, and so on ; then the series cannot go on without limit, but there must be a prime cause of the motion.[a] For suppose this is not so and the series has no limit : let A be kept in motion by B, B by C, C by D, and so on, each member of the series being kept in motion by the next. Now we are assuming that each mover, while it causes motion, is being kept in motion ; and since the movements of the mover and the moved must occur simultaneously (for the one moves and the other is moved at the same time [b]), it is obvious that the movements of A, B, C, and of every one of the moved movers will occur simultaneously. Take the movement of each member separately, and let E, F, G, H, represent respectively the motions of A, B, C, D ; for although

E	F	G	H

A	B	C	D

throughout the series each is being kept in motion by the next one, we may nevertheless assign to each a movement that is numerically one, because every movement is from 'here' to 'there' and is not unlimited in extent.[c] [d](By ' a movement that is numerically one' I mean a movement that proceeds from one and the same starting-point to one and the same goal in one and the same period of time. For a movement may be ' the same ' generically or specifically, as well as numerically : generically, if it belongs to the

[d] [This long parenthesis recapitulates the definition of a 'numerically single motion' given in Book V. In a modern book it would stand as a footnote.—C.]

211

242 a αὐτῆς κατηγορίας, οἷον οὐσίας ἢ· ποιότητος, εἴδει
δὲ ἡ ἐκ τοῦ αὐτοῦ τῷ εἴδει εἰς τὸ αὐτὸ τῷ εἴδει,
οἷον ἐκ λευκοῦ εἰς μέλαν ἢ ἐξ ἀγαθοῦ εἰς κακὸν
ἀδιάφορον τῷ εἴδει, ἀριθμῷ δὲ ἡ ἐξ ἑνὸς τῷ
242 b ἀριθμῷ εἰς ἓν τῷ ἀριθμῷ ἐν τῷ αὐτῷ χρόνῳ, οἷον
ἐκ τοῦδε τοῦ λευκοῦ εἰς τόδε τὸ μέλαν ἢ ἐκ τοῦδε
τοῦ τόπου εἰς τόνδε ἐν τῷδε τῷ χρόνῳ· εἰ γὰρ ἐν
4 ἄλλῳ, οὐκέτι ἔσται ἀριθμῷ μία κίνησις, ἀλλ᾽ εἴδει.
8 εἴρηται δὲ περὶ τούτων ἐν τοῖς πρότερον.) εἰλήφθω
δὲ καὶ ὁ χρόνος ἐν ᾧ κεκίνηται τὴν αὐτοῦ κίνησιν
τὸ Α, καὶ ἔστω ἐφ᾽ ᾧ Κ. πεπερασμένης δ᾽ οὔσης
τῆς τοῦ Α κινήσεως, καὶ ὁ χρόνος ἔσται πεπερασμένος. ἐπεὶ δ᾽ ἄπειρα τὰ κινοῦντα καὶ τὰ κινούμενα, καὶ ἡ κίνησις ἡ ΕΖΗΘ ἡ ἐξ ἁπασῶν ἄπειρος
15 ἔσται. (ἐνδέχεται μὲν γὰρ ἴσην εἶναι τὴν τοῦ Α καὶ
τοῦ Β καὶ τὴν τῶν ἄλλων, ἐνδέχεται δὲ μείζους τὰς
τῶν ἄλλων, ὥστε εἴτε ἴσαι εἴτε μείζους,[1] ἀμφοτέρως ἄπειρος ἡ ὅλη· λαμβάνομεν γὰρ τὸ ἐνδεχόμενον.) ἐπεὶ δ᾽ ἅμα κινεῖται τὸ Α καὶ τῶν ἄλλων
ἕκαστον, ἡ ὅλη κίνησις ἐν τῷ αὐτῷ χρόνῳ ἔσται
καὶ ἡ τοῦ Α· ἡ δὲ τοῦ Α ἐν πεπερασμένῳ· ὥστε
εἴη ἂν ἄπειρος ἐν πεπερασμένῳ, τοῦτο δ᾽ ἀδύνατον.
20 Οὕτω μὲν οὖν δόξειεν ἂν δεδεῖχθαι τὸ ἐξ ἀρχῆς·

---

[1] [εἴτε ἴσαι εἴτε μείζους Simpl. 1045. 8, Oxf. Trans.: εἰ ἀεί
τε μείζους, Par. 1859.—C.]

---

[a] [At 227 b 3 ff.—C.]
[b] [If we take either of the cases mentioned, the conclusion,
that the total movement is unlimited (*i.e.* an illimitable
aggregate of movements through limited distances), will
follow ; and since these are possible cases we are entitled to
deduce our conclusion from either. It is immaterial that the

same category of existence, (say) substance or quality; specifically, if the starting-point and the goal belong to the same species, for example black and white, or good and bad, where one of these is not distinguished from the other by any further specific difference; but it is numerically one when the passage occurs in a single unbroken period of time between terms which are each numerically one, *e.g.* from one particular whiteness to one particular blackness or from this particular place to that, in this particular period of time; for if the period occupied were different, the movement would have only specific, not numerical, unity. But all this has been set forth already.[a]) Let us now take the time in which A has completed its own movement, and represent that time by K. Since the movement of A is limited, the time will be limited. But since by hypothesis the series of movers and moved is unlimited, the movement EFGH composed of all their individual movements will likewise be unlimited (for it is possible to assume that the movements of A, B, and the rest are all equal or that the movements of the rest are greater than that of A: in either case the result will be that the whole movement is unlimited; and it is open to us to take any case that is possible[b]). And since the movements of A and of each of the rest are simultaneous, the total movement EFGH will occupy the same period as the movement of A: but the period occupied by A's movement was limited; consequently we shall have an unlimited movement in a limited time, which is impossible.

This might seem to establish the point we set out

conclusion might not follow, if, for example, the movements formed a convergent series.—C.]

12 b οὐ μὴν ἀποδείκνυται διὰ τὸ μηδὲν δείκνυσθαι
ἀδύνατον. ἐνδέχεται γὰρ ἐν πεπερασμένῳ χρόνῳ
ἄπειρον εἶναι κίνησιν, μὴ ἑνὸς ἀλλὰ πολλῶν· ὅπερ
συμβαίνει καὶ ἐπὶ τούτων, ἕκαστον γὰρ κινεῖται τὴν
ἑαυτοῦ κίνησιν, ἅμα δὲ πολλὰ κινεῖσθαι οὐκ
ἀδύνατον. ἀλλ᾿ εἰ τὸ κινοῦν πρῶτον[1] κατὰ τόπον
25 καὶ σωματικὴν κίνησιν ἀνάγκη ἢ ἅπτεσθαι ἢ
συνεχὲς εἶναι τῷ κινουμένῳ (καθάπερ ὁρῶμεν ἐπὶ
πάντων), ἀνάγκη τὰ κινούμενα καὶ τὰ κινοῦντα
συνεχῆ εἶναι ἢ ἅπτεσθαι ἀλλήλων, ὥστ᾿ εἶναί τι
ἐξ ἁπάντων ἕν. τοῦτο δὲ εἴτε πεπερασμένον εἴτε
ἄπειρον, οὐδὲν διαφέρει πρὸς τὸ νῦν· πάντως γὰρ
ἡ κίνησις ἔσται ἄπειρος ἀπείρων ὄντων, εἴπερ
ἐνδέχεται καὶ ἴσας εἶναι καὶ μείζους ἀλλήλων· ὃ
30 γὰρ ἐνδέχεται ληψόμεθα ὡς ὑπάρχον. εἰ οὖν τὸ
μὲν ἐκ τῶν Α, Β, Γ, Δ ἄπειρόν τί ἐστιν, κινεῖται
δὲ τὴν ΕΖΗΘ κίνησιν ἐν τῷ χρόνῳ τῷ Κ, οὗτος
δὲ πεπέρανται, συμβαίνει ἐν πεπερασμένῳ χρόνῳ
ἄπειρον διιέναι ἢ τὸ πεπερασμένον ἢ τὸ ἄπειρον.
ἀμφοτέρως δὲ ἀδύνατον· ὥστε ἀνάγκη ἵστασθαι καὶ

---

[1] [πρῶτον Simplic. 1046. 4 (lemma); cf. ibid. 9 πρῶτον,
τοῦτ᾿ ἔστι προσεχῶς καὶ μὴ δι᾿ ἄλλου, and below 243 a 3 and
245 a 8 τὸ πρῶτον κινοῦν : πρώτως al.—C.]

---

[a] [' Physical, as contrasted with the action of a psycho-
logical ' motive.'—C.]
[b] See note a on 244 a 15.
[c] What is meant by illimitable motion in Bk. VI. ch. vii.
is traversing illimitable distance ; and the demonstration
there is intended to show that this cannot be accomplished
in a limited time by either a limited or a limitless mobile.   In
the present passage there is no question of an illimitable
distance being traversed either by the illimitable aggregate
or by any limited member of it : what is meant by illimitable

to prove : that there must be a prime cause of motion. But there is as yet no *reductio ad absurdum*, for in a finite time there may be infinite movement, if it is movement not of one thing but of many ; and this is so in the present case : each thing accomplishes its own movement, and there is no impossibility in many things being in motion simultaneously. But since the immediate and direct cause of a physical[a] movement in space must (as we see in all cases) be either in contact or continuous with the thing it moves,[b] our series of movers and moved must be either continuous or in contact with one another so as to form one thing composed of them all. For our present purpose it makes no difference whether this one thing is limited or unlimited ; for in any case, since they are unlimited in number, the whole movement will be unlimited, if we assume as actual what is theoretically possible, namely, that each movement is either equal to or greater than the one prior to it. If then, A, B, C, D, etc. make up an unlimited magnitude which accomplishes its motion EFGH in the limited time K, this involves the conclusion that an unlimited movement is gone through in a finite time by something which is either limited or unlimited ; and, whichever it is, the conclusion is an impossibility.[c] The series must therefore come to

movement here, is a motion of an illimitable magnitude which brings a different limited stretch of it over against a definite object. So far from this being shown to be impossible, it is taken for granted that it can happen, in the former passage (see pp. 165 *sq.*). So that the present contention is not only unsupported but implicitly denied by the former argument. It was unfortunately accepted by mediaeval writers, including Aquinas, who refers it to Aristotle ; but this passage (unauthentic in the opinion of the translator) seems to be the only place in which it is to be found.

243 a εἶναί τι πρῶτον κινοῦν καὶ κινούμενον. οὐδὲν γὰρ
διαφέρει τὸ συμβαίνειν ἐξ ὑποθέσεως τὸ ἀδύνατον·
ἡ γὰρ ὑπόθεσις εἴληπται ἐνδεχομένη, τοῦ δ'
ἐνδεχομένου τεθέντος οὐδὲν προσήκει γίγνεσθαι
διὰ τοῦτο ἀδύνατον.

CHAPTER II

ARGUMENT

[*The cause of movement or change must be in direct touch
with the thing moved or changed by it, i.e. there must be
nothing between them. This principle applies to all kinds of
change : of place, or quality, or quantity* (243 a 3–11).

(1) *All locomotion caused by an external agent can be
reduced to either pushing or pulling* (a 11–244 a 4). *And
since in pushing or pulling there must be direct contact with
the load, this is true of all local movement* (a 4–b 2).

(2) *Modification of quality means change in those sensible
characteristics which distinguish one body from another,
effected by sensible characteristics of the same kind. In
animate beings such change may be accompanied by sensation
and perception. In all such cases there is direct contact*

243 a 3 Τὸ δὲ πρῶτον κινοῦν—μὴ ὡς τὸ οὗ ἕνεκεν, ἀλλ'
ὅθεν ἡ ἀρχὴ τῆς κινήσεως—ἅμα τῷ κινουμένῳ
5 ἐστί· λέγω δὲ τὸ ἅμα, ὅτι οὐδέν ἐστιν αὐτῶν
μεταξύ. τοῦτο γὰρ κοινὸν ἐπὶ παντὸς κινουμένου
καὶ κινοῦντός ἐστιν. ἐπεὶ δὲ τρεῖς αἱ κινήσεις—
ἥ τε κατὰ τόπον καὶ ἡ κατὰ τὸ ποιὸν καὶ ἡ κατὰ
10 τὸ ποσόν—ἀνάγκη καὶ τὰ κινοῦντα τρία εἶναι, τό
τε φέρον καὶ τὸ ἀλλοιοῦν καὶ τὸ αὖξον ἢ φθίνον.

Πρῶτον οὖν εἴπωμεν περὶ τῆς φορᾶς· πρώτη
γὰρ αὕτη τῶν κινήσεων. ἅπαν δὴ τὸ φερόμενον

an end, and there must be a first moved mover.[a]
This impossibility, it is true, depends on an assumption [b]; but that does not matter, because the
assumption is theoretically possible and from such
an assumption no impossibility ought to result.

   [a] [And, of course, beyond this first *moved* mover, an
unmoved mover to move it.—C.]
   [b] [Viz. that each movement is either equal to or greater
than the preceding one.—C.]

CHAPTER II

ARGUMENT (*continued*)

*between the object, the medium (if any) such as air, and the
subject* (b 2–245 a 11).
   (3) *Change of quantity, increase or decrease, is effected by
direct contact* (a 11–16).
   *Thus in every kind of change the extremities of agent and
patient must be together, with nothing between* (a 16–b 2).—
C.]

TAKING the initiator of movement to mean not that
for the sake of which the movement takes place,
but that which sets it going, we may say that the
initiator must be in direct touch with the thing
it immediately moves; and by this I mean that
there can be nothing between them. This is true
of every mover and the moved it directly acts
upon. And since there are three kinds of motion,
(1) local, (2) qualitive, and (3) quantitive, there must
be three kinds of mover respectively causing local
transference, change of attribute, and growth or
shrinkage.
   So let us begin with (1) local movement, for it
takes natural precedence of the others. Everything

217

243 a ἢ ὑφ᾿ αὑτοῦ κινεῖται ἢ ὑπ᾿ ἄλλου.   ὅσα μὲν οὖν
αὐτὰ ὑφ᾿ αὑτῶν κινεῖται, φανερὸν ἐν τούτοις ὅτι
ἅμα τὸ κινούμενον καὶ τὸ κινοῦν ἐστιν· ἐνυπάρχει
15 γὰρ αὐτοῖς τὸ πρῶτον κινοῦν, ὥστ᾿ οὐδέν ἐστιν
ἀναμεταξύ.   ὅσα δ᾿ ὑπ᾿ ἄλλου κινεῖται, τετραχῶς
ἀνάγκη γίγνεσθαι· τέτταρα γὰρ εἴδη τῆς ὑπ᾿
ἄλλου φορᾶς—ἕλξις, ὦσις, ὄχησις, δίνησις.

Ἅπασαι γὰρ αἱ κατὰ τόπον κινήσεις ἀνάγονται
εἰς ταύτας.   ἡ μὲν γὰρ ἔπωσις ὦσίς τίς ἐστιν,
ὅταν τὸ ἀφ᾿ αὑτοῦ[1] κινοῦν ἐπακολουθοῦν ὠθῇ, ἡ
20 δ᾿ ἄπωσις, ὅταν μὴ ἐπακολουθῇ κινῆσαν, ἡ δὲ
243 b ῥῖψις, ὅταν σφοδροτέραν ποιήσῃ τὴν ἀφ᾿ αὑτοῦ[1]
κίνησιν τῆς κατὰ φύσιν φορᾶς καὶ μέχρι τοσούτου
φέρηται ἕως ἂν κρατῇ ἡ κίνησις.   πάλιν ἡ δίωσις
καὶ σύνωσις ἄπωσις καὶ ἕλξις εἰσίν· ἡ μὲν γὰρ
δίωσις ἄπωσις (ἢ γὰρ ἀφ᾿ αὑτοῦ ἢ ἀπ᾿ ἄλλου
5 ἐστὶν ἡ ἄπωσις), ἡ δὲ σύνωσις ἕλξις (καὶ γὰρ πρὸς
αὑτὸ καὶ πρὸς ἄλλο ἡ ἕλξις)· ὥστε καὶ ὅσα τούτων
εἴδη, οἷον σπάθησις καὶ κέρκισις· ἡ μὲν γὰρ
σύνωσις, ἡ δὲ δίωσις.   ὁμοίως δὲ καὶ αἱ ἄλλαι
συγκρίσεις καὶ διακρίσεις (ἅπασαι γὰρ ἔσονται
διώσεις ἢ συνώσεις), πλὴν ὅσαι ἐν γενέσει καὶ

---

[1] [ἀφ᾿ αὑτοῦ Oxf. Trans.; cf. Simplic. 1049. 20.—C.]

---

[a] Note that the natural movement of the elements is not included.

[b] e.g. down a slope, over an edge, or just falling where it stands.

that is in local motion is being moved by itself or by
something else. In the former case it is obvious
that the moving principle and that which it moves
are immediately in touch with each other, for since
the source of movement is inherently contained in
what it moves, there can be nothing intermediate
between them.[a] Whereas things that are moved by
an external agent, are so moved either by pulling
or pushing or carrying or turning.

To these four all possible ways of moving can be
reduced. For pushing is pushing, whether you have
to push continuously, always following up the load,
or whether the push starts the load on a course of its
own [b] ; and throwing is a push that causes the load
to go off with an impulse, stronger than its natural
movement, by which it is taken along so long as the
impulse is the stronger. And again pushing apart and
pushing together are a pushing away and a pulling ;
for pushing apart is included in pushing away, since
one may push a thing away from something else as
well as from oneself ; and pushing together is included in pulling, since one may pull a thing towards
another thing as well as towards oneself. And
consequently, pushing and pulling will cover all the
sub-species of pushing together and pushing apart,
such as the action of the reed and that of the heald,[c]
the former pressing the threads together and the
latter lifting the threads apart. And other unions
and separations come under the same head (for they
are all of them pushing something away from something else, or to it), with the exception of union and

[c] The heald separates the threads of the warp to enable the
shuttle to pass between them ; the reed brings together the
threads of the woof.

243 b 10 φθορᾷ εἰσιν. ἅμα δὲ φανερὸν ὅτι οὐδ' ἔστιν ἄλλο
τι γένος κινήσεως ἢ σύγκρισις καὶ διάκρισις·
ἅπασαι γὰρ διανέμονται εἴς τινας τῶν εἰρημένων.
ἔτι δ' ἡ μὲν εἰσπνοὴ ἕλξις, ἡ δ' ἐκπνοὴ ὦσις·
ὁμοίως δὲ καὶ ἡ πτύσις καὶ ὅσαι ἄλλαι διὰ τοῦ
σώματος ἢ ἐκκριτικαὶ ἢ ληπτικαὶ κινήσεις· αἱ μὲν
15 γὰρ ἕλξεις εἰσίν, αἱ δ' ἀπώσεις.

Δεῖ δὲ καὶ τὰς ἄλλας τὰς κατὰ τόπον ἀνάγειν·
ἅπασαι γὰρ πίπτουσιν εἰς τέσσαρας ταύτας, τούτων
δὲ πάλιν ἡ ὄχησις καὶ ἡ δίνησις εἰς ἕλξιν καὶ
ὦσιν. ἡ μὲν γὰρ ὄχησις κατὰ τούτων τινὰ τῶν
τριῶν τρόπων ἐστίν· τὸ μὲν γὰρ ὀχούμενον κινεῖται
20 κατὰ συμβεβηκός, ὅτι ἐν κινουμένῳ ἐστὶν ἢ ἐπὶ
244 a κινουμένου τινός, τὸ δ' ὀχοῦν ὀχεῖ ἢ ἑλκόμενον ἢ
ὠθούμενον ἢ δινούμενον, ὥστε κοινή ἐστιν ἁπασῶν
τῶν τριῶν ἡ ὄχησις. ἡ δὲ δίνησις σύγκειται ἐξ
ἕλξεώς τε καὶ ὤσεως· ἀνάγκη γὰρ τὸ δινοῦν τὸ
μὲν ἕλκειν τὸ δ' ὠθεῖν· τὸ μὲν γὰρ ἀφ' αὑτοῦ τὸ
δὲ πρὸς αὑτὸ ἄγει.

5 Ὥστ' εἰ τὸ ὠθοῦν καὶ τὸ ἕλκον ἅμα τῷ ὠθου-
μένῳ καὶ τῷ ἑλκομένῳ, φανερὸν ὅτι τοῦ κατὰ τόπον
κινουμένου καὶ κινοῦντος οὐδέν ἐστι μεταξύ. ἀλλὰ

---

^a If you are speaking absolutely, genesis cannot be a
'bringing' together (as some have maintained it is), for it
would be a bringing something to something indeed, not
however 'away from something else' but 'away from
nothingness.' And analogously with perishing. [When
two or more of the four elements are brought together to
form a (homoeomerous) substance, such as flesh, something
new comes into being, which was not there before. So the
coming-into-being (or perishing) of flesh, though it involves
a bringing together (or separation) of pre-existing elements,
is not completely accounted for by that process of local
movement.—C.]

separation as involved in genesis and perishing.[a] And now that we see that union and separation are synonymous with bringing together and setting apart, we see that all motions can be reduced to these antithetical terms.[b] Further, inhaling is a drawing in, and breathing out an expulsion; and so with spitting and all the excretive and assimilating movements, since they are indrawings and outthrustings respectively.

Moreover, we must reduce the remaining forms of local movement to these two. For all of them come under one of the enumerated four, and of these again carrying and turning can be reduced to pulling and pushing. For being carried is distributed amongst all the other three forms, since the load moves incidentally to the motion of the carrier in or on which it is placed, and the carrier moves because it is either pulled or pushed or turned, so that carrying may be referred to any of the three. And turning can be resolved into pulling and pushing, for the agent that turns the subject does so by pulling one part towards itself and pushing another part away from itself.[c]

It is clear, then, that in all cases of local movement there will be nothing between the mover and the moved, if it can be shown that the pushing or pulling agent must be in direct contact with the load. But

[b] I follow a suggestion made by Simplicius in interpreting this difficult passage. [It must be remembered that κίνησις here means locomotion only. *Cf.* the second text here, καὶ πᾶσα δὴ κίνησις ἡ κατὰ τόπον σύγκρισις καὶ διάκρισίς ἐστιν.—C.]

[c] Obviously, as Simplicius notes, this assertion is made on the strength of the action of the mill-girl, or whoever it may be, that pulls and pushes the mill-stone by the handle as she grinds.

244 a μὴν τοῦτο δῆλον καὶ ἐκ τῶν ὁρισμῶν· ὧσις μὲν
γάρ ἐστιν ἡ ἀφ' αὑτοῦ ἢ ἀπ' ἄλλου πρὸς ἄλλο
κίνησις, ἕλξις δὲ ἡ ἀπ' ἄλλου πρὸς αὐτὸ ἢ πρὸς
10 ἄλλο, ὅταν[1] θάττων ἡ κίνησις ᾖ τοῦ ἕλκοντος τῆς
χωριζούσης ἀπ' ἀλλήλων τὰ συνεχῆ· οὕτω γὰρ
συνεφέλκεται θάτερον. (τάχα δὲ δόξειεν ἂν εἶναί
τις ἕλξις καὶ ἄλλως· τὸ γὰρ ξύλον ἕλκει τὸ πῦρ
οὐχ οὕτως.   τὸ δ' οὐθὲν διαφέρει κινουμένου τοῦ
ἕλκοντος ἢ μένοντος ἕλκειν· ὁτὲ μὲν γὰρ ἕλκει οὗ
15 ἔστιν, ὁτὲ δὲ οὗ ἦν.) ἀδύνατον δὲ ἢ ἀφ' αὑτοῦ
244 b πρὸς ἄλλο ἢ ἀπ' ἄλλου πρὸς αὐτὸ κινεῖν μὴ
ἁπτόμενον· ὥστε φανερὸν ὅτι τοῦ κατὰ τόπον
κινουμένου καὶ κινοῦντος οὐδέν ἐστι μεταξύ.

'Αλλὰ μὴν οὐδὲ τοῦ ἀλλοιουμένου καὶ τοῦ
ἀλλοιοῦντος. τοῦτο δὲ δῆλον ἐξ ἐπαγωγῆς· ἐν
ἅπασι γὰρ συμβαίνει ἅμα εἶναι τὸ ἔσχατον ἀλλοιοῦν

---

[1] [ὅταν . . . συνεχῆ. The reading of Simplicius 1054. 7
and 27, adopted by the Oxf. Trans.—C.]

---

^a The wood draws the fire to itself, whereas the natural
movement of fire is upwards. So much is clear. But what
underlies this curious interpolation (known to Simplicius,
but not the mediaeval Latin translation) is something much
more than this. To Simplicius and to Aquinas the more
obvious case of the magnet known to Aristotle (and even to
Thales) but strangely neglected by him, seemed to present
the strange (to them as to most modern minds) phenomenon
of the *actio in distans* which contradicted the very thesis
which our present author is endeavouring to prove, viz. that
an agent cannot act upon any subject with which it is not in
physical contact. Perhaps no metaphysical prejudice has
ever entangled the mind of man more mischievously than
this. Albertus and Aquinas escaped it by attributing to the
heavenly bodies the power of *actio in distans* and allowing

this follows directly from our definitions, for pushing moves things away (either from the agent or from something else) to some other place, and pulling moves things from some other place either to the agent or to something else, the motion of the pulling agent itself being faster than the motion which tends to separate the two continuous things from one another ; for in that case the second is towed along by the first. (It may well seem, however, that there is some other kind of 'drawing' than that which we have dealt with ; for wood draws fire to itself without itself moving at all. But it does not really make any difference whether the pulling agent is in motion itself (in the direction of the motion it imparts) or not ; for if stationary it draws the mobile to where it is, if in motion, to where it was.) *a* But in any case the agent cannot move anything from itself to somewhere else or from somewhere else to itself, unless it is in contact with it. So it is obvious that there is no intermediary between the mover and the moved in the case of local movement.

(2) No more can there be anything between the agent and patient in qualitive modifications. This can be shown by going through the possible cases, for in all of them we shall find that the extremes of the active and passive correlatives are in contact.

the magnet to share in this celestial power and so help to maintain a continuity in the whole scheme of nature. Ancient thinkers found no such escape and modern thinkers are only now, if now, emancipating themselves from it. Here our interpolator having raised the question and being unable to answer it, contents himself with the dogmatic reassertion that no such action as appears to manifest itself here is really possible. [For the analysis of the magnet's action see 267 a 1.—C.]

244 b 5 καὶ τὸ πρῶτον ἀλλοιούμενον. ⟨ὑπόκειται γὰρ
ἡμῖν τὸ τὰ ἀλλοιούμενα κατὰ τὰς παθητικὰς
λεγομένας ποιότητας πάσχοντα ἀλλοιοῦσθαι. τὸ
γὰρ ποιὸν ἀλλοιοῦται τῷ αἰσθητὸν εἶναι, αἰσθητὰ
δ' ἐστὶν οἷς διαφέρουσι τὰ σώματα ἀλλήλων (ἅπαν
γὰρ σῶμα σώματος διαφέρει τοῖς αἰσθητοῖς ἢ
πλείοσιν ἢ ἐλάττοσιν ἢ τῷ μᾶλλον καὶ ἧττον τοῖς
αὐτοῖς). ἀλλὰ μὴν καὶ ἀλλοιοῦται τὸ ἀλλοιού-
μενον⟩[1] ὑπὸ τῶν εἰρημένων· ταῦτα γάρ ἐστι πάθη
τῆς ὑποκειμένης ποιότητος. ἢ γὰρ θερμαινόμενον
ἢ γλυκαινόμενον ἢ πυκνούμενον ἢ ξηραινόμενον
ἢ λευκαινόμενον ἀλλοιοῦσθαί φαμεν, ὁμοίως τὸ
ἄψυχον καὶ τὸ ἔμψυχον λέγοντες, καὶ πάλιν τῶν
10 ἐμψύχων τά τε μὴ αἰσθητικὰ τῶν μερῶν καὶ αὐτὰς
τὰς αἰσθήσεις. ἀλλοιοῦνται γάρ πως καὶ αἱ
αἰσθήσεις· ἡ γὰρ αἴσθησις ἡ κατ' ἐνέργειαν
κίνησίς ἐστι διὰ σώματος, πασχούσης τι τῆς
αἰσθήσεως. καθ' ὅσα μὲν οὖν τὸ ἄψυχον ἀλλοιοῦται, καὶ τὸ ἔμψυχον· καθ' ὅσα δὲ τὸ ἔμψυχον, οὐ
15 κατὰ πάντα τὸ ἄψυχον· οὐ γὰρ ἀλλοιοῦται κατὰ
245 a τὰς αἰσθήσεις, καὶ τὸ μὲν λανθάνει τὸ δ' οὐ λανθάνει πάσχον (οὐδὲν δὲ κωλύει καὶ τὸ ἔμψυχον
λανθάνειν ὅταν μὴ κατὰ τὰς αἰσθήσεις γίγνηται ἡ
ἀλλοίωσις). εἴπερ οὖν ἀλλοιοῦται τὸ ἀλλοιού-

---

[1] [The clauses in brackets were supplied by Prantl from
Simplicius 1057. 24 and the second text in six of Bekker's
MSS.—C.]

---

[a] [*Categories*, ch. viii. distinguishes four classes of Qualities:
(1) *habits and dispositions* (some of which are discussed here
in the next chapter); (2) *inborn capacities and incapacities*;
(3) *shape and form* (see 245 b 10 ff.); (4) *affective qualities*,

224

For we are assuming that things undergo qualitive
modification in virtue of some action which affects
what are called their ' affective qualities.' [a] That
which is of a certain quality is modified in so far as
it is perceptible to some sense, sensible characteristics being those which distinguish one body from
another according as any body possesses more or
fewer such characteristics or the same characteristics
in a greater or less degree. And it is these sensible
characteristics that produce the qualitive modification ; for they are affections of the ' affective quality '
we have assumed above. Thus we say that a thing
is being modified when it is becoming warm or sweet
or dense or dry or white. Moreover, we speak of all
these processes taking place both in animate and
inanimate beings, and in animate beings as occurring
not only in parts that have no sense but in the senses
themselves. For the process of sensation involves a
kind of qualitive modification, actual sensation being
a motion transmitted through the body when the
sense-organ is affected in a certain way. Accordingly,
all the modifications that the inanimate patient can
experience are common to the animate, but the
animate subject experiences modifications which are
not shared by the inanimate. For the inanimate
does not experience modifications of sensation, nor
is it aware of its modifications, as the animate is—
though the animate too, for that matter, may be
unconscious of such modifications as do not affect
the senses. Since, then, qualitive modification is

viz. those which are the objects of the five senses as constituting the contrarieties of touch, taste, smell, hearing, vision.
They are called ' affective' as having the power to modify
contrary qualities in other things, and as producing ' affections ' ($\pi\acute{a}\theta\eta$) of our senses.—C.]

225

245 a μενον ὑπὸ τῶν αἰσθητῶν, ἐν ἅπασί γε τούτοις
5 φανερὸν ὅτι ἅμα ἐστὶ τὸ ἔσχατον ἀλλοιοῦν καὶ
τὸ πρῶτον ἀλλοιούμενον. τῷ μὲν γὰρ συνεχὴς ὁ
ἀήρ, τῷ δ' ἀέρι τὸ σῶμα. πάλιν δὲ τὸ μὲν χρῶμα
τῷ φωτί, τὸ δὲ φῶς τῇ ὄψει. τὸν αὐτὸν δὲ τρόπον
καὶ ἡ ἀκοὴ καὶ ἡ ὄσφρησις, τὸ γὰρ πρῶτον κινοῦν
10 ὁμοίως·[a] ἅμα γὰρ τῇ γεύσει ὁ χυμός. ὡσαύτως δὲ
πρὸς τὸ κινούμενον ὁ ἀήρ. καὶ ἐπὶ τῆς γεύσεως
καὶ ἐπὶ τῶν ἀψύχων καὶ ἀναισθήτων. ὥστ' οὐδὲν
ἔσται μεταξὺ τοῦ ἀλλοιουμένου καὶ τοῦ ἀλλοιοῦντος.

Οὐδὲ μὴν τοῦ αὐξανομένου τε καὶ αὔξοντος. αὐξά-
νει γὰρ τὸ πρῶτον αὖξον προσγιγνόμενον, ὥστε
ἓν γίγνεσθαι τὸ ὅλον· καὶ πάλιν φθίνει τὸ φθίνον
15 ἀπογιγνομένου τινὸς τῶν τοῦ φθίνοντος.[b] ἀνάγκη
οὖν συνεχὲς εἶναι καὶ τὸ αὖξον καὶ τὸ φθίνον, τῶν
δὲ συνεχῶν οὐδὲν μεταξύ.

245 b Φανερὸν οὖν ὅτι τοῦ κινουμένου καὶ τοῦ κινοῦντος
πρώτου καὶ ἐσχάτου πρὸς τὸ κινούμενον οὐδέν
ἐστιν ἀνὰ μέσον.

---

[a] [*Literally*, ' for the cause of movement that is proximate
with reference to the thing moved is the air (in contact with
the sense-organ).'—C.]
[b] [The process of growth is exhaustively analysed in *De
gen. et corr.* i. 5.—C.]

effected by sensible characteristics, it is clear that
in all cases of modification one extreme of the
modifier is in contact with the other extreme of the
modified. For in touch, air is in contact with the
source of warmth, and the body in contact with the
air. And again, colour is in contact with the light,
and the light with the organ of vision. And so too
with hearing and smelling, for the air is in contact
both with the object that provokes the sensation and
the organ that feels the stimulus.[a] And with taste
too, the savour is in contact with the organ of taste.
And the principle holds equally with inanimate
things that have no senses. The conclusion is that
in no case is there anything between the modifier
and the modified.

(3) Further, it is true of that which causes and
that which experiences growth. For that from which
the growth is ultimately derived is so assimilated to
the growing body that the whole becomes one. And
that which causes shrinkage, again, causes it by some
portion of that which shrinks coming away from it.
Necessarily, then, that which causes growth or
shrinkage must be continuous with that upon which
it acts ; and if things are continuous there is nothing
between them.[b]

Clearly then nothing intervenes between the
corresponding extremes of agent and patient in any
kind of passing from this to that.

CHAPTER III

ARGUMENT

[*This chapter elaborates the statement made in the last,
that change of quality is always effected by sensible characteristics and confined to things which can be affected by
them, viz. physical bodies* qua *possessing such characteristics,
and the sentient faculty of the soul. It will be shown that
certain cases which might be regarded as exceptions are not
really such* (245 b 3–9).

(1) *The shaping of material into a complete form is not a
qualitive modification, as may be seen from the use of
language* (b 9–246 a 9).

(2) *Habits, whether bodily or mental, and the acquisition
or loss of them, are not qualitive modifications. An excellence
is a perfection of the thing's nature, a defect a departure
from such perfection* (a 10–b 2). *All excellences are condi-*

245 b 3 ΄Ότι δὲ τὸ ἀλλοιούμενον ἅπαν ἀλλοιοῦται ὑπὸ
τῶν αἰσθητῶν, καὶ ἐν μόνοις ὑπάρχει τούτοις
5 ἀλλοίωσις ὅσα καθ' αὑτὰ λέγεται πάσχειν ὑπὸ τῶν
αἰσθητῶν, ἐκ τῶνδε θεωρητέον. τῶν γὰρ ἄλλων
μάλιστ' ἄν τις ὑπολάβοι ἔν τε τοῖς σχήμασι καὶ
ταῖς μορφαῖς καὶ ἐν ταῖς ἕξεσι καὶ ταῖς τούτων
λήψεσι καὶ ἀποβολαῖς ἀλλοίωσιν ὑπάρχειν· ἐν
οὐδετέροις δ' ἔστιν.

10 Τὸ μὲν γὰρ σχηματιζόμενον ὅταν ἐπιτελεσθῇ,
οὐ λέγομεν ἐκεῖνο ἐξ οὗ ἐστιν, οἷον τὸν ἀνδριάντα
χαλκὸν ἢ τὴν πυραμίδα κηρὸν ἢ τὴν κλίνην ξύλον,
ἀλλὰ παρωνυμιάζοντες τὸ μὲν χαλκοῦν τὸ δὲ
κήρινον τὸ δὲ ξύλινον. τὸ δὲ πεπονθὸς καὶ ἠλ-

---

^a [This meaning of πυραμίς (which I owe to the Oxford
translation) might be recognized at *De gen. et corr.* 334 a 32
ὥσπερ ἐκ κηροῦ γένοιτ' ἂν ἐκ μὲν τουδὶ τοῦ μέρους σφαῖρα ('ball,'

CHAPTER III

ARGUMENT (*continued*)

tions determined by some particular relation. (a) *Bodily excellences, health, strength, beauty, etc., and the corresponding defects are good or bad dispositions with relation to elements in the physical constitution or influences in the environment. A modification of these factors is involved in, but not the same thing as, the formation of an excellence or defect* (b 2–20). (b) *Moral virtues and vices similarly depend on relations to physical pleasures and pains* (b 20–247 a 19). (c) *Intellectual excellences are not modifications and are not the result of a process of becoming ; and even more than moral habits they depend on a particular relation* (b 1–248 a 6).

It appears, then, that qualitive modification occurs only in the field of sensible characteristics and in the sentient part of the soul (a 6–9).—C.]

THE following considerations will show us that whatever suffers qualitive modification is so modified by things perceptible by the senses, and that such modifications take place only in such things as can be said to be affected directly and in themselves by things so perceptible. What one would be most inclined to suppose exceptions to this rule are such things as (1) shapes or forms, and (2) habits and their acquisition and loss. But neither of these two classes of things constitutes an exception.

For (1) when any material has been completely shaped or arranged into a structure, we no longer call it by its own name but by a derivative : the statue is not brass but brazen, the candle[a] not wax but waxen, the bench not wood but wooden. Where-

not ' sphere '), πυραμὶς (' candle,' not ' pyramid ') δ' ἐξ ἄλλου τινός.—C.]

245 b λοιωμένον προσαγορεύομεν· ξηρὸν γὰρ καὶ ὑγρὸν
καὶ θερμὸν καὶ σκληρὸν τὸν χαλκὸν λέγομεν καὶ
15 τὸν κηρόν. καὶ οὐ μόνον οὕτως, ἀλλὰ καὶ τὸ
ὑγρὸν καὶ τὸ θερμὸν χαλκὸν λέγομεν, ὁμωνύμως
246 a τῷ πάθει προσαγορεύοντες τὴν ὕλην. ὥστ' εἰ
κατὰ μὲν τὸ σχῆμα καὶ τὴν μορφὴν οὐ λέγεται
τὸ γεγονὸς ἐν ᾧ ἐστι τὸ σχῆμα, κατὰ δὲ τὰ πάθη
καὶ τὰς ἀλλοιώσεις λέγεται, φανερὸν ὅτι οὐκ ἂν
εἶεν αἱ γενέσεις αὗται ἀλλοιώσεις. ἔτι δὲ καὶ
5 εἰπεῖν οὕτως ἄτοπον ἂν δόξειεν, ἠλλοιῶσθαι τὸν
ἄνθρωπον ἢ τὴν οἰκίαν ἢ ἄλλο ὁτιοῦν τῶν γεγενη-
μένων· ἀλλὰ γίγνεσθαι μὲν ἴσως ἕκαστον ἀναγκαῖον
ἀλλοιουμένου τινός (οἷον τῆς ὕλης πυκνουμένης ἢ
μανουμένης ἢ θερμαινομένης ἢ ψυχομένης), οὐ
μέντοι τὰ γιγνόμενά γε ἀλλοιοῦται, οὐδ' ἡ γένεσις
αὐτῶν ἀλλοίωσίς ἐστιν.

10 Ἀλλὰ μὴν οὐδ' αἱ ἕξεις οὔθ' αἱ τοῦ σώματος
οὔθ' αἱ τῆς ψυχῆς ἀλλοιώσεις. αἱ μὲν γὰρ ἀρεταὶ
αἱ δὲ κακίαι τῶν ἕξεων, οὐκ ἔστι δὲ οὔτε ἡ ἀρετὴ
οὔτε ἡ κακία ἀλλοίωσις, ἀλλ' ἡ μὲν ἀρετὴ τελείωσίς
τις—ὅταν γὰρ λάβῃ τὴν ἑαυτοῦ ἀρετήν, τότε
15 λέγεται τέλειον ἕκαστον· τότε γὰρ μάλιστα ἔστι
τὸ κατὰ φύσιν (ὥσπερ κύκλος τέλειος ὅταν

─────────

ᵃ [That is, molten brass can be described as ' the liquid,'
230

as, if it is really a qualitive modification that the material has undergone, we still say that the brass or the wax is dry or liquid or hot or hard ; and, what is more, we speak of the liquid or hot stuff as brass, giving the same name to the material that we give to the quality.[a] Since, then, having regard to the shape or form, the thing which has been formed cannot be called by the name of the material in which the form has come to exist, whereas having regard to qualitive affections and modifications we do call the thing by the name of the material, it is evident that a process of production of this kind— the shaping of material—is not a qualitive alteration. Again, it would be recognized as absurd to say that a man or a house or anything that comes into existence had come to be by being qualitively modified. Though it may well be that some qualitive modification of material by thickening or dilating or heating or cooling may be necessary for the production of anything, the things themselves that come into being do not suffer qualitive modification, nor is their genesis such a modification.

(2) Nor are habits,[b] whether bodily or mental, qualitive modifications. Some habits are excellences, others are defects, and neither excellence nor defect is a modification ; but excellence is a kind of perfection, since a thing is said to be perfect when it has acquired its appropriate excellence, for it is then in most complete conformity to its own nature (as a circle becomes perfect in proportion as it becomes

and we can say ' this liquid ' or ' this brass ' denoting the same thing.—C.]

[b] [' Habit ' means a comparatively permanent condition, either of body or soul, established by the constant exercise of some function.—C.]

246 a μάλιστα γένηται κύκλος βέλτιστος¹)—ἡ δὲ κακία
φθορὰ τούτου καὶ ἔκστασις. ὥσπερ οὖν οὐδὲ τὸ
τῆς οἰκίας τελείωμα λέγομεν ἀλλοίωσιν (ἄτοπον
γὰρ εἰ ὁ θριγκὸς καὶ ὁ κέραμος ἀλλοίωσις ἢ εἰ
θριγκουμένη καὶ κεραμουμένη ἀλλοιοῦται ἀλλὰ
20 μὴ τελειοῦται ἡ οἰκία), τὸν αὐτὸν τρόπον καὶ ἐπὶ
246 b τῶν ἀρετῶν καὶ τῶν κακιῶν καὶ τῶν ἐχόντων ἢ
λαμβανόντων· αἱ μὲν γὰρ τελειώσεις αἱ δὲ ἐκστάσεις
εἰσίν, ὥστ' οὐκ ἀλλοιώσεις.

Ἔτι δὲ καί φαμεν ἁπάσας εἶναι τὰς ἀρετὰς ἐν
τῷ πρός τί πως ἔχειν. τὰς μὲν γὰρ τοῦ σώματος,
5 οἷον ὑγίειαν καὶ εὐεξίαν, ἐν κράσει καὶ συμμετρίᾳ
θερμῶν καὶ ψυχρῶν τίθεμεν ἢ αὐτῶν πρὸς αὐτὰ
τῶν ἐντὸς ἢ πρὸς τὸ περιέχον· ὁμοίως δὲ καὶ τὸ
κάλλος καὶ τὴν ἰσχὺν καὶ τὰς ἄλλας ἀρετὰς καὶ
κακίας. ἑκάστη γὰρ ἔστι τῷ πρός τί πως ἔχειν
καὶ περὶ τὰ οἰκεῖα πάθη εὖ ἢ κακῶς διατίθησι τὸ
10 ἔχον· οἰκεῖα δ' ὑφ' ὧν γίγνεσθαι καὶ φθείρεσθαι
πέφυκεν. ἐπεὶ οὖν τὰ πρός τι οὔτε αὐτά ἐστιν
ἀλλοιώσεις οὔτε αὐτῶν ἔστιν ἀλλοίωσις οὐδὲ
γένεσις οὐδ' ὅλως μεταβολὴ οὐδεμία, φανερὸν ὅτι
οὔθ' αἱ ἕξεις οὔθ' αἱ τῶν ἕξεων ἀποβολαὶ καὶ
λήψεις ἀλλοιώσεις εἰσίν, ἀλλὰ γίγνεσθαι μὲν ἴσως

¹ [βέλτιστος Par. 1859: καὶ ὅταν βέλτιστος al. The sense
required is: 'For this above all is the moment when something that realizes its nature is in existence, as a circle is
called " perfect " precisely from the moment when (the process
of constructing it ends and) it becomes a circle (realizes its
nature).' The point is that a circle is called perfect when it
is a circle, not 'when it is a *very good* circle.' *Cf.* the second
text 246 b (19) καθάπερ ὁ κύκλος τότε μάλιστα κατὰ φύσιν ἐστίν,
ὅταν μάλιστα κύκλος ᾖ. The sense can be obtained by omitting βέλτιστος and so eliminating the suggestion that one
circle can be 'better' than another, or the same circle better

the best possible circle); and defect is losing and departing from the same. Accordingly just as we do not call the completion of a house a qualitive modification of it (for who would call the coping and tiling of a house a qualitive modification of it, or say that the house had been 'modified' by the addition of them instead of 'completed'?), so is it with excellences and defects and with those who have or acquire them: the former are completions and the other lapses from such, and neither of them modifications.

Again, we say that all the excellences are conditions determined by some particular relation. Thus (*a*) bodily excellences such as health and fitness we ascribe to the mingling of the warm and cold humours in due proportion, in relation either to each other or to the environment. And so too with beauty and strength and all other excellences and defects; each consists in being in a certain condition in relation to something and puts its possessor into favourable or unfavourable dispositions with reference to its peculiar affections, by which I mean those affections which, according to the natural constitution of the thing, tend to promote or to destroy its being. Since, then, relations are neither themselves qualitive modifications nor yet subjects of such modification or of coming-into-being or of any kind of change at all, it is clear that neither are habits such, nor the acquisition or loss of them; though it may be that, just as

---

at one time than at another. An alternative is to read καὶ τότε βέλτιστος: 'as a circle is called "perfect" precisely from the moment when it becomes a circle, and then it is at its best' (having passed out of the imperfect stage of being under construction and 'attained its excellence').—C.]

246 b 15 αὐτὰς καὶ φθείρεσθαι ἀλλοιουμένων τινῶν ἀνάγκη
(καθάπερ καὶ τὸ εἶδος καὶ τὴν μορφήν), οἷον θερμῶν
καὶ ψυχρῶν ἢ ξηρῶν καὶ ὑγρῶν ἢ ἐν οἷς τυγ-
χάνουσιν οὖσαι πρώτοις. περὶ ταῦτα γὰρ ἑκάστη
λέγεται κακία καὶ ἀρετή, ὑφ' ὧν ἀλλοιοῦσθαι
πέφυκε τὸ ἔχον· ἡ μὲν γὰρ ἀρετὴ ποιεῖ ἢ ἀπαθὲς
20 ἢ ὡς δεῖ παθητικόν, ἡ δὲ κακία παθητικὸν ἢ
ἐναντίως ἀπαθές.

247 a Ὁμοίως δὲ καὶ ἐπὶ τῶν τῆς ψυχῆς ἕξεων·
ἅπασαι γὰρ καὶ αὗται τῷ πρός τί πως ἔχειν, καὶ
αἱ μὲν ἀρεταὶ τελειώσεις αἱ δὲ κακίαι ἐκστάσεις·
ἔτι ἡ μὲν ἀρετὴ εὖ διατίθησι πρὸς τὰ οἰκεῖα πάθη,
ἡ δὲ κακία κακῶς. ὥστ' οὐδ' αὗται ἔσονται
5 ἀλλοιώσεις, οὐδὲ δὴ αἱ ἀποβολαὶ καὶ λήψεις αὐτῶν·
γίγνεσθαι δ' αὐτὰς ἀναγκαῖον ἀλλοιουμένου τοῦ
αἰσθητικοῦ μέρους. ἀλλοιοῦται δ' ὑπὸ τῶν αἰσθητῶν. ἅπασα γὰρ ἡ ἠθικὴ ἀρετὴ περὶ ἡδονὰς καὶ
λύπας τὰς σωματικάς, αὗται δ' ἢ ἐν τῷ πράττειν
10 ἢ ἐν τῷ μεμνῆσθαι ἢ ἐν τῷ ἐλπίζειν. αἱ μὲν οὖν
ἐν τῇ πράξει κατὰ τὴν αἴσθησίν εἰσιν, ὥσθ' ὑπ'
αἰσθητοῦ τινος κινεῖσθαι, αἱ δ' ἐν τῇ μνήμῃ καὶ
ἐν τῇ ἐλπίδι ἀπὸ ταύτης (ἢ γὰρ οἷα ἔπαθον μεμνη-
μένοι ἥδονται ἢ ἐλπίζοντες οἷα μέλλουσιν)· ὥστ'
ἀνάγκη πᾶσαν τὴν τοιαύτην ἡδονὴν ὑπὸ τῶν
15 αἰσθητῶν γίγνεσθαι. ἐπεὶ δ' ἡδονῆς ἢ λύπης
ἐγγιγνομένης καὶ ἡ κακία καὶ ἡ ἀρετὴ ἐγγίγνεται

234

with the characteristics or forms we have already
spoken of, the formation or destruction of habits may
involve the modification of certain factors, (say) the
heat or cold or dryness or moisture of the physical
elements, or the proper seats of the habits, whatever
they may be. For excellence and defect are in every
case concerned with influences whereby their possessor is, according to its natural constitution, liable
to be modified : the result of excellences is that the
thing is either not affected at all by these influences
or affected in the right way ; the result of defect, that
it is affected or else not affected when it ought to be.

The same is true of (b) the moral habits, for they
too consist in conditions determined by certain relations, and the virtues are perfections of nature, the
vices departures from it. Moreover, virtue disposes
a man rightly towards the affections peculiar to his
own being, and vice evilly. So neither are these
qualitive modifications, nor yet is the acquisition or
loss of them such ; but, all the same, the sensitive
faculties of the soul must necessarily suffer modification before the moral habits can come into existence.
And the sensitive faculties can only be affected by
objects of sense. For all the moral virtues are concerned with bodily pleasures and pains, either in
present experience or in memory or in hope. Present
pleasure or pain is a matter of sensations, and must
therefore be stirred by some sensible object, and the
pleasures and pains of memory or hope are dependent
upon those of experience (for they accompany the
memory of past pleasure or the expectation of
pleasure in the future), so that all such pleasure must
spring from objects of sense. And since vice and
virtue come into being in presence of pleasure and

247 a (περὶ ταύτας γάρ εἰσιν), αἱ δ' ἡδοναὶ καὶ αἱ λῦπαι
ἀλλοιώσεις τοῦ αἰσθητικοῦ, φανερὸν ὅτι ἀλλοιουμένου τινὸς ἀνάγκη καὶ ταύτας ἀποβάλλειν καὶ
λαμβάνειν. ὥσθ' ἡ μὲν γένεσις αὐτῶν μετ' ἀλλοιώσεως, αὐταὶ δ' οὐκ εἰσὶν ἀλλοιώσεις.

247 b Ἀλλὰ μὴν οὐδ' αἱ τοῦ νοητικοῦ μέρους ἀλλοιώσεις, οὐδ' ἔστιν αὐτῶν γένεσις. πολὺ γὰρ μᾶλλον[1]
τὸ ἐπιστῆμον ἐν τῷ πρός τί πως ἔχειν λέγομεν·
ἔτι δὲ καὶ φανερὸν ὅτι οὐκ ἔστιν αὐτῶν γένεσις.
5 τὸ γὰρ κατὰ δύναμιν ἐπιστῆμον οὐδὲν αὐτὸ κινηθὲν
ἀλλὰ τῷ ἄλλο ὑπάρξαι γίγνεται ἐπιστῆμον· ὅταν
γὰρ γένηται τὸ κατὰ μέρος, ἐπίσταταί πως τῇ
καθόλου τὸ ἐν μέρει. πάλιν δὲ τῆς χρήσεως καὶ
τῆς ἐνεργείας οὐκ ἔστι γένεσις, εἰ μή τις καὶ τῆς
ἀναβλέψεως καὶ τῆς ἀφῆς οἴεται γένεσιν εἶναι καὶ
10 τὸ ἐνεργεῖν ὅμοιον τούτοις. ἡ δ' ἐξ ἀρχῆς λῆψις
τῆς ἐπιστήμης γένεσις οὐκ ἔστιν οὐδ' ἀλλοίωσις.
τῷ γὰρ ἠρεμῆσαι καὶ στῆναι τὴν διάνοιαν ἐπ-
ίστασθαι καὶ φρονεῖν λεγόμεθα, εἰς δὲ τὸ ἠρεμεῖν
οὐκ ἔστι γένεσις, ὅλως γὰρ οὐδεμιᾶς μεταβολῆς,

---

[1] [μᾶλλον Oxf. Trans.; cf. Simplic. 1074. 15: μάλιστα codd.
—C.]

---

[a] [This sentence seems meant to justify the statements
(1) that intellectual states are not modifications and (2) that
they consist in ' being in a certain state *in relation to something*,' viz. the object known. The faculty which is capable
of knowing is *not itself modified* (οὐδὲν αὐτὸ κινηθέν) when
it comes into the state of knowing, but this occurs by
something else (an object) coming *into relation with* it.
The following sentences argue that neither the exercise of
knowledge already acquired nor the original acquisition of
knowledge is a *genesis*.—C.]

[b] [The Greek word for knowledge (ἐπιστήμη) is etymologi-

pain (for their concern is all with them), and pleasure and pain are modifications of the sensitive part, it is obvious that virtue and vice can only be lost or gained conditionally on some qualitive modification of the sensitive part having come about. So although the coming into being of virtue and vice is concomitant with qualitive change, they themselves are not such changes.

Nor are (c) the states of the intellectual part qualitive modifications, nor do they ever come into existence in the primary and strict sense. For it is even more true of the state of knowing than it is of the moral virtues that it is a condition determined by a particular relation; and it is further evident that these intellectual states have no proper genesis. [a] For that which knows potentially comes to know actually, not in virtue of any motion of its own, but because something not itself is now newly presented to it; when the particular is presented to it, it gets such knowledge as it can have of the particular by means of knowledge of the universal. And again the enjoyment and actualizing of knowledge is not the result of a process of coming-into-being, unless you choose to say the same of every act of seeing or touching and consider the actualizing of knowing as analogous to such. Nor is the original acquisition of knowledge a process of becoming or a modification. For it is when the understanding has come to rest [b] at its goal that we are said to know and possess a truth, and there is no process of becoming leading to the terminal pause, nor indeed to any kind of change, as has al-

cally connected with ' coming to a stand ' ($\sigma\tau\hat{\eta}\nu\alpha\iota$). *Cf.* Plato, *Phaedo* 96 B, *Cratylus* 437 A, Aristot. *Post. Anal.* 100 a 1 ff. —C.]

247 b καθάπερ εἴρηται πρότερον. ἔτι δ' ὥσπερ ὅταν ἐκ
τοῦ μεθύειν ἢ καθεύδειν ἢ νοσεῖν εἰς τἀναντία
15 μεταστῇ τις οὔ φαμεν ἐπιστήμονα γεγονέναι πάλιν
(καίτοι ἀδύνατος ἦν τῇ ἐπιστήμῃ χρῆσθαι πρότερον), οὕτως οὐδ' ὅταν ἐξ ἀρχῆς λαμβάνῃ τὴν ἕξιν.
τῷ γὰρ καθίστασθαι τὴν ψυχὴν ἐκ τῆς φυσικῆς
ταραχῆς φρόνιμόν τι γίγνεται καὶ ἐπιστῆμον (διὸ
καὶ τὰ παιδία οὔτε μανθάνειν δύναται οὔτε κατὰ
248 a τὰς αἰσθήσεις ὁμοίως κρίνειν τοῖς πρεσβυτέροις·
πολλὴ γὰρ ἡ ταραχὴ καὶ ἡ κίνησις). καθίσταται
δὲ καὶ ἠρεμίζεται πρὸς ἔνια μὲν ὑπὸ τῆς φύσεως
αὐτῆς, πρὸς ἔνια δ' ὑπ' ἄλλων, ἐν ἀμφοτέροις δὲ
5 ἀλλοιουμένων τινῶν τῶν ἐν τῷ σώματι, καθάπερ
ἐπὶ τῆς χρήσεως καὶ τῆς ἐνεργείας ·ὅταν νήφων
γένηται καὶ ἐγερθῇ.

Φανερὸν οὖν ἐκ τῶν εἰρημένων ὅτι τὸ ἀλλοιοῦσθαι
καὶ ἡ ἀλλοίωσις ἔν τε τοῖς αἰσθητοῖς γίγνεται καὶ
ἐν τῷ αἰσθητικῷ μέρει τῆς ψυχῆς, ἐν ἄλλῳ δ'
οὐδενὶ πλὴν κατὰ συμβεβηκός.

ᵃ [In Bk. V. chap. ii. Also at 230 a 4 ' coming to a
stand ' (ἠρέμησις) was defined as a *movement*.—C.]

ᵇ [*Cf.* Plato, *Timaeus* 44 ᴀ ff.—C.]

ᶜ [The implied point of this sentence describing the acquisition of the state of knowledge is that it is not a process of
qualitative modification (it has already been shown that it

CHAPTER IV

ARGUMENT

*In this chapter the question is discussed : what conditions
must be satisfied if two changes are to be ' comparable,' i.e.
such that they can be called equal to, or greater or less than,
one another ? Special consideration is given to the two kinds*

ready been shown.[a] Again, just as we do not say that a man has come to have knowledge again when he emerges from drunkenness or sleep or disease (although it is true that his power of realizing the knowledge has been suspended), so likewise we should not say that when he originally acquires the state he is ' coming to be ' possessed of knowledge. For the condition of understanding or knowing results from the soul coming to a state of stillness out of the turbulence natural to it (this is why children cannot acquire knowledge or pass judgements as to things of sense as grown men can, for their bodies are in a state of great turbulence and instability [b]). And the soul is quieted and stilled, in some respects by nature herself in her normal course, in other respects by external influences ; and in either case it is only a qualitive modification of certain bodily organs that is involved,[c] as in the case of the recovered power of employing and exercising the intellect, when a man becomes sober or wakes from sleep.

It is clear, then, that qualitive modification and susceptibility to it are proper to things perceptible by the senses and to the sensitive factor in the soul, and occur in naught else, save by implication with these.

is not a genesis), though it *involves* a modification of bodily organs.—C.]

CHAPTER IV

ARGUMENT (*continued*)

of local motion, viz. (a) *rotation, designated as ' circular ' (i.e. ' angular ') motion, and* (b) *' translation,' designated as ' rectilinear ' motion. The two kinds of ' local distance ' corresponding to these two kinds of motion are* (a) *circular*

ARGUMENT (continued)

(angular) distance—measured on a circular scale in angular
degrees—and (b) rectilinear distance—measured on a rectilinear scale in degrees of length. The discussion is very
obscure and is 'dialectical,' that is to say, the final answer is
reached by putting forward a series of tentative suggestions,
showing why each of them is inadequate, and so gradually
collecting a definition of the conditions required.

1st suggestion : that every change is comparable with every
other. If (as would then be the case) changes in every sphere
could be reduced to a common measure (it would then be
possible to turn round, to go straight on, and to change in
quality with equal velocity) [a]: and if ' moving with equal
velocity' means covering an equal stretch in an equal time, it
would follow not only that an angle and a length, but also a
stretch of qualitive change, could be equal to one another.
But this is not so, and therefore all kinds of change are not
comparable (248 a 10–18).

2nd suggestion : that the motions of all things which are
' moving' in the same sense of the word are comparable.
But if all local motions were comparable then again all local
' distances' would be so, and an angle could be equal to a
length (a 18–b 6).

3rd suggestion : that motions are comparable when the
same term (e.g. ' quick') can be applied unequivocally to both of
them. But even a term like ' much' or ' double' which

---

[a] This link in the argument is omitted in the text, but it must be
understood in order for the next step to follow.

248 a 10   ᾿Απορήσειε δ᾽ ἄν τις πότερόν ἐστι κίνησις πᾶσα

πάσῃ συμβλητὴ ἢ οὔ. εἰ δή ἐστι πᾶσα συμβλητὴ

καὶ ὁμοταχὲς τὸ ἐν ἴσῳ χρόνῳ ἴσον κινούμενον,

ἔσται περιφερής τις ἴση εὐθείᾳ, καὶ μείζων δὴ καὶ

ἐλάττων. ἔτι ἀλλοίωσις καὶ φορά τις ἴση, ὅταν

15 ἐν ἴσῳ χρόνῳ τὸ μὲν ἀλλοιωθῇ τὸ δ᾽ ἐνεχθῇ. ἔσται

PHYSICS, VII. iv.

ARGUMENT (*continued*)

*admits of no equivocality in itself may yet have an ambiguous
meaning when applied to subjects with different natures (e.g.
water and air); for the ambiguity in its meaning is in this
case inherent in the subject, not in the term itself* (b 6–21).

This brings us to the
*4th suggestion : that it is the nature of the subject to which
it is applied which makes a term ambiguous. But if it lay
only there, attributes themselves would never be equivocal*
(b 21–249 a 3).

*It appears, then, that if two things are to be comparable
with respect to any attribute, the attribute must be unambiguous, and this involves (not only that it must be manifested in a specific subject such as a surface but also) that it
must itself be specific, e.g. 'white,' not merely 'a colour'*
(a 3–8).

*Only changes of the same kind can have equal velocities.
Changes are not only differentiated according to whether
they are qualitive, quantitive, or local, but according to subdivisions of these classes.*

*If the velocities of two qualitive changes are to be equal it
is not only necessary for a like affection to change in the same
degree but also for it to affect an equal amount of a like
subject in each case* (a 8–b 19).

*Analogous problems present themselves with respect to
generation and perishing* (b 19–26).

THE question may be raised whether every kind of
motion or change is comparable with every other.
If so, and if two things moving with equal velocities
move each as far as the other in the same time,
then it will follow that a circular distance may be
equal to a rectilinear distance, or greater or smaller.
Again, we shall have a modification and a local
motion equal to each other when the modification
of one thing and the motion of another from place
to place occupy the same time. This means that

241

ARISTOTLE

248 a ἄρα ἴσον πάθος μήκει· ἀλλ' ἀδύνατον. ἀλλ' ἄρα
ὅταν ἐν ἴσῳ ἴσον κινηθῇ, τότε ἰσοταχές, ἴσον δὲ
οὐκ ἔστι πάθος μήκει; ὥστε οὐκ ἔστιν ἀλλοίωσις
φορᾷ ἴση, οὐδὲ ἐλάττων· ὥστε οὐ πᾶσα συμ-
βλητή.

Ἐπὶ δὲ τοῦ κύκλου καὶ τῆς εὐθείας πῶς συμ-
20 βήσεται; ἄτοπόν τε γὰρ εἰ μὴ ἔστι κύκλῳ ὁμοίως
τουτὶ κινεῖσθαι καὶ τοῦτο ἐπὶ τῆς εὐθείας ἀλλ'
εὐθὺς ἀνάγκη ἢ θᾶττον ἢ βραδύτερον, ὥσπερ εἰ
κάταντες, τὸ δ' ἄναντες. ἔτι οὐδὲ διαφέρει οὐδὲν[1]
τῷ λόγῳ, εἴ τις φήσειεν ἀνάγκην εἶναι θᾶττον
εὐθὺς ἢ βραδύτερον κινεῖσθαι· ἔσται γὰρ μείζων
25 καὶ ἐλάττων ἡ περιφερὴς τῆς εὐθείας, ὥστε καὶ
ἴση. εἰ γὰρ ἐν τῷ Α χρόνῳ τὸ μὲν τὴν Β διῆλθε
248 b τὸ δὲ τὴν Γ, μείζων ἂν εἴη ἡ Β τῆς Γ· οὕτω
γὰρ τὸ θᾶττον ἐλέγετο. οὐκοῦν καὶ εἰ ἐν ἐλάττονι

---

[1] [οὐδὲ διαφέρει οὐδὲν two mss. of First Text, Prantl: οὐδὲν
διαφέρει οὐδ' ἐν (οὐδ' ἐν om. F), Second Text, Bekker.—C.]

---

[a] [This is the correct solution in the case of changes of
different kinds ; but it does not suffice to solve the difficulty
about two movements of the same kind (*e.g.* circular and
rectilinear locomotion) being incomparable.—C.]

[b] [*Or*, ' But how will this conclusion (that the two movements are incomparable) result in the case of the circle and
the straight line? For it is absurd that one thing should not be
able to move on a circular track at the same rate (*cf.* Simplic.
1083. 31 ὁμοίως καὶ ἰσοταχῶς) as another on a rectilinear one,
if we take that as at once implying that it must be going either
faster or slower than the other—as if one were going uphill,
the other down.' The point of the last sentence is the ambiguity of ' not of equal velocity.' This may mean : (1) that,
while the two velocities are comparable, one is greater or
less than the other. Taking that sense, it is absurd to say

242

a qualitive affection will be equal to a distance in space : which is impossible. However (in order to escape this difficulty) shall we say that, while two things are indeed of equal velocity when they move over equal stretches or intervals in a given time, the stretch covered by a qualitive change is not 'equal' to the stretch (length) covered by a local movement ? Hence a qualitive modification (though it may occupy the same time, is not 'of equal velocity' with, and so) is not 'equal' to a local motion, nor is it less (or greater) ; and consequently not every kind of change or movement is comparable with every other.[a]

[b] How is it, then, with the circular and the rectilinear distance ? It would be monstrous to maintain that one thing could not be moving on a rectilinear track and another on a circular one in the same sense, namely that of local motion, just as in the case of up and down and so forth. And the first impression is that if so, one may be swifter or slower than the other ; just as in the case of motion up and down. And it makes no difference in principle whether we say swifter or slower or equal ; for if swifter or slower, then the circular distance will be greater or less than the rectilinear, and whenever that relation exists it implies the possibility of equality between the two. For if in the time A the swifter mobile (B) moves through an arc β, and the slower (C) a straight line c, one would say that β was greater than c, for having a higher velocity means travelling a great distance in the same time. Therefore the swifter mobile (B)

our two movements could not be of equal velocity. Or (2) that the two velocities are not equal (or less or greater) because not comparable at all. This is actually the case in our instance, as will appear later.—C.]

ARISTOTLE

248 b ἴσον, θᾶττον· ὥστ' ἔσται τι μέρος τοῦ Α ἐν ᾧ τὸ
Β τοῦ κύκλου τὸ ἴσον δίεισι, καὶ τὸ Γ ἐν ὅλῳ τῷ
5 Α τὴν Γ. ἀλλὰ μὴν εἰ ἔστι συμβλητά, συμβαίνει
τὸ ἄρτι ῥηθέν, ἴσην εὐθεῖαν εἶναι κύκλῳ. ἀλλ'
οὐ συμβλητά· οὐδ' ἄρα αἱ κινήσεις.

ἀλλ' ὅσα μὴ ὁμώνυμα, πάντα συμβλητά.[1] οἷον
διὰ τί οὐ συμβλητόν, πότερον ὀξύτερον τὸ γραφεῖον
ἢ ὁ οἶνος ἢ ἡ νήτη; ὅτι ὁμώνυμα, οὐ συμβλητά·
ἀλλ' ἡ νήτη τῇ παρανήτῃ συμβλητόν, ὅτι ταὐτὸ
10 σημαίνει τὸ ὀξὺ ἐπ' ἀμφοῖν. ἆρ' οὖν οὐ ταὐτὸν
τὸ ταχὺ ἐνταῦθα κἀκεῖ; πολὺ δ' ἔτι ἧττον ἐν
ἀλλοιώσει καὶ φορᾷ. ἢ πρῶτον μὲν τοῦτο οὐκ
ἀληθές, ὡς εἰ μὴ ὁμώνυμα συμβλητά· τὸ γὰρ πολὺ
ταὐτὸ σημαίνει ἐν ὕδατι καὶ ἀέρι, καὶ οὐ συμβλητά·
εἰ δὲ μή, τό γε διπλάσιον ταὐτὸ (δύο γὰρ πρὸς ἕν),
15 καὶ οὐ συμβλητά.[a] ἢ καὶ ἐπὶ τούτων ὁ αὐτὸς

---

[1] [Simplic. 1086. 20 records two variants ('with the same meaning'): ἀλλ' ὅσα μὴ συνώνυμα, ἅπαντα ἀσυμβλητά (MSS. collated by Shute): ἀλλ' ἀρά γε ὅσα μὴ ὁμώνυμα ἅπαντα συμβλητά ('transferred here by some from the other Bk. VII.').—C.]

---

[a] [Or, we cannot speak of an amount of water being 'twice as much as a given amount of air.' The two substances have properties, other than volume, which make them not comparable.—C.]

[b] [More literally, 'Or does the same thing (above said about 'sharp') hold also of these terms ('much' and 'double')—for 'much' too is an ambiguous word—only (with this difference) that in some cases (such as 'much' and 'double,' not only the words, as in the case of 'sharp,' but) also the definitions of the words are ambiguous?'—C.]

244

would cover an equal distance in less time, so that
there must be some portion of the time A in which B
traverses a part of the arc β, equal to the whole line
c, which C takes the whole of the time A to traverse.
But if the two can be so equated, we arrive at the
same conclusion, namely that an arc may be equal to
a straight line. But they cannot be compared, and
therefore our first impression, that rates of motion
through them can be so compared, is false.

Then (it may be thought) things can be compared
if they can be described without equivocation as of
the same order. Thus : Why can we not say which
is sharpest, this pencil, this wine, or this musical
note ? Because ' sharp ' is equivocal, so the several
sharpnesses cannot be compared ; but we can compare
the highest note in the scale with the leading note,
because ' sharp ' means the same thing for both. May
it be, then, that the word ' quick ' has not the same
meaning when applied to rectilinear motion as when
applied to circular motion, and still less when one
movement is a qualitive modification and the other
a local movement ? But does this take us far enough ?
Or are there even some cases in which things that
bear the same name without equivocation are, nevertheless, not comparable ? Take the term ' much.'
In ' much water,' and ' much air,' ' much ' has the
same meaning ; but you cannot say whether this
much air is equal to this much water, or which is
greater. Or if you deny that ' much ' means the
same in both cases, at any rate ' double ' would seem
to admit no ambiguity, for in every case it is the ratio
of two to one. Yet here twice as much water and
twice as much air are not comparable.[a] [b] But then
too the same argument employed above will show

248 b λόγος—καὶ γὰρ τὸ πολὺ ὁμώνυμον—ἀλλ' ἐνίων
καὶ οἱ λόγοι ὁμώνυμοι, οἷον εἰ λέγοι τις ὅτι τὸ
πολὺ τὸ τοσοῦτον καὶ ἔτι, ἄλλο τὸ τοσοῦτον· καὶ
τὸ ἴσον ὁμώνυμον· καὶ τὸ ἓν δέ, εἰ ἔτυχεν, εὐθὺς
20 ὁμώνυμον, εἰ δὲ τοῦτο, καὶ τὰ δύο. ἐπεὶ διὰ τί
τὰ μὲν συμβλητὰ τὰ δὲ οὔ, εἴπερ ἦν μία φύσις;

Ἢ ὅτι ἐν ἄλλῳ πρώτῳ δεκτικῷ; ὁ μὲν οὖν
ἵππος καὶ ὁ κύων συμβλητά, πότερον λευκότερον·
ἐν ᾧ γὰρ πρώτῳ, τὸ αὐτό, ἡ ἐπιφάνεια· καὶ κατὰ
25 μέγεθος ὡσαύτως· ὕδωρ δὲ καὶ φωνὴ οὔ· ἐν
ἄλλῳ γάρ. ἢ δῆλον ὅτι ἔσται οὕτω γε πάντα ἓν
249 a ποιεῖν, ἐν ἄλλῳ δὲ ἕκαστον φάσκειν εἶναι, καὶ
ἔσται ταὐτὸν ἴσον καὶ γλυκὺ καὶ λευκόν, ἀλλ' ἄλλο

---

a [For τὸ τοσοῦτον καὶ ἔτι in this sense the Oxf. Trans.
compares *Met.* 1021 a 6 τὸ δὲ ὑπερέχον πρὸς τὸ ὑπερεχόμενον
τοσοῦτόν τέ ἐστι καὶ ἔτι. *Cf.* also *De caelo* 273 b 31.—C.]

b [The ambiguity of terms expressing differences of quantity has suggested that the cause of incomparability lies in the
natures or constitutions (as distinct from the magnitudes or
volumes) of the substances concerned. This suggestion is
pursued in the next paragraph, but will be found inadequate.
—C.]

c [Simplicius takes the objection to be that, if we make the
cause of incomparability reside always and solely in a difference of kind between the subjects having the attribute, then
we shall do away with the distinction between ambiguous and
unambiguous attributes used above (248 b 7) to explain *some*
cases of incomparability : we shall no longer say that ' sweet '
has different meanings as applied to water and to a voice.
Translate : ' But obviously on this showing it will be possible
to make out that all attributes are unambiguous (ἕν) and to
allege (as a reason for incomparability, merely) that any one

246

that if 'much' cannot bring water and air on to a scale of comparison, neither can double. The fact is that sometimes definitions themselves are ambiguous. Thus if 'much' be defined as 'so much and more,' [a] 'so much' will mean a different amount in different cases ; and 'equal' or 'the same amount' is similarly ambiguous, and ('equal' being the ratio of one to one) that at once implies that it may very well happen that 'one' is ambiguous, and if 'one' is ambiguous, so is 'two' or 'double.' For why, when some things are comparable, should others not be so, if there were no difference in the nature of the things of which the various amounts are taken ? [b]

Shall we say it is because the direct and primary seat of the attributes in question is different in kind ? Thus we can say whether a horse or a dog is the whiter, for the seat of the colour is the same in both cases, to wit the surface ; and in like manner you can say which is greater, because magnitude or volume in each case is the measure of body ; but you cannot say whether this volume of water is greater or less than this volume of sound, for one volume is material and the other qualitive. [c] But obviously if you take difference in the recipient to be the sole cause of incomparability, you will be driven to the doctrine of ideal unities and material diversities, so that there will be an absolute 'same' and 'equal' and 'sweet' and 'white,' of which diverse recipients partake

of them is in a subject that is different in kind : 'equal' or 'sweet' or 'white' will be unambiguous, only different instances of any one of them will be in subjects different in kind. (This is absurd ;) and moreover, not any and every subject is capable of a given attribute, but one attribute belongs to one kind of subject in the primary sense.' (Water is not capable of the kind of sweetness that can belong to a voice.)—C.]

249 a ἐν ἄλλῳ. ἔτι δεκτικὸν οὐ τὸ τυχόν ἐστιν, ἀλλ᾽
ἐν ἑνὸς τὸ πρῶτον.

᾽Αλλ᾽ ἆρα οὐ μόνον δεῖ τὰ συμβλητὰ μὴ ὁμώνυμα
εἶναι ἀλλὰ καὶ μὴ ἔχειν διαφορὰν μήτε ὃ μήτ᾽
5 ἐν ᾧ; λέγω δὲ οἷον χρῶμα ἔχει διαίρεσιν· τοιγαροῦν
οὐ συμβλητὸν κατὰ τοῦτο, οἷον πότερον κεχρωμά-
τισται μᾶλλον (μὴ κατά τι χρῶμα ἀλλ᾽ ᾗ χρῶμα),
ἀλλὰ κατὰ τὸ λευκόν. οὕτω καὶ περὶ κίνησιν
ὁμοταχὲς τὸ ἐν ἴσῳ χρόνῳ κινηθὲν ἴσον τοσονδί.
10 εἰ δὴ τοῦ μήκους ἐν τῳδὶ τὸ μὲν ἠλλοιώθη τὸ δὲ
ἠνέχθη, ἴση ἄρα αὕτη ἡ ἀλλοίωσις καὶ ὁμοταχὴς
τῇ φορᾷ; ἀλλ᾽ ἄτοπον· αἴτιον δ᾽ ὅτι ἡ κίνησις ἔχει
εἴδη. ὥστε εἰ τὰ ἐν τῷ ἴσῳ χρόνῳ ἐνεχθέντα ἴσον
μῆκος ἰσοταχῆ ἔσται, ἴση ἡ εὐθεῖα καὶ ἡ περιφερής.
πότερον οὖν αἴτιον, ὅτι ἡ φορὰ γένος ἢ ὅτι ἡ
15 γραμμὴ γένος; (ὁ μὲν γὰρ χρόνος ὁ αὐτός.[1]) ἂν

---

[1] [ὁ αὐτός Simplic. 1092. 30, Oxf. Trans.—C.]

---

[a] See Vol. I. Introd. p. xliv.

[b] And the impossibility of this consequence proves that the antecedent supposition of their equal velocities is also impossible. [The Greek is very obscure, and the Oxf. Trans. suggests a lacuna. It is certainly hard to get out of ὥστε εἰ, κτλ. the required meaning, which seems to be as follows : ' And so (if we eliminate such a difference in kind between the movements and take a case where both movements are of the same generic kind—locomotion, and) if we are to say that things which move locally over an equal distance in the same time are of equal velocity, then (on the supposition that straight-moving and circular-moving bodies can be of equal velocity, we get the impossible conclusion :) the rectilinear distance will be equal to the circular distance. Which, then, of two possible ambiguities is responsible for this impossible conclusion—is it the fact that " locomotion " is a genus (not an indivisible species), or is it the fact that " line " (track) is a genus? (It must be one or the other or both,) for time is

diversely.[a] Moreover, we must note that a receptive factor of one kind cannot receive any impress at random, but each such receptive factor is susceptible only of one corresponding order of participation.

May we then conclude that, in order to be comparable with each other, the terms compared must not only be unequivocal, but must also have no specific differentia from each other either in themselves or in that in which they are manifested? I mean that ' colour ' for instance, is susceptible of specific division. Therefore you cannot say which of two things is the more ' coloured,' in the generic sense of ' colour '; but you can say which is the whiter. So too in the case of motion or passing : two things are moving at the same rate if they take an equal time to accomplish a certain equal amount of motion. Suppose then that one half of a body's length suffers a qualitive modification and the other a change of place in a certain time, is the modification of the one equal to the local movement of the other, and their velocities equal ? Manifestly not ; and the reason is that there are distinguishable kinds of passing from this to that. So that if it were really true that a mobile moving on a circular track and one moving on a rectilinear one could have an equal velocity, then a circular and a rectilinear track might be equal.[b] Why then cannot they have equal velocity? Is it that 'local movement' is a genus and not a species, or that 'line' (track) is? (It must be one or the other or both, for ' time ' is certainly an unequivocal term.) Both the movement certainly not divisible into species. (It is in fact both ; for) if there are specific differences of " line " (track), there must be specific differences of locomotion to correspond.' *Cf.* Simplic. 1092. 12 ff.—C.]

ARISTOTLE

249 a δὲ τῷ εἴδει ἢ ἄλλα, καὶ ἐκεῖνα εἴδει διαφέρει· καὶ
γὰρ ἡ φορὰ εἴδη ἔχει, ἂν ἐκεῖνο ἔχῃ εἴδη ἐφ' οὗ
κινεῖται. ἔτι δὲ ἐὰν ᾧ, οἷον εἰ πόδες, βάδισις, εἰ δὲ
πτέρυγες, πτῆσις; ἢ οὔ, ἀλλὰ τοῖς σχήμασιν ἡ
φορὰ ἄλλη. ὥστε τὰ ἐν ἴσῳ χρόνῳ ταὐτὸ μέγεθος
20 κινούμενα ἰσοταχῆ· τὸ αὐτὸ δὲ ἀδιάφορον εἴδει
καὶ κινήσει ἀδιάφορον.

Ὥστε τοῦτο σκεπτέον, τίς διαφορὰ κινήσεως.
καὶ σημαίνει ὁ λόγος οὗτος ὅτι τὸ γένος οὐχ ἕν
τι, ἀλλὰ παρὰ τοῦτο λανθάνει πολλά. εἰσί τε τῶν
ὁμωνυμιῶν αἱ μὲν πολὺ ἀπέχουσαι, αἱ δὲ ἔχουσαί
τινα ὁμοιότητα, αἱ δ' ἐγγὺς ἢ γένει ἢ ἀναλογίᾳ,
25 διὸ οὐ δοκοῦσιν ὁμωνυμίαι εἶναι οὖσαι.

Πότε οὖν ἕτερον τὸ εἶδος—ἐὰν ταὐτὸ ἐν ἄλλῳ, ἢ
ἂν ἄλλο ἐν ἄλλῳ; καὶ τίς ὅρος; ἢ τῷ κρινοῦμεν
ὅτι ταὐτὸν τὸ λευκὸν καὶ τὸ γλυκὺ ἢ ἄλλο; ὅτι
ἐν ἄλλῳ φαίνεται ἕτερον; ἢ ὅτι ὅλως οὐ ταὐτό;

Περὶ δὲ δὴ ἀλλοιώσεως πῶς ἔσται ἰσοταχὴς

---

^a [Simplicius takes ἀλλὰ τοῖς σχήμασιν ἡ φορὰ ἄλλη to refer
to differences between walking, flying, etc. ' We may dismiss such distinctions as involving only a difference in the
fashion of the movement' (which would not affect the
question whether the speeds were comparable).—C.]

^b White and sweet were used as examples of ambiguous
attributes above (248 b 20 ff.), and it was stated that not
only has 'sweet' a different meaning as applied to water
and to a voice, but it must have a subject of a different
kind.—C.]

^c These questions of course are rhetorical. In either case
the other-in-themselves and received-by-different-corre-
spondents is supposed to be the obvious answer.

250

and the track in question are equivocal, for since the tracks are specifically different so are the movements that follow them. Are we to add that the instruments of locomotion establish specific differences in the motions themselves, walking with feet, and flying with wings ? We may dismiss such distinctions and confine ourselves to the formation of the track,[a] and say that the equal velocity means passing the *same distance* in equal time, only the ' sameness' must be specific in the case of the track and (consequently) in the case of the movement.

We must consider, then, what constitutes a specific difference in the case of motion. The above argument indicates that the genus is not indivisible, but that, besides the genus, there are a number of varieties concealed in it. When a term is equivocal, the senses covered by it may be widely removed, or they may have some resemblance, or they may, in fact or by the closeness of their analogies, draw so near to each other that the ambiguity of the term that includes them all, though very real, easily escapes our notice.

What constitutes a difference of kind then ? Is it a difference in the several participants of the same nature, or rather a difference in that which is participated, to which the difference in the participants corresponds ? And how do we determine the existence of a specific difference ? Or by what means are we to decide that ' white ' or ' sweet ' is (specifically) the same or different (in a variety of cases) ?[b] Is it by noting only that they are manifested in different subjects, or because in both respects, in themselves and their recipients alike, they are different ?[c]

Turning, then, to modifications of quality, we must

ARISTOTLE

249 a 30 ἑτέρᾳ ἑτέρα; εἰ δή ἐστι τὸ ὑγιάζεσθαι ἀλλοιοῦσθαι,
ἔστι τὸν μὲν ταχὺ τὸν δὲ βραδέως ἰαθῆναι, καὶ
249 b ἅμα τινάς· ὥστ' ἔστιν ἀλλοίωσις ἰσοταχής, ἐν ἴσῳ
γὰρ χρόνῳ ἠλλοιώθη. ἀλλὰ τί ἠλλοιώθη; τὸ γὰρ
ἴσον οὐκ ἔσται ἐνταῦθα λεγόμενον, ἀλλ' ὡς ἐν τῷ
ποσῷ ἰσότης, ἐνταῦθα ὁμοιότης. ἀλλ' ἔστω
5 ἰσοταχὲς τὸ ἐν ἴσῳ χρόνῳ τὸ αὐτὸ μεταβάλλον.
πότερον οὖν ἐν ᾧ τὸ πάθος ἢ τὸ πάθος δεῖ συμ-
βάλλειν; ἐνταῦθα μὲν δὴ ὅτι ἡ ὑγίεια ἡ αὐτή,
ἔστι λαβεῖν ὅτι οὔτε μᾶλλον οὔτε ἧττον ἀλλ'
ὁμοίως ὑπάρχει. ἐὰν δὲ τὸ πάθος ἄλλο ᾖ, οἷον
10 ἀλλοιοῦται τὸ λευκαινόμενον καὶ τὸ ὑγιαζόμενον,
τούτοις οὐδὲν τὸ αὐτὸ οὐδ' ἴσον οὐδ' ὅμοιον, ᾗ
ἤδη ταῦτα εἴδη ποιεῖ ἀλλοιώσεως, καὶ οὐκ ἔστι
μία ὥσπερ οὐδ' αἱ φοραί. ὥστε ληπτέον πόσα
εἴδη ἀλλοιώσεως καὶ πόσα φορᾶς. εἰ μὲν οὖν τὰ
κινούμενα εἴδει διαφέρει ὧν εἰσιν αἱ κινήσεις καθ'
αὐτὰ καὶ μὴ κατὰ συμβεβηκός, καὶ αἱ κινήσεις εἴδει
διοίσουσιν· εἰ δὲ γένει, γένει· εἰ δὲ ἀριθμῷ, ἀριθμῷ.
15 ἀλλὰ δὴ πότερον εἰς τὸ πάθος δεῖ βλέψαι, ἐὰν ᾖ

---

[a] [The Oxf. Trans. takes τί as accusative and the question as meaning : What qualification are we to introduce into our definition of ' equal velocity ' in the case of modification of quality corresponding to the ' equal distance (or ' same magnitude ') covered ' (249 a 19) in the case of locomotion ? We must substitute for ' equality ' ' likeness ' or specific identity. —C.]

[b] [' Them,' *i.e.* the two *subjects* just mentioned—the surface which is growing white, the body which is regaining health. The difference between whiteness and health is such as to imply a difference of kind between their respective subjects, which accordingly offer no ground of comparison, and the modifications they undergo must be specifically different. —C.]

252

ask under what conditions can velocities in change
of quality be equal to each other ? Now regaining
health is a modification of quality, and it is possible
for one man to gain health quickly and another
slowly, and for two men to be doing so at the same
time. So equal velocities of recovery must be
possible, since the recoveries may occupy the same
time. But what is the nature of that which is being
modified ? [a] The term ' equal ' cannot be used of
a *quale* : in that category what corresponds to
equality in the category of quantity is *likeness*. Let
us take ' equal velocity,' then, to mean ' making
the same change in the same time.' Are we then to
compare the seat of the affections, or the affections
themselves ? In our present illustration, it is because health (the affection) is the same that we are
able to ascertain that it is present neither more
nor less but in a like degree in the two subjects.
But if the affection were different in each case—
if one subject were whitened, for instance, and the
other restored to health—there is no sameness or
equality or likeness between them,[b] and this in
itself establishes the two modifications as specifically different, nor are they of one kind any more
than the various species of locomotion we have
examined. So we must ask how many species of
qualitive modification there are, and how many of
locomotion. If, then, the things which are directly
and essentially (not merely accidentally) the subjects of change or modification differ specifically,
the movements or progress will differ specifically,
and if generically generically, if individually individually. But is it enough to consider the nature of the
affection and its identity or similarity if the modifi-

249 b ταὐτὸν ἢ ὅμοιον, εἰ ἰσοταχεῖς αἱ ἀλλοιώσεις, ἢ
εἰς τὸ ἀλλοιούμενον, οἷον εἰ τοῦ μὲν τοσονδὶ λελεύ-
κανται τοῦ δὲ τοσονδί; ἢ εἰς ἄμφω· καὶ ἡ αὐτὴ
μὲν ἢ ἄλλη τῷ πάθει, εἰ τὸ αὐτὸ ⟨ἢ μὴ τὸ αὐτό⟩,[1]
ἴση δ᾽ ἢ ἄνισος, εἰ ἐκεῖνο ⟨ἴσον ἢ⟩ ἄνισον.

Καὶ ἐπὶ γενέσεως δὲ καὶ φθορᾶς τὸ αὐτὸ σκεπτέον
20 —πῶς ἰσοταχὴς ἡ γένεσις; εἰ ἐν ἴσῳ χρόνῳ τὸ
αὐτὸ καὶ ἄτομον, οἷον ἄνθρωπος ἀλλὰ μὴ ζῷον·
θάττων δέ, εἰ ἐν ἴσῳ ἕτερον. (οὐ γὰρ ἔχομέν τινα
δύο, ἐν οἷς ἡ ἑτερότης ὡς ἡ ἀνομοιότης.[2] καὶ εἰ
ἔστιν ἀριθμὸς ἡ οὐσία, πλείων καὶ ἐλάττων ἀριθμὸς
25 ὁμοειδής· ἀλλ᾽ ἀνώνυμον τὸ κοινὸν καὶ τὸ ἑκάτερον,
ὥσπερ τὸ πλεῖον πάθος ἢ τὸ ὑπερέχον μᾶλλον, τὸ
δὲ ποσὸν μεῖζον).

---

[1] [I have adopted the correction proposed by the Oxf.
Trans. which renders: 'That is to say, the alterations are
the same or different according as the affections are
the same or different, while they are equal or unequal according
as the things altered are equal or unequal.'—C.]

[2] [The stop after ἀνομοιότης might be removed: 'For we
have not two terms to convey this difference in the way that
unlikeness in quality is conveyed (by "more" and "less")
or, on the theory that substance is number, a number (may
be called) "greater" or "less" than another of the same
kind; but etc.'—C.]

---

[a] ['Equal' or 'unequal'—terms appropriate to the category of quantity—cannot be applied to the 'affection'
(quality), but only to the subject, as having magnitude.—C.]

[b] Simplicius seems to be right in understanding this to
mean if the embryo (of the same species) were brought to
perfection in less time in one of the compared cases.

[c] [Jaeger, *Aristoteles* (1923) p. 313, sees a reference to
the Platonic and Academic doctrine of substances as Ideal
Numbers and refers to *Met.* M 7, 1080 b 37 ff.: the question
whether the monads composing Ideal Numbers are com-

cations it endures are to be regarded as of equal
velocity, or are we also to take into consideration
the seat or patient of the change, whether the same
area has been whitened, for instance, in each case ?
Clearly both, so as to judge of identity by the affection, but of equality by the area.[a]

The same inquiry should be made as to genesis
and perishing. What constitutes equal velocities of
generation ? If the times are equal, the things
generated must be *the same* and of the same infima
species, both men for instance, not merely both
animals. It would be quicker if in the same time
a *different* result were produced.[b] (I use the terms
'same' and 'different' because we have no pair
of terms to convey this difference in the case of
a generation of a substance in the same way
that in the case of alteration of quality unlikeness is conveyed by the terms 'more' and 'less.'
If indeed being were number,[c] then there might be
a 'more' or 'less' of number (*i.e.* being) of the same
kind; but we have had to call it 'otherness' for
want of a general word[d] that can rank each being,
as we rank the 'more' or 'less' (or rather excessive
or defective) in quality and the 'greater' in
quantity.)

parable (συμβληταί) or not, etc. If a number is to be comparable (equal to, or greater or less than another) it must be
of the same kind or order, ὁμοειδής. *Cf.* the use of this term
at *Met.* 991 b 21.—C.]

[d] [There is no special word (more precise than the wide
expression 'difference') corresponding to 'unlikeness' in
quality or 'inequality' in quantity to cover both relations
(κοινόν), nor any word for each relation severally (τὸ ἑκάτερον),
like 'more' and 'less' in quality, 'greater' and 'smaller' in
quantity.—C.]

ARISTOTLE

CHAPTER V

ARGUMENT

[*This chapter states some simple principles of mechanics. A force which can move a given load a certain distance in a certain time can move half the load either twice as far in the same time or the same distance in half the time* (249 b 27–250 a 4).

Also, if the load is reduced by half, half the force will suffice to move it the whole distance in the whole time (a 4–9).

Also, half the force can move the whole load, taken half at a time, half the distance in the whole time. But, if the load has to be moved as a whole, half the force will not necessarily be able to move it half the distance or even to move it at all (a 9–19).

249 b 27 Ἐπεὶ δὲ τὸ κινοῦν κινεῖ τι ἀεὶ καὶ ἔν τινι καὶ μέχρι του (λέγω δὲ τὸ μὲν ἔν τινι, ὅτι ἐν χρόνῳ, τὸ δὲ μέχρι του, ὅτι ποσόν τι μῆκος· ἀεὶ γὰρ ἅμα
30 κινεῖ καὶ κεκίνηκεν, ὥστε ποσόν τι ἔσται ὃ ἐκινήθη, καὶ ἐν ποσῷ), εἰ δὴ τὸ μὲν Α τὸ κινοῦν, τὸ δὲ Β
250 a τὸ κινούμενον, ὅσον δὲ κεκίνηται μῆκος τὸ Γ, ἐν ὅσῳ δὲ ὁ χρόνος ἐφ' οὗ Δ, ἐν δὴ τῷ ἴσῳ χρόνῳ ἡ ἴση δύναμις ἡ ἐφ' οὗ Α τὸ ἥμισυ τοῦ Β διπλασίαν τῆς Γ κινήσει, τὴν δὲ τὸ Γ ἐν τῷ ἡμίσει τοῦ Δ· οὕτω γὰρ ἀνάλογον ἔσται.
5 Καὶ εἰ ἡ αὐτὴ δύναμις τὸ αὐτὸ ἐν τῳδὶ τῷ χρόνῳ τοσήνδε κινεῖ καὶ τὴν ἡμίσειαν ἐν τῷ ἡμίσει, καὶ ἡ ἡμίσεια ἰσχὺς τὸ ἥμισυ κινήσει ἐν τῷ ἴσῳ χρόνῳ τὸ ἴσον. οἷον τῆς Α δυνάμεως ἔστω ἡμίσεια ἡ τὸ

ᵃ [Sir T. Heath (*Greek Math.* i. 345) remarks that the axiom which is regarded as containing the germ of the principle of virtual velocities is enunciated here and in the *De caelo* (301 b 4, 11) in the slightly different form : ' A smaller

CHAPTER V

ARGUMENT (*continued*)

This explains the fallacy of Zeno's contention that if a bushel of millet makes a noise in falling, every grain must make its proportionate noise (19–25).

But, if two forces can separately move two loads so far in a given time, then when combined they can move the combined load the same distance in the same time (a 25–28).

The same principles apply to forces causing alteration of quality or increase of quantity (a 28–b 7).—C.]

THAT which is causing motion is always moving something in something and up to somewhere. (By the something ' in which ' I mean time, and by the ' up to somewhere ' the measure of the distance traversed ; for if a thing is now causing motion, it has already caused motion before now, so that there is always a distance that has been covered and a time that has been taken.) If, then, A is the moving agent, B the mobile, C the distance traversed and D the time taken, then

A will move ½ B over the distance 2 C in time D,
and A   ,,   ½ B   ,,   ,,   C ,,   ½ D;
for so the proportion will be observed.[a]

Again, if

A will move B over distance C in time D
     and A   ,,   B   ,,   ½ C ,,   ½ D,
then E (= ½ A) ,, F (= ½ B) ,,   C ,,   D ;
for the relation of the force E (½ A) to the load F (½ B) in the last proposition is the same as the

and lighter weight will be given more movement if the force acting on it is the same. . . . The speed of the lesser body will be to that of the greater as the greater body is to the lesser.'—C.]

257

250 a Ε καὶ τοῦ Β τὸ Ζ ἥμισυ· ὁμοίως δὴ ἔχουσι καὶ
ἀνάλογον ἡ ἰσχὺς πρὸς τὸ βάρος, ὥστε ἴσον ἐν ἴσῳ
χρόνῳ κινήσουσιν.

10 Καὶ εἰ τὸ Ε τὸ Ζ κινεῖ ἐν τῷ Δ τὴν Γ, ἀναγκαῖον[1] ἐν τῷ ἴσῳ χρόνῳ τὸ ἐφ' οὗ Ε τὸ διπλάσιον
τοῦ Ζ κινεῖν τὴν ἡμίσειαν τῆς Γ. εἰ δὲ[2] τὸ Α τὸ
Β[3] κινήσει ἐν τῷ Δ ὅση ἡ τὸ Γ, τὸ ἥμισυ τοῦ Α
(τὸ ἐφ' οὗ Ε) τὸ Β[3] οὐ κινήσει ἐν τῷ χρόνῳ ἐφ'
ᾧ Δ, οὐδ' ἔν τινι τοῦ Δ, τὶ τῆς[4] Γ ἀνάλογον πρὸς
15 τὴν ὅλην τὴν Γ ὡς τὸ Α πρὸς τὸ Ε. ὅλως γάρ,
εἰ ἔτυχεν, οὐ κινήσει οὐδέν· οὐ γὰρ εἰ ἡ ὅλη ἰσχὺς
τοσήνδε ἐκίνησεν, ἡ ἡμίσεια οὐ κινήσει οὔτε ποσὴν
οὔτ' ἐν ὁποσῳοῦν· εἰς γὰρ ἂν κινοίη τὸ πλοῖον,
εἴπερ ἥ τε τῶν νεωλκῶν τέμνεται ἰσχὺς εἰς τὸν
ἀριθμὸν καὶ τὸ μῆκος ὃ πάντες ἐκίνησαν.

---

[1] [ἀναγκαῖον ΕΚ, Simplicius (1105. 15 τῆς μὲν δυνάμεως πάλιν
τὸ ἥμισυ λαμβάνει, βάρος δὲ τὸ ἐξ ἀρχῆς, καὶ χρόνον ἐκεῖνον τὸν Δ.
καὶ λέγει ὅτι τὸ ἥμισυ κινήσει τοῦ Γ μήκους): οὐκ ἀνάγκη cett.,
Bekker, Prantl; Simplic. 1106. 1 records with approval a
variant reading containing οὐκ. This sentence has been misunderstood by those who inserted οὐκ and by the editors
who have followed them. With οὐκ the sentence becomes a
duplicate of the next (in which εἰ δὴ is awkwardly substituted
for εἰ δέ); it ought to begin with εἰ δὲ or ἀλλ' εἰ, not with καὶ
εἰ; and there seems to be no reason why 'the same load'
(as Simplicius calls it) should be called here τὸ διπλάσιον τοῦ
Ζ and in the next sentence τὸ Β. The loads intended are not
the same, twice one not being for all purposes the same as
two. τὸ διπλάσιον τοῦ Ζ means 'twice F' in the sense of two
halves of B taken separately. As the next sentence says,
the half-force E cannot cope with B *as a whole*, but our
sentence says it can cope with it if allowed to move first one
half and then the other. If two colliers (Λ) carry two sacks

relation of the force A to the load B in the first, and accordingly the same distance (C) will be covered in the same time (D).

Also if E ($\frac{1}{2}$ A) will move F ($\frac{1}{2}$ B) over distance C in time D, it follows that in the same time E will move 2 F's over half the distance C.[a] But if A will move B over the whole distance C in time D, half A (E) will not be able to move B, in time D or in any fraction of it, over a part of C bearing the same proportion to the whole of C that E bears to A. Because it may well happen that E cannot move B at all ; for it does not follow that if the whole force could move it so far, half the force could move it either any particular distance or in any time whatever ; for if it were so, then a single man could haul the ship through a distance whose ratio to the whole distance is equal to the ratio of his individual force to the whole force of the gang.[b]

---

[a] [See critical note 1.—C.]

[b] [*Literally*, ' otherwise one man could move the ship, since both the force of the haulers and the distance over which all of them together make it move are divisible into the (same) number (of parts as there are men).'—C.]

---

of coal (B) a mile in an hour, one collier (E) cannot carry *two sacks at once* (B) at all, but he can carry *two sacks, one at a time* (2 F's) half-a-mile within the hour. This principle —that the fractional force can deal with a multiple of its proper load if allowed to take it piecemeal—will explain another much misunderstood passage in Book VIII., 266 a 15 ff.—C.

2 [δὲ EK : δὴ cett.—C.]

3 [τὸ B Oxf. Trans. ; *cf.* Simplic. 1106. 27 ff. : τὴν τὸ B codd.—C.]

4 [τὶ τῆς Prantl (*cf.* Simplic. 1107. 2 μόριόν τι τοῦ Γ διαστήματος), Oxf. Trans. : τις τῆς K : τῆς cett.—C.]

250 a 20   Διὰ τοῦτο ὁ Ζήνωνος λόγος οὐκ ἀληθής, ὡς ψοφεῖ
τῆς κέγχρου ὁτιοῦν μέρος· οὐδὲν γὰρ κωλύει μὴ κινεῖν
τὸν ἀέρα ἐν μηδενὶ χρόνῳ τοῦτον ὃν ἐκίνησε πεσὼν
ὁ ὅλος μέδιμνος. οὐδὲ δὴ τοσοῦτον μόριον, ὅσον ἂν
κινήσειε τοῦ ὅλου, εἰ εἴη καθ' αὑτὸ τοῦτο, οὐ κινεῖ·
οὐδὲ γὰρ οὐδέν ἐστιν ἀλλ' ἢ δυνάμει ἐν τῷ ὅλῳ.

25   Εἰ δὲ τὰ δύο,[1] ἑκάτερον δὲ τῶνδε ἑκάτερον κινεῖ
τοσόνδε ἐν τοσῷδε, καὶ συντιθέμεναι αἱ δυνάμεις
τὸ σύνθετον ἐκ τῶν βαρῶν τὸ ἴσον κινήσουσι μῆκος
καὶ ἐν ἴσῳ χρόνῳ· ἀνάλογον γάρ.

  Ἆρ' οὖν οὕτω καὶ ἐπ' ἀλλοιώσεως καὶ ἐπ'
αὐξήσεως; τὶ μὲν γὰρ τὸ αὖξον, τὶ δὲ τὸ αὐξανό-
30 μενον, ἐν ποσῷ δὲ χρόνῳ καὶ ποσὸν τὸ μὲν αὔξει
τὸ δὲ αὐξάνεται. καὶ τὸ ἀλλοιοῦν καὶ τὸ ἀλλοιού-
250 b μενον ὡσαύτως, τὶ καὶ ποσὸν κατὰ τὸ μᾶλλον
καὶ τὸ ἧττον ἠλλοίωται καὶ ἐν ποσῷ χρόνῳ—ἐν
διπλασίῳ διπλάσιον ⟨ἢ ἐν ἡμίσει ἡμίσυ⟩,[2] καὶ τὸ

---

[1] [Fort. εἰ δὲ τὰ ⟨κινοῦντα⟩ δύο. *Cf.* Philop. 881. 18 εἰ δύc
τινὰ εἶεν κινοῦντα καὶ ἑκάτερον αὐτῶν κινῇ, κτλ.— C.]

[2] [In the mss. this clause stands after τὸ δ' ἥμισυ ἐν ἡμίσει
χρόνῳ. In this sentence τὸ διπλάσιον and τὸ ἥμισυ mean
'twice the thing that is altered' and 'half the thing that
is altered'; while διπλάσιον and ἥμισυ are adverbial with
ἀλλοιοῦται understood, and mean twice and half the amount
of change. (Here I differ from the Oxford Translation,
which treats ἥμισυ as sometimes equivalent to τὸ ἥμισυ.) The
last clause ἢ ἐν ἴσῳ διπλάσιον must have τὸ ἥμισυ for its
subject. Either τὸ ἥμισυ must be inserted in it, or the
clause which precedes it in the mss., ἢ ἐν ἡμίσει ἥμισυ (the
subject of which is *not* τὸ ἥμισυ), must be transposed where
I have put it, so as to allow the τὸ ἥμισυ in τὸ δ' ἥμισυ ἐν
ἡμίσει χρόνῳ to serve as subject to the last clause.—C.]

[a] [It appears from Simplicius 1108. 18 that Aristotle is here
referring not to Zeno's own writings but to some early dialogue
(Diels suggests the Φυσικός of Alcidamas, *Vors.*[4] 19 Α 29) in
which Zeno was represented as arguing with Protagoras.—C.

And in this lies the fallacy of Zeno's [a] contention
that every grain of millet must make a sound as it
falls (if the whole measure is to do so). For it may
well be that in no period of time could the one grain
make such a stir in the air [b] as the whole measure does.
Nor need it be able, if alone, to effect that portion of
the total movement which may be assigned to it in
accordance with its proportion to the whole mass [c]; for
it cannot be regarded, except potentially, as having
any several action in the total movement effected.

On the other hand, if two separate agents can each
of them move one of two loads in so much time, then
if united they would move the combined load the
same distance in the same time ; for the proportions
would hold.

And it is the same with qualitive modifications and
with growth. For there is something that causes the
growth and something that is made to grow, and the
process takes so much time, and the growth effected
and acquired is so much. So too with the qualitive
modification and the quality modified, for a certain
' so much,' as measured by ' more and less,' is modified, and in ' so much ' time. Thus if

      A alters B to a degree   C in time D,

then   A ,,   ,,   ,, 2 C ,,   2 D

---

[b] [*Literally*, ' move that air that the whole bushel moves '
i.e. such an amount of air as we may suppose necessary to
cause the whole sound.—C.]

[c] [Just as one out of 100 ship-haulers cannot by himself
move the ship $\frac{1}{100}$th of the distance. So Simplicius (1109. 2) ;
but the sentence can more easily be construed to mean : ' Indeed (when it forms a part of the whole bushel) it does not
even move such a part of the whole amount of air as it would
move if it were by itself ; for no part so much as exists (as a
distinct moving agent) in the whole otherwise than potentially.' *Cf.* Oxf. Trans.—C.]

250 b διπλάσιον ἐν διπλασίῳ, τὸ δ' ἥμισυ ἐν ἡμίσει
χρόνῳ ἢ ἐν ἴσῳ διπλάσιον.

Εἰ δὲ τὸ ἀλλοιοῦν ἢ αὖξόν τι¹ τοσόνδε ἐν τῷ
⁵ τοσῷδε ἢ αὔξει ἢ ἀλλοιοῖ² ⟨καὶ τὸ ἥμισυ ἐν ἡμίσει
ἢ ἐν ἡμίσει ἥμισυ⟩, οὐκ ἀνάγκη ⟨καὶ τὸ ἥμισυ
ἐν διπλασίῳ⟩, ἀλλ' οὐδέν, εἰ ἔτυχεν, ἀλλοιώσει ἢ
αὐξήσει, ὥσπερ καὶ ἐπὶ τοῦ βάρους.

¹ [τι: τὸ MSS. τὸ τοσόνδε should mean 'an object (area or volume) of a certain magnitude,' but some mention of 'a certain amount' of change seems needed; cf. 250 a 25. Perhaps τὸ τοσόνδε ⟨τοσόνδε⟩.—C.]

² [The MS. reading ἀλλοιοῖ, οὐκ ἀνάγκη καὶ τὸ ἥμισυ ἐν ἡμίσει καὶ ἐν ἡμίσει τὸ ἥμισυ, ἀλλ' οὐδέν, κτλ. is nonsense. In the clause καὶ τὸ ἥμισυ ἐν ἡμίσει, where it stands in the MSS., if τὸ ἥμισυ means τὸ ἥμισυ τοῦ ἀλλοιοῦντος (½ A), it is nonsense, for no one could expect the force to do the work in half the time; if it means τὸ ἥμισυ τοῦ ἀλλοιουμένου (½ B), the statement is false, for then the subject is τὸ ἀλλοιοῦν (A) and A will change ½ B in half the time. The other clause καὶ ἐν ἡμίσει τὸ ἥμισυ is a mere repetition, which should in any case be corrected from Simplicius to ἢ ἐν ἡμίσει ἥμισυ.

The remedy adopted is based on Simplicius's paraphrase (1111. 18): οὐκέτι μέντοι εἰ τὸ τοσόνδε ὑπὸ τοῦ τοσοῦδε ἠλλοίωται τήνδε τινὰ τὴν ἀλλοίωσιν ἢ ηὔξηται τήνδε τὴν αὔξησιν, ἀνάγκη καὶ τὸ ἥμισυ ἐν ἡμίσει ἢ (sic) ἐν ἡμίσει ἥμισυ (sic) ἀλλοιοῦσθαι ἢ αὔξεσθαι ὑπὸ τῆς ἡμισείας δυνάμεως ἢ ὑπὸ τῆς ἡμισείας τὸ ὅλον ἐν διπλασίῳ χρόνῳ ἀλλοιωθήσεται. οὐδὲ γὰρ τοῦ ὅλου πάντως κινητικὴ ἡ ἡμίσεια δύναμις, ἀλλ' εἰ ἔτυχε τοσαύτη ἐστὶν ἡ ἡμίσεια ὡς μὴ ἰσχύειν ἔτι ἀλλοιοῦν ὅλως ἢ αὔξειν. This suggests that Simplicius read: οὐκ ἀνάγκη καὶ τὸ ἥμισυ (= ὑπὸ τῆς ἡμισείας δυνάμεως) τὸ ἥμισυ ἐν ἡμίσει ἢ ἐν ἡμίσει ἥμισυ, ἢ τὸ ἥμισυ (= ὑπὸ τῆς ἡμισείας) ἐν διπλασίῳ, and understood it to mean 'It does not follow that ½ A will change ½ B by amount C in time ½ D (nonsense) or change B by amount ½ C in time ½ D (nonsense); otherwise (ἢ) ½ A will change B by amount C in 2 D; (and this will not do,) for the half-force may

or	A alters	B to a degree	$\frac{1}{2}$ C	in time	$\frac{1}{2}$ D
and	A ,,	2 B	,,	C ,,	2 D
while	A ,,	$\frac{1}{2}$ B	,,	C ,,	$\frac{1}{2}$ D
or	A ,,	$\frac{1}{2}$ B	,,	2 C ,,	D.[a]

If, on the other hand, there is a force A causing alteration or growth, and if

	A alters	B to a degree	C	in time	D
and	A ,,	$\frac{1}{2}$ B	,,	C ,,	$\frac{1}{2}$ D
or	A ,,	B	,,	$\frac{1}{2}$ C ,,	$\frac{1}{2}$ D,

it does not necessarily follow that $\frac{1}{2}$ A will alter B to a degree C in 2 D,[b] but it may well happen that $\frac{1}{2}$ A will effect no change or growth whatever, just as in the case of the load.

[a] [With the transposition made in the text the sentence becomes logical, and the use of ἤ (not καί, twice) correctly indicates alternative effects that may happen to the same subject. To make the statement symmetrical and complete, it would be necessary to add (after καὶ τὸ διπλάσιον ἐν διπλασίῳ) ἤ ἐν ἴσῳ ἥμισυ, i.e. '2 B will be altered $\frac{1}{2}$ C in D.' But the omission may be Aristotle's.—C.]

[b] [Nor, it might be added, will $\frac{1}{2}$ A necessarily alter B by amount $\frac{1}{2}$ C in time D (=ἤ ἐν ἴσῳ ἥμισυ). (Cf. above, 250 a 10.)—C.]

not be able to change the whole B at all.' This is still nonsense, but may be taken as evidence for the existence of the words ἤ τὸ ἥμισυ ἐν διπλασίῳ, which are not in our MSS. These words (with καί for ἤ), if placed after ἀνάγκη, express what is wanted—a consequence that might be expected, but does not necessarily follow. My correction assumes that they have been ousted by the other clauses, καὶ τὸ ἥμισυ ἐν ἡμίσει ἤ ἐν ἡμίσει ἥμισυ, which, placed after ἀλλοιοῖ, make sense that is both good and relevant to the argument. The last clause might be completed thus: οὐκ ἀνάγκη καὶ τὸ ἥμισυ ἐν διπλασίῳ ἤ ἐν ἴσῳ ἥμισυ, but the last four words are not represented in Simplicius.—C.]

BOOK VIII

INTRODUCTION

[This Book leads up to the conclusion that all change and motion in the universe are ultimately caused by a Prime Mover that is itself unchanging and unmoved and is not dimensional.

Chapter I. proves that motion in the universe is eternal : there can never have been a time before any motion existed, and there never will be a time when all motion will have ceased. Some objections are answered in Chapter II., especially the objection that animals in a state of rest can make a clear beginning of motion in themselves by the self-moving power of the soul : so why should not the universe, if we suppose it animate, have passed at some moment from rest to motion ? This apparent self-motion of animals is really caused from without.

But the problem remains: how is it that transition from rest to motion or from motion to rest does occur ? In Chapter III. theories which deny this obvious fact are refuted, and Aristotle undertakes to establish that some things are always in motion, some things always at rest, and some can either move or rest.

The demonstration occupies the next three chapters. Chapter IV. proves that the primary agent of any motion or change is distinguishable from the primary patient. But there cannot be an unlimited series of things, each of which is moved by the one before it and moves the one after it. The series must terminate in an original

PHYSICS, VIII. INTRODUCTION

agent that is either unmoved or self-moved; and when
we analyse 'self-motion' we find that it involves an unmoved agent. Hence the primary agent of all motion
is unmoved (Chapter V.). If, as we have proved, there
is eternal motion, there must be at least one eternal
unmoved mover, and it is superfluous to assume more
than one. In seeking for the Prime Cause of motion,
'continuous' (i.e. everlasting, uninterrupted, and uniform)
movements and also varying and intermittent movements
must be taken into account. In each case the one eternal
and unmoved agent is shown to be the cause. It causes
the uniform proper movements and the regular but not
uniform derivative and compound movements of the
heavenly bodies; and also, through a chain of celestial
and terrestrial intermediaries, the variable and intermittent movements of terrestrial things (Chapter VI.).

Chapter VII. makes a fresh start. The motion caused
by the primary mover must be both prior to all other
forms of change and such that it can continue for ever.
Locomotion is the only form of change which satisfies
both conditions. Chapters VIII. and IX. add that, of
all species of locomotion, rotation is the only one that
can be everlasting and continuous. This conclusion is
supported by the testimony of all earlier philosophers.

Chapter X. reaches the final conclusion that, since the
Prime Mover cannot be either a finite or an infinite
magnitude, it is not a magnitude at all and has no parts,
but is immaterial and not in space, though its operation
is directly *felt* at the circumference of the universe.—C.]

Θ

CHAPTER I

ARGUMENT

[*Do motion and change exist at all times, or had they a beginning and will they have an end ? (250 b 11–15).*

All physicists (as opposed to the Eleatics) admit the existence of motion. The Atomists hold it to be everlasting, for they believe in innumerable cosmoi always coming into existence and perishing. Of believers in a single cosmos, some hold that the cosmos and motion had no beginning in time ; some (Anaxagoras) that they began at some moment after an indefinite duration of motionlessness ; others (Empedocles) that periods in which a cosmos and motion exist alternate with periods of motionlessness (b 15–251 a 8).

Motion being the actualizing of a potential movable, there must be movables if there is to be actual motion ; but we cannot suppose that they existed in a state of immobility up to a moment when motion or change began. Suppose they did so, they must either (a) have come into being or (b) have been ungenerated (a 8–17). If (a), then their coming into being was itself a change ; so we should have a change earlier than the first change (a 17–20). If

250 b 11 Πότερον δὲ γέγονέ ποτε κίνησις οὐκ οὖσα πρότερον, καὶ φθείρεται πάλιν οὕτως ὥστε κινεῖσθαι μηδέν, ἢ οὔτ᾽ ἐγένετο οὔτε φθείρεται ἀλλ᾽ ἀεὶ ἦν καὶ ἀεὶ

266

BOOK VIII

CHAPTER I

ARGUMENT (*continued*)

(*b*), *some change must have occurred to release them from immobility—again a change before the first change* (a 20–28); *for the withdrawal of a negative hindrance is a change, which converts what merely ' has the possibility ' of movement into something ' actually able ' to move* (a 28–b 10). *Also there could not ever be a time when there is no motion, because time is defined as the measure of motion* (b 10–28).

By the same reasoning it is impossible to conceive in the future a time after all motion has ceased. Motion is, therefore, everlasting (b 28–252 a 5).

Empedocles' alternate periods of motion and rest do at least provide for some order in natural changes, such as is lacking in Anaxagoras. But Empedocles fails to account for the alternation. Democritus too does not account for motion when he simply declares it to be an eternal fact (a 5–b 5).

So much in proof that there never was nor will be a time without motion (b 5–6).—C.]

DID motion itself ever come into existence, never having been before? And will it in like manner cease to be, so that nothing will move thereafter? Or did it never begin to be and will it never cease to be, so that there always has been and always will

267

250 b ἔσται, καὶ τοῦτ' ἀθάνατον καὶ ἄπαυστον ὑπάρχει
15 τοῖς οὖσιν, οἷον ζωή τις οὖσα τοῖς φύσει συνεστῶσι
πᾶσιν;

Εἶναι μὲν οὖν κίνησιν πάντες φασὶν οἱ περὶ
φύσεώς τι λέγοντες, διὰ τὸ κοσμοποιεῖν καὶ περὶ
γενέσεως καὶ φθορᾶς εἶναι τὴν θεωρίαν πᾶσιν
αὐτοῖς, ἣν ἀδύνατον ὑπάρχειν μὴ κινήσεως οὔσης.
20 ἀλλ' ὅσοι μὲν ἀπείρους τε κόσμους εἶναί φασι καὶ
τοὺς μὲν γίγνεσθαι τοὺς δὲ φθείρεσθαι τῶν κόσμων,
ἀεί φασιν εἶναι κίνησιν (ἀναγκαῖον γὰρ τὰς γενέσεις
καὶ τὰς φθορὰς εἶναι μετὰ κινήσεως αὐτῶν)· ὅσοι
δὲ ἕνα ἢ μὴ ἀεί,[1] καὶ περὶ τῆς κινήσεως ὑποτίθενται
κατὰ λόγον.

Εἰ δὴ ἐνδέχεταί ποτε μηδὲν κινεῖσθαι, διχῶς
ἀνάγκη τοῦτο συμβαίνειν· ἢ γὰρ ὡς Ἀναξαγόρας
25 λέγει (φησὶ γὰρ ἐκεῖνος, ὁμοῦ πάντων ὄντων καὶ
ἠρεμούντων τὸν ἄπειρον χρόνον, κίνησιν ἐμποιῆσαι
τὸν Νοῦν καὶ διακρῖναι) ἢ ὡς Ἐμπεδοκλῆς, ἐν μέρει
κινεῖσθαι καὶ πάλιν ἠρεμεῖν—κινεῖσθαι μὲν ὅταν ἡ
Φιλία ἐκ πολλῶν ποιῇ τὸ ἓν ἢ τὸ Νεῖκος πολλὰ

---

[1] [ἕνα ἢ μὴ ἀεί. The Oxf. Trans. infers that Themistius
read ἕνα ἢ ἀεί ἢ μὴ ἀεί 'one world whether everlasting or
not.'—C.]

---

[a] [The Atomists, Leucippus and Democritus, whose view
was adopted, after Aristotle's time, by Epicurus. There
is, in my opinion, no satisfactory evidence for this doctrine
being held by any other Pre-Socratic school. Cf. " Innumerable Worlds in Pre-Socratic Philosophy," *Class. Quarterly*,
Jan. 1934.—C.]

[b] [Believers in a single cosmos (all except the Atomists)
fall into three classes : (a) Heracleitus and Aristotle himself,
who believed in a single cosmos having no beginning or
end in time. So, it is generally held, did Plato, though in
the *Timaeus* he describes in mythical form a generation of
the cosmos. For these motion had no beginning in time;

268

be motion, belonging to all things as their deathless and never-failing property and constituting a kind of life for everything that is constituted by nature ?

To begin with, all who have discoursed on nature admit that there is such a thing as motion. And so they must, since they are all of them concerned with the formation of the cosmos and the genesis of things and their evanishment, which could not be at all were there no movement. But whereas those *a* who believe in innumerable cosmoi, some coming into being and others passing out of it, say that motion is ever-existing, for the genesis and evanishment of these cosmoi must needs involve motion, those, on the other hand, who believe that there is a single cosmos, and perhaps that there is not always a cosmos in existence,*b* hold views as to motion consonant with their general theory.

Now if it is possible that there should ever be a complete absence of motion it can only be conceived in one of the two ways set forth respectively by Anaxagoras and Empedocles. The former holds that, all things having remained congested and motionless for an unlimited period, ' Mind ' imposed motion upon them and separated them out ; whereas Empedocles conceived of alternations between movement and its absence, holding that things are in motion when ' attraction ' is drawing them into unity from plurality or ' repulsion ' is thrusting them

(*b*) Anaxagoras and others, who held that our cosmos is the only one that has ever existed, but that it had a beginning in time, and (*c*) Empedocles, who had a series of single cosmoi separated by intervals in which no cosmos or motion exists. For the last two classes there is ' not always a cosmos ' and they have (*b*) one or (*c*) more beginnings of motion in time.—C.]

250 b ἐξ ἑνός, ἠρεμεῖν δὲ ἐν τοῖς μεταξὺ χρόνοις, λέγων
οὕτως,

30   ᾗ μὲν ἓν ἐκ πλεόνων μεμάθηκε φύεσθαι
      ἠδὲ πάλιν διαφύντος ἑνὸς πλέον' ἐκτελέθουσι,
251 a   τῇ μὲν γίγνονταί τε καὶ οὔ σφισιν ἔμπεδος αἰών·
       ᾗ δὲ τάδ' ἀλλάσσοντα διαμπερὲς οὐδαμὰ λήγει,
       ταύτῃ δ' αἰὲν ἔασιν ἀκίνητοι κατὰ κύκλον·[1]

το γὰρ ' ᾗ δὲ τάδ' ἀλλάσσοντα ' ἐνθένδε ἐκεῖσε λέγειν
5 αὐτὸν ὑποληπτέον.[2] σκεπτέον δὴ περὶ τούτων πῶς
ἔχει· πρὸ ἔργου γὰρ οὐ μόνον πρὸς τὴν περὶ φύσεως θεωρίαν ἰδεῖν τὴν ἀλήθειαν, ἀλλὰ καὶ πρὸς τὴν
μέθοδον τὴν περὶ τῆς ἀρχῆς τῆς πρώτης.
    Ἀρξώμεθα δὲ πρῶτον ἐκ τῶν διωρισμένων ἡμῖν
ἐν τοῖς Φυσικοῖς πρότερον. φαμὲν δὴ τὴν κίνησιν
10 εἶναι ἐντελέχειαν τοῦ κινητοῦ ᾗ κινητόν. ἀναγ-

---

[1] [Empedocles, frag. 26. 8 ff. Cf. frag. 17. 9 ff., where
the same lines are repeated with διαλλάσσοντα (which appears
in FI here) for ᾗ δ' ἀλλάσσοντα. Though the first line quoted
began with οὕτως, the οὕτως in our text may belong to
Aristotle (with λέγων).—C.]

[2] [τὸ γὰρ ᾗ δὲ (τῆδε FI) τάδ' ἀλλάσσοντα (διαλάσσοντα I)
ἐνθένδε . . . ὑποληπτέον FHII Oxf. Trans.: δεῖ γὰρ ὑπολαβεῖν
λέγειν αὐτὸν ᾗ δὲ τάδ' ἐνθένδε τὰ ἀλλάσσοντα cett., Bekker,
Prantl.—C.]

---

a [We must distinguish (a) what Empedocles meant in
these lines and (b) what Aristotle makes them mean.
    (a) Empedocles had a cycle of 4 periods. In (1) the Reign
of Love and (3) the Reign of Strife, no cosmos or motion
exists. In (2) and (4) cosmoi are formed by the operation
respectively of Strife breaking the ' one ' into ' many '
and Love drawing the ' many ' into ' one.' These lines
answer the question : In what sense are the four immutable
elements (Earth, Water, Air, Fire) involved in a process of
' becoming ' ? The answer is : in so far as (by their motion,

270

into plurality from unity, but that all is motionless in the intermediate periods. These are his words :

" In as far as the one is wont to spring out of the many, and reversely the many to rise out of the dis-integrating one, in so far they ' become ' and their life is not stable ; but inasmuch as the succession of these reversals never comes to an end at all, there is always a periodical recurrence of the motion-less state."

For we must understand him to be speaking of the reversals from the one process to the other.[a] So we must look into this question of whether there was a beginning of motion ; for it is worth while to get at the truth not only with a view to our specula-tions as to nature, but also for its bearing on our study of the first principle.

Let us start from the points established in the earlier part of our Physics. We said [b] that motion is the actualizing of the potentiality of the mobile as

rushing through one another and combining to form various substances, inorganic or organic) they *come to be* a formed world, in so far they may be said to ' become ' and change (' their life is not stable ') ; but the elements themselves do not *come into being* or change but ' in so far as they *never cease* in their perpetual alternation, in that sense they *exist for ever unchangeable* (ἀκίνητοι) in their cycle.' There is no reference to the motionless conditions (1) and (3).

(b) But Aristotle, with his usual carelessness in quoting the Pre-Socratics, apparently takes the last two lines as containing such a reference. The translation above is intended to convey this false construction (which the words will hardly bear), justified by Aristotle in the following sentence : ' For by the expression " in so far as these alter-nating, etc." we must take Empedocles to mean " alter-nating from the one process of world-formation to the other." '—C.]

[b] [At Book III. chap. i., 201 a 10.—C.]

251 a καίον ἄρα ὑπάρχειν τὰ πράγματα τὰ δυνάμενα
κινεῖσθαι καθ᾽ ἑκάστην κίνησιν. καὶ χωρὶς δὲ τοῦ
τῆς κινήσεως ὁρισμοῦ, πᾶς ἂν ὁμολογήσειεν ἀναγκαῖον εἶναι κινεῖσθαι τὸ δυνατὸν κινεῖσθαι καθ᾽
15 ἑκάστην κίνησιν—οἷον ἀλλοιοῦσθαι μὲν τὸ ἀλλοιω-
τόν, φέρεσθαι δὲ τὸ κατὰ τόπον μεταβλητόν—ὥστε
δεῖ πρότερον καυστὸν εἶναι πρὶν κάεσθαι, καὶ
καυστικὸν πρὶν κάειν. οὐκοῦν καὶ ταῦτα ἀναγκαῖον
ἢ γενέσθαι ποτὲ οὐκ ὄντα ἢ ἀΐδια εἶναι.

Εἰ μὲν τοίνυν ἐγένετο τῶν κινητῶν ἕκαστον,
20 ἀναγκαῖον πρότερον τῆς ληφθείσης ἄλλην γενέσθαι
μεταβολὴν καὶ κίνησιν, καθ᾽ ἣν ἐγένετο τὸ δυνατὸν
κινηθῆναι ἢ κινῆσαι.

Εἰ δ᾽ ὄντα προυπῆρχεν ἀεὶ κινήσεως μὴ οὔσης,
ἄλογον μὲν φαίνεται καὶ αὐτόθεν ἐπιστήσασιν, οὐ
μὴν ἀλλὰ μᾶλλον ἔτι προιοῦσι τοῦτο συμβαίνειν
ἀναγκαῖον. εἰ γάρ, τῶν μὲν κινητῶν ὄντων τῶν
25 δὲ κινητικῶν, ὁτὲ μὲν ἔσται τι πρῶτον κινοῦν τὸ
δὲ κινούμενον, ὁτὲ δὲ οὐδὲν ἀλλ᾽ ἠρεμεῖ, ἀναγκαῖον

* Each of these being a kind of motion, for they are
qualitive modifications of their material.
272

such. The necessary presupposition of motion of any kind, then, is that things capable of motion of that kind should already be in existence. And apart from the definition, everyone would admit that what is in motion must be that which is capable of movement in the particular sense of the word in point—if the movement of modification, then the modifiable, if of transference that which is capable of changing its place—so that there must be something combustible before there can be combustion and something that can burn before there can be burning.[a] And so these things capable of movement either (a) must have come into existence at a definite moment, not previously having been there, or (b) must always be there eternally.

Now if (a) every one of these 'movables' came into existence, there must have been some other change or movement, prior to the one under consideration, which prior movement marked the coming into existence of this very object, capable of experiencing or causing movement, which we have seen must itself be prior to movement.

On the other hand to suppose (b) that entities capable of being moved and agents capable of moving them had been in existence from everlasting but that no motion had taken place, will at once strike anyone who thinks as unreasonable, and when he goes on to examine it the irrationality will become clearer yet. For if we are to suppose that there was a time when the potentially-moved and potential movers were in existence but all was at rest and no movement took place, and then there came a time when first some potential mover actually moved something movable, there must necessarily have been

ARISTOTLE

251 a τοῦτο μεταβάλλειν πρότερον· ἦν γάρ τι αἴτιον τῆς
ἠρεμίας, ἡ γὰρ ἠρέμησις στέρησις τῆς κινήσεως.
ὥστε πρὸ τῆς πρώτης μεταβολῆς ἔσται μεταβολὴ
προτέρα.

Τὰ μὲν γὰρ κινεῖ μοναχῶς, τὰ δὲ καὶ τὰς ἐναντίας
30 κινήσεις, οἷον τὸ μὲν πῦρ θερμαίνει ψύχει δ' οὔ,
ἡ δὲ ἐπιστήμη δοκεῖ τῶν ἐναντίων εἶναι μία.
φαίνεται μὲν οὖν κἀκεῖ τι εἶναι ὁμοιότροπον· τὸ
γὰρ ψυχρὸν θερμαίνει στραφέν πως καὶ ἀπελθόν,
ὥσπερ καὶ ἁμαρτάνει ἑκὼν ὁ ἐπιστήμων ὅταν
251 b ἀνάπαλιν χρήσηται τῇ ἐπιστήμῃ. ἀλλ' οὖν ὅσα
γε δυνατὰ ποιεῖν καὶ πάσχειν ἢ κινεῖν, τὰ δὲ
κινεῖσθαι, οὐ πάντως δυνατά ἐστιν ἀλλ' ὡδὶ ἔχοντα

---

a [*Literally*, ' this (τοῦτο, *i.e.* the subject of ἠρεμεῖ, the
movable which was at rest before actual motion started)
must previously have been in process of change ' : something
must have happened to it, to release it from arrest. If
the potential agent and patient were previously too far
apart for one to move the other, they must have come
nearer ; if there was some obstacle, it must have been removed (Themistius).—C.]

b [This paragraph justifies the rather paradoxical assertion that the potential agents and patients cannot suddenly
pass from immobility to exercise of their activity without
some previous change, viz. the removal of some ' cause '
of arrest. It is true that some ' powers ' (δυνάμεις) capable
of causing change can positively cause change only in one
direction (fire can only heat, snow can only cool) ; but
negatively they can cause change the other way : snow
causes warmth by its removal. So the presence of a mere
negative obstacle to action can be said to ' cause ' the arrest
and its withdrawal to ' cause ' the action so released.—C.]

c The commentators instance a physician who should
destroy a man's health or the dialectician who should pur-

274

some antecedent change.[a] For there must have been
some cause of that stopping short of actual motion
which constitutes being at rest ; so before motion
could take place, there must have been some change
which prevented that cause from any longer hinder-
ing motion. Thus before the supposed first change
there must have been another change.

[b] For some moving principles can only cause movement in one direction, while others can reverse the
direction of their action : thus fire can heat but
cannot chill, whereas it seems that one and the same
mental skill may act in opposite directions. There
appears, however, to be something analogous to this
reverse action even in the former class, since coldness
may cause warmth by turning away and departing,
just as the expert may do mischief on purpose if he
reverse the direction in which to exercise his skill.[c]
At any rate,[d] nothing that ' has the possibility ' of
producing motion or of being moved or, more generally, of acting or being acted on, can actualize these
potentialities under all circumstances but only when
they are suitably disposed and approximated to each

posely give currency to false beliefs. [Aristotle alludes,
in particular, to the paradoxical conclusion of the argument
between Socrates and Hippias in the *Hippias Minor* of
Plato, p. 376 в ὁ ἄρα ἑκὼν ἁμαρτάνων . . . εἴπερ τίς ἐστιν
οὗτος, οὐκ ἂν ἄλλος εἴη ἢ ὁ ἀγαθός (= ὁ ἐπιστήμων).—C.]

[d] [It is now explained that to describe our potential
movers and moved in the supposed previous condition of
rest as ' capable ' (δυνατά) of moving or being moved is to
use an ambiguous phrase. They may not be ' actually
able ' (δυνάμενα) to move or be moved unless some arresting
cause is withdrawn. So we justify the *reductio ad absurdum*
that a change—the withdrawal of the hindrance—would
have to occur before the (*ex hypothesi*) first actual motion
could occur.—C.]

251 b καὶ πλησιάζοντα ἀλλήλοις. ὥσθ᾽ ὅταν πλησιάσῃ
κινεῖ, τὸ δὲ κινεῖται, καὶ ὅταν ὑπάρξῃ ὡς ἦν[1] τὸ
5 μὲν κινητικὸν τὸ δὲ κινητόν. εἰ τοίνυν μὴ ἀεὶ
ἐκινεῖτο, δῆλον ὡς οὐχ οὕτως εἶχον ὡς ἦν δυνάμενα τὸ μὲν κινεῖσθαι τὸ δὲ κινεῖν, ἀλλ᾽ ἔδει μεταβάλλειν θάτερον αὐτῶν· ἀνάγκη γὰρ ἐν τοῖς πρός
τι τοῦτο συμβαίνειν, οἷον εἰ μὴ ὂν διπλάσιον νῦν
διπλάσιον, μεταβάλλειν, εἰ μὴ ἀμφότερα, θάτερον.
10 ἔσται ἄρα τις προτέρα μεταβολὴ τῆς πρώτης.

Πρὸς δὲ τούτοις, τὸ πρότερον καὶ ὕστερον πῶς
ἔσται, χρόνου μὴ ὄντος, ἢ ὁ χρόνος, μὴ οὔσης
κινήσεως; εἰ δή ἐστιν ὁ χρόνος κινήσεως ἀριθμὸς
ἢ κίνησίς τις, εἴπερ ἀεὶ χρόνος ἔστιν, ἀνάγκη καὶ
κίνησιν ἀΐδιον εἶναι. ἀλλὰ μὴν περί γε χρόνου,
15 ἔξω ἑνός, ὁμονοητικῶς ἔχοντες φαίνονται πάντες·
ἀγένητον γὰρ εἶναι λέγουσι. καὶ διὰ τοῦτο Δημό-
κριτός γε δείκνυσιν ὡς ἀδύνατον ἅπαντα γεγο-
νέναι· τὸν γὰρ χρόνον ἀγένητον εἶναι. Πλάτων
δ᾽ αὐτὸν γεννᾷ μόνος· ἅμα μὲν γὰρ αὐτὸν τῷ
οὐρανῷ γεγονέναι, τὸν δὲ οὐρανὸν γεγονέναι φησίν.
20 εἰ οὖν ἀδύνατόν ἐστι καὶ εἶναι καὶ νοῆσαι χρόνον
ἄνευ τοῦ νῦν, τὸ δὲ νῦν ἐστι μεσότης τις καὶ ἀρχὴν
καὶ τελευτὴν ἔχον ἅμα—ἀρχὴν μὲν τοῦ ἐσομένου
χρόνου, τελευτὴν δὲ τοῦ παρελθόντος—ἀνάγκη ἀεὶ
εἶναι χρόνον· τὸ γὰρ ἔσχατον τοῦ τελευταίου

---

[1] [ὡς ἦν E Oxf. Trans.: ὡς εἶναι cett.—C.]

[a] Compare the definition of time in Book IV. 219 b 3 ff.
[b] [*Timaeus* 38 B. But Plato's own followers maintained
that he was here using the language of ' myth ' and really
regarded the visible universe and time as having no beginning.
—C.]

other. Motion takes place, then, when there exists
a mobile and a potential motor and they are so
approximated that the one really is able to act and
the other to be acted on. So if they had been there
eternally but without motion, it must obviously
have been because they were not in such relations
as to make them *actually able* to cause motion or
to be moved. For motion to supervene, therefore,
it must be necessary that one or the other should
experience a change, for this must be so where we are
dealing with any pair of related factors—for instance
if A is now twice B and was not so before, either one
or both must have changed. So there would have
to be a change anterior to the supposed first change.

And besides this, how could there be any before or
after at all if time were not, or time itself be if there
were no motion ? For surely if time is the numerical
aspect of movement [a] or is itself a movement, it
follows that, if there has always been time, there
must always have been movement ; and as to that
it seems that, with a single exception, all thinkers
agree that time never came into existence but was
always there. It is thus that Democritus shows how
impossible it is that everything can have had an
origin — because time has not. (Plato alone assigns
an origin to time, for he says it came into existence
simultaneously with the universe [b] and he assigns
an origin to that). Well then, if it is impossible for
time to exist or to be conceived without the 'present now,' and if this 'now' is a kind of midmostness,
which combines beginning and end—the beginning,
to wit, of future and the end of past time—then there
must always have been time ; for however far back

ARISTOTLE

251 b λῃφθέντος χρόνου ἔν τινι τῶν νῦν ἔσται (οὐδὲν γὰρ
25 ἔστι λαβεῖν ἐν τῷ χρόνῳ παρὰ τὸ νῦν), ὥστε ἐπεί
ἐστιν ἀρχή τε καὶ τελευτὴ τὸ νῦν, ἀνάγκη αὐτοῦ
ἐπ᾿ ἀμφότερα εἶναι ἀεὶ χρόνον. ἀλλὰ μὴν εἴγε
χρόνον, φανερὸν ὅτι ἀνάγκη εἶναι καὶ κίνησιν,
εἴπερ ὁ χρόνος πάθος τι κινήσεως.

Ὁ δ᾿ αὐτὸς λόγος καὶ περὶ τοῦ ἄφθαρτον εἶναι
30 τὴν κίνησιν. καθάπερ γὰρ ἐπὶ τοῦ γενέσθαι κίνησιν συνέβαινε προτέραν εἶναί τινα μεταβολὴν τῆς
πρώτης· οὕτως ἐνταῦθα ὑστέραν τῆς τελευταίας·
οὐ γὰρ ἅμα παύεται κινούμενον καὶ κινητὸν ὂν
(οἷον καόμενον καὶ καυστὸν ὄν, ἐνδέχεται γὰρ
252 a καυστὸν εἶναι μὴ καόμενον) οὐδὲ κινητικὸν καὶ
κινοῦν. καὶ τὸ φθαρτικὸν[1] δὲ δεήσει φθαρῆναι,
ὅταν φθαρῇ, καὶ τὸ τούτου φθαρτικὸν πάλιν ὕστερον·
καὶ γὰρ ἡ φθορὰ μεταβολή τίς ἐστιν. εἰ δὴ ταῦτ᾿

---

[1] [φθαρτικὸν EK Simplic,: φθαρτὸν cett.—C.]

[a] [The reading is uncertain and the argument obscure.
The previous argument about genesis (251 a 16 ff.) was a
dilemma. The corresponding dilemma here would be as
follows : if there will ever be a time when there is no motion
or change, then the things capable of causing or suffering
change (τὰ κινητικὰ καὶ κινητά) must either (a) perish after
the last change has occurred or (b) endure unchanged for
ever. Both suppositions should lead to an impossibility,
viz. a change (destruction) occurring after what is *ex hypothesi*
the last change.

The sentence οὐ γὰρ ἅμα παύεται κτλ. seems to refer to
supposition (a) and to mean that ceasing to be (or to exist
as) a thing *capable* of causing or suffering change (τὸ παύεσθαι
κινητικὸν ἢ κινητὸν ὄν) is a change that will have to follow
ceasing to be a thing that is *actually* causing or suffering
change (τὸ παύεσθαι κινοῦν ἢ κινούμενον), *i.e.* the ceasing-
to-be of potential agents and patients of change will be a
change later than the last actual change they cause or suffer.

Does this sentence also prove the impossibility of the

278

you go in time past, the extreme limit you take must be a certain 'now' (for in time there is nothing else to take except a 'now'), and since every now is an end as well as a beginning, it follows that time stretches from it in both directions. And if time, then motion, inasmuch as time is but an aspect or affection of motion.

The same line of argument further shows that movement is imperishable. For as we have seen that if we suppose movement to have had an origin we shall have to suppose that there was a change anterior to the first change, so also if we suppose it to cease we shall have to admit a change posterior to the last change. For what is movable does not cease to be movable because it is no longer being moved, nor does that which is capable of causing motion cease to have that capacity because it is not moving anything ; for instance the combustible if it is not being burnt (for it may still be combustible all the same) or the potential agent of local shifting when it is shifting nothing. And so, if all the destructible were destroyed that would not destroy the destroying agent, which would remain for destruction in its turn, and when it was destroyed its destroyer would remain ; and being destroyed is a kind of change.[a]

alternative supposition (b) : that the potential agents and patients should endure unchanged for ever ? Can it mean that the shift from being ' actually able ' to cause and suffer change to perpetual immobility could only be effected by some change that rendered agents and patients permanently incapable of affecting one another—e.g. put them out of range (cf. 251 b 1 ff.)—and this would be a change in their condition coming later than the last change ? Then the ambiguous phrase τὸ ⟨παύεσθαι κινητικὸν ἢ κινητὸν ὄν would mean (not being simply blotted out, but) ' ceasing to be things actually capable of causing or suffering change.'

Unless we interpret so, alternative (b) seems to be ignored,

ARISTOTLE

252 a ἀδύνατα, δῆλον ὡς ἔστιν ἀίδιος κίνησις, ἀλλ' οὐχ
5 ὁτὲ μὲν ἦν ὁτὲ δ' οὔ· καὶ γὰρ ἔοικε τὸ οὕτω λέγειν
πλάσματι μᾶλλον.

Ὁμοίως δὲ καὶ τὸ λέγειν ὅτι πέφυκεν οὕτως
καὶ ταύτην δεῖ νομίζειν εἶναι ἀρχήν, ὅπερ ἔοικεν
Ἐμπεδοκλῆς ἂν εἰπεῖν, ὡς τὸ κρατεῖν καὶ κινεῖν
ἐν μέρει τὴν Φιλίαν καὶ τὸ Νεῖκος ὑπάρχει τοῖς
πράγμασιν ἐξ ἀνάγκης, ἠρεμεῖν δὲ τὸν μεταξὺ
10 χρόνον. τάχα δὲ καὶ οἱ μίαν ἀρχὴν ποιοῦντες,
ὥσπερ Ἀναξαγόρας, οὕτως ἂν εἴποιεν. ἀλλὰ μὴν
οὐδέν γε ἄτακτον τῶν φύσει καὶ κατὰ φύσιν· ἡ
γὰρ φύσις αἰτία πᾶσι τάξεως. τὸ δ' ἄπειρον πρὸς
τὸ ἄπειρον οὐδένα λόγον ἔχει· τάξις δὲ πᾶσα λόγος.
15 τὸ δ' ἄπειρον χρόνον ἠρεμεῖν, εἶτα κινηθῆναί ποτε,
τούτου δὲ μηδεμίαν εἶναι διαφοράν, ὅτι νῦν μᾶλλον
ἢ πρότερον, μηδ' αὖ τινα τάξιν ἔχειν, οὐκέτι
φύσεως ἔργον. ἢ γὰρ ἁπλῶς ἔχει τὸ φύσει καὶ
οὐχ ὁτὲ μὲν οὕτως ὁτὲ δὲ ἄλλως—οἷον τὸ πῦρ ἄνω
φύσει φέρεται καὶ οὐχ ὁτὲ μὲν ὁτὲ δὲ οὔ—ἢ λόγον
20 ἔχει τὸ μὴ ἁπλοῦν. διόπερ βέλτιον ὡς Ἐμπεδοκλῆς, κἂν εἴτις ἕτερος εἴρηκεν οὕτως ἔχειν, ἐν

---

for the next sentence καὶ τὸ φθαρτικόν, κτλ. cannot (with
any ms. reading) be construed as referring to it. It
appears to be an afterthought. If the κινητικά and κινητά are
to be either destroyed or reduced to permanent incapacity,
there must be something capable of destroying or immobiliz-
ing them (φθαρτικόν). ' And likewise that which is capable
of destroying them will have to perish after they are destroyed, and what is capable of destroying *it* will have to
perish in turn still later ; for perishing is a kind of change '
(and this change, or series of changes, will follow the last
change).—C.]

ᵃ For it is as good as saying there was a time when time

And if all this is impossible, it is evident that movement is eternal, and is not something which now was
and now was not. Indeed to assert the opposite is
very like a contradiction in terms.[a]

Nor does it help matters to say that that is how
things were made and that we must take that as a
principle, as Empedocles [b] seems to imply that the
alternating power of attraction and repulsion effectively to move things was always there of necessity
and the periods of rest between. And one may take
it that those who believe in one active principle
only, such as Anaxagoras, would take the same line.[c]
Well, but nothing natural or accordant with nature
is without order ; for nature is the universal determinant of order. And the unlimited bears no proportion to the unlimited, whereas all orderly succession implies proportion. Thus for there to be an
unlimited period of rest, and then at a certain point
for motion to supervene,[d] there being no principle of
distinction to determine its ' now ' from any previous
point, so that all orderly succession is excluded—
this, I say, by the mere statement is excluded from
the works of nature. For what is natural is either
absolute, not now thuswise and now otherwise (just
as fire always tends upwards, not sometimes so and
sometimes not) or, if not absolute, is determined by
some intelligible principle. Thus Empedocles (or
others who may adopt his theories) has the advantage

was not. For the exact meaning of πλάσμα cf. De caelo
289 a 6 and b 25.
    [b] [Empedocles, *frag.* 17. 29 ἐν δὲ μέρει κρατέουσι περι-
πλομένοιο χρόνοιο. *Cf. frag.* 26. 1.—C.]
    [c] Namely that that's how things were and there's an
end.
    [d] [The view attributed to Anaxagoras above, 250 b 24.—C.]

ARISTOTLE

252 a μέρει τὸ πᾶν ἠρεμεῖν καὶ κινεῖσθαι πάλιν· τάξιν
γὰρ ἤδη τιν' ἔχει τὸ τοιοῦτον. ἀλλὰ καὶ τοῦτο
δεῖ τὸν λέγοντα μὴ φάναι μόνον, ἀλλὰ καὶ τὴν
αἰτίαν αὐτοῦ λέγειν, καὶ μὴ τίθεσθαι μηδὲν μηδ'
25 ἀξιοῦν ἀξίωμ' ἄλογον, ἀλλ' ἢ ἐπαγωγὴν ἢ ἀπό-
δειξιν φέρειν. αὐτὰ μὲν γὰρ οὐκ αἴτια τὰ ὑπο-
τεθέντα, οὐδὲ τοῦτ' ἦν τὸ Φιλότητι ἢ Νείκει εἶναι,
ἀλλὰ τῆς μὲν τὸ συνάγειν τοῦ δὲ τὸ διακρίνειν·
εἰ δὲ προσοριεῖται τὸ ἐν μέρει, λεκτέον ἐφ' ὧν
οὕτως, ὥσπερ ὅτι ἔστι τι ὃ συνάγει τοὺς ἀνθρώ-
30 πους, ἡ φιλία, καὶ φεύγουσιν οἱ ἐχθροὶ ἀλλήλους·
τοῦτο γὰρ ὑποτίθεται καὶ ἐν τῷ ὅλῳ εἶναι· φαίνεται
γὰρ ἐπί τινων οὕτω. τὸ δὲ καὶ δι' ἴσων χρόνων
δεῖται λόγου τινός. ὅλως δὲ τὸ νομίζειν ἀρχὴν
εἶναι ταύτην ἱκανήν, ὅτι ἀεὶ ἢ ἔστιν οὕτως ἢ
γίγνεται, οὐκ ὀρθῶς ἔχει ὑπολαβεῖν. ἐφ' ὃ Δημό-
35 κριτος ἀνάγει τὰς περὶ φύσεως αἰτίας, ὡς οὕτω
252 b καὶ τὸ πρότερον ἐγίγνετο· τοῦ δὲ ἀεὶ οὐκ ἀξιοῖ
ἀρχὴν ζητεῖν, λέγων ἐπί τινων ὀρθῶς, ὅτι δ' ἐπὶ

---

[a] αἰτίαν, the word usually translated ' cause.'
[b] [And both these forces might operate simultaneously in a perpetual ' harmony of opposite tensions,' as in the system of Heracleitus. *Cf.* Plato, *Soph.* 242 E.—C.]
[c] [Empedocles, *frag.* 17. 21, does assert that the power of 'Love' at work among the physical elements is the same that is recognized as causing sexual union in living creatures. —C.]
[d] [*Cf.* Plut. *Strom.* 7 (Diels, *Dox.* 581) Δημόκριτος . . . μηδεμίαν ἀρχὴν ἔχειν τὰς αἰτίας τῶν νῦν γιγνομένων, ἄνωθεν δ' ὅλως ἐξ ἀπείρου χρόνου προκατέχεσθαι τῇ ἀνάγκῃ πάνθ' ἁπλῶς τὰ γεγονότα καὶ ἐόντα καὶ ἐσόμενα.—C.]

282

of Anaxagoras, in that he alternates cessation and recurrence of motion, for this at least gives us an ordered succession. But even so it is not enough for anyone to assert that this particular succession actually takes place unless he can point out its determining principle[a] : he must not lay down or claim as an axiom a groundless assumption; on the contrary he must produce some inductive or deductive proof of his assertion. Now the principles alleged by Empedocles do not in themselves determine an alternation of activities, nor is any such alternation included in the essential notion of either, since the action of one (attraction) is to draw together and of the other (repulsion) to thrust apart.[b] So that if you are to add an explanation of their alternation, you must give instances where such a thing occurs; just as you can show that there is such a thing as ' attraction ' because you can see men drawn together by it, and in like manner can see 'repulsion' at work when men mutually avoid each other, and since this obtains in some cases, you propose to apply it to the universe.[c] But even if you had shown that attraction and repulsion alternate, you would have to explain why each acts over an equal length of time. Nor yet (to take a more general ground) is it sound reasoning to conclude that you have reached a fundamental principle when you have shown that this or that always is, or always occurs, thus and no otherwise. Democritus, it is true, held it to be enough for the establishing of determining principles to have shown that this or that has been so in all former times,[d] and did not feel bound to seek any deeper principle behind what has always been. But this took him right in

252 b πάντων, οὐκ ὀρθῶς. καὶ γὰρ τὸ τρίγωνον ἔχει
δυσὶν ὀρθαῖς ἀεὶ τὰς γωνίας ἴσας, ἀλλ᾽ ὅμως ἔστι
τι τῆς ἀιδιότητος ταύτης ἕτερον αἴτιον· τῶν μέντοι
5 ἀρχῶν οὐκ ἔστιν ἕτερον αἴτιον, ἀιδίων οὐσῶν.

῞Οτι μὲν οὖν οὐδεὶς ἦν χρόνος, οὐδ᾽ ἔσται, ὅτε
κίνησις οὐκ ἦν ἢ οὐκ ἔσται, εἰρήσθω τοσαῦτα.

---

^a The property in question is not regarded as axiomatic but
as derived from a truth of higher order in which it is shown
to be involved.   This is not so with an axiom or first principle,
which cannot be proved at all but irresistibly asserts itself
as true on its own merits.

CHAPTER II

ARGUMENT

[*Three objections might be made to the doctrine of the previous chapter :* (1) *No change can be everlasting, since every
change is between extremes which put a limit to it ;* (2) *A
clear beginning of motion is seen in inanimate things which,
after being completely at rest, are set in motion ;* (3)
*Animals, completely at rest, can initiate motion in them-
selves, and why should not the same happen in the universe ?*
(252 b 7–28).   *These objections are replied to as follows :*
(1) *It is true that a single movement between opposites
cannot go on for ever ; but that does not exclude the possi-*

252 b 7 Τὰ δ᾽ ἐναντία τούτοις οὐ χαλεπὸν λύειν. δόξειε
δ᾽ ἂν ἐκ τῶν τοιῶνδε σκοποῦσιν ἐνδέχεσθαι μάλιστα
κίνησιν εἶναί ποτε μὴ οὖσαν ὅλως, πρῶτον μὲν
10 ὅτι οὐδεμία ἀίδιος μεταβολή· μεταβολὴ γὰρ ἅπασα

certain cases only, and not in all. For instance the angles of a triangle are always equal to two right angles, but a reason can be assigned for the eternity of this property that lies behind the fact itself.[a] But a first principle can have no such other cause behind it, since principles are eternal on their own merits.

Let this suffice to demonstrate that there never was nor will be a time when movement was not or will not be.

CHAPTER II

ARGUMENT (continued)

bility of any sort of continuous and eternal motion (b 28–253 a 2).

(2) *There is no difficulty in the motion of inanimate things being started by an external agent which comes into action. A more serious question is : why some things that are at rest are not always at rest and others that are in motion are not always in motion* (a 2–7).

(3) *The apparently self-originated motion of animals may be caused by changes in the environment or inside the body* (a 7–21).—C.]

THE arguments on the other side are not difficult to refute. The chief considerations that might lead one to think it possible for motion to start absolutely *de novo*, there having been no such thing before, are as follows. (1) It is said that no change can go

252 b πέφυκεν ἔκ τινος εἴς τι, ὥστε ἀνάγκη πάσης μεταβολῆς εἶναι πέρας τἀναντία ἐν οἷς γίγνεται, εἰς
ἄπειρον δὲ κινεῖσθαι μηδέν. ἔτι ὁρῶμεν ὅτι δυνατὸν κινηθῆναι μήτε κινούμενον μήτε ἔχον ἐν
ἑαυτῷ μηδεμίαν κίνησιν, οἷον ἐπὶ τῶν ἀψύχων
15 ὧν οὔτε μέρος οὐδὲν οὔτε τὸ ὅλον κινούμενον ἀλλ'
ἠρεμοῦν κινεῖταί ποτε· προσῆκε δὲ ἢ ἀεὶ κινεῖσθαι
ἢ μηδέποτε, εἴπερ μὴ γίγνεται οὐκ οὖσα. πολὺ
δὲ μάλιστα τὸ τοιοῦτον ἐπὶ τῶν ἐμψύχων εἶναι
φανερόν· οὐδεμιᾶς γὰρ ἐν ἡμῖν ἐνούσης κινήσεως
ἐνίοτε ἀλλ' ἡσυχάζοντες ὅμως κινούμεθά ποτε,[a]
20 καὶ ἐγγίνεται ἐν ἡμῖν ἐξ ἡμῶν αὐτῶν ἀρχὴ κινήσεως[1]
κἂν μηδὲν ἔξωθεν κινήσῃ. τοῦτο γὰρ ἐπὶ τῶν
ἀψύχων οὐχ ὁρῶμεν ὁμοίως, ἀλλ' ἀεί τι κινεῖ αὐτὰ
τῶν ἔξωθεν ἕτερον· τὸ δὲ ζῷον αὐτό φαμεν ἑαυτὸ
κινεῖν. ὥστ' εἴπερ ἠρεμεῖ ποτε πάμπαν, ἐν ἀκινήτῳ
κίνησις ἂν γένοιτο ἐξ αὐτοῦ καὶ οὐκ ἔξωθεν. εἰ
25 δ' ἐν ζῴῳ τοῦτο δυνατὸν γενέσθαι, τί κωλύει τὸ
αὐτὸ συμβῆναι καὶ κατὰ τὸ πᾶν; εἰ γὰρ ἐν μικρῷ
κόσμῳ γίγνεται, καὶ ἐν μεγάλῳ· καὶ εἰ ἐν τῷ

---

[1] [κινήσεως EK Prantl : κινήσεως ἐνίοτε cett. Bekker.—C.]

---

[a] [Or ' for sometimes, when we are still and no motion is
occurring in us, we none the less move at a given moment :
a motion begins in us which has its source in ourselves,
though nothing external may set us moving.' The self-
originated motion attributed to living things is described
in contrast with the passivity of the inanimate in the next
sentence.—C.]

[b] [Diels, *Vors.*[4] 55 B 34 accepts the evidence of the
Armenian philosopher David that Democritus spoke of

PHYSICS, VIII. 11.

on for ever ; for every change must needs be from
this to that, so that the extreme opposites in the
kind wherein the change occurs constitute a limit
that prevents the change extending indefinitely.
(2) Further, we see that things which are neither
in motion relatively to other things nor experience
internal movements within themselves can nevertheless be set in motion. This is the case with any
inanimate object which, being at rest and not in
motion as a whole or as to any of its parts, is set
moving at some definite moment ; whereas it ought
either to be eternally in motion or eternally at rest,
if motion cannot have a beginning of being. (3) But
far more important yet is the belief that in the case
of animate beings some such thing is actually in
evidence ; for (they say) when nothing is moving
within us, but all is still, we nevertheless find ourselves in motion at a given moment, and sometimes,
even though nothing *outside* us either sets us off,
the initiation of motion comes up in us out of ourselves.[a] Now this we never witness in inanimate
things, for it is always something other than and
outside themselves that moves them ; but we say
that a living thing moves itself. And, according to
this, if a living thing is ever absolutely at rest, we
shall have a motionless thing in which motion is
originated by the thing itself and not from without.
If this can happen to a living thing, why not to the
universe ? And if in a lesser cosmos,[b] why not in a
greater, and if in *the* cosmos, why not in the un-

man as a 'small world' or microcosm. G. P. Conger,
Theories of Macrocosms and Microcosms, New York (1922)
p. 6, casts doubt upon it as unsupported, and cites our
passage as the first authentic occurrence of the term, though
he recognizes that Aristotle must be quoting somebody.—C.]

287

252 b κόσμῳ, κἂν τῷ ἀπείρῳ, εἴπερ ἐνδέχεται κινεῖσθαι
τὸ ἄπειρον καὶ ἠρεμεῖν ὅλον.

Τούτων δὴ τὸ μὲν πρῶτον λεχθέν, τὸ μὴ τὴν αὐ-
30 τὴν ἀεὶ καὶ μίαν τῷ ἀριθμῷ εἶναι τὴν κίνησιν τὴν
εἰς τὰ ἀντικείμενα, ὀρθῶς λέγεται. τοῦτο μὲν γὰρ
ἴσως ἀναγκαῖον, εἴπερ μὴ ἀεὶ μίαν καὶ τὴν αὐτὴν
εἶναι δυνατὸν τὴν τοῦ αὐτοῦ καὶ ἑνὸς κίνησιν·
λέγω δ' οἷον πότερον τῆς μιᾶς χορδῆς εἷς καὶ ὁ αὐτὸς φθόγγος, ἢ ἀεὶ ἕτερος, ὁμοίως ἐχούσης καὶ κι-
35 νουμένης. ἀλλ' ὅμως, ὁποτέρως ποτ' ἔχει, οὐδὲν
253 a κωλύει τὴν αὐτὴν εἶναί τινα τῷ συνεχῆ εἶναι καὶ
ἀίδιον· δῆλον δ' ἔσται μᾶλλον ἐκ τῶν ὕστερον.

Τὸ δὲ κινεῖσθαι μὴ κινούμενον οὐδὲν ἄτοπον, ἐὰν
ὁτὲ μὲν ᾖ τὸ κινῆσαν ἔξωθεν, ὁτὲ δὲ μή. τοῦτο
μέντοι πῶς ἂν εἴη, ζητητέον—λέγω δὲ ὥστε τὸ
5 αὐτὸ ὑπὸ τοῦ αὐτοῦ κινητικοῦ ὄντος ὁτὲ μὲν
κινεῖσθαι ὁτὲ δὲ μή· οὐδὲν γὰρ ἄλλ' ἀπορεῖ ὁ
τοῦτο λέγων ἢ διὰ τί οὐκ ἀεὶ τὰ μὲν ἠρεμεῖ τῶν
ὄντων τὰ δὲ κινεῖται.

Μάλιστα δ' ἂν δόξειε τὸ τρίτον ἔχειν ἀπορίαν,

---

a [The unlimited mass of unordered matter, such as
figures in the systems of Anaximander, Anaximenes, Anaxagoras, before the cosmos arises.—C.]

b [Literally, ' This may be said to be an inevitable conclusion, provided it be possible for the motion of one and
the same thing to be not always one and the same motion.'
In Book V. chap. iv. (227 b 21 ff.) a movement was said to
be ' one and the same' when (1) the thing moved is one
and the same individual thing, (2) the motion of a kind
that cannot be subdivided into species, and (3) the time
unintermittent. The string of an instrument tuned to a
constant pitch (ὁμοίως ἐχούσης) and kept continuously in
vibration yields an apparently continuous sound. The
question Aristotle raises seems to be whether the motion
288

limited ?—if ' the unlimited ' [a] as a whole be susceptible of motion or rest.

Now as to (1), it is perfectly true that no identical and numerically single motion *from opposite to opposite* can go on for ever. [b] And this, I take it, would be conclusive if it were shown to be impossible for there to be *any* one and identical motion of an identical mobile.[c] I mean, the question may arise whether, if a vibrating chord be kept in uniform action between the limits of its vibration, the note produced is to be regarded as one and continuous or as a succession of separate sounds ; but whatever answer we give to this question it does not exclude the possibility of there being such a thing as motion, *not* from opposites to opposites, but continuously identical and so eternal. On this we shall get more light as we proceed.[d]

As to (2), we need not wonder that things pass from rest to motion when something that was not there before comes from outside to move them ; but what we have to ask is whether it is possible for the same mobile, when continuously within the range of the same motor, to pass at a certain time out of a previous state of rest into motion ; for he who asserts that it can is concerned with naught else than the question why things at rest are not at rest for ever, and those in motion in motion for ever.

So it seems that the most serious question is the

causing such a sound can be regarded as *not* ' one and the same,' though it may appear to conform to the above definition. It will be shown in chap. viii. that a vibratory movement is not a single continuous movement.—C.]

[c] Aristotle has in mind the rotation of a sphere. *Cf.* chap. viii.

[d] [In chap. viii.—C.]

253 a 10 ὡς ἐγγιγνομένης οὐκ ἐνούσης πρότερον κινήσεως,
τὸ συμβαῖνον ἐπὶ τῶν ἐμψύχων· ἠρεμοῦν γὰρ πρότερον μετὰ ταῦτα βαδίζει, κινήσαντος τῶν ἔξωθεν
οὐδενός, ὡς δοκεῖ. τοῦτο δ' ἐστὶ ψεῦδος. ὁρῶμεν
γὰρ ἀεί τι κινούμενον ἐν τῷ ζῴῳ τῶν συμφύτων·
15 τούτου δὲ τῆς κινήσεως οὐκ αὐτὸ τὸ ζῷον αἴτιον
ἀλλὰ τὸ περιέχον ἴσως. αὐτὸ δέ φαμεν ἑαυτὸ
κινεῖν οὐ πᾶσαν κίνησιν ἀλλὰ τὴν κατὰ τόπον.
οὐδὲν οὖν κωλύει, μᾶλλον δ' ἴσως ἀναγκαῖον, τῷ
σώματι πολλὰς ἐγγίγνεσθαι κινήσεις ὑπὸ τοῦ
περιέχοντος, τούτων δ' ἐνίας τὴν διάνοιαν ἢ τὴν
ὄρεξιν κινεῖν, ἐκείνην δὲ τὸ ὅλον ἤδη ζῷον κινεῖν—
20 ὁποῖον συμβαίνει περὶ τοὺς ὕπνους· αἰσθητικῆς
μὲν γὰρ οὐδεμιᾶς ἐνούσης κινήσεως, ἐνούσης μέντοι
τινός, ἐγείρεται τὰ ζῷα πάλιν. ἀλλὰ γὰρ φανερὸν
ἔσται καὶ περὶ τούτων ἐκ τῶν ἑπομένων.

---

a [The *De somno*, chap. iii., explains that sleep is caused
by ' the evaporation attendant on the process of nutrition,'
and that a person awakes when digestion is completed and
he is released from the heaviness consequent on taking food.
These are internal processes, not involving the perception of
any change in the external environment.—C.]

CHAPTER III

ARGUMENT

[*With a view to the problem, why some things are now at
rest, now in motion, we review all the possibilities :* (1)
All things always at rest, (2) *All things always in motion,*
(3) *Some things moving, others at rest; in which case either*
(a) *the things in motion are always in motion, those at*

PHYSICS, VIII. ii.–iii.

third (3), which asks : If motion never starts *de
novo* in that which was at rest, how are we to understand what takes place in animate creatures ? For
a quiescent animal starts walking when there seems
to be nothing outside it to produce the movement.
But this is just the mistake. For we observe that
motion is always going on in some organ of the living
creature, and the movement of such an organ is not
determined by the animal itself, but (as I take it)
by its environment. For when we say that an
animal 'moves itself' we are referring to local
movement and nothing else ; and it may well be,
or rather I would say it must be, that many movements within the body are determined by changes
in the environment, and some of these movements
prompt conceptions or impulses which in their turn
stir the whole animal. We can detect this in respect
to sleep, for it is at the prompting of some internal
motion (that must be there, though it is not a change
in any organ of perception) that sleeping animals
wake up again.[a] But here again more light will be
shed on the matter in the sequel.[b]

[b] [In chap. vi., 259 b 1 ff.—C.]

CHAPTER III

ARGUMENT (*continued*)

rest always at rest, or (b) *anything can be either moving or
at rest, or* (c) *some things are always moving, some always
at rest, others can either move or rest. This last alternative
we shall establish* (253 a 22–32).

(1) *To assert all things always at rest contradicts the
fundamental assumption of Physics* (a 32–b 6).

ARISTOTLE

(2) *It is held by some physicists that all things are always in motion, though it may not be perceptible. This can be refuted by taking the several kinds of movement separately* (b 6–254 a 3).

(3 a) *The view that there is nothing that is sometimes at rest and sometimes in motion denies obvious facts and can be refuted on similar grounds* (a 3–15).

253 a 22 Ἀρχὴ δὲ τῆς σκέψεως ἔσται ἥπερ καὶ περὶ τῆς λεχθείσης ἀπορίας, διὰ τί ποτε ἔνια τῶν ὄντων ὁτὲ μὲν κινεῖται ὁτὲ δὲ ἠρεμεῖ πάλιν.

25 Ἀνάγκη δ᾽ ἤτοι πάντα ἠρεμεῖν ἀεί, ἢ πάντ᾽ ἀεὶ κινεῖσθαι, ἢ τὰ μὲν κινεῖσθαι τὰ δὲ ἠρεμεῖν· καὶ πάλιν τούτων ἤτοι τὰ μὲν κινούμενα κινεῖσθαι ἀεὶ τὰ δ᾽ ἠρεμοῦντα ἠρεμεῖν, ἢ πάντα πεφυκέναι ὁμοίως κινεῖσθαι καὶ ἠρεμεῖν, ἢ τὸ λοιπὸν ἔτι καὶ τρίτον· ἐνδέχεται γὰρ τὰ μὲν ἀεὶ τῶν ὄντων ἀκίνητα

30 εἶναι, τὰ δ᾽ ἀεὶ κινούμενα, τὰ δ᾽ ἀμφοτέρων μεταλαμβάνειν. ὅπερ ἡμῖν λεκτέον ἐστίν· τοῦτο γὰρ ἔχει λύσιν τε πάντων τῶν ἀπορουμένων, καὶ τέλος ἡμῖν ταύτης τῆς πραγματείας ἐστίν.

Τὸ μὲν οὖν πάντ᾽ ἠρεμεῖν, καὶ τούτου ζητεῖν λόγον ἀφέντας τὴν αἴσθησιν, ἀρρωστία τίς ἐστι διανοίας, καὶ περὶ ὅλου τινὸς ἀλλ᾽ οὐ περὶ μέρους

35 ἀμφισβήτησις· οὐδὲ μόνον πρὸς τὸν φυσικόν, ἀλλὰ

ᵃ [Raised above, at 253 a 5.—C.]

ARGUMENT (*continued*)

*It appears, then, that at least some things are now in
motion, now at rest. It remains to consider whether
(3 b) this is true of all things, or (3 c) only of some,
while of the remainder some are always moving, some always
at rest. The alternatives are again reviewed, with a view
to establishing (3 c) (a 15–b 6).—C.]*

Now this very point [a]—why certain things are sometimes in motion and sometimes again at rest—is
the hinge on which the whole investigation we are
entering upon must turn.

One of three alternatives must necessarily be
accepted : either (1) everything is always at rest,
or (2) everything is always in motion, or (3) some
things are in motion and some at rest. And the
last of these alternatives, again, includes three
possibilities ; either (*a*) the things that move at all
are always moving, and the things that are ever at
rest are always at rest, or (*b*) everything is naturally
capable both of motion and rest, or (the only
alternative left), it may be possible (*c*) that there
are some things that never move at all, some that
are always in motion, and some that pass from one
state to the other ; and it is this last hypothesis
that we ourselves accept, for this alone solves all
the problems, and brings our whole business here to
a conclusion.

Well then (1) to adopt the thesis that all things
are at rest, and (ruling sense-perception out of court)
to attempt to prove it by reasoning, really amounts
to paralysing intelligence itself, and this not only
on the particular field in question but universally,
since it affects not Physics only but, if I may say so,

ARISTOTLE

253 b πρὸς πάσας τὰς ἐπιστήμας, ὡς εἰπεῖν, καὶ πάσας
τὰς δόξας, διὰ τὸ κινήσει χρῆσθαι πάσας. ἔτι δ᾽
αἱ περὶ τῶν ἀρχῶν ἐνστάσεις, ὥσπερ ἐν τοῖς περὶ
τὰ μαθήματα λόγοις οὐδέν εἰσι πρὸς τὸν μαθη-
ματικόν (ὁμοίως δὲ καὶ τῶν ἄλλων), οὕτως οὐδὲ
5 περὶ τοῦ νῦν ῥηθέντος πρὸς τὸν φυσικόν· ὑπόθεσις
γὰρ ὅτι ἡ φύσις ἀρχὴ τῆς κινήσεως.

Σχεδὸν δέ τι καὶ τὸ φάναι πάντα κινεῖσθαι ψεῦδος
μέν, ἧττον δὲ τούτου παρὰ τὴν μέθοδον· ἐτέθη μὲν
γὰρ ἡ φύσις ἐν τοῖς Φυσικοῖς ἀρχή, καθάπερ
κινήσεως, καὶ ἠρεμίας, ὅμως[1] δὲ φυσικὸν ⟨μᾶλλον⟩
10 ἡ κίνησις· καί φασί τινες κινεῖσθαι τῶν ὄντων οὐ
τὰ μὲν τὰ δ᾽ οὔ, ἀλλὰ πάντα καὶ ἀεί, ἀλλὰ λανθάνειν τοῦτο τὴν ἡμετέραν αἴσθησιν. πρὸς οὓς
καίπερ οὐ διορίζοντας ποίαν κίνησιν λέγουσιν, ἢ
πάσας, οὐ χαλεπὸν ἀπαντῆσαι. οὔτε γὰρ αὐξάνε-
σθαι οὔτε φθίνειν οἷόν τε συνεχῶς, ἀλλ᾽ ἔστι καὶ τὸ
15 μέσον. ἔστι δ᾽ ὅμοιος ὁ λόγος τῷ περὶ τοῦ τὸν
σταλαγμὸν κατατρίβειν καὶ τὰ ἐκφυόμενα τοὺς

[1] [ὅμως Pacius: ὁμοίως codd. The necessary sense can be
restored by reading οὐχ ὁμοίως (i.e. ᾽ in a more special sense ᾽),
as suggested in the Oxf. Trans. note, or by inserting μᾶλλον,
cf. Philop. 825. 21 and 27 (paraphr.) ἀλλὰ μᾶλλον ἐν κινήσει
τὰ τῆς φύσεως ἔργα θεωρεῖται, 883. 24 πλὴν ἐπειδὴ μᾶλλον ἔργον
φαίνεται τῆς φύσεως ἡ κίνησις. Simplic. 1195. 35 ἀλλὰ καθ᾽
ὅσον ἡ κίνησις οἰκειοτέρα τῇ φύσει μᾶλλον τῆς ἠρεμίας is compatible with either reading or with ὅμως δὲ φυσικ⟨ώτερ⟩ον ἡ
κίνησις.—C.]

---

a [Cf. 184 b 25 ff.—C.]
b [Cf. the definition of ' nature ' in Book II. chap. i.,
192 b 20.—C.]   c [At 192 b 21.—C.]
d ' Rest ' being only the negation of movement in things
capable of moving.
e [Simplicius 1196. 8 mentions the Heracleiteans (cf.

294

every science and even every received opinion, since they all assume motion; and—not only in mathematics but in all other studies also—the expert has nothing to say to the man who denies his axioms.[a] So in this case, the physicist is not concerned to argue with the man who denies the existence of motion, for he starts with the datum that Nature is the principle of movement.[b]

As to (2), it is about right to say that it is palpably false, but not quite so defiant of the whole discipline of Physics as the other; for though in our discourse on Physics [c] it was laid down that Nature is the principle of rest as well as motion, yet it is motion that is primarily germane to the matter; [d] and there are, as a matter of fact, physicists who maintain that everything is always in motion, though some movements are on too small a scale to be observed by our senses.[e] These last, though they do not define what kind of motion they refer to, or whether to every kind,[f] are not hard to deal with. For neither growth nor decay can go on perpetually, but there is also what comes between.[g] The argument is analogous to that concerning the wearing of a stone by dropping water, or the splitting of a rock

Plato's description of them at *Theaetetus* 179 D ff.); Alexander (*ibid.*) saw a reference to the Atomists, who held that the atoms are always in motion, though imperceptibly. But the Atomists unquestionably meant local motion only (265 b 23 ff.), and Aristotle's arguments seem rather to be directed against a theory that apparent rest is infinitesimally slow motion, so that the transition from motion to apparent rest really only marks the point where motion becomes too slow to be perceived.—C.]

[f] *i.e.* whether they include qualitive changes and growth or only local movement.

[g] *i.e.* the point at which growth must stop and decay set in.

253 b λίθους διαιρεῖν· οὐ γὰρ εἰ τοσόνδε ἐξέωσεν ἢ ἀφεῖλεν
ὁ σταλαγμός, καὶ τὸ ἥμισυ ἐν ἡμίσει χρόνῳ πρό-
τερον· ἀλλ' ὥσπερ ἡ νεωλκία, καὶ οἱ σταλαγμοὶ
οἱ τοσοιδὶ τοσονδὶ κινοῦσι, τὸ δὲ μέρος αὐτῶν
20 ἐν οὐδενὶ χρόνῳ τοσοῦτον. διαιρεῖται μὲν οὖν τὸ
ἀφαιρεθὲν εἰς πλείω, ἀλλ' οὐδὲν αὐτῶν ἐκινήθη
χωρίς, ἀλλ' ἅμα. φανερὸν οὖν ὡς οὐκ ἀναγκαῖον
ἀεί τι ἀπιέναι, ὅτι διαιρεῖται ἡ φθίσις εἰς ἄπειρα,
ἀλλ' ὅλον ποτὲ ἀπιέναι. ὁμοίως δὲ καὶ ἐπ' ἀλλοιώσεως ὁποιασοῦν· οὐ γὰρ εἰ μεριστὸν εἰς
25 ἄπειρον τὸ ἀλλοιούμενον, διὰ τοῦτο καὶ ἡ ἀλλοίωσις,
ἀλλ' ἀθρόα γίγνεται πολλάκις, ὥσπερ ἡ πῆξις.
ἔτι ὅταν τις νοσήσῃ, ἀνάγκη χρόνον γενέσθαι ἐν
ᾧ ὑγιασθήσεται, καὶ μὴ ἐν πέρατι χρόνου μετα-
βάλλειν· ἀνάγκη δὲ εἰς ὑγίειαν μεταβάλλειν καὶ εἰς
ἄλλο μηδέν. ὥστε τὸ φάναι συνεχῶς ἀλλοιοῦσθαι
30 λίαν ἐστὶ τοῖς φανεροῖς ἀμφισβητεῖν· εἰς τοὐναντίον

ᵃ [The reference is to Book VII., 250 a 9 ff. : if force A
can move B a distance C in time D, it does not follow that
half A can move B over half C in any time whatsoever, any
more than one of (say) 100 ship-haulers can by himself
drag the ship one hundredth part of the distance. The growing root must accumulate just enough pressure to overpower
the resisting forces and then it will suddenly ' dislodge a
certain amount' of rock. So it may take nothing less
than a dropping that lasts a certain time to produce the
minimum erosion. And if a certain number of drops (like
the certain number of ship-haulers) is required to produce
a certain amount of erosion, a fraction (μέρος) of that number may not produce a corresponding fraction (τοσοῦτον, cf.
Simplic. 1197. 17 οὐκ ἀνάγκη ἕκαστον σταλαγμὸν τὸ τοσοῦτον
μέρος ἀφελεῖν ὅσον αὐτός ἐστι τῶν πάντων) of the effect 'in any
period of time' (i.e. in the corresponding fraction, however

by roots in its crevices ; for if in so much time the
root has made a certain split or the dripping removed
a certain portion it does not follow that they had
already produced half the effect when half the time
had elapsed ; rather it is like the case of hauling
the ship : it may be that a certain number of drops
can produce a definite movement, whereas half of
them could not produce it in any length of time.[a]
Thus it is true that the amount removed is capable of
multiplex division, but no part of it has been moved
separately, but only in conjunction with the rest.[b]
It is clear then that even though a given amount
of shrinkage be capable of indefinite subdivision, it
does not follow that the actual subtraction has been
continuous, for it may all have taken place at once.
The case of any kind of modification is similar.
For though the entity modified be divisible without
limit, it does not follow that the modification itself
is so ; for it may take place all at once, as in the case
of freezing. Again, when a man is sick he must
have time in which to recover and he cannot make
the change *at* the limit of some period ; and also
recovery is a change from sickness to health, and
not to something else.[c] So to suppose modifications
to be continuous and unceasing is a too violent
departure from the manifest phenomena, since all
change must be a receding from one opposite and

large that may be, of the time required by dripping at the
same rate to cause the erosion).—C.]

[b] [Compare the argument about the grains of millet,
Book VII. chap. v., 250 a 19.—C.]

[c] [And, health being a terminus (an ' opposite,' as it is
called in the next sentence), when it is reached, the process
of becoming healthy—an example of ' modification '—cannot
go further.—C.]

253 b γὰρ ἡ ἀλλοίωσις. ὁ δὲ λίθος οὔτε σκληρότερος
γίγνεται οὔτε μαλακώτερος. κατά τε τὸ φέρεσθαι
θαυμαστὸν εἰ λέληθεν ὁ λίθος κάτω φερόμενος ἢ
μένων ἐπὶ τῆς γῆς. ἔτι δ' ἡ γῆ καὶ τῶν ἄλλων
ἕκαστον ἐξ ἀνάγκης μένουσι μὲν ἐν τοῖς οἰκείοις
35 τόποις, κινοῦνται δὲ βιαίως ἐκ τούτων· εἴπερ οὖν
254 a ἔνι' αὐτῶν ἐστιν ἐν τοῖς οἰκείοις τόποις, ἀνάγκη
μηδὲ κατὰ τόπον πάντα κινεῖσθαι. ὅτι μὲν οὖν
ἀδύνατον ἢ ἀεὶ πάντα κινεῖσθαι ἢ ἀεὶ πάντα
ἠρεμεῖν, ἐκ τούτων καὶ ἄλλων τοιούτων πιστεύσειεν
ἄν τις.

Ἀλλὰ μὴν οὐδὲ τὰ μὲν ἀεὶ ἐνδέχεται ἠρεμεῖν
5 τὰ δ' ἀεὶ κινεῖσθαι, ποτὲ δ' ἠρεμεῖν καὶ ποτὲ κινεῖσθαι μηδέν. λεκτέον δ' ὅτι ἀδύνατον, ὥσπερ ἐπὶ
τῶν εἰρημένων πρότερον, καὶ ἐπὶ τούτων· ὁρῶμεν
γὰρ ἐπὶ τῶν αὐτῶν γιγνομένας τὰς εἰρημένας
μεταβολάς· καὶ πρὸς τούτοις ὅτι μάχεται τοῖς
φανεροῖς ὁ ἀμφισβητῶν· οὔτε γὰρ ἡ αὔξησις οὔθ'
10 ἡ βίαιος ἔσται κίνησις, εἰ μὴ κινήσεται παρὰ φύσιν
ἠρεμοῦν πρότερον. γένεσιν οὖν ἀναιρεῖ καὶ φθορὰν
οὗτος ὁ λόγος. σχεδὸν δὲ καὶ τὸ κινεῖσθαι γίγ-
νεσθαί τι καὶ φθείρεσθαι δοκεῖ πᾶσιν· εἰς ὃ μὲν
γὰρ μεταβάλλει, γίγνεται τοῦτο ἢ ἐν τούτῳ, ἐξ

---

^a [A change in the specific hardness or softness of (say)
a diamond, if it were constantly occurring, ought to be
perceptible in a sufficient length of time. The last sentence
may mean : it would be strange if we could not perceive
whether a stone on the ground were really at rest or moving
downwards (with its natural motion) with infinitesimal slowness, as the theory asserts.—C.]

an approach to the other. Besides, stones do not grow either harder or softer ; nor is it easy to believe we are deceived in thinking that a stone is moving when it is falling but is at rest when it lies upon the earth.[a] Besides, it is a natural necessity that earth or anything else should rest in the place proper to it and only move out of it under force ; so that if some things actually are in the places proper to them, it follows that all things cannot always be in motion. So from these and other considerations one might well be confident that neither are all things always in motion nor are they all always at rest.

(3) But neither is it possible (a) that some things are always in motion and other things always at rest, but nothing in motion at one time and at rest at another. We may affirm this on the same grounds on which we have rested in the other cases, for we actually observe certain things passing to and fro between the states of rest and motion. Moreover, to deny that things can pass from motion to rest and from rest to motion is to deny the manifest fact of growth [b] ; and also that of forcible movement, if what was at rest in the place proper to it cannot be set in the motion not proper to it by force. The contention is further incompatible with the genesis and evanishment of things, and it comes near to denying motion [c] altogether, for all motion is universally regarded as, in a sort, a coming-to-be and evanishment, since the goal of movement is a coming to 'this' or 'here,' and it starts by passing

---

[b] [Because it is an essential feature of the growth of living things that it stops when full development is reached.—C.]

[c] [Or 'movement' (change of quality, quantity, or place) as distinct from genesis proper.—C.]

254 a οὗ δὲ μεταβάλλει, φθείρεται τοῦτο ἢ ἐντεῦθεν.
15 ὥστε δῆλον ὅτι τὰ μὲν κινεῖται, τὰ δ' ἠρεμεῖ ἐνίοτε.
Τὸ δὲ πάντα ἀξιοῦν ὁτὲ μὲν ἠρεμεῖν ὁτὲ δὲ
κινεῖσθαι, τοῦτ' ἤδη συναπτέον πρὸς τοὺς πάλαι
λόγους. ἀρχὴν δὲ πάλιν ποιητέον ἀπὸ τῶν νῦν
διορισθέντων, τὴν αὐτὴν ἥνπερ ἠρξάμεθα πρότερον.
20 ἢ γάρ τοι πάντα ἠρεμεῖ, ἢ πάντα κινεῖται, ἢ τὰ
μὲν ἠρεμεῖ τὰ δὲ κινεῖται τῶν ὄντων. καὶ εἰ τὰ
μὲν ἠρεμεῖ τὰ δὲ κινεῖται, ἀνάγκη ἤτοι πάντα ὁτὲ
μὲν ἠρεμεῖν ὁτὲ δὲ κινεῖσθαι, ἢ τὰ μὲν ἀεὶ ἠρεμεῖν
τὰ δὲ ἀεὶ κινεῖσθαι, ⟨ἢ τὰ μὲν ἀεὶ ἠρεμεῖν τὰ δ'
ἀεὶ κινεῖσθαι⟩¹ αὐτῶν τὰ δ' ὁτὲ μὲν ἠρεμεῖν ὁτὲ δὲ
κινεῖσθαι. ὅτι μὲν τοίνυν οὐχ οἷόν τε πάντ' ἠρεμεῖν,
εἴρηται μὲν καὶ πρότερον, εἴπωμεν δὲ καὶ νῦν. εἰ
25 γὰρ κατ' ἀλήθειαν οὕτως ἔχει, καθάπερ φασί τινες
εἶναι τὸ ὂν ἄπειρον καὶ ἀκίνητον, ἀλλ' οὔτι φαίνεταί
γε κατὰ τὴν αἴσθησιν, ἀλλὰ κινεῖσθαι πολλὰ τῶν
ὄντων. εἴπερ οὖν ἔστι δόξα ψευδὴς ἢ ὅλως δόξα,
καὶ κίνησίς ἔστι, κἂν εἰ φαντασία, κἂν εἰ ὁτὲ μὲν

---

¹ [⟨ἢ τὰ μὲν . . . κινεῖσθαι⟩ inserted by Prantl after αὐτῶν,
here by the Oxf. Trans. An alternative would be to insert
ἢ τὰ μὲν ἠρεμοῦντα ἠρεμεῖν ἀεὶ τὰ δὲ κινούμενα κινεῖσθαι after
ὁτὲ δὲ κινεῖσθαι in l. 21: cf. the statement of this possibility
at 253 a 26.—C.]

ᵃ [Literally, ' for a thing comes to be that to which it
changes (e.g. it becomes a white thing in quality or a large
thing in quantity) or (in the case of locomotion) it comes to
be in that (place) to which it shifts ; and it ceases to be that
(quality or quantity) from which it changes or (in locomotion)
ceases to be in the place it leaves.' What really comes to
be or ceases to be is this-thing-with-this-quality (or quantity)
or ' this-thing-in-this-place.' The phrase φθείρεται τοῦτο
seems to mean ' it ceases to be (of) this (quality etc.).'
Cf. 263 b 22 ἐφθείρετο λευκόν 'it ceased to be white,' as

away out of ' that ' and ' there.' [a] Evidently then there are certain things that move after being at rest, and certain things that rest after being in motion.

It is now time to take (b) the assertion that there is nothing that is not sometimes at rest, sometimes in motion, in connexion with the arguments we used a short while ago.[b] We must take our start once more from the alternatives set out at the opening of the discussion. Either (1) everything is motionless, or (2) everything is in motion, or (3) some things are at rest and some in motion. And if the third alternative is to be accepted, then either (b) everything is sometimes at rest and sometimes in motion, or (a) those at rest are always at rest, those in motion always in motion, or (c) some things are always motionless and some always in motion and some now motionless and now in motion. Now (1) it has already been said that all things cannot be motionless. But let us repeat it here ; for even though it be true, as some [c] say, that the existent is unlimited and motionless, yet our senses at any rate contradict it and assert that many things are in motion ; so if false opinion exists (as Melissus and the other Eleatics must admit) or indeed any opinion, then motion also exists ; and so it does if imagination

the opposite of ἐγίγνετο λευκόν ' it began to be white.' γίγνεται λευκόν has two meanings : (1) ' (a) white (thing) comes into existence,' (2) ' a thing (already existing) comes to have the quality white.' Aristotle, straining ordinary usage, makes φθείρεται λευκόν serve as the opposite of (2) as well as of (1).—C.]

[b] [For πάλαι referring to what has been said only a page or two before cf. 267 b 13, Pol. 1262 b 29, 1282 a 15, Aesch. Agam. 587.—C.]

[c] [Melissus ; cf. 184 b 16, 185 a 32.—C.]

254 a οὕτως δοκεῖ εἶναι, ὁτὲ δ' ἑτέρως· ἡ γὰρ φαντασία
30 καὶ ἡ δόξα κινήσεις τινὲς εἶναι δοκοῦσιν. ἀλλὰ
τὸ μὲν περὶ τούτου σκοπεῖν, καὶ ζητεῖν λόγον ὧν
βέλτιον ἔχομεν ἢ λόγου δεῖσθαι, κακῶς κρίνειν
ἐστὶ τὸ βέλτιον καὶ τὸ χεῖρον καὶ τὸ πιστὸν καὶ
τὸ μὴ πιστὸν καὶ ἀρχὴν καὶ μὴ ἀρχήν. ὁμοίως
δὲ ἀδύνατον καὶ τὸ πάντα κινεῖσθαι, ἢ τὰ μὲν ἀεὶ
35 κινεῖσθαι τὰ δ' ἀεὶ ἠρεμεῖν. πρὸς ἅπαντα γὰρ
254 b ταῦτα ἱκανὴ μία πίστις· ὁρῶμεν γὰρ ἔνια ὁτὲ μὲν
κινούμενα ὁτὲ δ' ἠρεμοῦντα. ὥστε φανερὸν ὅτι
ἀδύνατον ὁμοίως τὸ πάντα ἠρεμεῖν καὶ τὸ πάντα κινεῖσθαι συνεχῶς τῷ τὰ μὲν ἀεὶ κινεῖσθαι τὰ δὲ
ἠρεμεῖν ἀεί. λοιπὸν οὖν θεωρῆσαι πότερον πάντα
5 τοιαῦτα οἷα κινεῖσθαι καὶ ἠρεμεῖν, ἢ ἔνια μὲν οὕτως,
ἔνια δ' ἀεὶ ἠρεμεῖ, ἔνια δ' ἀεὶ κινεῖται· τοῦτο γὰρ
δεικτέον ἡμῖν.

ᵃ *i.e.* changes or geneses in the mind.

CHAPTER IV

ARGUMENT

[*The first step in the demonstration promised at the end of
the last chapter is now taken by establishing that all motion
or change is due to the action of some agent distinguishable
from the thing moved or changed. (This point was obscurely
demonstrated in Book VII. Chapter i., 241 b 24–242 a 16).*

exists or if opinions change from time to time; for imagination and opinion are held to be movements of a kind.[a] But in truth to examine such speculations and to seek proofs of that of which we have too direct assurance to need any proof, is to confound the better and the worse, the credible and the incredible, that which is axiomatic and that which is not. Again it is equally impossible (2) that everything is always in motion, or (3 a) that all things are divided into such as are always in motion and such as are always at rest. For to all these contentions there is the one convincing reply that we can see some things now in motion and now at rest. Thus that all things should be in *unbroken* motion, or all things in *unbroken* rest, is just as impossible as that all things should be exhaustively divided between such as are eternally in motion and such as are eternally at rest. It remains then to consider whether (3 b) all things are of a nature to move now and now to be motionless, or (3 c) whether some things be of this nature, whereas others are eternally motionless and yet others eternally in motion. And it is this last alternative that we are now to demonstrate as the truth.

CHAPTER IV

ARGUMENT (*continued*)

We are not concerned with ' accidental ' motion, but only with what moves or is moved per se (254 b 7–12).
Things moved per se *can be classified by a cross division*

ARISTOTLE

as follows : (a) *self-moved* (i.e. *animate beings*), (b) *moved by something external* (i.e. *inanimate things*): *either of these can be moved* (1) *naturally or* (2) *unnaturally. Thus* (a) *the self-moved animal is moved* (1) *naturally by a source of motion within itself, but its body can also be moved* (2) *unnaturally. Also* (b) *things moved from without can have* (2) *an unnatural motion, as when earthy things are forced upward. Here it is obvious that motion is caused by something other than the thing moved, and the same truth could be made plain in the case of* (a 1) *the natural movements of self-moving animals* (b 12–33).

This truth is most difficult to see in the remaining case, (b 1) *the natural movements of things moved from without,* e.g. *the movements of the elements to their proper places* (b 33–255 a 5).

Such movement is not ' self-motion ' ; for this is proper to animals and could not occur in substances whose nature is continuous and without internal distinctions. Such things must be moved by something other than themselves, which analysis will reveal (a 5–20).

254 b 7 Τῶν δὴ κινούντων καὶ κινουμένων τὰ μὲν κατὰ συμβεβηκὸς κινεῖ καὶ κινεῖται, τὰ δὲ καθ' αὑτά—κατὰ συμβεβηκὸς μὲν οἷον ὅσα τε τῷ ὑπάρχειν **10** τοῖς κινοῦσιν ἢ κινουμένοις καὶ τὰ κατὰ μόριον, τὰ δὲ καθ' αὑτὰ ὅσα μὴ τῷ ὑπάρχειν τῷ κινοῦντι ἢ κινουμένῳ μηδὲ τῷ μόριόν τι αὐτῶν κινεῖν ἢ κινεῖσθαι.

---

[a] As anything which makes a red ball move indirectly causes its colour to move, since the ball cannot move without it, but it does not make the redness move by exercising direct pressure on it, like that which it exerts on its material mass as such.

[b] As the whole scythe is moved because the handles have been set in motion by the mower.

304

ARGUMENT (continued)

The distinction of 'natural' and 'unnatural' applies to the agents of motion or change : the natural agent is that which is actually so-and-so operating on what is potentially so-and-so. Similarly the natural patient is that which is potentially of such and such a quality (quantity etc.). So an element, such as fire, is moved naturally by something else when its own inherent potentiality (of upward motion) is called into activity (a 20–30).

The reason why the agent of such changes is hard to distinguish is that there is more than one stage of potentiality before we reach full activity, which follows upon the final stage in the absence of extraneous hindrance (a 30–b 13).

Our question is : why light and heavy things move to their proper places. The answer is : they have a natural tendency to move in their respective directions, which constitutes the essence of lightness or heaviness. But, as we have seen, there is more than one stage of potentiality, and the final activity—actual motion to the proper place— may be hindered by an obstacle. To remove the obstacle is to ' cause ' the motion only in an incidental sense. What is clear is that the things in question are not self-moved, but possess the quality of being set in motion by a suitably situated agent (b 13–31).

Conclusion : It is true in the case of all the four classes of things subject to motion or change, that they are moved or changed by some agent distinguishable from themselves (b 31–256 a 3).—C.]

THAT which produces motion or in which motion is produced may be the immediate seat of the action or passion in question, in which case it is, itself, the primary and proper mover or moved ; or it may be involved by implication either because it is implicated in the proper mover or moved, as the subject in which it inheres,[a] or because it is a whole of which the proper mover or moved is a part.[b]

305

254 b Τῶν δὲ καθ᾽ αὑτὰ τὰ μὲν ὑφ᾽ ἑαυτοῦ τὰ δὲ ὑπ᾽
ἄλλου, καὶ τὰ μὲν φύσει τὰ δὲ βίᾳ καὶ παρὰ φύσιν.
15 τό τε γὰρ αὐτὸ ὑφ᾽ αὑτοῦ κινούμενον φύσει κινεῖται,
οἷον ἕκαστον τῶν ζῴων· κινεῖται γὰρ τὸ ζῷον αὐτὸ
ὑφ᾽ αὑτοῦ, ὅσων δ᾽ ἡ ἀρχὴ ἐν αὐτοῖς τῆς κινήσεως,
ταῦτα φύσει φαμὲν κινεῖσθαι. διὸ τὸ μὲν ζῷον ὅλον
φύσει αὐτὸ ἑαυτὸ κινεῖ, τὸ μέντοι σῶμα ἐνδέχεται
20 καὶ φύσει καὶ παρὰ φύσιν κινεῖσθαι· διαφέρει γὰρ
ὁποίαν τε ἂν κίνησιν κινούμενον τύχῃ καὶ ἐκ ποίου
στοιχείου συνεστηκός. καὶ τῶν ὑπ᾽ ἄλλου κινουμένων τὰ μὲν φύσει κινεῖται τὰ δὲ παρὰ φύσιν—
παρὰ φύσιν μὲν οἷον τὰ γεηρὰ ἄνω καὶ τὸ πῦρ κάτω.
ἔτι δὲ τὰ μόρια τῶν ζῴων πολλάκις κινεῖται παρὰ
φύσιν, παρὰ τὰς θέσεις καὶ τοὺς τρόπους τῆς
25 κινήσεως. καὶ μάλιστα τὸ ὑπό τινος κινεῖσθαι
τὸ κινούμενον ἐν τοῖς παρὰ φύσιν κινουμένοις ἐστὶ
φανερὸν διὰ τὸ δῆλον εἶναι ὑπ᾽ ἄλλου κινούμενον.
μετὰ δὲ τὰ παρὰ φύσιν τῶν κατὰ φύσιν τὰ αὐτὰ ὑφ᾽
αὑτῶν, οἷον τὰ ζῷα· οὐ γὰρ τοῦτ᾽ ἄδηλον, εἰ ὑπό

---

a [attitudes: a man may walk on his hands; modes of
motion: he may roll along on the ground instead of walking
(Simplicius).—C.]

b This elaborate expansion of τὸ ὑπό τινος κινεῖσθαι τὸ
κινούμενον is intended to bring out the important distinction between a thing that has been set in motion, having had
a cause to initiate that motion, and what Aristotle unhappily
regards as the fact that whatever is in a state of motion
must so long as it is moving be under continuous and direct
action of its moving cause. On this devastating failure on
Aristotle's part to recognize the principle of inertia cf. Vol. I.
p. 196.

Of the proper subjects of motion some are moved by themselves and others by something not themselves, and some have a movement natural to themselves and others have a movement forced upon them which is not natural to them. Thus the self-moved has a natural motion. Take, for instance, any animal : the animal moves itself, and we call every movement natural, the principle of which is internal to the body in motion. Wherefore the animal, as an organic whole, can only be moved by itself according to movements natural to it, whereas its body (considered apart from its vital force) may be moved on the lines natural to it or such as do it violence. It all depends on the nature of the movement and the elements of which the body is composed. So also in things that are not animate and do not move themselves it is possible for movements to be produced not only in harmony with their nature but in opposition to it, as when earth is made to move upwards and fire to move downwards. Moreover the several limbs of animals are often moved contrary to their nature in consequence of their attitudes and the modes of motion in question.[a] Now the fact that an object in motion must be under the present influence of something that is acting upon it [b] is most obvious in the case of unnatural movements, for then it is plain that the motion is caused by an external agent. And after forced movements the next most obvious example of the same principle is those natural movements in which a thing in motion is being moved by itself, to wit the natural movements of animals ; for in these cases there is no doubt as to there being an active factor in the animal that

254 b τινος κινεῖται, ἀλλὰ πῶς δεῖ διαλαβεῖν αὐτοῦ τὸ
30 κινοῦν καὶ τὸ κινούμενον· ἔοικε γὰρ ὥσπερ ἐν τοῖς
πλοίοις καὶ τοῖς μὴ φύσει συνισταμένοις, οὕτω
καὶ ἐν τοῖς ζῴοις εἶναι διῃρημένον τὸ κινοῦν καὶ
τὸ κινούμενον, καὶ οὕτω τὸ ἅπαν αὐτὸ αὑτὸ κινεῖν.

Μάλιστα δ' ἀπορεῖται τὸ λοιπὸν τῆς εἰρημένης
τελευταίας διαιρέσεως· τῶν γὰρ ὑπ' ἄλλου κινου-
35 μένων τὰ μὲν παρὰ φύσιν ἐθήκαμεν κινεῖσθαι, τὰ
255 a δὲ λείπεται ἀντιθεῖναι ὅτι φύσει. ταῦτα δ' ἐστὶν
ἃ τὴν ἀπορίαν παράσχοι ἂν ὑπὸ τίνος κινεῖται, οἷον
τὰ κοῦφα καὶ τὰ βαρέα. ταῦτα γὰρ εἰς μὲν τοὺς
ἀντικειμένους τόπους βίᾳ κινεῖται, εἰς δὲ τοὺς
οἰκείους—τὸ μὲν κοῦφον ἄνω, τὸ δὲ βαρὺ κάτω—
5 φύσει· τὸ δ' ὑπὸ τίνος οὐκέτι φανερόν, ὥσπερ
ὅταν κινῶνται παρὰ φύσιν.

Τό τε γὰρ αὐτὰ ὑφ' αὑτῶν φάναι ἀδύνατον
ζωτικόν τε γὰρ τοῦτο καὶ τῶν ἐμψύχων ἴδιον, καὶ
ἱστάναι ἂν ἐδύνατο αὐτά (λέγω δ' οἷον, εἰ τοῦ

---

[a] So that by definition it is only incidentally that the animal moves itself.

is causing movement and a passive one that is experiencing it. The only problem is clearly to demark what factor in the animal it is that is in the proper and primary sense the producer of the movement and what that in which the movement is primarily and directly produced ; for it would appear that what is obvious with a man-in-a-boat, or wherever we are dealing with things not naturally organized as wholes, is also really true with animals, viz. that we must distinguish between that which moves and that which is moved and can only say that the whole animal moves itself because both mover and moved are parts of that whole self.[a]

The real difficulty then is narrowed down to those movements of things that are not self-moving which we have not yet dealt with ; for in pronouncing some of the movements of things which are not self-moving to be contrary to their nature, we have by inference laid down that the rest are natural; and it is here that we come to grips with the real difficulty, viz. the question what is the agent of the natural movements of bodies heavy and light. For such bodies can be forced to move in directions opposite to those natural to them ; but whereas it is obvious that light things go up and heavy ones down ' by nature,' we have not yet arrived at any clear conception as to what is the agent of this ' natural ' movement, as we have done in the case of the enforced and unnatural movements.

For we cannot say that such bodies, when moving naturally, ' move themselves,' for this is proper to animals that have life, and if light and heavy bodies moved themselves up and down they would be able to stop themselves also—I mean that if an animal

309

255 a βαδίζειν αἴτιον αὐτῷ, καὶ τοῦ μὴ βαδίζειν), ὥστ'
10 εἰ ἐπ' αὐτῷ τὸ ἄνω φέρεσθαι τῷ πυρί, δῆλον
ὅτι ἐπ' αὐτῷ καὶ τὸ κάτω. ἄλογον δὲ καὶ τὸ μίαν
κίνησιν κινεῖσθαι μόνην ὑφ' αὐτῶν, εἴγε αὐτὰ
ἑαυτὰ κινοῦσιν. ἔτι πῶς ἐνδέχεται συνεχές τι
καὶ συμφυὲς αὐτὸ ἑαυτὸ κινεῖν; ᾗ γὰρ ἓν καὶ
συνεχὲς μὴ ἁφῇ, ταύτῃ ἀπαθές· ἀλλ' ᾗ κεχώρισται,
15 ταύτῃ τὸ μὲν πέφυκε ποιεῖν τὸ δὲ πάσχειν. οὔτ'
ἄρα τούτων οὐθὲν αὐτὸ ἑαυτὸ κινεῖ—συμφυῆ γάρ—
οὔτ' ἄλλο συνεχὲς οὐδέν, ἀλλ' ἀνάγκη διῃρῆσθαι
τὸ κινοῦν ἐν ἑκάστῳ πρὸς τὸ κινούμενον, οἷον ἐπὶ
τῶν ἀψύχων ὁρῶμεν, ὅταν κινῇ τι τῶν ἐμψύχων
αὐτά. ἀλλὰ συμβαίνει καὶ ταῦτα ὑπό τινος ἀεὶ
20 κινεῖσθαι· γένοιτο δ' ἂν φανερὸν διαιροῦσι τὰς
αἰτίας.

Ἔστι δὲ καὶ ἐπὶ τῶν κινούντων λαβεῖν τὰ
εἰρημένα· τὰ μὲν γὰρ παρὰ φύσιν αὐτῶν κινητικά
ἐστιν—οἷον ὁ μοχλὸς οὐ φύσει τοῦ βάρους κινητικός
—τὰ δὲ φύσει, οἷον τὸ ἐνεργείᾳ θερμὸν κινητικὸν

---

[a] [Or 'could only move with a single *kind* of motion,'
whereas an animal can walk, run, leap, dance and move
up or down (Themistius). As the text stands, this sentence
seems to contain a separate objection, though the logic
would be improved if the clause ὥστ' εἰ . . . τὸ κάτω (ll. 9–10)
were transposed after ἑαυτὰ κινοῦσιν (l. 11).—C.]

[b] Cf. 227 a 15.

[c] [Or ' So none of these things (such as fire etc., which
have a natural motion) moves itself—for they are of naturally
coherent substance (cf. De gen. et corr. 327 a 1 συμφυὲς
ἕκαστον καὶ ἓν ὂν ἀπαθές)—nor yet does anything else that is
continuous, but the moving element in every case must
be distinct from the moved, with such a distinction as can
be actually seen in the case of an inanimate object (e.g. a
boat) moved by an animate (a man rowing it).—C.]

can make itself march it can also make itself stop marching—so that if fire makes itself move upwards it should be able to make itself move downwards also. If they moved themselves there would be no sense in saying that they could only move in one direction.[a] Again what can be meant by a continuous and homogeneous body ' moving itself ' ? For in so far as it is one and continuous (otherwise than by contact [b]) it cannot be affected by itself ; it is only if it can be analysed into parts or factors that it can be self-affected, by one of its elements being the agent and another the patient. [c] Thus in the movement of such bodies there is no single constituent which is at once the primary agent and the primary patient (nor can there be, since each constituent is homogeneous in itself). And the argument applies to all properly ' continuous ' bodies. So in every case the mover and the moved must be distinguished, just as we see that they are when a living thing as agent moves a lifeless thing as patient. These continuous bodies are, in fact, always moved by something else ; what this something is would become clear if we were to distinguish the causes involved.

The above-mentioned distinctions can be drawn in the case of the agents of motion : some of them are capable of causing motion unnaturally (a lever, for instance, is not by nature capable of moving a load [d]), others naturally ; thus a body that is actually hot is capable of causing a change in one that is

---

[d] A bar of iron is heavy, and so its inherent tendency is to pull or push things downwards. But it may be used as a lever and so made to impart a motion contrary to its own nature.

255 a τοῦ δυνάμει θερμοῦ· ὁμοίως δὲ καὶ ἐπὶ τῶν ἄλλων
25 τῶν τοιούτων. καὶ κινητὸν δ' ὡσαύτως φύσει
τὸ δυνάμει ποιὸν ἢ ποσὸν ἤ που, ὅταν ἔχῃ τὴν
ἀρχὴν τὴν τοιαύτην ἐν αὑτῷ καὶ μὴ κατὰ συμβεβηκός (εἴη γὰρ ἂν τὸ αὐτὸ καὶ ποιὸν καὶ ποσόν,
ἀλλὰ θατέρῳ θάτερον συμβέβηκε καὶ οὐ καθ' αὑτὸ
30 ὑπάρχει). τὸ δὴ πῦρ καὶ ἡ γῆ κινοῦνται ὑπό τινος
βίᾳ μέν, ὅταν παρὰ φύσιν, φύσει δέ, ὅταν εἰς τὰς
αὑτῶν ἐνεργείας δυνάμει ὄντα.

’Επεὶ δὲ τὸ δυνάμει πλεοναχῶς λέγεται, τοῦτ'
αἴτιον τοῦ μὴ φανερὸν εἶναι ὑπὸ τίνος τὰ τοιαῦτα
κινεῖται, οἷον τὸ πῦρ ἄνω καὶ ἡ γῆ κάτω. ἔστι
δὲ δυνάμει ἄλλως ὁ μανθάνων ἐπιστήμων καὶ ὁ
ἔχων ἤδη καὶ μὴ θεωρῶν. ἀεὶ δ', ὅταν ἅμα τὸ
35 ποιητικὸν καὶ τὸ παθητικὸν ὦσι, γίγνεται ἐνίοτε
255 b ἐνεργείᾳ τὸ δυνατόν, οἷον τὸ μανθάνον ἐκ δυνάμει
ὄντος ἕτερον γίγνεται δυνάμει· ὁ γὰρ ἔχων ἐπιστήμην μὴ θεωρῶν δὲ δυνάμει ἐστὶν ἐπιστήμων
πως, ἀλλ' οὐχ ὡς καὶ πρὶν μαθεῖν. ὅταν δ' οὕτως
ἔχῃ, ἐὰν μή τι κωλύῃ, ἐνεργεῖ καὶ θεωρεῖ, ἢ ἔσται

---

a I follow Simplicius in understanding this to be the
implication of ἐνίοτε. The alternative would be to omit
it with IF and the copies reported by Alexander (Simplic.
1214. 10). [Cf. note in Oxford Translation. The apparent
contradiction between ἀεί and ἐνίοτε can be explained by
taking the sentence (as above) to mean ' It is a rule without
exception (ἀεί) that, agent and patient being in contact,
under certain (i.e. favourable) circumstances (ἐνίοτε) etc.'
Cf. the use of ἀεί at 266 a 26. The circumstances are unfavourable, if action is prevented by some extraneous obstacle
(cf. b 4 ἐὰν μή τι κωλύῃ).—C.]

potentially hot ; and so with other kinds of change. And it is the same with what is capable of suffering change : the natural subject of change is that which is potentially of a certain quality or quantity or in a certain place, when it contains the principle of the modification in question in itself and not accident- ally—' not accidentally,' because a thing that comes to have a certain quality may also grow to a certain size at the same time, but the change of size is incidental to the change of quality and is not an essential property of the thing *qua* capable of quali- tive change. So, then, when fire and earth are moved by some agent, whereas the motion is forcible when it is contrary to their nature, it is natural when they actually engage in their proper move- ments, the potentiality for which was already in- herent in them.

Now the reason why the agent of such movements as that of fire upwards and earth downwards is not obvious is this : there are different stages of potenti- ality. The learner is a potential thinker in any given science in a different sense from that in which he is a potential thinker in it when he has learned its principles but is not thinking about it. And whenever the agent and patient are in effective [a] contact some kind of potentiality is developed into actuality ; for instance the learner rises to a higher kind of potentiality, which he did not actually possess at first, for the expert's expertness is still in a sense a potentiality rather than an actuality when he is not exercising it, but not in the same sense as it was before he had learned the skill. When he has acquired this second degree of potenti- ality he will actualize it in the positive exercise of

ARISTOTLE

255 b 5 ἐν τῇ ἀντιφάσει καὶ ἀγνοίᾳ. ὁμοίως δὲ ταῦτ'
ἔχει καὶ ἐπὶ τῶν φυσικῶν· τὸ γὰρ ψυχρὸν δυνάμει
θερμόν, ὅταν δὲ μεταβάλῃ, ἤδη πῦρ, καίει δέ, ἂν
μή τι κωλύῃ καὶ ἐμποδίζῃ. ὁμοίως δ' ἔχει καὶ
περὶ τὸ βαρὺ καὶ κοῦφον· τὸ γὰρ κοῦφον γίγνεται
10 ἐκ βαρέος, οἷον ἐξ ὕδατος ἀήρ· τοῦτο γὰρ δυνάμει
πρῶτον, καὶ ἤδη κοῦφον, καὶ ἐνεργήσει γ' εὐθύς,
ἂν μή τι κωλύῃ· ἐνέργεια δὲ τοῦ κούφου τὸ πού
εἶναι καὶ ἄνω, κωλύεται δ' ὅταν ἐν τῷ ἐναντίῳ
τόπῳ ᾖ. καὶ τοῦθ' ὁμοίως ἔχει καὶ ἐπὶ τοῦ ποσοῦ
καὶ ἐπὶ τοῦ ποιοῦ.

Καίτοι τοῦτο ζητεῖται, διὰ τί ποτε κινεῖται εἰς
15 τὸν αὐτῶν τόπον τὰ κοῦφα καὶ τὰ βαρέα. αἴτιον
δ' ὅτι πέφυκέ ποι, καὶ τοῦτ' ἐστὶ τὸ κούφῳ καὶ
βαρεῖ εἶναι, τὸ μὲν τῷ ἄνω τὸ δὲ τῷ κάτω διωρισμέ-
νον. δυνάμει δ' ἐστὶ κοῦφον καὶ βαρὺ πολλαχῶς,
ὥσπερ εἴρηται· ὅταν τε γὰρ ᾖ ὕδωρ, δυνάμει γέ
πώς ἐστι κοῦφον, καὶ ὅταν ἀήρ, ἔστιν ἔτι δυνάμει·
20 ἐνδέχεται γὰρ ἐμποδιζόμενον μὴ ἄνω εἶναι, ἀλλ'
ἐὰν ἀφαιρεθῇ τὸ ἐμποδίζον, ἐνεργεῖ καὶ ἀεὶ ἀνωτέρω
γίγνεται. ὁμοίως δὲ καὶ τὸ ποιὸν εἰς τὸ ἐνεργείᾳ
εἶναι μεταβάλλει· εὐθὺς γὰρ θεωρεῖ τὸ ἐπιστῆμον,
ἂν μή τι κωλύῃ. καὶ τὸ ποσὸν ἐκτείνεται, ἐὰν
μή τι κωλύῃ. ὁ δὲ τὸ ὑφιστάμενον καὶ κωλῦον
25 κινήσας ἔστι μὲν ὡς κινεῖ ἔστι δ' ὡς οὔ, οἷον ὁ

ᵃ Not continuously, but whenever he sees sufficient cause. Aristotle omits this qualification because his mind has already travelled on to the case of light and heavy bodies in which the challenge to the patient to actualize its potentiality *is* continuous.

314

his power [a] (unless there is some obstacle), else he were still in the ignorance which is the contradiction of this higher potentiality. Now this later stage of potentiality is what we meet in Physics ; for the cold which is potentially hot, when it has completed the change and is effectively fire, actualizes its new potentiality and burns things, if not prevented. And so with heavy and light ; for the light is developed out of the heavy, as air out of water, for it too is at first (as water) only potentially light, but then (as air) becomes effectively light, and straightway actualizes its new potentiality, unless hindered. The actuality of a light thing is to be somewhere, namely above, and the hindrance is whatever keeps it below. The analogy holds for quality and quantity as well as for position.

If the question is still pressed why light and heavy things tend to their respective positions, the only answer is that they are natured so, and that what we mean by heavy and light as distinguished and defined is just this downward or upward tendency. As we have said, here too there are different stages of potentiality. When a substance is water it is already in a way potentially light, and when it is air it may still be only potentially in the position proper to it, for its ascent may be hindered, but if the hindrance be removed it actualizes the potentiality and continuously mounts. And likewise the potentially ' such ' tends to its actual realization ; even as knowledge becomes straightway active if not impeded ; and so likewise are the potential dimensions of a thing realized if there be no hindrance. If anyone removes the obstacle he may be said in one sense (but in another not) to cause the movement ;

315

255 b τὸν κίονα ὑποσπάσας ἢ ὁ τὸν λίθον ἀφελὼν ἀπὸ
τοῦ ἀσκοῦ ἐν τῷ ὕδατι· κατὰ συμβεβηκὸς γὰρ
κινεῖ, ὥσπερ καὶ ἡ ἀνακλασθεῖσα σφαῖρα οὐχ ὑπὸ
τοῦ τοίχου ἐκινήθη ἀλλ' ὑπὸ τοῦ βάλλοντος. ὅτι
μὲν τοίνυν οὐδὲν τούτων αὐτὸ κινεῖ ἑαυτό, δῆλον·
30 ἀλλὰ κινήσεως ἀρχὴν ἔχει, οὐ τοῦ κινεῖν οὐδὲ τοῦ
ποιεῖν, ἀλλὰ τοῦ πάσχειν.

Εἰ δὴ πάντα τὰ κινούμενα ἢ φύσει κινεῖται ἢ
παρὰ φύσιν καὶ βίᾳ, καὶ τά τε βίᾳ καὶ παρὰ φύσιν
πάντα ὑπό τινος καὶ ὑπ' ἄλλου, τῶν δὲ φύσει πάλιν
35 τά θ' ὑφ' αὑτῶν κινούμενα ὑπό τινος κινεῖται καὶ
256 a τὰ μὴ ὑφ' αὑτῶν (οἷον τὰ κοῦφα καὶ τὰ βαρέα· ἢ
γὰρ ὑπὸ τοῦ γεννήσαντος καὶ ποιήσαντος κοῦφον ἢ
βαρύ, ἢ ὑπὸ τοῦ τὰ ἐμποδίζοντα καὶ κωλύοντα
λύσαντος), ἅπαντα ἂν τὰ κινούμενα ὑπό τινος
κινοῖτο.

for instance if he removes a column from beneath
the weight it was supporting, or cuts the string that
attached a bladder, under water, to the stone that
holds it down, for he incidentally determines the
moment at which the potential motion becomes
actual, just as the wall from which a ball rebounds
determines the direction in which the ball rebounds,
though it is the player and not the wall that is the
cause of its motion. So it is now clear that in no
one of these cases does the thing that is in motion
move itself; but it has the passive (though not
the active and efficient) principle of movement inherent in itself.

Since then all things that are in motion either
move according to their proper nature or in viola-
tion of it and under compulsion; and all things
whose movement is unnatural are set in motion by
some agent external to them; and things whose
movement is natural are also set in motion
by some agent, whether (like animals) they move
themselves (in the sense that they embrace both
the active and the passive factors of motion in their
organism), or do not move themselves, as for instance
light and heavy substances, which are moved either
directly by what agent soever generates them and
makes them light or heavy, or incidentally by the
agent that removes the obstruction or hindrance—
if all this is so, I say it follows that all things in
motion are moved by some agent.

ARISTOTLE

CHAPTER V

ARGUMENT

[It will now be shown that the primary agent of motion is itself unmoved. We have said that whatever is in motion must be moved by some agent. This may be either an intermediate, itself moved by the agent proper, or the agent proper, which may act either directly on the thing moved or through one or more intermediates (256 a 4–13).

If the agent is always something that is in motion, since there cannot be an infinite series of intermediates which both move something and are moved by something else, the series must terminate in a first moved mover which is moved not by anything else but by itself (a 13–21).

The same argument stated in another form (a 21–b 3).

Again, if whatever is in motion is moved by an agent that is itself moved by something else, this fact that the agent is so moved is either (a) accidental or (b) essential to its operation as agent. If (a) it is accidental, then it would be logically possible that at some time motion should not exist at all ; but that we have disproved in chap. i. (b 3–13). If (b) it is essential to the agent that it should be moved by another, this motion must either be of the same kind as it imparts or of one of the other two kinds. Either supposition leads to impossibilities (b 27–257 a 14).

Further it is impossible to suppose that whatever is capable of causing motion must be capable of suffering it (a 14–25).

Conclusion : There cannot be an unlimited series of agents

256 a 4 Τοῦτο δὲ διχῶς· ἢ γὰρ οὐ δι' αὐτὸ τὸ κινοῦν
5 ἀλλὰ δι' ἕτερον ὃ κινεῖ τὸ κινοῦν, ἢ δι' αὐτό· καὶ
τοῦτο ἢ πρῶτον μετὰ τὸ ἔσχατον ἢ διὰ πλειόνων,
οἷον ἡ βακτηρία κινεῖ τὸν λίθον καὶ κινεῖται ὑπὸ
τῆς χειρὸς κινουμένης ὑπὸ τοῦ ἀνθρώπου, οὗτος δ'
οὐκέτι τῷ ὑπ' ἄλλου κινεῖσθαι. ἄμφω δὴ κινεῖν φα-
10 μεν—καὶ τὸ τελευταῖον καὶ τὸ πρῶτον τῶν κινούν-
318

CHAPTER V

ARGUMENT (*continued*)

each moved by something else : the series must terminate in
an agent which is either unmoved or self-moved (a 25–31).

We must next consider in what sense self-motion is possible.
(1) A thing cannot move itself in its entirety. It must
contain a factor that moves and a factor that is moved (a 31–
b 13). *(2) It cannot be that each factor moves the other, reci-*
procally (b 13–26). *And what is primarily self-moving*
cannot contain a factor, or factors, that are self-moving (b 26–
258 a 1). *Conclusion : Whatever is self-moved contains an*
unmoved moving factor and a moved factor (a 1–2).

This conclusion further elaborated (a 2–27).

A possible objection answered (a 27–b 3).

Final conclusion : The primary agent of motion is unmoved (b 3–9).

⟨*This conclusion is such as we should expect from general*
considerations (256 b 13–27).⟩ See Vol. I. p. lxvii.—C.]

Now the thing moved may be moved by the true
agent either directly or by some intermediate which
itself is moved by the true agent directly.[a] And the
true agent may immediately precede the intermediate agent which acts directly upon the patient,
or there may be a chain of several intermediates.
Thus the staff (used as a lever) which shifts a stone
may itself be moved by the hand that in its turn is
moved by the man whose hand it is. But the man
is not moved by anything other than himself. Accordingly we say both that the last in the chain of
movers moves the load, and that the first does.
But if pushed we should say that it is really the first

[a] It must be remembered that, according to Aristotle,
motion is not only initiated but has to be maintained by the
present action of the agent. See Vol. I. p. 196, note *b*.

ARISTOTLE

256 a τῶν—ἀλλὰ μᾶλλον τὸ πρῶτον· ἐκεῖνο γὰρ κινεῖ τὸ
τελευταῖον, ἀλλ' οὐ τοῦτο τὸ πρῶτον, καὶ ἄνευ μὲν
τοῦ πρώτου τὸ τελευταῖον οὐ κινήσει, ἐκεῖνο δ'
ἄνευ τούτου, οἷον ἡ βακτηρία οὐ κινήσει μὴ
κινοῦντος τοῦ ἀνθρώπου.

15 Εἰ δὴ ἀνάγκη πᾶν τὸ κινούμενον ὑπό τινός τε
κινεῖσθαι καὶ ἢ ὑπὸ κινουμένου ὑπ' ἄλλου ἢ μή,
καὶ εἰ μὲν ὑπ' ἄλλου κινουμένου, ἀνάγκη τι εἶναι
κινοῦν ὃ οὐχ ὑπ' ἄλλου πρῶτον, εἰ δὲ τοιοῦτο τὸ
πρῶτον, οὐκ ἀνάγκη θάτερον (ἀδύνατον γὰρ εἰς
ἄπειρον ἰέναι τὸ κινοῦν καὶ κινούμενον ὑπ' ἄλλου
αὐτό· τῶν γὰρ ἀπείρων οὐκ ἔστιν οὐδὲν πρῶτον)—
20 εἰ οὖν ἅπαν μὲν τὸ κινούμενον ὑπό τινος κινεῖται,
τὸ δὲ πρῶτον κινοῦν κινεῖται μὲν οὐχ ὑπ' ἄλλου
δέ, ἀνάγκη αὐτὸ ὑφ' αὑτοῦ κινεῖσθαι.

Ἔτι δὲ καὶ ὧδε τὸν αὐτὸν τοῦτον λόγον ἔστιν
ἐπελθεῖν. πᾶν γὰρ τὸ κινοῦν τί τε κινεῖ καὶ τινί·
ἢ γὰρ αὐτῷ κινεῖ τὸ κινοῦν ἢ ἄλλῳ, οἷον ἄνθρωπος
ἢ αὐτὸς ἢ τῇ βακτηρίᾳ, καὶ ὁ ἄνεμος κατέβαλεν
25 ἢ αὐτὸς ἢ ὁ λίθος ὃν ἔωσεν. ἀδύνατον δὲ κινεῖν
ἄνευ τοῦ αὐτὸ αὑτῷ κινοῦντος τὸ ᾧ κινεῖ· ἀλλ' εἰ
μὲν αὐτὸ αὑτῷ κινεῖ, οὐκ ἀνάγκη ἄλλο εἶναι ᾧ

---

a [*Literally*, 'and if (it is moved) by something that is
moved by something else, then there must be at the beginning
of the series (πρῶτον) some mover not moved by something
else, whereas if the immediate mover (τὸ πρῶτον) is of this
description, there is no necessity for the other thing (for any
intermediate between it and the thing moved).' In either
case we shall arrive—mediately or immediately—at a prime
self-moved mover.—C.]

320

and original mover, for the first moves the last (mediately) but the last does not move the first at all ; moreover it could not move anything without the primary mover, but the primary mover could move things without it. In our example the staff could not move the stone unless the man moved the staff itself.

If then everything that is in motion must be moved by something, and that something must either be moved in its turn by something else or not, ^a and in the latter case it is the true agent and we need go no further, but in the other case we must run it back until we do reach a primary mover not moved by something else (for it is impossible to run back to infinity through movers that are themselves moved by something else, for there is no beginning at all of such an unlimited series)—why then it follows that if everything that is in motion is moved by some agent, and if the primary agent itself is in motion but is not moved by anything *else*, it must be moved by *itself*.

Or (reversing the order of the demonstration) we may repeat the argument in this way. Every mover sets something in motion by some instrumentality, either its own or other than its own : the man for instance either by the instrumentality of his own hand or by that of the staff, and the wind either by its own impact or by loosening a stone that moves whatever it may be. And when the primary mover employs an instrument sejunct from itself, that sejunct instrument cannot act without the primary mover that moves by its own instrumentality. But the primary mover can apply its own instrumentality without having to employ any other ; whereas an

321

256 a κινεῖ, ἂν δὲ ᾖ ἕτερον τὸ ᾧ κινεῖ, ἔστι τι ὃ κινήσει
οὐ τινὶ ἀλλ' αὑτῷ, ἢ εἰς ἄπειρον εἶσιν. εἰ οὖν
κινούμενόν τι κινεῖ, ἀνάγκη στῆναι καὶ μὴ εἰς
30 ἄπειρον ἰέναι· εἰ γὰρ ἡ βακτηρία κινεῖ τῷ κινεῖσθαι
ὑπὸ τῆς χειρός, ἡ χεὶρ κινεῖ τὴν βακτηρίαν· εἰ δὲ καὶ
ταύτην[1] ἄλλο κινεῖ, καὶ ταύτην ἕτερόν τι τὸ κινοῦν.
ὅταν δή τινι κινῇ ἀεὶ ἕτερον, ἀνάγκη εἶναι πρότερον
τὸ αὐτὸ αὑτῷ κινοῦν. εἰ οὖν κινεῖται μὲν τοῦτο,
μὴ ἄλλο δὲ τὸ κινοῦν αὐτό, ἀνάγκη αὐτὸ αὑτὸ
256 b κινεῖν· ὥστε καὶ κατὰ τοῦτον τὸν λόγον ἤτοι εὐθὺς
τὸ κινούμενον ὑπὸ τοῦ αὐτὸ κινοῦντος κινεῖται, ἢ
ἔρχεταί ποτε εἰς τὸ τοιοῦτον.

Πρὸς δὲ τοῖς εἰρημένοις καὶ ὧδε σκοποῦσι ταὐτὰ
συμβήσεται ταῦτα. εἰ γὰρ ὑπὸ κινουμένου κινεῖται
5 τὸ κινούμενον πᾶν, ἤτοι τοῦτο ὑπάρχει τοῖς πράγ-
μασι κατὰ συμβεβηκός, ὥστε κινεῖν μὲν κινούμενον,
οὐ μέντοι διὰ τὸ κινεῖσθαι αὐτὸ ἀεί, ἢ οὔ, ἀλλὰ
καθ' αὑτό. πρῶτον μὲν οὖν εἰ κατὰ συμβεβηκός,
οὐκ ἀνάγκη κινεῖσθαι τὸ κινούμενον· εἰ δὲ τοῦτο,
δῆλον ὡς ἐνδέχεταί ποτε μηδὲν κινεῖσθαι τῶν ὄντων·
10 οὐ γὰρ ἀναγκαῖον τὸ συμβεβηκός, ἀλλ' ἐνδεχόμενον
μὴ εἶναι. ἐὰν οὖν θῶμεν τὸ δυνατὸν εἶναι, οὐδὲν

---

[1] [ταύτην codd.: ταύτῃ conj. Oxf. Trans. If ταύτην is
retained, the clause means: 'if the hand itself is moved by
something else (not by itself),' *i.e.* if we have not yet reached
a self-moving mover, then there must be another mover,
which is self-moved, beyond it and distinct from it.—C.]

---

[a] [*i.e.* an agent that is moved *by something else*. This
is what the following dilemma will prove impossible. But
(as appears from the conclusion 257 a 25) the possibility that
the first agent may be moved *by itself* remains open, as well
as the possibility that it is *unmoved*.—C.]

instrument sejunct from a primary must (to be in action) have somewhere behind it some primary agent (or the search for one would run back with no limit). If, then, the agent of motion is in motion itself, we must come to stand somewhere and not go on without limit ; for if the staff moves the load because it is itself moved by the hand, the hand indeed moved the staff, but if the hand itself is moved by something else, what moves the hand is in turn a distinct thing. However long the chain, therefore, of things that produce motion by an instrumentality other than their own, there must lie behind it an agent that produces the movement by its own instrumentality. So that if this primary agent is in motion, and there is no agent behind it to set it in motion, it must of necessity be moving itself. So this line of argument again leads to the conclusion that if anything is in motion it must either be set in motion by a self-moving agent immediately, or must send us back through a chain of intermediaries until we come to such an agent.

Yet further, the same conclusions will result from another line of reasoning. For if it be true that everything that is in motion is moved by an agent that is in motion itself,^{a} either (a) this is inherent in the relation of mover to moved, or (b) it is only through some incidental connexion, so that although the mover always is as a matter of fact in motion, it is not in its capacity as motor that it is so. But in this latter case (b), motion would not be an eternal necessity, and it immediately follows that there would be a possibility of a total cessation of motion in things, for a connexion that is incidental may possibly cease. Now if any supposition we

ARISTOTLE

256 b ἀδύνατον συμβήσεται, ψεῦδος δ' ἴσως. ἀλλὰ τὸ
κίνησιν μὴ εἶναι ἀδύνατον· δέδεικται γὰρ πρότερον
ὅτι ἀνάγκη κίνησιν ἀεὶ εἶναι.

13 [Καὶ εὐλόγως . . . ἀμιγὴς ὤν.]¹

27 Ἀλλὰ μὴν εἰ μὴ κατὰ συμβεβηκὸς ἀλλ' ἐξ
ἀνάγκης κινεῖται τὸ κινοῦν, εἰ δὲ μὴ κινοῖτο οὐκ
30 ἂν κινοίη, ἀνάγκη τὸ κινοῦν, ᾗ κινεῖται, ἤτοι οὕτω
κινεῖσθαι ὡς τὸ² κατὰ τὸ αὐτὸ εἶδος τῆς κινήσεως,
ἢ καθ' ἕτερον· λέγω δὲ ἤτοι τὸ θερμαῖνον καὶ αὐτὸ
θερμαίνεσθαι καὶ τὸ ὑγιάζον ὑγιάζεσθαι καὶ τὸ
φέρον φέρεσθαι, ἢ τὸ ὑγιάζον φέρεσθαι, τὸ δὲ
φέρον αὔξεσθαι. ἀλλὰ φανερὸν ὅτι ἀδύνατον· δεῖ
257 a γὰρ μέχρι τῶν ἀτόμων διαιροῦντα λέγειν, οἷον εἴ
τι διδάσκει γεωμετρεῖν, τοῦτο διδάσκεσθαι γεωμετρεῖν τὸ αὐτό, ἢ εἰ ῥιπτεῖ, ῥιπτεῖσθαι τὸν αὐτὸν
τρόπον τῆς ῥίψεως· ἢ οὕτω μὲν μή, ἄλλο δ' ἐξ
5 ἄλλου γένους, οἷον τὸ φέρον μὲν αὔξεσθαι, τὸ δὲ
τοῦτο αὖξον ἀλλοιοῦσθαι ὑπ' ἄλλου, τὸ δὲ τοῦτο
ἀλλοιοῦν ἑτέραν τινὰ κινεῖσθαι κίνησιν. ἀλλ'
ἀνάγκη στῆναι· πεπερασμέναι γὰρ αἱ κινήσεις. τὸ
δὲ πάλιν ἀνακάμπτειν καὶ τὸ ἀλλοιοῦν φάναι φέρε-

---

¹ [The paragraph here omitted is transferred to the end of the chapter. See note 2 on p. 336.—C.]
² [ὡς τὸ Oxf. Trans.: ὥστε τὸ E : ὥστε cett.—C.]

ᵃ [In Bk. VII. chap. i.—C.]

324

choose to make is not inherently impossible, then
no deductions legitimately drawn from it can be
inherently impossible either, though they may be
contrary to fact. But it is inherently impossible for
all motion to cease, since we have proved [a] the eternal
necessity of its persistence.

But if on the other alternative (a) it is not incidentally but primarily and of necessity that the
mover as such is itself in motion, so that if it were
not in motion it would not cause motion, then of
necessity the movement which the mover as such
itself experiences must be either of the same order
as that which it imparts or of some other. I mean
that either the heater must itself be growing hot
and the curative itself becoming healthy and what
causes local transference be itself in local transit, or
the curative be (say) in local transit, or that which
causes local transference be itself in process of growth.
But obviously this will not work. For we should
have to carry it down into the furthest detail, to say
for instance that the teacher of geometry must be
in process of himself learning the very theorem of
geometry he is teaching, or that the thrower must
be in act of being himself thrown after the same
fashion ; or else (taking the other alternative) to
say that one kind of change depends on another—
for example that what causes local transference is
itself growing and that whatever makes it grow is
itself being modified, and what causes this modification is experiencing some other kind of change. But
this can not go on indefinitely, for the orders of change
are limited in number. And to suppose that (in our
example) the producer of the modification in the
thing that is growing is itself in local transit would

325

257 a σθαι τὸ αὐτὸ ποιεῖν ἐστι κἂν εἰ εὐθὺς ἔφη τὸ φέρον
10 φέρεσθαι καὶ διδάσκεσθαι τὸ διδάσκον. δῆλον
γὰρ ὅτι κινεῖται καὶ ὑπὸ τοῦ ἀνωτέρω κινοῦντος
τὸ κινούμενον πᾶν, καὶ μᾶλλον ὑπὸ τοῦ προτέρου
τῶν κινούντων. ἀλλὰ μὴν τοῦτό γε ἀδύνατον· τὸ
διδάσκον γὰρ συμβαίνει μανθάνειν, ὧν τὸ μὲν μὴ
ἔχειν τὸ δ᾽ ἔχειν ἐπιστήμην ἀναγκαῖον.

15 Ἔτι δὲ μᾶλλον τούτων ἄλογον, ὅτι συμβαίνει
πᾶν τὸ κινητικὸν κινητόν, εἴπερ ἅπαν ὑπὸ κινουμένου κινεῖται τὸ κινούμενον· ἔσται γὰρ κινητὸν
ὥσπερ εἴ τις λέγοι πᾶν τὸ ὑγιαστικὸν καὶ ὑγιάζον
ὑγιαστὸν εἶναι, καὶ τὸ οἰκοδομητικὸν οἰκοδομητόν,
20 ἢ εὐθὺς ἢ διὰ πλειόνων (λέγω δ᾽ οἷον εἰ κινητὸν
μὲν ὑπ᾽ ἄλλου πᾶν τὸ κινητικόν, ἀλλ᾽ οὐ ταύτην
τὴν κίνησιν κινητὸν ἣν κινεῖ τὸ πλησίον ἀλλ᾽
ἑτέραν—οἷον τὸ ὑγιαστικὸν μαθητόν—ἀλλὰ τοῦτο
ἐπαναβαῖνον ἥξει ποτὲ εἰς τὸ αὐτὸ εἶδος, ὥσπερ
εἴπομεν πρότερον). τὸ μὲν οὖν τούτων ἀδύνατον,
τὸ δὲ πλασματῶδες· ἄτοπον γὰρ τὸ ἐξ ἀνάγκης τὸ
25 ἀλλοιωτικὸν αὐξητὸν εἶναι.

Οὐκ ἄρα ἀνάγκη ἀεὶ κινεῖσθαι τὸ κινούμενον

---

a [The supposition stated at 256 b 4 and disproved by the
foregoing dilemma.—C.]
326

be to make the series re-entrant into itself, so that we might as well have said at first that what causes local transference must itself be in local transit, and the teacher must himself be in process of being taught what he is teaching. Nay, better say so, for as you go back through the series of antecedent movers you find them all causes of the movement you started from, and the further you go back the more truly causal the cause you have reached. But this co-incidence of teacher and taught, for example, is self-contradictory, for by hypothesis the one has the knowledge and the other has it not.

Further, if everything that is in motion is moved by an agent that is itself in motion,[a] a consequence still more unreasonable will follow, namely that anything capable of causing a change must be capable of suffering change. This is as much as to say that whatever can heal, or is healing, must itself be capable of being healed, and the builder capable of being built. It will be capable of suffering the change either directly or through a chain of intermediate links. (By this latter alternative I mean the supposition that whatever can cause change is capable of suffering change, but not the same change as it conveys to its neighbour but a different one—what can heal, let us say, can be taught : but even so the circle of varied kinds of movement must at some point be re-entrant, as already said, and lead back to the same kind of change.) Now the direct connexion is impossible, and the indirect, as well as involving the direct, rests on a purely fantastic conception ; for how could there be any necessity in an agent that modifies being itself capable of growth ?

In conclusion, then, it is false to say that every-

257 a ὑπ' ἄλλου, καὶ τούτου κινουμένου· στήσεται ἄρα.
ὥστε ἤτοι ὑπὸ ἠρεμοῦντος κινήσεται τὸ κινούμενον
πρῶτον, ἢ αὐτὸ ἑαυτὸ κινήσει. ἀλλὰ μὴν καὶ εἴ
γε δέοι σκοπεῖν πότερον αἴτιον κινήσεως καὶ ἀρχὴ
τὸ αὐτὸ αὑτὸ κινοῦν ἢ τὸ ὑπ' ἄλλου κινούμενον,
30 ἐκεῖνο πᾶς ἂν θείη· τὸ γὰρ αὐτὸ καθ' αὑτὸ ὂν
αἴτιον ἀεὶ πρότερον τοῦ καθ' ἕτερον καὶ αὐτοῦ
ὄντος.

Ὥστε τοῦτο σκεπτέον λαβοῦσιν ἄλλην ἀρχήν,
εἴ τι κινεῖ αὐτὸ αὑτό, πῶς κινεῖ καὶ τίνα τρόπον.
ἀναγκαῖον δὴ τὸ κινούμενον ἅπαν εἶναι διαιρετὸν
εἰς ἀεὶ διαιρετά· τοῦτο γὰρ δέδεικται πρότερον
257 b ἐν τοῖς καθόλου περὶ φύσεως, ὅτι πᾶν τὸ καθ'
αὑτὸ κινούμενον συνεχές. ἀδύνατον δὴ τὸ αὐτὸ
αὑτὸ κινοῦν πάντῃ κινεῖν αὐτὸ αὑτό· φέροιτο γὰρ
ἂν ὅλον καὶ φέροι τὴν αὐτὴν φοράν, ἓν ὂν καὶ
ἄτομον τῷ εἴδει, ἢ ἀλλοιοῖτο καὶ ἀλλοιοῖ, ὥστε
5 διδάσκοι ἂν καὶ διδάσκοιτο ἅμα, καὶ ὑγιάζοι καὶ
ὑγιάζοιτο τὴν αὐτὴν ὑγίειαν. ἔτι διώρισται ὅτι
κινεῖται τὸ κινητόν· τοῦτο δ' ἐστὶ δυνάμει κινού-

ᵃ [Simplicius says this was shown in Book V. (referring
perhaps to 228 a 20 ff.), but the proof he quotes is given in
Book VI. chap. iv.—C.]

thing in motion is moved by something else that
is itself moved by something else ; and it is true to
say that such a series must terminate. Consequently its first member must be moved either
by an agent which is not in motion at all, or
by itself. Now (reserving the alternative of the
first mover being itself not in motion) it is
obvious enough in itself (though we have carefully
established it if it were not) that if anyone had
to determine whether the cause and principle of
movement is to be found in that which moves itself
or in that which is moved by something else, he would
declare for the former, on the general principle that
a cause which is causative in itself must be prior to
that which derives its causative power from some other
cause which is itself also derivatively causative only.

We must, then, start afresh and examine the
question : If there is any self-moving agent of
motion, how does it move itself and with what kind
of motion ? Well then, all divisions of a mobile must
themselves be divisible without limit ; for it has been
shown already, in our general treatment of the
principles of Physics,[a] that whatever can, primarily
and on its own account, be in motion, must be continuous. Hence it follows (1) that if a thing moves
itself it cannot do so integrally in both capacities ;
for that would amount to saying that, being one and
indivisible specifically, it was, in its integrity, both
agent and patient of the same identical transference,
or both the modifier and the modified in respect of
the same modification, so that it might be teacher
and taught simultaneously, or agent and patient of
the same healing. Moreover, it must by definition
be some mobile that is set in motion, and the mobile,

ARISTOTLE

257 b μενον, οὐκ ἐντελεχείᾳ· τὸ δὲ δυνάμει εἰς ἐντελέχειαν βαδίζει, ἔστι δὲ ἡ κίνησις ἐντελέχεια
κινητοῦ ἀτελής. τὸ δὲ κινοῦν ἤδη ἐνεργείᾳ ἐστίν,
10 οἷον θερμαίνει τὸ θερμὸν καὶ ὅλως γεννᾷ τὸ
ἔχον τὸ εἶδος. ὥσθ᾽ ἅμα τὸ αὐτὸ κατὰ τὸ αὐτὸ
θερμὸν ἔσται καὶ οὐ θερμόν. ὁμοίως δὲ καὶ τῶν
ἄλλων ἕκαστον, ὅσων τὸ κινοῦν ἀνάγκη ἔχειν τὸ
συνώνυμον. τὸ μὲν ἄρα κινεῖ τὸ δὲ κινεῖται τοῦ
αὐτὸ αὐτὸ κινοῦντος.

Ὅτι δ᾽ οὐκ ἔστι τὸ αὐτὸ αὐτὸ κινοῦν[1] οὕτως
15 ὥσθ᾽ ἑκάτερον ὑφ᾽ ἑκατέρου κινεῖσθαι, ἐκ τῶνδε
φανερόν. οὔτε γὰρ ἔσται πρῶτον κινοῦν οὐδέν,
εἴ γε ἑκάτερον κινήσει ἑκάτερον· τὸ γὰρ πρότερον
αἰτιώτερον τοῦ κινεῖσθαι τοῦ ἐχομένου καὶ κινήσει
μᾶλλον· διχῶς γὰρ κινεῖν ἦν, τὸ μὲν τὸ ὑπ᾽ ἄλλου
κινούμενον αὐτό, τὸ δ᾽ αὑτῷ· ἐγγύτερον δὲ τὸ
20 πορρώτερον τοῦ κινουμένου τῆς ἀρχῆς ἢ τὸ μεταξύ.
ἔτι οὐκ ἀνάγκη τὸ κινοῦν κινεῖσθαι εἰ μὴ ὑφ᾽
αὑτοῦ· κατὰ συμβεβηκὸς ἄρα ἀντικινεῖ θάτερον.
ἔλαβον τοίνυν ἐνδέχεσθαι μὴ κινεῖν· ἔσται ἄρα τὸ

---

[1] [τὸ αὐτὸ αὐτὸ κινοῦν Simplic. 1237. 3 (lemma): αὐτὸ αὐτὸ κινοῖν EK : αὐτὸ αὐτὸ κινεῖν al.—C.]

---

[a] Cf. Book III. chapters i. and ii. The *mobile* is capable (i.) of being set in motion (transitional or first actualizing), and (ii.) of completing the movement in question and reaching the goal (complete or final actualizing).
[b] [Cf. 202 a 9.—C.]
[c] The reservation apparently is to meet such cases as the favourite ' man is generated by man and the sun,' in which a general cause of the conditions under which a specific cause can produce a specific effect is sometimes spoken of as producing that specific effect itself.
[d] Which exclusion cannot falsify my conclusion. *Cf.* 256 b 10.

330

as such, is potentially, not actually, in motion ; and the potential is still only on its way to actuality (movement being an actualizing, though not a complete one [a]), whereas the mover must already be actualized ; that which heats, for instance, must already be hot, and, universally, the generator must already be in possession of the characteristics to be conferred upon the generated.[b] Thus the ' self-heating ' would have to be both hot and not hot at the same time and in the same respect. And so in all other cases in which producer and produced bear the same denomination.[c] It follows, then, that if anything moves itself, the factor that causes the movement is distinguishable from the factor that is moved.

But (2) that such a case cannot be regarded as one of reciprocal action and passion between the factors concerned may be shown as follows. There would not really be any primary motor at all if each moved the other, for the primacy of causation falls to the agent that is prior to the next most primary and is therefore entitled better than it to be called the source of motion ; for we have seen that ' causing motion ' may be assigned to an agent in two senses, to wit to the agent that is set in motion by something else or to the one set in motion by itself, and that one further back from the object ultimately moved is nearer to the principle of movement than is an intermediate between it and that object. Moreover, there is no necessity for either moving factor to be put in motion by anything but itself ; so it would only be by incidental concomitance that the other moves it in return. I choose then hypothetically to exclude this contingency,[d] and we are left with one element

ARISTOTLE

257 b μὲν κινούμενον, τὸ δὲ κινοῦν ἀκίνητον. ἔτι οὐκ
ἀνάγκη τὸ κινοῦν ἀντικινεῖσθαι, ἀλλ' ἢ ἀκίνητόν
25 γέ τι κινεῖν ἀνάγκη ἢ αὐτὸ ὑφ' αὑτοῦ κινούμενον,
εἴπερ ἀνάγκη ἀεὶ κίνησιν εἶναι. ἔτι ἣν κινεῖ κίνησιν
καὶ κινοῖτ' ἄν, ὥστε τὸ θερμαῖνον θερμαίνεται.

Ἀλλὰ μὴν οὐδὲ τοῦ πρώτως αὐτὸ αὑτὸ κινοῦντος
οὔτε ἓν μόριον οὔτε πλείω κινήσει αὐτὸ αὐτὸ
ἕκαστον. τὸ γὰρ ὅλον εἰ κινεῖται αὐτὸ ὑφ' αὑτοῦ,
30 ἤτοι ὑπὸ τῶν αὑτοῦ τινος κινήσεται ἢ ὅλον ὑφ'
ὅλου. εἰ μὲν οὖν τῷ κινεῖσθαί τι μόριον αὐτὸ ὑφ'
αὑτοῦ, τοῦτ' ἂν εἴη τὸ πρῶτον αὐτὸ αὑτὸ κινοῦν·
χωρισθὲν γὰρ τοῦτο μὲν κινήσει αὐτὸ αὑτό, τὸ δὲ
ὅλον οὐκέτι. εἰ δὲ ὅλον ὑφ' ὅλου κινεῖται, κατὰ
συμβεβηκὸς ἂν ταῦτα κινοῖ αὐτὰ ἑαυτά. ὥστ' εἰ
258 a μὴ ἀναγκαῖον, εἰλήφθω μὴ κινούμενα ὑφ' αὑτῶν.

Τῆς ὅλης ἄρα τὸ μὲν κινήσει ἀκίνητον ὄν, τὸ δὲ
κινηθήσεται· μόνως γὰρ οὕτως οἷόν τέ τι αὐτο-
κίνητον εἶναι.

Ἔτι εἴπερ ἡ ὅλη αὐτὴ αὑτὴν κινεῖ, τὸ μὲν
κινήσει αὐτῆς, τὸ δὲ κινήσεται· ἡ ἄρα ΑΒ ὑφ'
5 αὑτῆς τε κινήσεται καὶ ὑπὸ τῆς Α. ἐπεὶ δὲ κινεῖ
τὸ μὲν κινούμενον ὑπ' ἄλλου τὸ δ' ἀκίνητον ὄν, καὶ

ᵃ Cf. Chapter i.
ᵇ Not receiving heat from the source and passing it on instrumentally or as a mediator to a recipient, but being itself both actually hot so as to heat its neighbour and under ' shortage ' of heat so as to be heated by it.
ᶜ This paragraph is a supplementary afterthought, the proof being complete and the discussion closed without it. It is an alternative form of (2) just above.

that is set in motion and another that moves it but
is not itself in motion at all. Moreover the established fact [a] of the eternity of motion cannot be
appealed to as establishing in its turn any such
reciprocal action ; for all that it establishes is that
there must be either some unmoving cause of motion,
or some self-moving one. And yet again, if there
were such a reciprocal causation of movement it would
have to be of the type 'that which is causing heat is,
qua cause, receiving heat.' [b]

But in truth there cannot be, in that which *primarily*
moves itself, either a single part that moves itself or
a number of parts each of which moves itself. For
if, as we are assuming, the whole is self-moved, it
must be either (2) moved by some part of itself or
(1) moved as a whole by itself as a whole. If then
(2) its motion is due to the self-motion of one of its
parts, this part would be the *primary* self-mover ;
for if isolated from the whole this part would still
move itself, while the whole would do so no longer.
But if (1) the whole is moved by itself as a whole, the
self-motion of the parts will be an accidental circum-
stance ; and since it is not necessary, we are at liberty
to suppose that they do not move themselves.

All the other alternatives being exhausted, then,
we conclude that one factor of whatever is self-moved
causes motion without being in motion and the other
is moved, for only so is self-movement possible.

[c] Again, if the whole moves itself, it must (as we
have just seen) include a factor that causes motion
and another that is moved ; so if the whole AB is
to be described as ' moving itself,' we may also say
that it is moved by the moving factor A. Now
since the motor may either be in motion itself

258 a κινεῖται τὸ μὲν κινοῦν τὸ δὲ οὐθὲν κινοῦν, τὸ αὐτὸ
αὑτὸ κινοῦν ἀνάγκη ἐξ ἀκινήτου εἶναι κινοῦντος δέ,
καὶ ἔτι ἐκ κινουμένου μὴ κινοῦντος δ' ἐξ ἀνάγκης
ἀλλ' ὁπότερ' ἔτυχεν. ἔστω γὰρ τὸ Α κινοῦν μὲν
10 ἀκίνητον δέ, τὸ δὲ Β κινούμενόν τε ὑπὸ τοῦ Α
καὶ κινοῦν τὸ ἐφ' ᾧ Γ, τοῦτο δὲ κινούμενον μὲν
ὑπὸ τοῦ Β, μὴ κινοῦν δὲ μηδέν (εἴπερ γὰρ καὶ διὰ
πλειόνων ἥξει ποτὲ εἰς τὸ Γ, ἔστω δι' ἑνὸς μόνου).
τὸ δὴ ἅπαν ΑΒΓ αὐτὸ ἑαυτὸ κινεῖ. ἀλλ' ἐὰν
ἀφέλω τὸ Γ, τὸ μὲν ΑΒ κινήσει αὐτὸ ἑαυτό—τὸ
μὲν Α κινοῦν, τὸ δὲ Β κινούμενον—τὸ δὲ Γ οὐ
15 κινήσει αὐτὸ ἑαυτό, οὐδ' ὅλως κινήσεται. ἀλλὰ
μὴν οὐδ' ἡ ΒΓ κινήσει αὐτὴ ἑαυτὴν ἄνευ τοῦ Α·
τὸ γὰρ Β κινεῖ τῷ κινεῖσθαι ὑπ' ἄλλου, οὐ τῷ ὑφ'
αὑτοῦ τινος μέρους. τὸ ἄρα ΑΒ μόνον αὐτὸ ἑαυτὸ
κινεῖ. ἀνάγκη ἄρα τὸ αὐτὸ ἑαυτὸ κινοῦν ἔχειν
20 τὸ κινοῦν ἀκίνητον δὲ καὶ τὸ κινούμενον μηδὲν δὲ
κινοῦν ἐξ ἀνάγκης, ἁπτόμενα ἤτοι ἄμφω ἀλλήλων
ἢ θατέρου θάτερον. εἰ μὲν οὖν συνεχές ἐστι τὸ
κινοῦν—τὸ γὰρ κινούμενον ἀναγκαῖον εἶναι συνεχές
—δῆλον ὅτι τὸ πᾶν αὐτὸ ἑαυτὸ κινεῖ οὐ τῷ αὐτοῦ
τι εἶναι τοιοῦτον οἷον αὐτὸ ἑαυτὸ κινεῖν, ἀλλ' ὅλον
25 κινεῖ αὐτὸ ἑαυτό, κινούμενόν τε καὶ κινοῦν τῷ
αὑτοῦ τι εἶναι τὸ κινοῦν καὶ τὸ κινούμενον. οὐ
γὰρ ὅλον κινεῖ οὐδ' ὅλον κινεῖται, ἀλλὰ κινεῖ μὲν

---

[a] [The argument is more easily followed in a concrete
illustration : let A be a man's soul, B his body, C his clothes.
—C.]

[b] The reservation is because if the agent is immaterial it
is said to touch the patient but the patient is not said to touch
it. *Cf. De gen. et corr.* 323 a 25 ff.

(under the action of another motor) or may not be
in motion at all, and since the thing moved may in
its turn either be moving something else or moving
nothing, the self-mover must embrace a factor that
causes motion but is itself unmoved and also a factor
that is in motion and that may or may not, as the
case may be, convey motion to something else. Let
A then be the unmoved mover, B what is moved
by A and in its turn moves C, which is moved by B
but itself moves nothing.[a] (There may of course
be any number of links between B and C, but, as it
makes no difference, we suppose one only.) Then
ABC taken as a whole group moves itself. But
if I take away C out of the group, AB will still move
itself, A being the mover and B the moved ; but C
will neither move itself nor be moved at all. And
neither will BC move itself without A, for B can only
move anything at all in virtue of being moved by
something else, not by any factor it contains in
itself. It is then only AB that really moves itself.
The self-mover, then, must embrace a motor that
cannot itself be a motum, and a motum that need not
itself be a motor ; and motor and motum must be in
contact, either reciprocal or at least in the direction
from motor to motum.[b] If then the motor is continuous[c] (as the motum must necessarily be), obviously the whole self-mover does not move itself in
virtue of some self-moving principle that pervades
it continuously, but moves itself as a whole that
is both suffering and causing motion in virtue of
embracing as factors of itself that which causes
motion and that which suffers it ; for not all of it is
motor, nor all of it motum, but A is the motor and

[a] *i.e.* dimensional, and therefore material.

258 a τὸ Α, κινεῖται δὲ τὸ Β μόνον· τὸ δὲ Γ ὑπὸ τοῦ
Α οὐκέτι· ἀδύνατον γάρ.¹

’Απορίαν δὲ ἔχει, ἐὰν ἀφέλῃ τις ἢ τῆς Α (εἰ συνεχὲς
τὸ κινοῦν μὲν ἀκίνητον δέ) ἢ τῆς Β τῆς κινουμένης·
30 ἡ λοιπὴ ἆρα κινήσει τῆς Α ἢ τῆς Β κινηθήσεται; εἰ
γὰρ τοῦτο, οὐκ ἂν εἴη πρώτως κινουμένη ὑφ’ αὑτῆς
ἡ ΑΒ· ἀφαιρεθείσης γὰρ ἀπὸ τῆς ΑΒ, ἔτι κινήσει
ἑαυτὴν ἡ λοιπὴ ΑΒ. ἢ δυνάμει μὲν ἑκάτερον
258 b οὐδὲν κωλύει ἢ θάτερον τὸ κινούμενον διαιρετὸν
εἶναι, ἐντελεχείᾳ δὲ ἀδιαίρετον· ἐὰν δὲ διαιρεθῇ,
μηκέτι εἶναι ἔχον τὴν αὐτὴν δύναμιν. ὥστ’ οὐδὲν
κωλύει ἐν διαιρετοῖς δυνάμει πρώτως ἐνεῖναι.

Φανερὸν τοίνυν ἐκ τούτων ὅτι ἐστὶ τὸ πρώτως
5 κινοῦν ἀκίνητον· εἴτε γὰρ εὐθὺς ἵσταται τὸ κινούμενον ὑπό τινος δὲ κινούμενον εἰς ἀκίνητον τὸ
πρῶτον, εἴτε εἰς κινούμενον μὲν αὐτὸ δ’ αὑτὸ
κινοῦν καὶ ἱστάν, ἀμφοτέρως συμβαίνει τὸ πρώτως
κινοῦν ἐν ἅπασιν εἶναι τοῖς κινουμένοις ἀκίνητον.

256 b 13 ²⟨Καὶ εὐλόγως δὲ τοῦτο συμβέβηκεν. τρία
15 γὰρ ἀνάγκη εἶναι, τό τε κινούμενον καὶ τὸ κινοῦν
καὶ τὸ ᾧ κινεῖ. τὸ μὲν οὖν κινούμενον ἀνάγκη

¹ [τὸ δὲ Γ . . . ἀδύνατον γάρ is omitted in E. It was un-
known to Alexander and absent in most copies known to
Simplicius (1245. 2).—C.]
² [I have followed Themistius (222. 23) in placing this
paragraph here. No further rearrangement of the text, such
as Alexander (Simplic. 1224. 26) said some critics desired,
is necessary. The conclusion (τοῦτο) which this paragraph
describes as having been reached and commends as reason-
able—that the first mover must be *unmoved*—has not even
been mentioned at the earlier place, and there is nothing
in the preceding context there for τοῦτο to refer to. The
paragraph is an afterthought which was somehow inserted
in the wrong place, where it interrupts the course of the
argument.—C.]

only B is the motum; for there will be no C in the whole (if it be rightly 'self-moving') of which A is the motor : there cannot be.[a]

But supposing A, the unmoved motor, to be continuous, it may be asked : " If we subtract something from A or from the motum B, will the remainder of A continue to act as motor or the remainder of B to be moved ? For if so, AB will not be the primary self-mover, since if you subtract something from it the remainder will still move itself." The answer is that either motor and motum alike or motum only may well be divisible potentially (*qua* dimensional) so long as they are indivisible in their actuality (*qua* entities); for it may be that if divided they would lose the capacities on which the self-moving relation is based. So there is no reason why the primary self-moving characteristic should not inhere in potentially divisible entities.

It is evident, then, from all that we have said that the primary motor is not itself a movable; for the thing in motion under some agent other than itself can always trace back its motion either to a primary unmoved mover or to an agent that is indeed moving but can itself initiate its movement or arrest it,[b] and either way alike the primary motor of anything that is in motion is found to be unmoved.

Now this conclusion is only what we should have expected ; for in the three links of mover, instrument of motion, object moved, the last must experience

---

[a] [Simplicius (1245. 5) thinks that, if this last remark is genuine, it means that AB constitutes a complete self-moving system. The addition of a C would be superfluous, for B may or may not have a C to move (258 a 8).—C.]

[b] *e.g.* a self-moving animal.

256 b μὲν κινεῖσθαι, κινεῖν δὲ οὐκ ἀνάγκη· τὸ δ' ᾧ κινεῖ
καὶ κινεῖν καὶ κινεῖσθαι (συμμεταβάλλει γὰρ τοῦτο
ἅμα καὶ κατὰ τὸ αὐτὸ τῷ κινουμένῳ ὄν· δῆλον δ'
ἐπὶ τῶν κατὰ τόπον κινούντων, ἅπτεσθαι γὰρ
20 ἀλλήλων ἀνάγκη μέχρι τινός), τὸ δὲ κινοῦν οὕτως
ὥστ' εἶναι μὴ ᾧ κινεῖ, ἀκίνητον. ἐπεὶ δ' ὁρῶμεν
τὸ ἔσχατον,[a] ὃ κινεῖσθαι μὲν δύναται, κινήσεως
δὲ ἀρχὴν οὐκ ἔχει, καὶ ὃ κινεῖται μέν, οὐχ ὑπ'
ἄλλου δὲ ἀλλ' ὑφ' αὑτοῦ, εὔλογον—ἵνα μὴ ἀναγκαῖον εἴπωμεν—καὶ τὸ τρίτον εἶναι ὃ κινεῖ ἀκίνη-
25 τον ὄν. διὸ καὶ Ἀναξαγόρας ὀρθῶς λέγει, τὸν
Νοῦν ἀπαθῆ φάσκων καὶ ἀμιγῆ εἶναι, ἐπειδήπερ
κινήσεως ἀρχὴν αὐτὸν ποιεῖ εἶναι· οὕτω γὰρ ἂν
μόνως κινοίη ἀκίνητος ὢν καὶ κρατοίη ἀμιγὴς ὤν.⟩

---

[a] This ἔσχατον is to be taken simply as ' the last of a
connected series '—in this case the series of divine and
immaterial motors, animate self-moving organisms, inanimate
mobilia.

[b] [Anaxagoras, *frag.* 12, so describes *Nous*, except that he
does not say that it is incapable of motion.—C.]

CHAPTER VI

INTRODUCTORY NOTE

The primal cause of all motion is itself motionless.
The primal motion (directly caused by it) is rotation;
all other motions are derivative and vary in complexity
according to their mode of derivation. Thus there is:

1. Uniform motion caused by an agent (A) which is
itself motionless.

2. Regular, but not uniform, motion caused by an
agent (B) which is itself moving with a uniform motion.

3. More complex motion caused by an agent (C) which
is itself moving with a regular, but not uniform, motion.

motion but need not cause it ; the middle term must be in motion itself as well as causing motion in something else (for it accompanies the changes of the thing it moves and keeps pace with it—patently so in the case of local movement where the instrument and the load must remain in (partial) contact somewhere) ; and so if the first term (which by hypothesis causes motion) is to be distinguished from an instrument, it cannot also be itself in motion. And since we find as the last term of the series[a] entities (inanimate objects, to wit) capable of being moved but not of initiating motion, and other entities (living organisms, to wit) including in themselves a factor capable of initiating motion and also one capable of being moved, does not analogy suggest—not to say insist—that there is a third order of entities capable of initiating motion but incapable of being moved ? So Anaxagoras[b] did well to say that ‘ Intelligence ’ was unaffected (by the material universe) and free from admixture, since he regarded it as the principle of movement, and it could only be so if itself motionless, and could only control it if itself unmingled with it.

CHAPTER VI

INTRODUCTORY NOTE (continued)

4. Still more complex motion caused by various combinations of the above (for the same subject can move with more than one motion. See 259 b 30).

The heavens consist of a nest of concentric spheres whose several axes are inclined at various angles to the Prime axis (that of the outermost) ; they and their motions are all eternal. The proper motion of each, viz. uniform

ARISTOTLE

rotation about its own axis, belongs to class 1, and this is
the only motion of the outermost sphere; that of each of
the others is compounded of motions belonging to 1, and
2 or 3: the two latter being derived from one (or more) of
the spheres above it. The sun, moon, and the various
planets (each of which is fixed on the equator of its
proper sphere) move therefore with various degrees of

ARGUMENT

*[We have seen that the primary agent of motion must be
unmoved. The next point is that, if there is to be eternal
and constant motion, there must be at least one eternal
primary unmoved mover. That is all we need to establish,
whether or not there is a plurality of such agents (258 b 10–16).*

*It might be alleged that the souls of animals are unmoved
sources of motion and that they exist at one time and not
at another and so are not eternal. But even so there must be
some eternal agent to account for the perpetual process of
coming into being and perishing and for the fact that souls
exist at some times and not at others (b 16–259 a 6).*

*Is there only one such eternal agent, or more than one?
The view that there is only one is to be preferred on grounds
of the economy of nature, and because a single constant
motion requires a single agent (a 6–20).*

*This conclusion can be supported by a review of the results
already reached with regard to the principles of motion and*

258 b 10   Ἐπεὶ δὲ δεῖ κίνησιν ἀεὶ εἶναι καὶ μὴ διαλείπειν,
ἀνάγκη εἶναί τι ἀίδιον ὃ πρῶτον κινεῖ, εἴτε ἓν εἴτε
πλείω, καὶ τὸ πρῶτον κινοῦν ἀκίνητον. ἕκαστον
μὲν οὖν ἀίδιον εἶναι τῶν ἀκινήτων μὲν κινούντων
δέ, οὐδὲν πρὸς τὸν νῦν λόγον· ὅτι δ' ἀναγκαῖον εἶναι

ᵃ The allusion is to the belief, attributed to the Platonists,

340

complexity. Thus it is easy to see that variable, contrary, and intermittent changes, including genesis and extinction in terrestrial things, may be caused by the influence of the ' stars.'

Cf. *De caelo* ii. 6, 8, 10, and 12, and Sir Th. Heath's *Aristarchus of Samos*, pp. 193 *sqq.*

a closer analysis of the self-motion ascribed to the souls of animals. The only kind of ' self-motion ' animals can be supposed to have is local movement, and strictly this is originated by external causes and therefore cannot be unceasingly maintained. Also the animal's soul moves itself only in the incidental sense that the body carries it from place to place. To cause continuous motion we need an agent that cannot be moved even incidentally (a 20–b 31).

It follows further that what is primarily and directly moved by such an agent—namely the heaven—must be eternal and possess a constant motion, whereas the heavenly bodies, which impart motion to earthly things, have compound and therefore variable motions (b 31–260 a 10).

We can now see why there is constant motion of that which is directly moved by the first unmoved agent, and also intermittent motion derived from variable agents (a 10–19).—C.]

WE have shown that motion must be eternal and can never cease ; so there must be some prime mover, whether singular or plural, that is eternal and not itself movable. The contention that *all* unmoved movers are eternal[a] is not to our present purpose, but the following considerations will show that there

that every ' soul,' *i.e.* the vital principle of every living thing, is immortal. [Plato, *Phaedrus* 245 c.—C.]

ARISTOTLE

258 b τι τὸ ἀκίνητον μὲν αὐτὸ πάσης ἐκτὸς μεταβολῆς
15 καὶ ἁπλῶς καὶ κατὰ συμβεβηκός, κινητικὸν δ᾽
ἑτέρου, δῆλον ὧδε σκοποῦσιν.

Ἔστω δ᾽, εἴ τις βούλεται, ἐπί τινων ἐνδεχόμενον
ὥστ᾽ εἶναί ποτε καὶ μὴ εἶναι ἄνευ γενέσεως καὶ
φθορᾶς (τάχα γὰρ ἀναγκαῖον, εἴ τι ἀμερὲς ὁτὲ
μὲν ἔστιν ὁτὲ δὲ μὴ ἔστιν, ἄνευ τοῦ μεταβάλλειν
20 ὁτὲ μὲν εἶναι ὁτὲ δὲ μὴ εἶναι πᾶν τὸ τοιοῦτον).
καὶ τῶν ἀρχῶν τῶν ἀκινήτων μὲν κινητικῶν δ᾽
ἐνίας ὁτὲ μὲν εἶναι ὁτὲ δὲ μὴ εἶναι, ἐνδεχέσθω καὶ
τοῦτο. ἀλλ᾽ οὔ τι πάσας γε δυνατόν· δῆλον γὰρ ὡς
αἴτιόν τι τοῖς αὐτὰ ἑαυτὰ κινοῦσίν ἐστι τοῦ ὁτὲ
μὲν εἶναι, ὁτὲ δὲ μή. τὸ μὲν γὰρ αὐτὸ ἑαυτὸ
25 κινοῦν ἅπαν ἔχειν ἀνάγκη μέγεθος, εἰ μηδὲν
κινεῖται ἀμερές· τὸ δὲ κινοῦν οὐδεμία ἀνάγκη ἐκ
τῶν εἰρημένων. τοῦ δὴ τὰ μὲν γίγνεσθαι τὰ δὲ
φθείρεσθαι, καὶ τοῦτ᾽ εἶναι συνεχῶς, οὐδὲν αἴτιον
τῶν ἀκινήτων μὲν μὴ ἀεὶ δ᾽ ὄντων, οὐδ᾽ αὖ τῶν
ἀεὶ μὲν ταδὶ κινούντων, τῶν¹ δ᾽ ἕτερα. τοῦ γὰρ
30 ἀεὶ καὶ συνεχοῦς οὔτε ἕκαστον αὐτῶν αἴτιον οὔτε
πάντα· τὸ μὲν γὰρ οὕτως ἔχειν ἀίδιον καὶ ἐξ ἀνάγ-

¹ [τῶν Simplic. 1252. 26, Oxf. Trans.: τούτων codd.—C.]

ᵃ [Aristotle has in view the objection that the souls of animals are unmoved causes of motion, but exist only for a time (though they may not undergo any *process* of coming into being or perishing) and consequently are not eternal. That may be so ; but none the less there must be *some* eternal unmoved mover.—C.]

ᵇ [Because, as shown in Book VI. chapter iv., anything that undergoes a process of change must be divisible into parts.—C.]

must be *something* that is not itself susceptible of any movement in the way of external change, either primarily or incidentally, while it is capable of causing movement in something else.

Let us grant (if anyone chooses to urge it) that there may conceivably be things which sometimes are and sometimes are not, without any process of becoming or perishing *a* (indeed if anything that has no parts exists at one time and not at another, it may be a necessary conclusion that it does so without undergoing any process of change *b*). Further, let us grant the possibility that *some* of the principles that cause motion but are not themselves susceptible of movement belong to this class of things that now are and now are not. But in no case can this be true of *all* such principles ; for it is evident that the coming and going of these intermittently present and not present self-movers must have some cause. For anything which moves itself must have magnitude *qua* mobile (for nothing that cannot be divided can be made to move), but nothing that we have said shows that a cause of motion as such must have magnitude. Accordingly the (prime) cause of the continual genesis and dissolution of the things that come into being and pass out of it cannot be found in any of the unmoved movers whose own existence is not eternal, nor in any group of causes some of which produce motion in certain things and others in certain other things. Neither (as is obvious) can any one of such be the cause of the everlasting and uninterrupted process, nor can the whole sum of them ; for that the process should be everlasting and uninterrupted is an eternal necessity, whereas the whole sum runs back without limit (so that we never

259 a κης, τὰ δὲ πάντα ἄπειρα, καὶ οὐχ ἅμα πάντα
ὄντα. δῆλον τοίνυν ὅτι, εἰ καὶ μυριάκις ἔνιαι
ἀρχαὶ τῶν ἀκινήτων μὲν κινουσῶν δέ, καὶ πολλὰ
τῶν αὐτὰ ἑαυτὰ κινούντων φθείρεται τὰ δ᾽ ἐπι-
γίνεται, καὶ τόδε μὲν ἀκίνητον ὂν τόδε κινεῖ,
ἕτερον δὲ τοδί, ἀλλ᾽ οὐδὲν ἧττον ἔστι τι ὃ περιέχει,
5 καὶ τοῦτο παρ᾽ ἕκαστον, ὅ ἐστιν αἴτιον τοῦ τὰ μὲν
εἶναι τὰ δὲ μὴ καὶ τῆς συνεχοῦς μεταβολῆς· καὶ
τοῦτο μὲν τούτοις, ταῦτα δὲ τοῖς ἄλλοις αἴτια
κινήσεως.

Εἴπερ οὖν ἀΐδιος ἡ κίνησις, ἀΐδιον καὶ τὸ κινοῦν
ἔσται πρῶτον, εἰ ἕν· εἰ δὲ πλείω, πλείω τὰ ἀΐδια.
ἓν δὲ μᾶλλον ἢ πολλὰ καὶ πεπερασμένα ἢ ἄπειρα
10 δεῖ νομίζειν. τῶν αὐτῶν γὰρ συμβαινόντων, ἀεὶ
τὰ πεπερασμένα μᾶλλον ληπτέον· ἐν γὰρ τοῖς
φύσει δεῖ τὸ πεπερασμένον καὶ τὸ βέλτιον, ἐὰν
ἐνδέχηται, ὑπάρχειν μᾶλλον. ἱκανὸν δὲ καὶ ἕν,
ὃ πρῶτον τῶν ἀκινήτων ἀΐδιον ὂν ἔσται ἀρχὴ τοῖς
ἄλλοις κινήσεως. φανερὸν δὲ καὶ ἐκ τοῦδε ὅτι
15 ἀνάγκη εἶναί τι ἓν καὶ ἀΐδιον τὸ πρῶτον κινοῦν.
δέδεικται γὰρ ὅτι ἀνάγκη ἀεὶ κίνησιν εἶναι. εἰ δὲ
ἀεί, ἀνάγκη συνεχῆ εἶναι· καὶ γὰρ τὸ ἀεὶ συνεχές,
τὸ δ᾽ ἐφεξῆς οὐ συνεχές. ἀλλὰ μὴν εἴ γε συνεχής,

ᵃ If (were such a thing possible) they were individually
eternal, and formed a group without limit in number, it
might be another matter. But, on the hypothesis we are
examining, they form an unlimited *succession*, each rising
out of its predecessor.

ᵇ [That the limited is (objectively) *better* than the unlimited
was a Pythagorean doctrine, and indeed a characteristically
Greek conviction. Simplicius (1254. 20) refers to 188 a 18,
where Empedocles' assumption of a small number of limited
elements was praised as ' better ' than the Atomists' and

come to a prime cause at all) and is not coexistent but successive.[a] It is clear, then, that though certain unmoved principles of motion may come and go any number of times, and many self-moving things may perish to be succeeded by others, one unmoving principle moving this mobile and another that, nevertheless there must be something which embraces them all and is distinct from any one of them, and is the cause of the others coming and going and of the continual change. This something, then, is what causes the movement of the first set of moving things, and they pass it on to the others.

So, inasmuch as motion is eternal, it follows that the prime mover, if it be single, or the prime movers, if plural, must likewise be eternal. And by preference we should regard it as one principle rather than many or as a limited rather than an unlimited plurality ; for if the consequences are the same it is always better to assume the more limited antecedent, since in the things of nature the limited, as being better, is sure to be found, wherever possible, rather than the unlimited.[b] And a single principle is adequate, which as the first of the unmoved entities and eternal will suffice as the principle of motion for all the rest. Another proof that there must be some single and eternal first mover is the following. We have shown that eternal movement exists of necessity. And for such movement to be eternal it must be continuous, for what constantly exists at all times is as such continuous, whereas the successive is discontinuous (and therefore not eternal). But for movement to be continuous it must be unified ; and

Anaxagoras's doctrine of an unlimited number of material particles. *Cf.* also 260 b 22.—C.]

259 a μία· μία δ' ἡ ὑφ' ἑνός τε τοῦ κινοῦντος καὶ ἑνὸς
20 τοῦ κινουμένου· εἰ γὰρ ἄλλο καὶ ἄλλο κινήσει, οὐ
συνεχὴς ἡ ὅλη κίνησις ἀλλ' ἐφεξῆς.

Ἔκ τε δὴ τούτων πιστεύσειεν ἄν τις εἶναί τι
πρῶτον ἀκίνητον, καὶ πάλιν ἐπιβλέψας ἐπὶ τὰς
ἀρχὰς τῶν κινούντων. τὸ μὲν δὴ εἶναι ἄττα τῶν
ὄντων ἃ ὁτὲ μὲν κινεῖται ὁτὲ δ' ἠρεμεῖ, φανερόν.
καὶ διὰ τούτου γέγονε δῆλον ὅτι οὔτε πάντα
25 κινεῖται οὔτε πάντα ἠρεμεῖ οὔτε τὰ μὲν ἀεὶ ἠρεμεῖ
τὰ δ' ἀεὶ κινεῖται· τὰ γὰρ ἐπαμφοτερίζοντα καὶ
δύναμιν ἔχοντα τοῦ ὁτὲ μὲν κινεῖσθαι ὁτὲ δὲ
ἠρεμεῖν δείκνυσι περὶ αὐτῶν. ἐπεὶ δὲ τὰ μὲν
τοιαῦτα δῆλα πᾶσι, βουλόμεθα δὲ δεῖξαι καὶ τοῖν
δυοῖν ἑκατέραν τὴν φύσιν, ὅτι ἔστι τὰ μὲν ἀεὶ
30 ἀκίνητα τὰ δ' ἀεὶ κινούμενα, προϊόντες δ' ἐπὶ
τοῦτο καὶ θέντες ἅπαν τὸ κινούμενον ὑπό τινος
κινεῖσθαι, καὶ τοῦτ' εἶναι ἢ ἀκίνητον ἢ κινούμενον,
καὶ κινούμενον ἢ ὑφ' αὐτοῦ ἢ ὑπ' ἄλλου ἀεί, προ-
ήλθομεν ἐπὶ τὸ λαβεῖν ὅτι τῶν κινουμένων ἐστὶν

---

[a] ' If movement is of necessity eternal, it must be continuous. If of necessity eternal and continuous, it must be
single. If of necessity eternal and continuous and single, it
must be the movement of one eternal mobile caused by one
eternal mover. Thus if there must be eternal movement there
must be a single eternal first mover. But the antecedent
has been demonstrated. Therefore the consequent is true.
And that eternal movement must be continuous he proves by
showing that its continuity is involved in its eternity ; for
if it were intermittent it would not be eternal.' Simplicius,
1254. 34 ff.   [b] [In chap. iii.—C.]

[c] [If ἐπεί has any apodosis, it must apparently begin at
259 b 3 ταῦτα δή (where E omits δή).—C.]

[d] [ὑπ' ἄλλου ἀεί. The force of ἀεί is : ' and that again by
something else, and so on.' Cf. Oxf. Trans. note.—C.]

for it to be unified it must be produced by a single
motor in a single mobile, for if the movement were
to be produced now by one thing now by another,
the whole movement would not be continuous but
successional.[a]

So from these considerations one would be led to
believe that there is a prime mover, itself unmoved ;
and the conviction is strengthened by a consideration
of the initiating principles of the (more familiar)
agents of motion. For that there are certain things
that are sometimes in motion and sometimes at rest
is a patent fact. And indeed it was this that com-
pelled us [b] to reject all the three hypotheses : (i.)
that everything is in motion, (ii.) that everything is
at rest, and (iii.) that some things are always in
motion and the remainder always at rest ; for all
these hypotheses are refuted by the existence of
things that are susceptible of either condition and
are now in motion and now at rest. And since [c]
these things that both move and rest are plainly to
be seen of all, it lay upon us to demonstrate the actual
existence of the two other kinds, namely those that
are (not only sometimes but) always without motion,
and those in like manner that are always in motion.
Advancing to which position and laying it down that
everything which is in motion must be moved by
something, that something being itself either unmoving or in motion, and if in motion either moved
by itself or by something else,[d] we arrived at this
conclusion as to the initiating principle of the motion
of moving things : in the cases in which such principle is itself (incidentally) involved in the motion it
causes, it lies (proximately) in a self-moving being ;

259 b ἀρχὴ κινουμένων μὲν¹ ὃ αὐτὸ ἑαυτὸ κινεῖ πάντων
δὲ τὸ ἀκίνητον, ὁρῶμεν δὲ καὶ φανερῶς ὄντα
τοιαῦτα ἃ κινεῖ αὐτὰ ἑαυτά, οἷον τὸ τῶν ἐμψύχων
καὶ τὸ τῶν ζῴων γένος,—ταῦτα δὴ καὶ δόξαν
5 παρεῖχε μή ποτ᾽ ἐνδέχεται κίνησιν ἐγγίγνεσθαι
μὴ οὖσαν ὅλως, διὰ τὸ ἐν τούτοις ὁρᾶν ἡμᾶς τοῦτο
συμβαῖνον· ἀκίνητα γάρ ποτε ὄντα κινεῖται πάλιν,
ὡς δοκεῖ. τοῦτο δὴ δεῖ λαβεῖν, ὅτι μίαν κίνησιν
αὐτὰ² κινεῖ, καὶ ὅτι ταύτην οὐ κυρίως. οὐ γὰρ
ἐξ αὐτοῦ τὸ αἴτιον, ἀλλ᾽ ἔνεισιν ἄλλαι κινήσεις
10 φυσικαὶ τοῖς ζῴοις, ἃς οὐ κινοῦνται δι᾽ αὐτῶν,
οἷον αὔξησις φθίσις ἀναπνοή, ἃς κινεῖται τῶν ζῴων
ἕκαστον ἠρεμοῦν καὶ οὐ κινούμενον τὴν ὑφ᾽ αὐτοῦ
κίνησιν· τούτου δ᾽ αἴτιον τὸ περιέχον καὶ πολλὰ
τῶν εἰσιόντων, οἷον ἐνίων τροφή· πεπτομένης
γὰρ καθεύδουσι, διακρινομένης δὲ ἐγείρονται καὶ
κινοῦσιν ἑαυτούς, τῆς πρώτης ἀρχῆς ἔξωθεν οὔσης.
15 διὸ οὐκ ἀεὶ κινοῦνται συνεχῶς ὑφ᾽ αὑτῶν· ἄλλο
γὰρ τὸ κινοῦν αὐτὸ κινούμενον καὶ μεταβάλλον

---

¹ [κινουμένων μὲν : κινουμένων E : κινούμενον μὲν K. Whether
κινουμένων or κινούμενον be read, it must be explained as by
Dr. Wicksteed: 'things moved has as its
source (κινουμένων μέν) among principles that are themselves
moved (or κινούμενον μέν, as a principle that is itself moved)
that which moves itself, but (as the ultimate principle of the
motion) of all things that which is unmoved.'—C.]

² [αὐτὰ Oxf. Trans. coll. Simplic. 1258. 13 : αὑτὰ codd.—C.]

ᵃ In interpreting and expanding this difficult passage I
follow Simplicius. The first κινουμένων refers to all material
entities that are in motion. The second κινουμένων (as
would be more easily seen if it had been preceded by ἀρχαί
instead of ἀρχή) refers to the class of *causes* of motion described above as κινούμενον, as opposed to ἀκίνητον. The
active factor in such causes shares incidentally in the essential

but the (ultimate and) universal cause lies in a principle that does not move at all.[a] That there really are beings that move themselves, to wit living things and (especially) animals, is plain to see, and accordingly they gave rise to the suggestion [b] that it is possible for there to be such a thing as the absolute initiation of movement *de novo*, as seen in these creatures ; for they seem to be without motion and then again to move. It is therefore important to note that this is only true at all of one order of their movements,[c] and not strictly true of that. For such motion in animals is not self-determined but due to other natural changes which occur in them not by their own agency : growth, decay, and breathing, for instance, go on naturally when they are at rest and not making the movements they themselves determine ; and the causes of these latter movements are found in the environment or in things that enter into the organism itself. Thus animals' food causes some of their motions, since they sleep while the food is being digested, and when it is being distributed they wake and move themselves, but on the initiation of an external cause. And this is why they do not maintain continuous and unceasing self-movements, since there is in every case another cause, of the order of movers that are themselves in motion, which changes when it acts upon the self-moving

movement which it provokes in the passive factor ; so that the concrete being is self-moved. But seeing that this active factor will be shown (in the immediate sequel) to be itself a link in a chain and not a true *initiator* of movement, it follows that the ultimate cause of all motion is itself exempt from any share (even incidental) in the motion it causes.
    [b] [This suggestion was provisionally rejected in chap. ii. 253 a 7 ff.—C.]   [c] [Namely, local movements.—C.]

ARISTOTLE

259 b πρὸς ἕκαστον τῶν κινούντων ἑαυτά. ἐν πᾶσι δὲ
τούτοις κινεῖται τὸ κινοῦν πρῶτον καὶ τὸ αἴτιον
τοῦ αὐτὸ ἑαυτὸ κινεῖν ὑφ' αὑτοῦ· κατὰ συμβεβηκὸς μέντοι, μεταβάλλει γὰρ τὸν τόπον τὸ σῶμα,
20 ὥστε καὶ τὸ ἐν τῷ σώματι ὂν καὶ τῇ μοχλείᾳ[1]
κινοῦν ἑαυτό. ἐξ ὧν ἔστι πιστεῦσαι ὅτι εἴ τί
ἐστι τῶν ἀκινήτων μὲν κινούντων δὲ καὶ αὐτῶν
κινουμένων κατὰ συμβεβηκός, ἀδύνατον συνεχῆ
κίνησιν κινεῖν. ὥστ' εἴπερ ἀνάγκη συνεχῶς εἶναι
κίνησιν, εἶναί τι δεῖ τὸ πρῶτον κινοῦν ἀκίνητον
25 καὶ[2] κατὰ συμβεβηκός, εἰ μέλλει (καθάπερ εἴπομεν) ἔσεσθαι ἐν τοῖς οὖσιν ἄπαυστός τις καὶ
ἀθάνατος κίνησις καὶ μενεῖν[3] τὸ ὂν αὐτὸ ἐν αὑτῷ
καὶ ἐν τῷ αὐτῷ· τῆς γὰρ ἀρχῆς μενούσης ἀνάγκη
καὶ τὸ πᾶν μένειν, συνεχὲς ὂν πρὸς τὴν ἀρχήν.
(οὐκ ἔστι δὲ τὸ αὐτὸ τὸ κινεῖσθαι κατὰ συμβεβηκὸς
ὑφ' αὑτοῦ καὶ ὑφ' ἑτέρου· τὸ μὲν γὰρ ὑφ' ἑτέρου
30 ὑπάρχει καὶ τῶν ἐν τῷ οὐρανῷ ἐνίαις ἀρχαῖς, ὅσα
πλείους φέρεται φοράς, θάτερον δὲ τοῖς φθαρτοῖς
μόνον.)

Ἀλλὰ μὴν εἴ γε ἔστι τι ἀεὶ τοιοῦτον, κινοῦν μέν
τι ἀκίνητον δὲ αὐτὸ καὶ ἀίδιον, ἀνάγκη καὶ τὸ
260 a πρῶτον ὑπὸ τούτου κινούμενον ἀίδιον εἶναι. ἔστι
δὲ τοῦτο δῆλον μὲν καὶ ἐκ τοῦ μὴ ἂν ἄλλως
εἶναι γένεσιν καὶ φθορὰν καὶ μεταβολὴν τοῖς

---

[1] [τῇ μοχλείᾳ HIK, Simplic. 1256. 32 (lemma): τὸ ἐν τῇ μοχλείᾳ al.—C.]
[2] [καὶ H, Simplic. 1260. 11: καὶ μὴ cett.—C.]
[3] [μενεῖν Oxf. Trans. coll. Them. 224. 21: μένειν codd.—C.]

---

[a] [Namely, the soul. If this changes its place, it does so
only as contained in a body which moves about carrying the
soul with it, and which the soul uses as a sort of lever.—C.]
350

organism. And in all these cases the active factor of movement,[a] the source of movement which is the cause of the whole organism being self-moving, is itself also set in motion by itself, but only incidentally ; for the body changes its place, and is accompanied in this change by that within the body which moves itself too with leverage it employs. Whence we may infer that no member of the class of the (essentially) unmoved causes of movement which is itself moved incidentally can be the cause of continuous movement. So that if there must needs be a continuous movement, there must be some primary mover which is not even incidentally moved, if, as we have said,[b] there is to be amongst things that exist a certain unceasing and deathless movement, and the universe is to abide self-contained and constant ; for only if the principle abides, the sum of things, being in continuous relation with it, must also abide. (But it is not the same for an agent to be incidentally moved by itself or by some other, for to be so moved by another applies to some principles of heavenly bodies, those to wit which are carried by several motions.[c] But the other alternative—that it should be incidentally self-moved—occurs only in perishable things.)

But if there really is such an existence (A), causing motion but itself unmoved and eternal, that (B) which is immediately moved by it must likewise be eternal. This is evident from the very fact that genesis and evanishment and change occur to all else for no other reason than that they are moved by something that

[b] [Chap. i.—C.]
[c] For the movements of the heavenly bodies see Vol. I. Introd. p. lxviii and Introd. Note to this chapter.

260 a ἄλλοις, εἰ μή τι κινήσει κινούμενον· τὸ μὲν γὰρ
ἀκίνητον ἀεὶ τὸν αὐτὸν κινήσει τρόπον καὶ μίαν
5 κίνησιν, ἅτε οὐδὲν αὐτὸ μεταβάλλον πρὸς τὸ
κινούμενον· τὸ δὲ κινούμενον ὑπὸ τοῦ κινουμένου
μέν, ὑπὸ τοῦ ἀκινήτου δὲ κινουμένου ἤδη, διὰ
τὸ ἄλλως καὶ ἄλλως ἔχειν πρὸς τὰ πράγματα,
οὐ τῆς αὐτῆς ἔσται κινήσεως αἴτιον, ἀλλὰ διὰ τὸ
ἐν ἐναντίοις εἶναι τόποις ἢ εἴδεσιν ἐναντίως παρ-
10 έξεται κινούμενον ἕκαστον τῶν ἄλλων, καὶ ὁτὲ
μὲν ἠρεμοῦν, ὁτὲ δὲ κινούμενον.

Φανερὸν δὴ γέγονεν ἐκ τῶν εἰρημένων καὶ ὃ κατ'
ἀρχὰς ἠποροῦμεν, τί δή ποτε οὐ πάντα ἢ κινεῖται
ἢ ἠρεμεῖ, ἢ τὰ μὲν κινεῖται ἀεὶ τὰ δ' ἀεὶ ἠρεμεῖ,
ἀλλ' ἔνια ὁτὲ μὲν ὁτὲ δ' οὔ. τούτου γὰρ τὸ αἴτιον
15 δῆλόν ἐστι νῦν, ὅτι τὰ μὲν ὑπὸ ἀκινήτου κινεῖται
ἀιδίου, διὸ ἀεὶ κινεῖται, τὰ δ' ὑπὸ κινουμένου καὶ
μεταβάλλοντος, ὥστε καὶ αὐτὰ ἀναγκαῖον μεταβάλλειν. τὸ δ' ἀκίνητον, ὥσπερ εἴρηται, ἅτε
ἁπλῶς καὶ ὡσαύτως καὶ ἐν τῷ αὐτῷ διαμένον,
μίαν καὶ ἁπλῆν κινήσει κίνησιν.

CHAPTER VII

ARGUMENT

[*A fresh start. Can any motion continue for ever without
interruption, and if so what motion ? And what form of
motion is prior to all others ? If motion is to be eternal, the
motion which is both continuous and primary must be that
caused by the primary mover (260 a 20–26).*

*Local motion is prior both to change of quality and to
change of quantity : such changes cannot occur without
movement in space (a 26–b 15).*
352

is itself in motion ; for the motion caused by the unmoved (A) will be a single motion caused always in the same way, since it in no way changes in relation to the mobile ; whereas that (C) which is moved by an agent (B) that is in motion, though that motion be immediately caused by the unmoving, inasmuch as it (C) changes its relation to the things (D) it moves, will not cause a uniform movement, but because of its contrasted positions or characteristics will produce contrary movements in each of the things it affects, and any such movements will be intermittent.

So now, from all that has been said, the answer is clear to the question from which we started : How comes it about that it is neither true that all things are in motion nor that all things are at rest, nor that some things are always in motion and the remainder always at rest, but that there are things which are sometimes in the one state and sometimes in the other ? The reason of this is now obvious, namely, that some things derive their motion from an eternal and immovable cause, and therefore their motion is constant, whereas others derive their motion from a cause which is itself in motion and changing, and therefore they also must necessarily be changing. The immovable, as we have said, being simple and unchanging and self-constant, causes an unbroken and simple motion.

CHAPTER VII

ARGUMENT (continued)

Local motion is prior to all other kinds of change in all the three senses of priority (b 15–19) : (1) *it can exist without the others, but the others cannot exist without it* (b 19–29);

353

ARGUMENT (*continued*)

(2) *it is prior in time, as the only motion possible to eternal things ; and locomotion must precede even ' coming-into-being '* (b 29–261 a 12) ; (3) *it is prior in the order of nature, as being last in the order of development of the perfect form* (a 13–26).

Locomotion, then, being prior to all other changes, what species of locomotion is primary ? The answer will establish what we have assumed—that a continuous eternal motion is possible (a 27–31).

No other kind of change can continue without interruption,

260 a 20   Οὐ μὴν ἀλλὰ καὶ ἄλλην ποιησαμένοις ἀρχὴν μᾶλλον ἔσται περὶ τούτων φανερόν. σκεπτέον γὰρ πότερον ἐνδέχεταί τινα κίνησιν εἶναι συνεχῆ ἢ οὔ, καὶ
εἰ ἐνδέχεται, τίς αὕτη, καὶ τίς πρώτη τῶν κινήσεων·
δῆλον γὰρ ὡς εἴπερ ἀναγκαῖον μὲν ἀεὶ κίνησιν εἶναι,
25   πρώτη δὲ ἥδε καὶ συνεχής, ὅτι τὸ πρῶτον κινοῦν
κινεῖ ταύτην τὴν κίνησιν, ἣν ἀναγκαῖον μίαν καὶ
τὴν αὐτὴν εἶναι καὶ συνεχῆ καὶ πρώτην.

Τριῶν δ' οὐσῶν κινήσεων, τῆς τε κατὰ μέγεθος
καὶ τῆς κατὰ πάθος καὶ τῆς κατὰ τόπον, ἣν καλοῦ-
μεν φοράν, ταύτην ἀναγκαῖον εἶναι πρώτην. ἀδύνα-
30   τον γὰρ αὔξησιν εἶναι ἀλλοιώσεως μὴ προϋπαρ-
χούσης· τὸ γὰρ αὐξανόμενον ἔστι μὲν ὡς ὁμοίῳ
αὐξάνεται, ἔστι δ' ὡς ἀνομοίῳ· τροφὴ γὰρ λέγεται
τῷ ἐναντίῳ τὸ ἐναντίον, προσγίγνεται δὲ πᾶν
γιγνόμενον ὅμοιον ὁμοίῳ. ἀνάγκη οὖν ἀλλοίω-
260 b   σιν εἶναι τὴν εἰς τἀναντία μεταβολήν. ἀλλὰ μὴν
εἴ γε ἀλλοιοῦται, δεῖ τι εἶναι τὸ ἀλλοιοῦν καὶ
ποιοῦν ἐκ τοῦ δυνάμει θερμοῦ τὸ ἐνεργείᾳ θερμόν.

---

[a] [This doctrine that nourishment involves qualitative assimilation is discussed in *De anima* 416 a 19 ff.—C.]

ARGUMENT (continued)

because all other kinds of change take place in opposite directions between contrary, or (in the case of genesis and perishing) contradictory, extremes. When the change reaches an extreme it must cease. Whether it is succeeded by a state of rest or by a contrary change does not matter ; what matters is that no change can coexist with either rest or the contrary change (a 31–b 26).—C.]

BUT conclusive as all this may be, it will be clearer yet if we start again and approach it from another direction. For we may ask ourselves whether it is possible for there to be any continuous motion at all, and if so of what nature such motion must be ; and also what kind of motion must be prior to all others. For it is obvious that if there must be eternal motion, and if some particular motion is primary and continuous, then that is just the motion which the prime mover causes—necessarily unbroken and uniform and everlasting and primary.

Now of the three kinds of motion (in the larger sense of change in general), to wit change of quantity, change of quality, and change of place, which we call ' locomotion,' this last named must come first. For growth cannot take place without change of qualities preceding it, for though that which grows may be said in one sense to increase by addition of its like, in another sense it grows by addition of its unlike ; for there is a contrast of unlikeness between the food and the fed, and every accession is caused by the unlike becoming like, which passage from unlikeness to likeness constitutes change of quality.[a] But if there is change of quality there must be something that causes the change and makes, for instance, what was susceptible of being heated

260 b δῆλον οὖν ὅτι τὸ κινοῦν οὐχ ὁμοίως ἔχει, ἀλλ' ὁτὲ
μὲν ἐγγύτερον ὁτὲ δὲ πορρώτερον τοῦ ἀλλοιουμένου
5 ἐστίν· ταῦτα δ' ἄνευ φορᾶς οὐκ ἐνδέχεται ὑπάρχειν.
εἰ ἄρα ἀνάγκη ἀεὶ κίνησιν εἶναι, ἀνάγκη καὶ φορὰν
ἀεὶ εἶναι πρώτην τῶν κινήσεων, καὶ φορᾶς, εἰ
ἔστιν ἡ μὲν πρώτη ἡ δ' ὑστέρα, τὴν πρώτην. ἔτι
δὲ πάντων τῶν παθημάτων ἀρχὴ πύκνωσις καὶ
10 μάνωσις—καὶ γὰρ βαρὺ καὶ κοῦφον καὶ μαλακὸν
καὶ σκληρὸν καὶ θερμὸν καὶ ψυχρὸν πυκνότητες
δοκοῦσι καὶ ἀραιότητες εἶναί τινες—πύκνωσις
δὲ καὶ μάνωσις σύγκρισις καὶ διάκρισις, καθ' ἃς
γένεσις καὶ φθορὰ λέγεται τῶν οὐσιῶν· συγκρινό-
μενα δὲ καὶ διακρινόμενα ἀνάγκη κατὰ τόπον
μεταβάλλειν. ἀλλὰ μὴν καὶ τοῦ αὐξανομένου καὶ
φθίνοντος μεταβάλλει κατὰ τόπον τὸ μέγεθος.
15 Ἔτι καὶ ἐντεῦθεν ἐπισκοποῦσιν ἔσται φανερὸν
ὅτι ἡ φορὰ πρώτη. τὸ γὰρ πρῶτον ὥσπερ καὶ ἐπὶ
τῶν ἄλλων, οὕτω καὶ ἐπὶ κινήσεως ἂν λέγοιτο
πλεοναχῶς· λέγεται δὲ πρότερον, οὗ τε μὴ ὄντος
οὐκ ἔσται τἆλλα, ἐκεῖνο δὲ ἄνευ τῶν ἄλλων, καὶ
τὸ τῷ χρόνῳ, καὶ τὸ κατ' οὐσίαν.

ᵃ Philoponus, Albertus Magnus, and Aquinas all insist
that Aristotle is here taking the Atomists on their own ground
but not committing himself to their doctrine. Hence the
reservations ' are taken to be ' and ' are supposed to be.'
[The reference may be to the Ionian Monists. At *Met.*
988 b 29 ff. they are criticized, as a group, for deriving the
qualitative differences of the four elements from the σύγκρισις
(*i.e.* πύκνωσις) of a single primary element without deciding
whether this is to be Fire or Air or Water. See Simplic.
Phys. 1319. 17 ff. *Cf.* 265 b 17–266 a 5, where Aristotle
says that all the physicists down to and including Plato

actually hot. And for this to come about the moving
cause obviously cannot remain just as it was, but
must approach or recede from that which it modifies ;
and that can only happen by local movement. If,
then, there must always be motion (in the larger
sense) there must always be local movement, which
takes precedence amongst all the kinds of motion ;
and if there is an order of precedence in the different
kinds of local movements, then it must be the primal
form of local movement that always continues.
Further, the principle of all changes of quality is
condensation and rarification, for heavy and light,
soft and hard, hot and cold are taken to be different
manifestations of condensation and rarification, and
condensation and rarification, again, to be identical
with the combination and resolution by which the
genesis and evanishment of things are supposed
to come about.[a] But combination and resolution
necessarily involve change of place. Moreover, all
that grows or shrinks changes locally in that it
changes in size.[b]

Yet again it can be proved that local motion takes
precedence of the others by the following considerations. In regard to motion, as in regard to everything else, 'priority' has several meanings : (1) that
has priority without which the things to which it is
said to be prior cannot exist, whereas it can exist
without them ; (2) the priority may be in time ; and
(3) in respect of perfection of nature.

implied that locomotion was the primary form of all
change.—C.]

[b] It has been shown that its nourishment changes in
quality and that this involves local changes. It is now added
that the mere occupying more or less room is itself a local
change.

ARISTOTLE

260 b 20 Ὥστ' ἐπεὶ κίνησιν μὲν ἀναγκαῖον εἶναι συνεχῶς,
εἴη δ' ἂν συνεχῶς ἢ ἡ συνεχὴς ἢ ἡ ἐφεξῆς, μᾶλλον
δ' ἡ συνεχής, καὶ βέλτιον συνεχῆ ἢ ἐφεξῆς εἶναι,
τὸ δὲ βέλτιον ἀεὶ ὑπολαμβάνομεν ἐν τῇ φύσει
ὑπάρχειν, ἂν ᾖ δυνατόν, δυνατὸν δὲ συνεχῆ εἶναι
(δειχθήσεται δὲ ὕστερον· νῦν δὲ τοῦθ' ὑποκείσθω),
25 καὶ ταύτην οὐδεμίαν ἄλλην οἷόν τ' εἶναι ἀλλ' ἢ
φοράν, ἀνάγκη τὴν φορὰν εἶναι πρώτην. οὐδεμία
γὰρ ἀνάγκη οὔτε αὔξεσθαι οὔτε ἀλλοιοῦσθαι τὸ
φερόμενον, οὐδὲ δὴ γίγνεσθαι ἢ φθείρεσθαι· τούτων
δὲ οὐδεμίαν ἐνδέχεται τῆς συνεχοῦς μὴ οὔσης, ἣν
κινεῖ τὸ πρῶτον κινοῦν.

30 Ἔτι χρόνῳ πρώτην· τοῖς γὰρ ἀιδίοις μόνον
ἐνδέχεται κινεῖσθαι ταύτην. ἀλλ' ἐφ' ἑνὸς μὲν
ὁτουοῦν τῶν ἐχόντων γένεσιν τὴν φορὰν ἀναγκαῖον ὑστάτην εἶναι τῶν κινήσεων· μετὰ γὰρ τὸ
γενέσθαι πρῶτον ἀλλοίωσις καὶ αὔξησις, φορὰ
261 a δ' ἤδη τετελειωμένων κίνησίς ἐστιν. ἀλλ' ἕτερον
ἀνάγκη κινούμενον εἶναι κατὰ φορὰν πρότερον, ὃ
καὶ τῆς γενέσεως αἴτιον ἔσται τοῖς γιγνομένοις,
οὐ γιγνόμενον, οἷον τὸ γεννῆσαν τοῦ γεννηθέντος.
ἐπεὶ δόξειέ γ' ἂν ἡ γένεσις εἶναι πρώτη τῶν
κινήσεων διὰ τοῦτο, ὅτι γενέσθαι δεῖ τὸ πρᾶγμα
5 πρῶτον· τὸ δ' ἐφ' ἑνὸς μὲν ὁτουοῦν τῶν γιγνομένων
οὕτως ἔχει, ἀλλ' ἕτερον ἀναγκαῖον πρότερόν τι

---

a i.e. either the same motion must go on continuously or
different motions must succeed one another without a pause.
b [Chap. viii.—C.]
c Animals and plants are primarily in Aristotle's mind.
d As manifested by self-movers.

Thus (1) since motion must necessarily go on without intermission, and to do so must either be continuous or successive,[a] of which continuity is to be preferred as the better, and since we must always assume the better, if it be not impossible, to be what actually occurs in nature, and since (as will be demonstrated hereafter,[b] and may be assumed meanwhile) continuity is not impossible in this case, and no other but local motion can be continuous, it follows that local motion has the priority in the first sense. For the fact that a thing is changing its place is no reason why it should also be growing or changing its qualities, or coming into existence or vanishing out of it ; whereas none of these other changes could take place, were it not for the continuous motion which the prime mover causes.

Further (2) it is first in time, for it is the only motion of which things eternal are capable. It is true that if we take any one individual thing that comes into being and vanishes out of it,[c] local movement must be the *last* which it experiences, for after it has begun to exist modification and growth are the first to set in, whereas local motion [d] is the characteristic movement of the 'accomplished' creature. On the other hand, all this must be preceded by some other cause which is locally in motion and acts as the cause of things coming into existence without itself being in process of coming into existence, as we see in the case of the begetter and the begotten. It might seem that genesis could claim the priority amongst movements, on the ground that the thing must be generated before all else ; but though this is so with respect to any one thing that comes to be, yet something which is not coming into existence

359

ARISTOTLE

261 a κινεῖσθαι τῶν γιγνομένων ὂν αὐτὸ καὶ μὴ γιγνόμενον, καὶ τούτου ἕτερον πρότερον. ἐπεὶ δὲ
γένεσιν ἀδύνατον εἶναι πρώτην (πάντα γὰρ ἂν εἴη
τὰ κινούμενα φθαρτά), δῆλον ὡς οὐδὲ τῶν ἐφεξῆς
10 κινήσεων οὐδεμία προτέρα—λέγω δ' ἐφεξῆς αὔξησιν,
εἶτ' ἀλλοίωσιν καὶ φθίσιν καὶ φθοράν—πᾶσαι γὰρ
ὕστεραι γενέσεως, ὥστ' εἰ μηδὲ γένεσις προτέρα
φορᾶς, οὐδὲ τῶν ἄλλων οὐδεμία μεταβολῶν.

Ὅλως δὲ φαίνεται τὸ γιγνόμενον ἀτελὲς καὶ ἐπ'
ἀρχὴν ἰόν, ὥστε τὸ τῇ γενέσει ὕστερον τῇ φύσει
πρότερον εἶναι. τελευταῖον δὲ φορὰ πᾶσιν ὑπάρχει
15 τοῖς ἐν γενέσει. διὸ τὰ μὲν ὅλως ἀκίνητα τῶν
ζώντων δι' ἔνδειαν τοῦ ὀργάνου, οἷον τὰ φυτὰ καὶ
πολλὰ γένη τῶν ζῴων, τοῖς δὲ τελειουμένοις
ὑπάρχει. ὥστ' εἰ μᾶλλον ὑπάρχει φορὰ τοῖς
μᾶλλον ἀπειληφόσι τὴν φύσιν, καὶ ἡ κίνησις αὕτη
πρώτη τῶν ἄλλων ἂν εἴη κατ' οὐσίαν, διά τε ταῦτα
20 καὶ διότι ἥκιστα τῆς οὐσίας ἐξίσταται τὸ κινούμενον τῶν κινήσεων ἐν τῷ φέρεσθαι· κατὰ μόνην
γὰρ οὐδὲν μεταβάλλει τοῦ εἶναι, ὥσπερ ἀλλοιουμένου μὲν τὸ ποιόν, αὐξανομένου δὲ καὶ φθίνοντος
τὸ ποσόν. μάλιστα δὲ δῆλον ὅτι τὸ κινοῦν αὐτὸ

360

but actually exists must in every case have been already moving before the inception of the thing which is coming into existence, and another again before that other. And since genesis cannot have been the absolute first (for if so all moving things would be perishable), it is clear that neither can any of the movements next in order (by which I mean growth, modification, decay, and passing away) take the precedence, since they are all subsequent to genesis ; so that if genesis does not precede local movement neither can any of the other forms of change do so.

Finally (3), taking broad ground, we may say that anything which is in process of coming into being proclaims itself as imperfect, and as making for some constituent principle which is already there in the nature of things, so that what it comes to last in its own genesis precedes it in the order of nature. Now local movement is the final characteristic that manifests itself in generated creatures. This is why some living creatures, such as plants and many kinds of animals, cannot move for lack of the appropriate organ, while others possess the power as they come to perfection. So if local movement characterizes things in proportion to the fulness of nature they have realized, this same kind of movement should take precedence of all others in respect of perfection of nature. And besides this, there is another reason, namely, that of all kinds of change local movement is the one which takes its subject least away from its essential nature, for it is the only one that affects no intimate characteristic, as modification affects quality and growth or shrinkage quantity. But most convincing of all is the fact that it is just this local move-

361

261 a 25 αὐτὸ μάλιστα ταύτην κινεῖ κυρίως τὴν κατὰ τόπον·
καίτοι φαμὲν τοῦτ' εἶναι τῶν κινουμένων καὶ
κινούντων ἀρχήν, καὶ πρῶτον τοῖς κινουμένοις τὸ
αὐτὸ αὑτὸ κινοῦν.

Ὅτι μὲν τοίνυν τῶν κινήσεων ἡ φορὰ πρώτη,
φανερὸν ἐκ τούτων· τίς δὲ φορὰ πρώτη, νῦν δεικτέον.
ἅμα δὲ καὶ τὸ νῦν καὶ πρότερον ὑποτεθέν, ὅτι
30 ἐνδέχεταί τινα κίνησιν εἶναι συνεχῆ καὶ ἀίδιον,
φανερὸν ἔσται τῇ αὐτῇ μεθόδῳ.

Ὅτι μὲν οὖν τῶν ἄλλων κινήσεων οὐδεμίαν
ἐνδέχεται συνεχῆ εἶναι, ἐκ τῶνδε φανερόν. ἅπασαι
γὰρ ἐξ ἀντικειμένων εἰς ἀντικείμενά εἰσιν αἱ κινήσεις καὶ μεταβολαί—οἷον γενέσει μὲν καὶ φθορᾷ
35 τὸ ὂν καὶ τὸ μὴ ὂν ὅροι, ἀλλοιώσει δὲ τἀναντία
πάθη, αὐξήσει δὲ καὶ φθίσει ἢ μέγεθος καὶ μι-
κρότης ἢ τελειότης μεγέθους καὶ ἀτέλεια—ἐναντίαι
261 b δ' αἱ εἰς τὰ ἐναντία. τὸ δὲ μὴ ἀεὶ κινούμενον τήνδε
τὴν κίνησιν, ὂν δὲ πρότερον, ἀνάγκη πρότερον
ἠρεμεῖν. φανερὸν οὖν ὅτι ἠρεμήσει ἐν τῷ ἐναντίῳ
τὸ μεταβάλλον. ὁμοίως δὲ καὶ ἐπὶ τῶν μεταβολῶν·

---

a [At 260 b 23 and 259 a 16.—C.]
b Such as hot and cold, light and heavy.
c [Hence its change cannot be continuous.—C.]
d [Cf. 225 a 31. Every ' movement ' (κίνησις, i.e. change of quality, quantity, or place) is a ' change ' (μεταβολή); becoming and perishing are ' changes,' not ' movements.'—C.]
362

ment and no other which is, properly speaking, made by the self-mover as such ; and it is just this self-mover that we have pronounced to be the principle, amongst things that are both in motion themselves and causes of motion in others, and the initiator of the movement of moving things.

That local motion takes precedence of the other motions has thus been demonstrated, and we must now go on to show what form of local movement itself takes precedence of the others ; in the course of which investigation we shall demonstrate what we have, in the present context and earlier,[a] laid down provisionally as to the possibility of there actually being a continuous and eternal movement.

To begin with, it is clear from the following considerations that no progression other than local movement can be continuous and perpetual. All the other progressions or changes are between one term and its opposite—for instance, existence and non-existence are the limiting terms of genesis and evanishment ; the extremes either way are the limits of qualitative modifications [b] ; and the greatest and least possible size, or maximum approach to, or defect from, the perfect norm of size, are the limits of growth and shrinkage — and movements directed to opposite limits are opposite to each other. Now a mobile which has not always been subject to a given movement, but was in existence before it began it, must then have been exempt from that movement ; so it is clear that that movement of the changing thing will cease when it reaches either extreme.[c] And so too with (pure) changes (that are not movements [d]) ;

ARISTOTLE

231 b 5 ἀντίκειται γὰρ ἡ φθορὰ καὶ γένεσις ἁπλῶς καὶ ἡ
καθ' ἕκαστον τῇ καθ' ἕκαστον· ὥστ' εἰ ἀδύνατον
ἅμα μεταβάλλειν τὰς ἀντικειμένας, οὐκ ἔσται
συνεχὴς ἡ μεταβολή, ἀλλὰ μεταξὺ ἔσται αὐτῶν
χρόνος. οὐδὲν γὰρ διαφέρει ἐναντίας ἢ μὴ ἐναντίας
10 εἶναι τὰς κατ' ἀντίφασιν μεταβολάς, εἰ μόνον
ἀδύνατον ἅμα τῷ αὐτῷ παρεῖναι· τοῦτο γὰρ τῷ
λόγῳ οὐδὲν χρήσιμον. οὐδ' εἰ μὴ ἀνάγκη ἠρεμῆσαι
ἐν τῇ ἀντιφάσει, μηδ' ἐστὶ μεταβολῇ ἠρεμία¹ ἐναντίον
—οὐ γὰρ ἴσως ἠρεμεῖ τὸ μὴ ὄν· ἡ δὲ φθορὰ εἰς τὸ
μὴ ὄν—ἀλλ' εἰ μόνον μεταξὺ γίγνεται χρόνος· οὕτω
γὰρ οὐκ ἔστιν ἡ μεταβολὴ συνεχής· οὐδὲ γὰρ ἐν
15 τοῖς πρότερον ἡ ἐναντίωσις χρήσιμον, ἀλλὰ τὸ μὴ
ἐνδέχεσθαι ἅμα ὑπάρχειν. οὐ δεῖ δὲ ταράττεσθαι
ὅτι τὸ αὐτὸ πλείοσιν ἔσται ἐναντίον, οἷον ἡ κίνησις
καὶ στάσει καὶ κινήσει τῇ εἰς τοὐναντίον, ἀλλὰ
μόνον τοῦτο λαμβάνειν, ὅτι ἀντίκειταί πως καὶ
τῇ κινήσει καὶ τῇ ἠρεμίᾳ ἡ κίνησις ἡ ἐναντία
20 (καθάπερ τὸ ἴσον καὶ τὸ μέτριον τῷ ὑπερέχοντι
καὶ τῷ ὑπερεχομένῳ), καὶ ὅτι οὐκ ἐνδέχεται ἅμα
τὰς ἀντικειμένας οὔτε κινήσεις οὔτε μεταβολὰς
ὑπάρχειν. ἔτι δ' ἐπί τε τῆς γενέσεως καὶ τῆς
φθορᾶς καὶ παντελῶς ἄτοπον ἂν εἶναι δόξειεν, εἰ

¹ [μεταβολῇ ἠρεμία HI, Oxf. Trans.: μεταβολὴ ἠρεμίᾳ cett.
—C.]
364

for genesis and evanishment taken absolutely are absolute opposites, and any specific genesis and evanishment are specifically opposite to each other ; and so, since nothing can be changing in opposite directions at the same time, a change in neither direction can be continuous, but there must be an interval of time between any two stretches of it. Nor does it make any difference whether you count these contradictory changes amongst ' contraries ' or not, for in any case, as long as changes in the two directions cannot coexist, this point does not affect the argument. Nor does it matter if there is no necessity for the thing to come to rest in the contradictory state, or if there is no state of rest opposed to the change : evanishment is passing into non-existence, and it may be true that the non-existent is not in a state of rest. All that matters is that there should be an interval of time ; for then the change is not continuous, just as in the other cases of change what mattered was not the contrariety between them but that they could not both occur in the same thing at the same time. Nor need we be troubled by one and the same thing being the contrary of more things than one, for instance one motion being opposed to ' station ' and also to the opposite motion. We may be content to take it that a motion may be opposed, under a certain aspect, either to the contrary motion or to absence of motion, just as equality or the mean may be contrasted either with what is short of it or what it is short of, and that neither opposite movements nor opposite changes can coexist in the same subject. Moreover, in the case of genesis and evanishment, it would surely be too monstrous to suppose that a thing must vanish

ARISTOTLE

261 b γενόμενον εὐθὺς ἀνάγκη φθαρῆναι καὶ μηδένα
25 χρόνον διαμεῖναι· ὥστε ἐκ τούτων ἂν ἡ πίστις
γένοιτο ταῖς ἄλλαις· φυσικὸν γὰρ τὸ ὁμοίως ἔχειν
ἐν πάσαις.

CHAPTER VIII

ARGUMENT

*We shall now show that everlasting, uniform and un-
interrupted motion does exist and that it is of necessity
rotatory (261 b 27–28).*

*All local motion is either circular or rectilinear or a
combination of these ; therefore if either of these is incapable
of being continuous no combination of them can be so.
Rectilinear motion cannot be continuous (i.e. uniform, uninterrupted and everlasting), because the mobile that goes on
moving when it reaches the end of the line divides its motion
into two specifically different ones by turning back and reversing the direction. Motion on a continuous path is continuous as long as the mobile does not stop moving. But if
it does stop and then go on again, the point at which it does so
marks the end of one movement and the beginning of another.
Motion is hindered by the mobile pausing at, but not by its
passing through, a point on its path. The pause makes the
point function dually as the end of one movement and the
beginning of another ; the mobile ' arrives there ' at the end
of the first and ' departs thence ' at the beginning of the second
movement, but not during one continuous movement.*

*This analysis does not apply to a point at which the mobile
turns back, for no pause is needed to give this point the
double function of the end of, say, a forward and the beginning
of a backward movement ; and the mobile ' arrives there ' at
the end of the first and ' departs thence ' at the beginning
of the second movement just as much as in the former case,
although the arrival and departure are here simultaneous
(b 28–263 a 1). [The difficulties suggested by the simultaneous
arrival and departure are dealt with at 263 b 9 sqq.]*

366

at the very instant of coming into existence and
not endure any time at all. This would plead, on
the principle of analogy that runs through nature,
for the belief that it is so in all the other cases.

CHAPTER VIII

ARGUMENT (continued)

*Conclusion : that rectilinear motion cannot go on for ever
without interruption (a 1–3).*

*The parallelism between time and space which solves Zeno's
Achilles and dichotomy dilemmas, as presented in Bk. VI. chs.
ii. and ix., does not touch the question of the passage of time itself : this is now shown to be a case of the distinction between the
potential and the actual : it is impossible to count (or to go
through) an illimitable number of actual points (or periods)
of time but not impossible to count or go through a period
whose potential divisibility is illimitable, if its actual extent
and the actual number of its parts are limited (a 3–b 9).*

*The instant which divides the past and future time per-
forms a double function : end of the past and beginning of the
future. But the point that divides states that counteract each
other—so that the object is always in either the one or the
other—has not a dual function, for to end the one is to begin
the other ; therefore at that point of time it is the other,
and has done being the first. So that instant belongs to
the future and not to the past (b 9–264 a 6).*

*Other considerations which also lead to the conclusion
that no rectilinear movement can be everlasting, uniform and
uninterrupted : (1) anything that moves continuously is
making for its goal from the beginning, but a mobile which
reverses the direction of its motion, moves away from what
it was formerly moving towards ; if then reverse movements
were continuous, it would still be moving towards what it
was now moving away from, which is impossible. (2) Anything capable of moving is capable of resting from motion,*

*and as a thing cannot move in opposite directions simul-
taneously it must rest from motion in one direction while
moving in the opposite one.*

Another example of (1) *in respect to change of quality*
(a 6–b 6)

*Continuity of time does not involve continuity of modi-
fication : for without pausing, a mobile can reverse the
direction of its motion and thereby break the continuity of
the modification* (b 6–9).

2G1 b 27   "Ότι δ' ἐνδέχεται εἶναί τινα ἄπειρον, μίαν οὖσαν
καὶ συνεχῆ, καὶ αὕτη ἐστὶν ἡ κύκλῳ, λέγωμεν νῦν.

Πᾶν γὰρ κινεῖται τὸ φερόμενον ἢ κύκλῳ ἢ
30 εὐθεῖαν ἢ μικτήν· ὥστ' εἰ μηδ' ἐκείνων ἡ ἑτέρα
συνεχής, οὐδὲ τὴν ἐξ ἀμφοῖν οἷόν τε εἶναι συγκειμένην. ὅτι δὲ τὸ φερόμενον τὴν εὐθεῖαν καὶ
πεπερασμένην οὐ φέρεται συνεχῶς, δῆλον. ἀνα-
κάμπτει γάρ· τὸ δ' ἀνακάμπτον τὴν εὐθεῖαν τὰς
ἐναντίας κινεῖται κινήσεις· ἐναντία γὰρ κατὰ τόπον
35 ἡ ἄνω τῇ κάτω, καὶ ἡ εἰς τὸ πρόσθεν τῇ εἰς τοὖπι-
σθεν, καὶ ἡ εἰς ἀριστερὰ τῇ εἰς δεξιά· τόπου γὰρ
262 a ἐναντιώσεις αὗται. τίς δ' ἐστὶν ἡ μία καὶ συνεχὴς

---

[a] *Cf.* Bk. VI. ch. x., 241 b 18.

[b] In speaking of a combination of the circle and the
straight line Aristotle no doubt had a spiral in his mind
(*cf.* 347 a 1). He never deals expressly with plane curves
other than the circle, but he would have had no difficulty in
explaining many of them, for example, as the track of a body
rotating round a point moving on a straight line in the plane
of its rotation (the movement of a point on the circumference
of the wheel of a carriage) or as the movement of a point on
the circumference of a circle the centre of which was itself
moving round the circumference of another circle (a point
on an epicycle) or as a circle seen obliquely ; and so
on. [*Cf.* chap. ix. *init.* where Aristotle says that any track of

ARGUMENT (*continued*)

*Continuity of rotatory motion involves no impossible con-
sequences, but any change between opposites must either stop
altogether or else reverse its direction when the mutabile
reaches either extreme. It cannot therefore go on for ever
without interruption* (b 9–265 a 1). *This disproves the view
that all sensible things are in continuous motion* (a 1–10).

*Rotatory locomotion then is the only change which can
be continuous, i.e. everlasting, uniform and uninterrupted*
(a 10–12).

WE are now to show that there actually is, in nature,
a motion ever-enduring, uniform, and uninterrupted ;
and that its nature is that of rotation.[a]

All local motion is circular or rectilinear or a
combination of the two,[b] so that if either of these
cannot be continuous, neither can any combination
of them be so.[c] Now it is obvious that the motion
of a body moving on a finite straight line cannot
be continuous. For to go on when it has come to
the end, it must turn back, and to go back along
the same line is to make the contrary motion, not
to go on with the same one ; for upward movement
is contrary to downward movement, movement
forward to movement backward, movement to right
to movement to left, these being the pairs of contraries in place. But we have already satisfied our-

locomotion must be either rectilinear or circular or a
compound of these two. Plato, *Parm.* 145 в καὶ σχήματος
δή τινος . . . μετέχοι ἂν τὸ ἕν, ἤτοι εὐθέος ἢ στρογγύλου ἢ
τινος μεικτοῦ ἐξ ἀμφοῖν.—C.]

[c] [Accordingly the claim of any compound motion to be
continuous can be disproved by showing that rectilinear
motion cannot be so; and this we proceed to do. Motion
on a *finite* straight line is alone considered because, according to Aristotle, no actual *infinite* straight line exists.—C.]

262 a κίνησις διώρισται πρότερον, ὅτι ἡ τοῦ ἑνὸς καὶ ἐν
ἑνὶ χρόνῳ καὶ ἐν ἀδιαφόρῳ κατ' εἶδος (τρία γὰρ ἦν—
τό τε κινούμενον, οἷον ἄνθρωπος ἢ θεός, καὶ ὅτε,
οἷον χρόνος, καὶ τρίτον τὸ ἐν ᾧ· τοῦτο δ' ἐστὶ τόπος
5 ἢ πάθος ἢ εἶδος ἢ μέγεθος)· τὰ δ' ἐναντία διαφέρει
τῷ εἴδει, καὶ οὐχ ἕν· τόπου δ' αἱ εἰρημέναι διαφοραί. σημεῖον δ' ὅτι ἐναντία κίνησις ἡ ἀπὸ τοῦ
Α πρὸς τὸ Β τῇ ἀπὸ τοῦ Β πρὸς τὸ Α, ὅτι ἱστᾶσι
καὶ παύουσιν ἀλλήλας, ἐὰν ἅμα γίγνωνται· καὶ
ἐπὶ κύκλου ὡσαύτως, οἷον ἡ ἀπὸ τοῦ Α ἐπὶ τὸ Β
10 τῇ ἀπὸ τοῦ Α ἐπὶ τὸ Γ· ἱστᾶσι γάρ, κἂν συνεχεῖς
ὦσι καὶ μὴ γίγνηται ἀνάκαμψις, διὰ τὸ τὰ ἐναντία
φθείρειν καὶ κωλύειν ἄλληλα· ἀλλ' οὐχ ἡ εἰς τὸ
πλάγιον τῇ ἄνω.

Μάλιστα δὲ φανερὸν ὅτι ἀδύνατον εἶναι συνεχῆ
τὴν ἐπὶ τῆς εὐθείας κίνησιν, ὅτι ἀνακάμπτον
15 ἀναγκαῖον στῆναι, οὐ μόνον ἐπ' εὐθείας, ἀλλὰ κἂν
κύκλον φέρηται· οὐ γὰρ ταὐτὸν κύκλῳ φέρεσθαι
καὶ κύκλον· ἔστι γὰρ ὁτὲ μὲν συνείρειν κινούμενον,
ὁτὲ δ' ἐπὶ τὸ αὐτὸ ἐλθὸν ὅθεν ὡρμήθη ἀνακάμψαι

---

^a [At 227 b 21 ff.—C.]

^b [Or 'in a field that is an indivisible species.' Cf.
227 b 29 καὶ ἐν ᾧ γὰρ ἓν δεῖ εἶναι καὶ ἄτομον (οἷον τὸ εἶδος).—C.]

^c πλάγιος, as usually in Aristotle, 'sideways' or 'across,'
not 'oblique.'

^d [So they do not annihilate one another.—C.] This
passage amounts to an express recognition of the principle
of 'virtual velocities,' and implicitly to the conception of
'resultant' movements.

selves [a] that a single and continuous movement must be that of a single mobile, uninterrmittent in time, and of a single kind [b] (for we must distinguish in *all* kinds of change, the subject affected, say a man or a god, and the temporal duration of the change, and thirdly the nature of the change itself, which must either be local translation, or change of affection or of the qualification which determines the kind of things, or change of dimension), and in the case of place the differences just mentioned constitute specifically different kinds of motion. That the movements on a straight line from A to B and from B to A are contrary is evidenced by the fact that they arrest and stop each other if they come at the same time. It is equally true that a circular movement in the direction of A to B is the contrary of a movement in the direction of A to C : they arrest each other, not only if the one movement is met and overpowered by a counter-movement so as to be reversed, but if the two are continuous, since contraries destroy or obstruct one another. On the other hand a sideways [c] motion is not the contrary of an upward motion.[d]

But the dominant consideration in declaring that movement along a straight line cannot be continuous is that the reversing of a movement involves stopping it. This is true not only of motion on a straight line but of motion on a circular track ; for it is not the same thing to move on a circular track and to go on moving round and round it, since it is possible either to go on continuously or, when you have come to the point of departure, to turn back again.

ARISTOTLE

πάλιν. ὅτι δ' ἀνάγκη ἵστασθαι, ἡ πίστις οὐ μόνον
ἐπὶ τῆς αἰσθήσεως ἀλλὰ καὶ ἐπὶ τοῦ λόγου. ἀρχὴ
20 δὲ ἥδε· τριῶν γὰρ ὄντων ἀρχῆς μέσου τελευτῆς,
τὸ μέσον πρὸς ἑκάτερον ἄμφω ἐστί, καὶ τῷ μὲν
ἀριθμῷ ἕν, τῷ λόγῳ δὲ δύο. ἔτι δὲ ἄλλο ἐστὶ τὸ
δυνάμει καὶ τὸ ἐνεργείᾳ. ὥστε τῆς εὐθείας τῶν
ἐντὸς τῶν ἄκρων ὁτιοῦν σημεῖον δυνάμει μὲν
ἔστι μέσον, ἐνεργείᾳ δ' οὐκ ἔστιν, ἐὰν μὴ διέλῃ
25 ταύτῃ καὶ ἐπιστὰν πάλιν ἄρξηται κινεῖσθαι· οὕτω
δὲ τὸ μέσον ἀρχὴ γίγνεται καὶ τελευτή, ἀρχὴ μὲν
τῆς ὑστέρου, τελευτὴ δὲ τῆς πρώτης· λέγω δ' οἷον
ἐὰν φερόμενον τὸ Α στῇ ἐπὶ τοῦ Β καὶ πάλιν
φέρηται ἐπὶ τὸ Γ. ὅταν δὲ συνεχῶς φέρηται, οὔτε
γεγονέναι οὔτε ἀπογεγονέναι οἷόν τε τὸ Α κατὰ τὸ
30 Β σημεῖον, ἀλλὰ μόνον εἶναι ἐν τῷ νῦν, ἐν χρόνῳ
δ' οὐδενὶ πλὴν οὗ τὸ νῦν διαίρεσίς ἐστιν ἐν τῷ ὅλῳ.
εἰ δὲ γεγονέναι τις θήσει καὶ ἀπογεγονέναι, ἀεὶ

---

[a] The point B divides the track into two parts, but these
parts are contiguous, and therefore the continuity of the track
is not broken. If the mobile pauses at B, though the two parts
of the track are contiguous, the two parts of the movement
are not; for they are separated by the pause in time, and
therefore the continuity of the movement is destroyed. If on
the other hand the mobile goes straight on without pausing,
then not only are the two parts of the track contiguous one
to the other, but so also are the two parts of the time and
the two parts of the movement, and there is no break in the
continuity of any of them. Therefore though any midway
point can be *made* into a terminus by the mobile pausing
there, it is not one by nature. It will be shown later
(262 b 22 *sqq.*) that the end of the track is by nature a
terminus in the movement (though not necessarily in the
time, for the mobile need not pause there, but may return
immediately on its track), for the *forward movement* must
cease at the end of the track whether it gives place to

We may convince ourselves that reversal of a movement involves stopping it, not only by observation,
but by reasoning, starting as follows. Take point A
as the beginning, point C as the end, and a point B

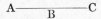

between them. This 'point between,' as soon as we
take it, divides AC into two, and itself constitutes
an end with respect to A and a beginning with
respect to C, and thus, while only single in place, it
is double in function. We shall see that the distinction between potentiality and actuality also comes
into play here, and so, whereas any point between
the extremities may be made to function dually in
the sense explained, it does not actually function
unless the mobile actually divides the line by
stopping and beginning to move again. Else there
were one movement, not two, for it is just this that
erects the 'point between' into a beginning and
an end, the beginning of the second and end of
the first movement—I mean just the fact of the
mobile stopping at B and then going on again to
C.[a] But if the movement be continuous, we must
note that we cannot with strict propriety say
either that the mobile 'has come' to B or that it
'has left' it, but only that it 'is there' *at* an instantaneous 'now,' and not *in* any space or period of
time at all—except in the sense that the 'now' was
included or embraced in the whole period of the
movement of which it marks a potential division. But
if anyone should say that it has 'arrived' at every
potential division in succession and 'departed' from

the reverse movement or to a state of rest (see 228 b *sqq.* and
216 a 27 *sqq.*).

ARISTOTLE

262 b στήσεται τὸ Α φερόμενον. ἀδύνατον γὰρ τὸ Α
ἅμα γεγονέναι τε ἐπὶ τοῦ Β καὶ ἀπογεγονέναι· ἐν
ἄλλῳ ἄρα σημείῳ χρόνου· χρόνος ἄρα ἔσται ὁ ἐν
μέσῳ· ὥστε ἠρεμήσει τὸ Α ἐπὶ τοῦ Β, ὁμοίως δὲ
καὶ ἐπὶ τῶν ἄλλων σημείων· ὁ γὰρ αὐτὸς λόγος
5 καὶ ἐπὶ πάντων. ὅταν δὲ χρήσηται τὸ φερόμενον
Α τῷ Β μέσῳ καὶ τελευτῇ καὶ ἀρχῇ, ἀνάγκη
στῆναι, διὰ τὸ δύο ποιεῖν ὥσπερ ἂν εἰ καὶ νοήσειεν.
ἀλλ' ἀπὸ μὲν τοῦ Α σημείου ἀπογέγονε τῆς ἀρχῆς,
ἐπὶ δὲ τοῦ Γ γέγονεν, ὅταν τελευτήσῃ καὶ στῇ,
διὸ καὶ πρὸς τὴν ἀπορίαν τοῦτο λεκτέον. ἔχει
10 γὰρ ἀπορίαν τήνδε· εἰ γὰρ εἴη ἡ τὸ Ε τῇ Ζ ἴση,
καὶ τὸ Α φέροιτο συνεχῶς ἀπὸ τοῦ ἄκρου πρὸς τὸ
Γ, ἅμα δ' εἴη τὸ Α ἐπὶ τῷ Β σημείῳ καὶ τὸ Δ
φέροιτο ἀπὸ τῆς Ζ ἄκρας πρὸς τὸ Η ὁμαλῶς καὶ
τῷ αὐτῷ τάχει τῷ Α, τὸ Δ ἔμπροσθεν ἥξει ἐπὶ
τὸ Η ἢ τὸ Α ἐπὶ τὸ Γ· τὸ γὰρ πρότερον ὁρμῆσαν

---

[a] [A is here the mobile which starts from the point A.
—C.]

[b] [Or ' But when the moving A does treat the intermediate
point B both as the end-point of one movement and the
starting-point of another, then A must come to a stand,
because it is making distinct use of the two aspects of B
which can be distinguished in thought. On the other hand
it has " departed from " the point A—the beginning (of the
finite line), and it " has arrived " at the point C (the end of the
finite line), when it stops at the end of its course.' This
last sentence distinguishes the two ends of the finite line as
actual starting- and finishing-points (since the line is actually
limited by them) from intermediate points, such as B, which

374

it, he will have to assert that as it moved it was
continually coming to a stand. For it cannot 'have
arrived' at a point (which implies that it is there)
and 'have departed' from it (which implies that it
is not there) at the same point of time. So there are
two points of time concerned, with a period of time
between them; and consequently A^a will be at rest
at B and equally at every other point, for it is the
same case with them all. It *would* stop everywhere,
then, if there was an actual division everywhere.
b But only when it actually does divide its course at
a 'point between' does it make that point both an
end and a beginning, and in that case it does actually
stop there and must do so in the very act of realizing
the conceptual duality. In such a case it 'has left'
its starting-point as soon as the movement has
begun and 'has arrived' at C when it 'makes an
end' there and stops. This reasoning will solve a
problem that suggests itself here. It may be said:
" Let the line from E equal the line from Z; and let
A move continuously from the extreme point E

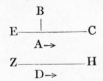

towards C; and at the time when A is *at* the point
B let D be moving from the extreme point Z towards
H uniformly and at the same rate as A: then D
will reach H before A reaches C, for the one that

are only *potential* starting- or finishing-points unless or until
A actually pauses at them.—C.]

262 b 15 καὶ ἀπελθὸν πρότερον ἐλθεῖν ἀνάγκη. οὐκ ἄρα ἅμα
γέγονε τὸ Α ἐπὶ τὸ Β καὶ ἀπογέγονεν ἀπ᾽ αὐτοῦ,
διὸ ὑστερίζει· εἰ γὰρ ἅμα, οὐχ ὑστεριεῖ, ἀλλ᾽
ἀνάγκη ἔσται ἵστασθαι. οὐκ ἄρα θετέον, ὅτε τὸ
Α ἐγένετο κατὰ τὸ Β, τὸ Δ ἅμα κινεῖσθαι ἀπὸ
τοῦ Ζ ἄκρου· εἰ γὰρ ἔσται γεγονὸς τὸ Α ἐπὶ τοῦ Β,
20 ἔσται καὶ τὸ ἀπογενέσθαι, καὶ οὐχ ἅμα· ἀλλ᾽ ἦν ἐν
τομῇ χρόνου καὶ οὐκ ἐν χρόνῳ. ἐνταῦθα μὲν οὖν
ἀδύνατον οὕτω λέγειν ἐπὶ τῆς συνεχοῦς· ἐπὶ δὲ τοῦ
ἀνακάμπτοντος ἀνάγκη λέγειν οὕτως. εἰ γὰρ ἡ
τὸ Η φέροιτο πρὸς τὸ Δ καὶ πάλιν ἀνακάμψασα
25 κάτω φέροιτο, τῷ ἄκρῳ ἐφ᾽ οὗ Δ τελευτῇ καὶ ἀρχῇ
κέχρηται—τῷ ἑνὶ σημείῳ ὡς δύο[1]· διὸ στῆναι
ἀνάγκη, καὶ οὐχ ἅμα γέγονεν ἐπὶ τῷ Δ καὶ ἀπ-
ελήλυθεν ἀπὸ τοῦ Δ· ἐκεῖ γὰρ ἂν ἅμα εἴη καὶ οὐκ
εἴη ἐν τῷ αὐτῷ νῦν. ἀλλὰ μὴν τήν γε πάλαι
λύσιν οὐ λεκτέον· οὐ γὰρ ἐνδέχεται λέγειν ὅτι

[1] [δύο: fort. δυσί. Cf. 263 a 24 and Simplic. 1286. 32.—C.]

---

[a] [Alexander (Simplic. 1285. 14) explains that D is supposed
to 'start and get away first' from a point on its own line
ZH corresponding to the point B on the other line EC. D
gets ahead because it is not supposed to 'arrive' at this point
at one moment and 'leave' it at another, as A is supposed to
arrive at and leave B and so to lose time there.—C.]

[b] [Viz. 'A *has arrived at*, or *has left*, an intermediate
point.'—C.]

[c] This appears to follow from the foregoing argument.
But in the next sentence Aristotle shows that this is not so,
and that the terms 'arrive' and 'depart' *can* be used in this
case: for though it is true that the end of the line is an
indivisible point in space, and that the mobile is only there
at an indivisible instant in time (if it reverses its motion there

376

starts and gets away first must arrive first."[a] This
argument implies that A has 'arrived' at B at one
instant and has 'left' B at another: that is the
reason why A gets left behind. If the arrival
and departure coincide at the same instant, A
will not be left behind; we have to suppose that
A comes to a stand at B. So the fallacy lies in
the supposition that at the same time that D was
moving from Z, A 'arrived' at B; for if A is to
be said to 'have arrived' at B, it will also have
to 'leave' B and the two events will not be
simultaneous; but the truth is that A is 'at B' only
at a sectional point (or potential division) of time and
does not *spend* any time there. In this case, then,
where the motion is continuous, we ought not to use
these expressions. [b] On the other hand they must be
used in the case of a mobile that turns back on its
course. For suppose a mobile H moves as far as D
and then turns back and moves down again: then it
has made the one point at which it turned function
both as a beginning and an end, and therefore as two.
It must therefore have stopped there; it cannot have
arrived at it and have departed from it simultaneously,
since that would involve being there and not being
there at the same instant.[c] The argument used to
solve the difficulty just above does not apply here:
we cannot say now, as we did then, that the mobile

without pausing)—so that on these two counts there is
nothing to distinguish it from a midway point—yet the end
of the line is by nature a terminus in the movement and the
midway point is not: for the forward motion *must* stop at
the end of the line, but need not stop at a midway point
(see p. 372 note a). The mobile can only, strictly speaking,
be said to 'arrive at' or 'depart from' a *terminus*; but as
we have just seen there is no need for it to *pause* at a terminus.

ARISTOTLE

232 b 30 ἐστὶ κατὰ τὸ Δ ἢ τὸ Η ἐν τομῇ, οὐ γέγονε δὲ
οὐδὲ ἀπογέγονεν· ἀνάγκη γὰρ ἐπὶ τέλος ἐλθεῖν τὸ
ἐνεργείᾳ ὄν, μὴ δυνάμει. τὸ μὲν οὖν ἐν μέσῳ
263 a δυνάμει ἐστί, τοῦτο δ' ἐνεργείᾳ, καὶ τελευτὴ μὲν
κάτωθεν, ἀρχὴ δὲ ἄνωθεν· καὶ τῶν κινήσεων ἄρα
ὡσαύτως.

'Ανάγκη ἄρα στῆναι τὸ ἀνακάμπτον ἐπὶ τῆς
εὐθείας. οὐκ ἄρα ἐνδέχεται συνεχῆ κίνησιν εἶναι
ἀίδιον[1] ἐπὶ τῆς εὐθείας.

Τὸν αὐτὸν δὲ τρόπον ἀπαντητέον καὶ πρὸς τοὺς
5 ἐρωτῶντας τὸν Ζήνωνος λόγον, [καὶ ἀξιοῦντας][2]
εἰ ἀεὶ τὸ ἥμισυ διέναι δεῖ, ταῦτα δ' ἄπειρα, τὰ δ'
ἄπειρα ἀδύνατον διεξελθεῖν, ἢ ὡς τὸν αὐτὸν τοῦτον
λόγον τινὲς ἄλλως ἐρωτῶσιν, ἀξιοῦντες ἅμα τῷ
κινεῖσθαι τὴν ἡμίσειαν πρότερον ἀριθμεῖν καθ'
ἕκαστον γιγνόμενον τὸ ἥμισυ, ὥστε διελθόντος
10 τὴν ὅλην ἄπειρον συμβαίνει ἠριθμηκέναι ἀριθμόν·
τοῦτο δ' ὁμολογουμένως ἐστὶν ἀδύνατον. ἐν μὲν
οὖν τοῖς πρώτοις λόγοις τοῖς περὶ κινήσεως ἐλύο-
μεν διὰ τοῦ τὸν χρόνον ἄπειρα ἔχειν ἐν αὑτῷ· οὐδὲν
γὰρ ἄτοπον εἰ ἐν ἀπείρῳ χρόνῳ ἄπειρα διέρχεταί
τις, ὁμοίως δὲ τὸ ἄπειρον ἔν τε τῷ μήκει ὑπάρχει

---

[1] [εἶναι ἀίδιον E²K, Simplic. 1287. 18 (lemma) a: ἀίδιον
εἶναι FHI, Simplic. ibid. A: ἴδιον (sic) post εὐθείας E¹. Fort.
εἶναι καὶ ἀίδιον: cf. Simplic. 1288. 28 (paraphr.) οὐκ ἄρα
ἐνδέχεται τὴν ἐπὶ τῆς εὐθείας κίνησιν συνεχῆ εἶναι καὶ ἀίδιον.—C.]
[2] [καὶ ἀξιοῦντας omitted by the Oxf. Trans. as probably ' a
gloss introduced under the influence of ἀξιοῦντες, l. 7.' The
words have no construction unless εἰ and δεῖ are omitted,
with K.—C.]

---

a [At 233 a 21 ff. and 239 b 11-29.—C.]

378

is only at the point D 'at' a sectional point of time, but has never 'arrived at it' or ' departed from it,' for the 'end' which it comes to must be an end in actuality, not in potentiality only. So a 'point between' the extremities of a continuous line is only potentially a beginning and an end, but this one is actual ; it is both the finishing-point as regarded from below and the starting-point as regarded from above, and so also the end-point of one motion and the beginning-point of the other.

The conclusion is that the motion of the mobile that turns back upon a straight line must stop. It is impossible, therefore, that there should be, on a straight line, continuous movement that is everlasting.

This reasoning, further, enables us to meet those who, in the terms of Zeno's argument, ask whether it is true that you must always go half-way to a point before you get there, and there is always a half-way point between the last half-way point that you have reached and the point itself that you are making for, and so you can never get there, because you would have to pass through an infinite number of points. Or, as others put it : If you count the first half of the journey and then the half of what is left and so on, you would have to count an infinite series of numbers before you got to the end of the journey ; which is admitted to be impossible. It is true that in our previous studies concerning movement[a] we solved this puzzle by pointing out that since time, just as much as space, is divisible without limit and with respect to this capacity is illimitable, there is no contradiction in a man passing through an infinite number of points in a time which is ' infinite ' in precisely the same sense as the distance to be tra-

ARISTOTLE

263 a 15 καὶ ἐν τῷ χρόνῳ. ἀλλ' αὕτη ἡ λύσις πρὸς μὲν τὸν
ἐρωτῶντα ἱκανῶς ἔχει—ἠρωτᾶτο γὰρ εἰ ἐν πεπερασμένῳ ἄπειρα ἐνδέχεται διεξελθεῖν ἢ ἀριθμῆσαι—
πρὸς δὲ τὸ πρᾶγμα καὶ τὴν ἀλήθειαν οὐχ ἱκανῶς.
ἂν γάρ τις, ἀφέμενος τοῦ μήκους καὶ τοῦ ἐρωτᾶν
20 εἰ ἐν πεπερασμένῳ χρόνῳ ἐνδέχεται ἄπειρα διεξελθεῖν, πυνθάνηται ἐπ' αὐτοῦ τοῦ χρόνου ταῦτα
(ἔχει γὰρ ὁ χρόνος ἀπείρους διαιρέσεις), οὐκέτι
ἱκανὴ ἔσται αὕτη ἡ λύσις, ἀλλὰ τὸ ἀληθὲς λεκτέον,
ὅπερ εἴπομεν ἐν τοῖς ἄρτι λόγοις. ἂν γάρ τις τὴν
συνεχῆ διαιρῇ εἰς δύο ἡμίση, οὗτος τῷ ἑνὶ σημείῳ
25 ὡς δυσὶ χρῆται—ποιεῖ γὰρ αὐτὸ ἀρχὴν καὶ τελευτήν
—οὕτω δὲ ποιεῖ ὅ τε ἀριθμῶν καὶ ὁ εἰς τὰ ἡμίση
διαιρῶν. οὕτω δὲ διαιροῦντος, οὐκ ἔσται συνεχὴς
οὔθ' ἡ γραμμὴ οὔθ' ἡ κίνησις· ἡ γὰρ συνεχὴς
κίνησις συνεχοῦς ἐστιν, ἐν δὲ τῷ συνεχεῖ ἔστι μὲν
ἄπειρα ἡμίση, ἀλλ' οὐκ ἐντελεχείᾳ ἀλλὰ δυνάμει.
30 ἂν δὲ ποιῇ ἐντελεχείᾳ, οὐ ποιήσει συνεχῆ ἀλλὰ
στήσει· ὅπερ ἐπὶ τοῦ ἀριθμοῦντος τὰ ἡμίση φανερόν
263 b ἐστιν ὅτι συμβαίνει· τὸ γὰρ ἓν σημεῖον ἀνάγκη
αὐτῷ ἀριθμεῖν δύο· τοῦ μὲν γὰρ ἑτέρου τελευτὴ
ἡμίσεος, τοῦ δ' ἑτέρου ἀρχὴ ἔσται, ἂν μὴ μίαν
ἀριθμῇ τὴν συνεχῆ ἀλλὰ δύο ἡμισείας. ὥστε

---

[a] [The solution given earlier got over the difficulty of
traversing an infinite number of points by appealing to the
infinite divisibility of the stretch of time taken. But the
objector may shift his ground and say : Leave the distance
traversed out of account and take merely a moving body
whose motion occupies a finite *time*. How can it get to
the end of the *time*, if it has to get through an infinite number of
subdivisions of that time ?—C.]

[b] It is the grammar only, not the sense, that is doubtful.
I follow Simplic. 1291. 14 *sqq.* If this is right, Aristotle uses
ἀριθμεῖν for ' taking the two functions of the point into consideration ' in 263 b 1, and for 'enumerating' the lines in b 2.

380

versed is. But this solution, though adequate as a
reply to the question (which was, whether it is possible
in a finite time to go through or to count an infinite
number of points), does not really settle the underlying truth or get at realities. For what if a man,
dropping the element of distance and the question
of the possibility of traversing an infinite number of
distances in a finite time, were to confine his question
to the time only ; for this contains an illimitable
number of divisions ? [a] It would then be no solution to
say that there is no limit to the divisibility of time itself,
but we should have to fall back upon the truth we have
just arrived at. For whoever divides the continuous
into two halves thereby confers a double function upon
the point of division, for he makes it both a beginning
and an end. And that is just what the counting
man, or the dividing man whose half-sections he
counts, is doing ; and by the very act of division
both the line and the movement cease to be continuous ; for the movement is not continuous unless
the mobile and the time and the track with which
it is concerned are continuous. And though it be
true that there is no limit to the potential dichotomy of any continuum, it is not true that it is
actually dichotomized to infinity. But to make
an actual bisection is to effect a motion that is not
continuous but interrupted, as is patent in the case
of one who counts the segments ; for he must take
the bisecting point twice, once as an end and once
as a beginning (which we have seen to involve an
interruption of continuity)—I mean if he does not
count the continuous line as one, but the separated
halves as two.[b] Accordingly, if we are asked whether

233 b λεκτέον πρὸς τὸν ἐρωτῶντα εἰ ἐνδέχεται ἄπειρα
5 διεξελθεῖν ἢ ἐν χρόνῳ ἢ ἐν μήκει, ὅτι ἔστιν ὥς,
ἔστι δ᾽ ὡς οὔ· ἐντελεχείᾳ μὲν γὰρ ὄντα οὐκ
ἐνδέχεται, δυνάμει δὲ ἐνδέχεται. ὁ γὰρ συνεχῶς
κινούμενος κατὰ συμβεβηκὸς ἄπειρα διελήλυθεν,
ἁπλῶς δ᾽ οὔ· συμβέβηκε γὰρ τῇ γραμμῇ ἄπειρα
ἡμίσεα εἶναι, ἡ δ᾽ οὐσία ἐστὶν ἑτέρα καὶ τὸ εἶναι.

Δῆλον δὲ καὶ ὅτι ἐὰν μή τις ποιῇ τοῦ χρόνου τὸ
10 διαιροῦν σημεῖον τὸ πρότερον καὶ ὕστερον ἀεὶ
τοῦ ὑστέρου τῷ πράγματι, ἔσται ἅμα τὸ αὐτὸ ὂν
καὶ οὐκ ὄν, καὶ ὅτε γέγονεν οὐκ ὄν. τὸ σημεῖον
μὲν οὖν ἀμφοῖν κοινόν, καὶ τοῦ προτέρου καὶ τοῦ
ὑστέρου, καὶ ταὐτὸν καὶ ἐν ἀριθμῷ, λόγῳ δ᾽ οὐ
ταὐτόν (τοῦ μὲν γὰρ τελευτή, τοῦ δὲ ἀρχή)· τῷ
15 δὲ πράγματι ἀεὶ τοῦ ὑστέρου πάθους ἐστίν. χρόνος ἐφ᾽ ᾧ ΑΓΒ, πρᾶγμα ἐφ᾽ ᾧ Δ· τοῦτο ἐν μὲν τῷ
Α χρόνῳ λευκόν, ἐν δὲ τῷ Β οὐ λευκόν. ἐν τῷ Γ
ἄρα λευκὸν καὶ οὐ λευκόν· ἐν ὁτῳοῦν γὰρ τοῦ Α

---

[a] Thus a movement which is uninterrupted is a single whole and has not the characteristics of multiplicity which would belong to it if it were interrupted and divided into segments. And we must distinguish between the sum of (rival) potentialities which include every alternative originally open to a thing (*e.g. either* unity *or* multiplicity but not both at once in the same respect) and those potentialities which actually are realized when the choice between alternatives has been made. *Cf.* 255 a 30: *De caelo* 281 b 15.

it is possible to go through an unlimited number of points, whether in a period of time or in a length, we must answer that in one sense it is possible but in another not. If the points are actual it is impossible, but if they are potential it is possible. For one who moves continuously traverses an illimitable number of points only in an accidental, not in an unqualified, sense ; it is an accidental characteristic of the line that it is an illimitable number of half-lengths ; its essential nature is something different.[a]

It is also evident that, when speaking of the subject of motion or change, unless we assign the instant that divides past and future time to the state into which that object turns and in which it will be for the future rather than to that which it turns out of and in which it was in the past, we shall have to say that the same thing both exists and does not exist at the same instant, and when it has become something it is not that something which it has become. It is true that in continuous time the point is common to the past and future and is one and the same numerically, though not in function, being the end of the one and the beginning of the other ; but as regards the subject of change it always belongs to the future and not to the past state of that subject. For suppose the time is represented by A and B, and the

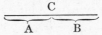

dividing 'now' by C, and call the thing that suffers change D, and suppose that D is white during the whole of A and not-white during the whole of B : then at the instant C it will be both white and not-white ; for if it really is white during the whole of A, it must

263 b λευκὸν ἀληθὲς εἰπεῖν, εἰ πάντα τὸν χρόνον τοῦτον
ἦν λευκόν, καὶ ἐν τῷ Β μὴ λευκόν, τὸ δὲ Γ ἐν
20 ἀμφοῖν. οὐκ ἄρα δοτέον ἐν παντί, ἀλλὰ πλὴν τοῦ
τελευταίου νῦν ἐφ' οὗ τὸ Γ· τοῦτο δ' ἤδη τοῦ
ὑστέρου[1]· καὶ εἰ ἐγίγνετο οὐ[2] λευκὸν καὶ εἰ ἐφθείρετο λευκὸν ἐν τῷ Α παντί, γέγονεν ἢ ἔφθαρται
ἐν τῷ Γ. ὥστε λευκὸν[3] ἢ μὴ λευκὸν ἐν ἐκείνῳ
πρῶτον ἀληθὲς εἰπεῖν, ἢ ὅτε γέγονεν οὐκ ἔσται
25 καὶ ὅτε ἔφθαρται ἔσται, ἢ ἅμα λευκὸν καὶ οὐ
λευκὸν καὶ ὅλως ὂν καὶ μὴ ὂν ἀνάγκη εἶναι.

Εἰ δ' ὃ ἂν ᾖ πρότερον μὴ ὄν, ἀνάγκη γίγνεσθαι
ὄν, καὶ ὅτε γίγνεται μὴ ἔστιν, οὐχ οἷόν τε εἰς
ἀτόμους χρόνους διαιρεῖσθαι τὸν χρόνον. εἰ γὰρ
ἐν τῷ Α χρόνῳ τὸ Δ ἐγίγνετο λευκόν, γέγονε δ'
30 ἅμα καὶ ἔστιν ἐν ἑτέρῳ ἀτόμῳ χρόνῳ ἐχομένῳ δὲ
ἐν τῷ Β, εἰ ἐν τῷ Α ἐγίγνετο, οὐκ ἦν, ἐν δὲ τῷ Β
ἐστί, γένεσιν δεῖ τινα εἶναι μεταξύ, ὥστε καὶ
264 a χρόνον ἐν ᾧ ἐγίγνετο. οὐ γὰρ ὁ αὐτὸς ἔσται
λόγος καὶ τοῖς μὴ ἄτομα λέγουσιν, ἀλλ' αὐτοῦ

[1] [τοῦ ὑστέρου Oxf. Trans. coll. Philop. 845. 31, Simplic.
1295. 23: τὸ ὕστερον codd.—C.]
[2] [οὐ om. I and apparently Simplic. 1295. 26.—C.]
[3] [ὥστε εἰ ἦν λευκόν E.—C.]

[a] [For this meaning of ἐφθείρετο λευκόν see note on 254 a
13.—C.]
[b] [The Oxf. Trans. renders : 'And so Γ is the first
moment at which it is true to call the thing white or not-
white respectively,' adding a note that 'only the latter case
has been mentioned above.' If λευκὸν ἢ μὴ λευκόν is to be
so construed, it would perhaps be better to suppose that
Aristotle has varied his illustration in the previous sentence
and to read there (l. 21) λευκόν for οὐ λευκόν, as it seems
Simplicius did, thus providing a mention of the former case
(becoming white). (In any case the καὶ εἰ before ἐφθείρετο
is difficult : why not ἢ ἐφθείρετο or εἴτε ἐγίγνετο . . . εἴτε

384

be true that it is white at any instant of A, and in B it is not-white, and C is in both A and B. So we must not allow that it is white at every point of A, but only at every point of A except the terminating instant C. This instant already belongs to B; and if D occupied the whole time A in the process of becoming not-white or of ceasing to be white,[a] either process was complete at the instant C. So unless we admit that a white thing [b] can be truly described as not-white at that instant for the first time, we shall either have to say that a thing does not exist at the instant when it has come to be and does exist at the instant when it has ceased to be, or else that it must be both white and not-white or (more generally) both existent and non-existent at the same instant.

Further, if what exists, having been previously non-existent, must come into existence, and if it does not exist while it is coming to be, it follows that time cannot be divided into atomic parts. For suppose D is getting to be white in the atom of time A and has become white as soon as ever it is in the next atom B; then, since in the time A it was not white, but was only becoming so, whereas in B it is white, some kind of genesis or act of becoming white must have taken place between A and B. And so there was time between them for the genesis to occur in (and consequently the two atoms are not contiguous). But this reasoning does not affect those (like ourselves) who deny that there are atoms of time. In

ἐφθείρετο? Perhaps εἰ before ἐφθείρετο should be omitted.) I have taken λευκόν (after ὥστε, l. 23) as standing outside the three alternatives ἤ . . . ἤ . . . ἤ and common to them all. This construction would be clearer and more regular if we read, with E, ὥστε εἰ ἦν λευκόν. (This paragraph has been re-written.)—C.]

264 a τοῦ χρόνου, ἐν ᾧ ἐγίγνετο, γέγονε καὶ ἔστιν ἐν
τῷ ἐσχάτῳ σημείῳ, οὗ οὐδὲν ἐχόμενόν ἐστιν οὐδ᾽
ἐφεξῆς· οἱ δ᾽ ἄτομοι χρόνοι ἐφεξῆς. φανερὸν
5 δ᾽ ὅτι εἰ ἐν τῷ Α ὅλῳ χρόνῳ ἐγίγνετο, οὐκ ἔστι
πλείων χρόνος ἐν ᾧ γέγονε καὶ ἐγίγνετο ἢ ἐν ᾧ
ἐγίγνετο μόνον παντί.

Οἷς μὲν οὖν ἄν τις ὡς οἰκείοις πιστεύσειε λόγοις,
οὗτοι καὶ τοιοῦτοί τινές εἰσι· λογικῶς δὲ ἐπι-
σκοποῦσι, κἂν ἐκ τῶνδε δόξειέ τῳ ταὐτὸ τοῦτο
συμβαίνειν.

10 Ἅπαν γὰρ τὸ κινούμενον συνεχῶς, ἂν ὑπὸ
μηδενὸς ἐκκρούηται, εἰς ὅπερ ἦλθε κατὰ τὴν φοράν,
εἰς τοῦτο καὶ ἐφέρετο πρότερον· οἷον εἰ ἐπὶ τὸ Β
ἦλθε, καὶ ἐφέρετο ἐπὶ τὸ Β, καὶ οὐχ ὅτε πλησίον
ἦν ἀλλ᾽ εὐθὺς ὡς ἤρξατο κινεῖσθαι· τί γὰρ μᾶλλον
15 νῦν ἢ πρότερον; ὁμοίως δὲ καὶ ἐπὶ τῶν ἄλλων. τὸ
δὴ ἀπὸ τοῦ Α ἐπὶ τὸ Γ φερόμενον, ὅταν ἐπὶ τὸ Γ
ἔλθῃ, πάλιν ἥξει ἐπὶ τὸ Α συνεχῶς κινούμενον.
ὅτε ἄρα ἀπὸ τοῦ Α φέρεται πρὸς τὸ Γ, τότε καὶ
εἰς τὸ Α φέρεται τὴν ἀπὸ τοῦ Γ κίνησιν· ὥσθ᾽ ἅμα

---

[a] For to say that the period of *becoming* is ended is only
another way of saying that the period of *being* has begun.
Cf. 235 b 6 ff.

[b] [The instant at which D has become white is a sectional
point of time terminating A, not a period the addition of
which to A would lengthen it. *Cf.* 235 b 19 ff.—C.]

[c] We might therefore proceed at once to the consideration
of purely rotatory motion. But it will be of interest to see
that what has been demonstrated of translation is equally
applicable to all changes from one opposite to the other.

[d] [*Literally*, ' Now we are to suppose that a body moving
from A to C will, when it has arrived at C, turn back and
reach A again *with a motion that is continuous* (throughout
the whole journey from A to C and back again). It follows
that at the time when it is moving from A to C, it is also

PHYSICS, VIII. viii.

their view D has become and is white at the terminal
point of the very period in which it was coming to be
so [a] ; and there is no contiguous point to that point,
nor any point between which and that point there
is no other point ; whereas if time could be divided
into atoms, there would be a next atom (either way)
to any given atom, with no atom between. And
it is clear that if the process of D's becoming
white occupied the whole time A, the time taken by
that process and its accomplishment—' D *has become*
white '—cannot be longer than the time entirely
occupied by the process alone.[b]

These and such as these are the arguments specially applicable to the demonstration that no motion
of translation and therefore no motion of combined
translation and rotation can be everlasting and
continuous.[c] But considerations affecting all forms
of change may be seen from the following arguments
to lead to the same result.

Anything that moves continuously is making for its
goal before it reaches it, provided that nothing diverts
it from its course : thus, if B is what it comes to, it
was making for B, and that not only when it came near
to B but from the instant when it first started ; since
you cannot assign any other instant at which to say
' now but not before.' And this holds for the other
kinds of change as well. [d]If, then, the mobile moves
from A to C and when it gets there returns to A with
a continuous movement, it will be moving from A to
A continuously and therefore it will be making for
A as soon as it begins to make for C ; and since move-
moving towards A with its (reverse) motion from C (since it is
making for A from the first moment of its motion). Hence
it will be making two contrary movements simultaneously.'—
C.]

387

ARISTOTLE

264 a τὰς ἐναντίας, ἐναντίαι γὰρ αἱ κατ᾽ εὐθεῖαν. ¹ἅμα δὲ
καὶ ἐκ τούτου μεταβάλλει ἐν ᾧ οὐκ ἔστιν. εἰ οὖν
20 τοῦτ᾽ ἀδύνατον, ἀνάγκη ἵστασθαι ἐπὶ τοῦ Γ. οὐκ ἄρα
μία ἡ κίνησις· ἡ γὰρ διαλαμβανομένη στάσει οὐ μία.
Ἔτι δὲ καὶ ἐκ τῶνδε φανερὸν καθόλου μᾶλλον
περὶ πάσης κινήσεως. εἰ γὰρ ἅπαν τὸ κινούμενον
τῶν εἰρημένων τινὰ κινεῖται κινήσεων καὶ ἠρεμεῖ
τῶν ἀντικειμένων ἠρεμιῶν (οὐ γὰρ ἦν ἄλλη παρὰ
ταύτας), τὸ δὲ μὴ ἀεὶ κινούμενον τήνδε τὴν κίνησιν
25 —λέγω δ᾽ ὅσαι ἕτεραι τῷ εἴδει, καὶ μὴ εἴ τι μόριόν
ἐστι τῆς ὅλης—ἀνάγκη πρότερον ἠρεμεῖν τὴν
ἀντικειμένην ἠρεμίαν (ἡ γὰρ ἠρεμία στέρησις τῆς
κινήσεώς ἐστιν)· εἰ οὖν ἐναντίαι μὲν κινήσεις αἱ
κατ᾽ εὐθεῖαν, ἅμα δὲ μὴ ἐνδέχεται κινεῖσθαι τὰς

¹ [Simplicius 1302. 37-39 here paraphrases an objection
which does not appear in our mss., and describes the objection in this sentence as the *third* which Aristotle brings
forward (εἶτα καὶ τρίτον ἄλλο ἄτοπον ἐπάγει). The paraphrase
ἐπὶ τὸ γενέσθαι ἐν ᾧ ἐστι κινηθήσεται· τοῦτο δὲ ἄτοπον. οὐδὲν
γὰρ κινεῖται διὰ τὸ γενέσθαι ἐν ᾧ ἐστι. τὸ γὰρ κινούμενον ποθέν
ποι κινεῖται suggests that he read ἅμα δὲ καὶ ⟨εἰς τοῦτο μεταβάλλει (? κινεῖται) ἐν ᾧ ἐστι καὶ⟩ ἐκ τούτου, κτλ. The moving
object is, *ex hypothesi*, all the time moving towards A; but
it is already at A when it starts, and it is absurd that a thing
should change its place in order to reach a place it already
occupies. But Themistius 230. 19 ff. and Philoponus 846. 20
appear to have had our text.—C.]

ᵃ [This sentence is ambiguous. Possible meanings are :
(1) ' *Its change starts from a position which it does not occupy.*'
Suppose a man at A throws a stone up to a height C, from
which it falls back to A. The stone really begins to fall from
C ; but if we are to say that the whole motion from A to C
and back to A is one *continuous* motion, we must say that
the falling starts from A—a position which the stone does
not in fact occupy when the falling-motion begins. (2) ' *It
shifts from a condition in which it is not.*' On reaching the
388

ments to and fro on a straight line are opposite movements, it will be moving in opposite directions at one and the same time. And moreover it would start its reverse movement from C back to A before it had got to C where it is reversed.[a] All this being impossible, then, it follows that the movement must stop at C. And so the movement is not a single one, for a movement that is severed by cessation is not one but two.

A further general consideration will establish the point for every kind of 'movement,' whether local or not. A thing susceptible of change, whether of quality, quantity, or position (and we have seen that there are no other ways of changing), is also susceptible of the corresponding stationary and unchanging state. [b]Also, if a change of any kind alters from time to time—I mean alters in direction, not merely as to the point it has reached—this adopting of a new direction involves the subject resting from change in the previous direction; for rest from change in any direction means 'privation of it.'[c] Granted, then, that changes to and fro on the same line are contrary and so cannot go on at the same

point C the stone shifts from moving away from A to moving towards A. But if the motion is one and continuous, it was always moving towards A and so was never in the condition of moving away from A. This interpretation would account for μεταβάλλει being used instead of φέρεται.—C.]

[b] [The assumption stated in this sentence can also be interpreted : ' If a thing that is undergoing, *otherwise than eternally*, some particular change—" particular " meaning not some particular part of the whole change, but a change belonging to one of the indivisible species of change—must have been previously in the state of rest opposite to that particular motion.'—C.]

[c] *i.e.* the absence of change in that direction in a subject naturally capable of such change.

ARISTOTLE

264 a 30 ἐναντίας, τὸ ἀπὸ τοῦ Α πρὸς τὸ Γ φερόμενον οὐκ
ἂν φέροιτο ἅμα καὶ ἀπὸ τοῦ Γ πρὸς τὸ Α· ἐπεὶ δὲ
οὐχ ἅμα φέρεται, κινήσεται δὲ ταύτην τὴν κίνησιν,
ἀνάγκη πρότερον ἠρεμῆσαι τὴν πρὸς τῷ Γ· αὕτη
γὰρ ἦν ἡ ἀντικειμένη ἠρεμία τῇ ἀπὸ τοῦ Γ κινήσει.
264 b δῆλον τοίνυν ἐκ τῶν εἰρημένων ὅτι οὐκ ἔστι συνεχὴς
ἡ κίνησις.

Ἔτι δὲ καὶ ὅδε ὁ λόγος μᾶλλον οἰκεῖος τῶν
εἰρημένων. ἅμα γὰρ ἔφθαρται τὸ οὐ λευκὸν καὶ
γέγονε λευκόν. εἰ οὖν συνεχὴς ἡ ἀλλοίωσις εἰς
λευκὸν καὶ ἐκ λευκοῦ καὶ μὴ μένει τινὰ χρόνον,
5 ἅμα ἔφθαρται τὸ οὐ λευκὸν καὶ γέγονε λευκὸν καὶ
γέγονεν οὐ λευκόν· τριῶν γὰρ ἔσται ὁ αὐτὸς χρόνος.

Ἔτι οὐκ εἰ συνεχὴς ὁ χρόνος, καὶ ἡ κίνησις, ἀλλ’
ἐφεξῆς. πῶς δ’ ἂν εἴη τὸ ἔσχατον τὸ αὐτὸ τῶν
ἐναντίων, οἷον λευκότητος καὶ μελανίας;

Ἡ δ’ ἐπὶ τῆς περιφεροῦς ἔσται μία καὶ συνεχής·
10 οὐθὲν γὰρ ἀδύνατον συμβαίνει. τὸ γὰρ ἐκ τοῦ Α
κινούμενον ἅμα κινήσεται εἰς τὸ Α κατὰ τὴν αὐτὴν
πρόθεσιν—εἰς ὃ γὰρ ἥξει, καὶ κινεῖται εἰς τοῦτο—
ἀλλ’ οὐχ ἅμα κινήσεται τὰς ἐναντίας οὐδὲ τὰς
ἀντικειμένας· οὐ γὰρ ἅπασα ἡ εἰς τοῦτο τῇ ἐκ
τούτου ἐναντία οὐδ’ ἀντικειμένη, ἀλλ’ ἐναντία μὲν

---

*[At 261 b 15, 264 a 25.—C.]

390

time, the movement from A to C cannot be going on simultaneously with the movement from C to A ; and since this latter motion, not being simultaneous, has still to occur, the motion towards C must first have stopped at C, this being, as we saw,[a] the ' rest ' which is opposite to motion from C. All this makes it plain that the movement which reverses its direction is not continuous.

Or (to generalize by taking an example of a change other than that of locality) suppose that a thing has ceased to be not-white and has become white at one and the same instant. If, then, the alteration to white and the reverse alteration from white are one continuous process and the white does not remain in existence for any time at all, that means that the having-ceased to be not-white and the having-become white have occurred at the same moment as the having-become not-white : the time of all these three events will be the same.

And note that the continuity of the time does not involve the continuity of the modification, but only that one modification succeeds the other (and counter) modification. And how can contraries like black and white have as their extreme the same point ?

Rotatory motion, on the other hand, we may suppose to be uniform and continuous without any impossible consequences. For a mobile revolving in a circle from point A round to point A again is maintaining one identical tenor in its movement, and so is moving all the time to the same point it is moving from until it actually reaches it ; but it will not be undergoing simultaneously two motions that are either contrary or opposite. The motion to a point is not always either contrary or opposite to the

ARISTOTLE

264 b 15 ἡ ἐπ' εὐθείας (ταύτῃ γάρ ἐστιν ἐναντία κατὰ τόπον,
οἷον ἡ κατὰ διάμετρον· ἀπέχει γὰρ πλεῖστον) ἀντικειμένη δὲ ἡ κατὰ τὸ αὐτὸ μῆκος. ὥστε οὐδὲν
κωλύει συνεχῶς κινεῖσθαι καὶ μηδένα χρόνον δια-
λείπειν· ἡ μὲν γὰρ κύκλῳ κίνησίς ἐστιν ἀπὸ τοῦ
αὐτοῦ εἰς αὐτό, ἡ δὲ κατ' εὐθεῖαν εἰς ἄλλο.[1] καὶ
20 ἡ μὲν ἐν τῷ κύκλῳ οὐδέποτε ἐν τοῖς αὐτοῖς, ἡ
δὲ κατ' εὐθεῖαν πολλάκις ἐν τοῖς αὐτοῖς· τὴν μὲν
οὖν ἀεὶ ἐν ἄλλῳ καὶ ἄλλῳ γιγνομένην ἐνδέχεται
κινεῖσθαι συνεχῶς· τὴν δ' ἐν τοῖς αὐτοῖς πολλάκις
οὐκ ἐνδέχεται, ἀνάγκη γὰρ ἅμα κινεῖσθαι τὰς
ἀντικειμένας. ὥστ' οὐδ' ἐν τῷ ἡμικυκλίῳ οὐδ' ἐν
25 ἄλλῃ περιφερείᾳ οὐδεμιᾷ ἐνδέχεται συνεχῶς κινεῖ-

---

[1] [Simplicius's paraphrase (1309. 13) shows that he read
ἀπὸ τοῦ αὐτοῦ εἰς αὐτό (though in the lemma (1308. 33) Diels
writes ἀφ' ἑαυτοῦ εἰς ἑαυτό), and his lemma reads ἡ δὲ κατ'
εὐθεῖαν εἰς ἄλλο. Themistius 231. 24 ἀπ' αὐτοῦ εἰς αὐτό, ἡ
δὲ κατ' εὐθεῖαν ἀπ' αὐτοῦ εἰς ἄλλο (ἀφ' αὐτοῦ εἰς αὐτό . . . ἀφ'
αὐτοῦ conj. Spengler). Our mss. have ἀφ' αὐτοῦ (or ἑαυτοῦ)
εἰς τὸ (τὸ om. FHI) αὐτό (ἑαυτό F), ἡ δὲ κατ' εὐθεῖαν ἀφ' αὐτοῦ
(or ἑαυτοῦ) εἰς ἄλλο. The Oxf. Trans. reads ἀφ' αὐτοῦ εἰς αὐτό
. . . ἀφ' αὐτοῦ εἰς ἄλλο. The choice lies between this and
Simplicius's reading.—C.]

---

[a] [In the diagram the motions along the diameter (A to B
and B to A) are both 'opposite' and 'contrary,' because
contraries in place are defined as 'being
at the maximum distance from each
other,' and this is true of the points A
and B on the line AB. The motions
along the arc (A to C and C to A) are
not 'contrary,' since A and C are not at
the maximum distance; but they are
'opposite' as traversing the same course in
opposite directions. But in travelling round the whole circle
from A back to A, the mobile is not undergoing two contrary or opposite motions *at the same time*, although it is all
the while travelling both from and to the same point.—C.]

392

motion from that same point : the two motions are *contrary* if they are on the same straight line—along the diameter of the circle, for instance, the one motion is in the local sense ' contrary ' to the other, in that the two ends of the diameter are at the greatest possible distance from each other—while the two motions are *opposite* only if, in going from and to the same point, they traverse the same line.[a] So there is nothing to prevent the movement of rotation from being perpetual and without interruption ; because in a circular movement the mobile is always going to the same point that it is coming from, but in a movement on a straight line it is always going to the point opposite to that which it is coming from. Also on a circle the progress of the movement is never at the same points, whereas the rectilinear movement is at the same points repeatedly.[b] So the movement that is always going forward to another and another may be continuous, but a movement which is at the same points repeatedly cannot, for that would involve moving in opposite directions at one and the same time. Thus it is impossible to move continuously upon a semi-circumference, or any other arc whatever, for that would

[b] [The Oxf. Trans. renders ἐν τοῖς αὐτοῖς ' localized within fixed limits,' following Themistius 231. 25 and others, who explain that whereas the straight line (or the arc) has an ' actual ' beginning and end, between which the motion must oscillate, there are no such limits anywhere on the circumference of a circle. But 240 a 33 τὰ μέρη (the parts of a rotating sphere) οὐκ ἔστιν ἐν τῷ αὐτῷ οὐδένα χρόνον, εἶτα καὶ τὸ ὅλον μεταβάλλει ἀεὶ εἰς ἕτερον suggests that ἐν τοῖς αὐτοῖς means ' at the same points '—the *movement* is always going on to ' another and another ' point of its progress, whereas a vibratory rectilinear movement recurs to the same points again and again.—C.]

264 b σθαι· πολλάκις γὰρ ἀνάγκη ταῦτα κινεῖσθαι καὶ τὰς
ἐναντίας μεταβάλλειν μεταβολάς· οὐ γὰρ συνάπτει
τῇ ἀρχῇ τὸ πέρας. ἡ δὲ τοῦ κύκλου συνάπτει, καὶ
ἔστι μόνη τέλειος.

Φανερὸν δὲ καὶ ἐκ ταύτης τῆς διαιρέσεως ὅτι
30 οὐδὲ τὰς ἄλλας ἐνδέχεται κινήσεις εἶναι συνεχεῖς.
ἐν ἁπάσαις γὰρ ταὐτὰ συμβαίνει κινεῖσθαι πολλάκις,
οἷον ἐν ἀλλοιώσει τὰ μεταξύ, καὶ ἐν τῇ τοῦ ποσοῦ
τὰ ἀνὰ μέσον μεγέθη, καὶ ἐν γενέσει καὶ φθορᾷ
ὡσαύτως· οὐδὲν γὰρ διαφέρει ὀλίγα ἢ πολλὰ
265 a ποιῆσαι ἐν οἷς ἐστιν ἡ μεταβολή, οὐδὲ μεταξὺ
θεῖναί τι ἢ ἀφελεῖν· ἀμφοτέρως γὰρ συμβαίνει
ταὐτὰ κινεῖσθαι πολλάκις.

Δῆλον οὖν ἐκ τούτων ὅτι οὐδ' οἱ φυσιολόγοι
καλῶς λέγουσιν οἱ πάντα τὰ αἰσθητὰ κινεῖσθαι
5 φάσκοντες ἀεί· κινεῖσθαι γὰρ ἀνάγκη τούτων τινὰ
τῶν κινήσεων, καὶ μάλιστα κατ' ἐκείνους ἐστὶν
ἀλλοιοῦσθαι· ῥεῖν γάρ φασιν ἀεὶ καὶ φθίνειν, ἔτι
δὲ καὶ τὴν γένεσιν καὶ τὴν φθορὰν ἀλλοίωσιν
λέγουσιν. ὁ δὲ λόγος νῦν εἴρηκε καθόλου περὶ
πάσης κινήσεως ὅτι κατ' οὐδεμίαν κίνησιν ἐνδέχεται κινεῖσθαι συνεχῶς, ἔξω τῆς κύκλῳ, ὥστε
10 οὔτε κατ' ἀλλοίωσιν οὔτε κατ' αὔξησιν.

---

[a] Which, as we have seen, must break the continuity.
[b] Which is a term you would not apply to mere changes
of local position.
[c] [Cf. 187 a 30.—C.]

involve recurrent retracing of the course and a series of changes in opposite directions,[a] inasmuch as on no such arc can the extreme limit of departure from the starting-point coincide with that starting-point itself ; whereas in the movement on a complete circumference that coincidence is realized, so that it alone is self-completing and re-entrant.

This analysis also makes it plain that none of the other kinds of change can be sustained in continuity, for all such changes do in fact retrace their movement repeatedly. In the case of change of quality all the intermediate stages would have to be retraced in the inverse order, and in quantitive changes the intermediate magnitudes, and analogously in genesis and evanishment ; for it makes no difference whether the recognized intermediary states are many or few, or whether we interpolate new ones or eliminate the accepted ones, since in any case the change must make its progress recurrently through them in the reverse direction if it is to be sustained.

From all this it follows that the physicists who say that all objects of sense are in uninterrupted motion and change are mistaken. For the motion or change they speak of must be one or another of those we have just shown to be intermittent ; and indeed the thinkers in question lay special stress on one of these very changes, namely the qualitive one ; for they say that all things are in a state of flux [b] and decay, and moreover they regard genesis and dissolution as mere qualitive modifications.[c] But our present argument has shown, of all motions in general, that there is no kind of sustained motion or change that can be continuous except that of rotation ; and this excludes both qualitive and quantitive change.

ARISTOTLE

265 a
"Ὅτι μὲν οὖν οὔτ᾽ ἄπειρός ἐστι μεταβολὴ οὐδεμία
οὔτε συνεχὴς ἔξω τῆς κύκλῳ φορᾶς, ἔστω τοσαῦθ᾽
ἡμῖν εἰρημένα.

CHAPTER IX

ARGUMENT

[*The priority of rotation to all other forms of locomotion is
easily shown. We may dismiss as compound and derivative
all species of locomotion except the rectilinear and the circular,
and of these the circular is prior, (1) as being simpler and
more complete and capable of never coming to an end (265 a
13–27). Also (2) on a circumference there is not (as on a
straight line) any definite starting-point or finishing-point
for the motion. The centre is the only beginning, middle, and
end, and the rotating body moves round, not towards, the
centre. Hence a sphere as a whole does not change its place,
though it moves continuously (a 27–b 8). (3) Rotation
must be primary because it is the measure of all other
motions, and conversely it must be the measure because
primary (b 8–11). (4) Rotation is the only motion that can
continue with a uniform velocity. Physical bodies moving
in a straight line increase their velocity as they approach
their proper place (and decrease their velocity as they are
forced away from it) (b 11–16).*

265 a 13
"Ὅτι δὲ τῶν φορῶν ἡ κυκλοφορία πρώτη, δῆλον.
πᾶσα γὰρ φορὰ (ὥσπερ καὶ πρότερον εἴπομεν) ἢ
15 κύκλῳ ἢ ἐπ᾽ εὐθείας ἢ μικτή. ταύτης δ᾽ ἀνάγκη
προτέρας εἶναι ἐκείνας· ἐξ ἐκείνων γὰρ συνέστηκεν.
τῆς δ᾽ εὐθείας ἡ κύκλῳ· ἁπλῆ γὰρ καὶ τέλειος
μᾶλλον. ἄπειρον μὲν γὰρ οὐκ ἔστιν εὐθεῖαν φέρε-

ᵃ [Consequently, from this point onwards, all movements
from place to place except rectilinear movement may be

396

Let this then suffice in proof that there can be no movement sustained without limit or continuously except rotatory locomotion.

CHAPTER IX

ARGUMENT (*continued*)

The primacy of locomotion over all other forms of change is supported by the testimony of all physical philosophers. Empedocles' Love and Strife and Anaxagoras' Mind cause change of all kinds by 'combining' or 'separating' (i.e. moving in space) material particles. The Atomists attribute only locomotion to their primary bodies or atoms. The Ionians explain the formation of a differentiated cosmos by 'condensation' and 'rarifaction' (i.e. bringing matter more or less closely together). The Platonists make the self-moving soul the principle of all kinds of change, and self-motion means locomotion. Finally in common usage locomotion is the strict and proper sense of 'motion'—the term we have used to cover locomotion, change of quality, and change of quantity (b 16–266 a 5).

Summary of conclusions reached in Chaps. I.-IX. (a 6–9). —C.]

It is easy to show that rotation is the primary form of locomotion. Local movement, as already said, is always either rectilinear or rotatory, or a combination of the two, and the things combined necessarily take precedence of the combination formed out of them.[a] And, of the two comparatively simple movements, rotation takes precedence of rectilinear motion, as being the simpler and more self-completing. For no mobile can travel all along

dismissed as derivative, and it will be enough to show that rotation is prior to rectilinear motion.—C.]

265 a σθαι· τὸ γὰρ οὕτως ἄπειρον οὐκ ἔστιν. ἀλλ' οὐδ'
εἰ ἦν, ἐκινεῖτ' ἂν οὐδέν· οὐ γὰρ γίγνεται τὸ ἀ-
20 δύνατον, διελθεῖν δὲ τὴν ἄπειρον ἀδύνατον. ἡ δ'
ἐπὶ τῆς πεπερασμένης εὐθείας ἀνακάμπτουσα μὲν
συνθετὴ καὶ δύο κινήσεις, μὴ ἀνακάμπτουσα δὲ
ἀτελὴς καὶ φθαρτή· πρότερον δὲ καὶ φύσει καὶ
λόγῳ καὶ χρόνῳ τὸ τέλειον μὲν τοῦ ἀτελοῦς, τοῦ
φθαρτοῦ δὲ τὸ ἄφθαρτον.   ἔτι προτέρα ἦν ἐν-
25 δέχεται ἀίδιον εἶναι τῆς μὴ ἐνδεχομένης· τὴν μὲν
οὖν κύκλῳ ἐνδέχεται ἀίδιον εἶναι, τῶν δ' ἄλλων
οὔτε φορὰν οὔτ' ἄλλην οὐδεμίαν· στάσιν γὰρ δεῖ
γίγνεσθαι, εἰ δὲ στάσις, ἔφθαρται ἡ κίνησις.

Εὐλόγως δὲ συμβέβηκε τὸ τὴν κύκλῳ μίαν εἶναι
καὶ συνεχῆ, καὶ μὴ τὴν ἐπ' εὐθείας. τῆς μὲν γὰρ
30 ἐπ' εὐθείας ὥρισται καὶ ἀρχὴ καὶ τέλος καὶ μέσον,
καὶ πάντ' ἔχει ἐν αὑτῇ, ὥστ' ἔστιν ὅθεν ἄρξεται
τὸ κινούμενον καὶ οὗ τελευτήσει (πρὸς γὰρ τοῖς
πέρασιν ἠρεμεῖ πᾶν, ἢ ὅθεν ἢ οὗ)· τῆς δὲ περιφεροῦς
ἀόριστα—τί γὰρ μᾶλλον ὁποιονοῦν πέρας τῶν ἐπὶ
τῆς γραμμῆς; ὁμοίως γὰρ ἕκαστον καὶ ἀρχὴ καὶ

---

[a] [Nothing can actually travel a rectilinear distance longer
than the diameter of the spherical universe.—C.]

[b] [The rectilinear movement is ' incomplete and must come
to an end ' *in either case*, for the movement which returns on
itself is nothing but two movements of which this is true.
It can *go no farther* when it has reached one extreme or the
other ; and it is *incomplete* or *imperfect* in that it cannot
' knit the end to the beginning ' (264 b 27) ; for the straight
line can always be extended, whereas the circle is once for all
complete.   *Cf. De caelo* 286 b 19.—C.]

[c] [ἄφθαρτον here seems to mean ' capable of not coming to
an end ' (rather than ' incapable of coming to an end '), as
the opposite of φθαρτόν ' incapable of not coming to an end ' ;
for rotation *can* stop, but need not ; whereas rectilinear

a straight line that has no limit ; in the first place
because there is no such line,[a] and in the second
place because, even if there were, no mobile would
effect the transit over it, for the impossible does not
happen, and it is impossible to traverse to the end
that which has no limit. And as to movement on
a finite straight line, if it returns upon itself it is
compound and consists of two movements, and if
it does not return upon itself it has no intrinsic
completeness and must be broken off.[b] Now that
which is fully developed precedes that which is un-
developed, alike in nature, in definition, and in time ;
and that which is capable of not being broken off[c]
in like manner precedes that which must be broken
off. Again, that which can be eternal precedes that
which cannot, and movement of rotation can be
eternal, whereas no other movement or change,
whether local or of any other kind, can be so. For
in all these other cases the movement must stop, that
is, be broken off and put an end to.

Nor is it anything strange that rotation should be
uniform and continuous and rectilinear motion not.
Motion on a straight line has a definite beginning,
middle, and end, all of which it contains in itself in
such a way that the mobile has a defined starting-
place and goal (for the limit of a movement, whether it
be its whither or its whence, always implies cessation).
Motion round a circumference, on the other hand, has
no such defined elements ; for why should any one
point on the line rather than another be regarded
as a limit ? Any point on the circumference is
indifferently a potential beginning, middle, or end

movement *must* stop. The next sentence puts it more
strongly : rotation is capable of *never* coming to an end.—C.]

265 b μέσον καὶ τέλος—ὥστ' ἀεί τέ τινα[1] εἶναι ἐν ἀρχῇ
καὶ ἐν τέλει καὶ μηδέποτε. διὸ κινεῖται καὶ ἠρεμεῖ
πως ἡ σφαῖρα· τὸν αὐτὸν γὰρ κατέχει τόπον. αἴτιον δ' ὅτι πάντα συμβέβηκε ταῦτα τῷ κέντρῳ—
καὶ γὰρ ἀρχὴ καὶ μέσον τοῦ μεγέθους καὶ τέλος
5 ἐστίν—ὥστε, διὰ τὸ ἔξω εἶναι τοῦτο τῆς περιφερείας, οὐκ ἔστιν ὅπου τὸ φερόμενον ἠρεμήσει
ὡς διεληλυθός· ἀεὶ γὰρ φέρεται περὶ τὸ μέσον, ἀλλ'
οὐ πρὸς τὸ ἔσχατον. διὰ δὲ τοῦτο μένει[2] ἀεί τε
ἠρεμεῖ πως τὸ ὅλον καὶ κινεῖται συνεχῶς.

Συμβαίνει δ' ἀντιστρόφως· καὶ γὰρ ὅτι μέτρον
τῶν κινήσεων ἡ περιφορά ἐστι, πρώτην ἀναγκαῖον
10 αὐτὴν εἶναι (ἅπαντα γὰρ μετρεῖται τῷ πρώτῳ)·
καὶ διότι πρώτη, μέτρον ἐστὶ τῶν ἄλλων.

---

[1] [τινα om. EK. Themistius's paraphrase is (232. 32) ἀεὶ
οὖν ἐν ἀρχῇ καὶ ἀεὶ ἐν τέλει, ignoring καὶ μηδέποτε. If τινα is
omitted, the subject of εἶναι is τὴν περιφερῆ κίνησιν.—C.]

[2] [The reading of the Tauchnitz edition διὰ δὲ τὸ τοῦτο (sc.
τὸ μέσον) μένειν might be supported by Themistius 233. 3
ἐπεὶ τοίνυν οὐκ ἐπὶ τὸ πέρας ἀλλὰ περὶ τὸ πέρας κινεῖται, τοῦτο δὲ
ἀεὶ ἐν ταὐτῷ μένει, κτλ., Philop. 849. 16 περὶ τὸ ἴδιον κέντρον
ἀκίνητον μένον, Simplic. 1316 22 μένοντος ἀεὶ τοῦ περὶ ὃ ἡ
κίνησις γίνεται. All three commentators feel the need to
mention that the centre does not move. E obtains this sense
by reading διὸ (in the late sense of ' because '=διότι) for διὰ.
But the other mss. read διὰ δὲ τοῦτο μένει ' for this reason the
sphere stays where it is,' i.e. does not move from place to
place. The point here is, not that the axis is stationary
while the rest of the sphere moves round it, but that the
sphere is stationary as a whole (ἠρεμεῖ πως τὸ ὅλον), and all the
time it is revolving 'occupies the same place' (τὸν αὐτὸν
κατέχει τόπον, l. 2).—C.]

---

* [τινα (if it should be retained at all) is ambiguous. Other
possible meanings are : (1) ' So that you can say that there
are always some *parts* of the rotating body at a starting-

PHYSICS, VIII. ix.

of a movement of rotation, so that any points you take are at beginning-and-end places potentially but none of them actually.[a] And thus a rotating sphere is moving in one sense, and (since as the frame of reference for internal positions it is constant) at rest in another.[b] The reason of which is that all the elements which are distinct in a straight line are attributes of the centre in a circle or sphere; for the centre is alike the beginning and middle and end of the measure of[c] a circular magnitude, so that, none of these limits being on the periphery, there is no position on that periphery at which the mobile must rest as having passed through to the end of its movement, for it is always being carried round the centre and never to any extreme point; and therefore the whole sphere is stationary and motionless in one sense, and moves continuously in another.

Note also this reciprocal relation. It is rotation (of the farthest heavenly sphere) that is the measure (in time) of all movements,[d] wherefore it must be primary, for it is by what is primary in their kind that all things are standardized or measured. And again it is because rotation is primary that it is the measure of all other kinds of movement or change.

point or at a goal, or you can equally well say that they are never at either.' (2) ' So that we can say of *certain things* (*sc.* things that rotate about an axis) both that they are always and that they never are at a starting-point and at a finishing-point ' (Oxf. Trans.).—C.]

[b] See Introd. to Bk. IV., Vol. I. p. 270.

[c] ['Of the space traversed' (Oxf. Tr.). Simplic. 1315. 12, the centre is ' *beginning* ' in that the circumference is everywhere at an equal distance *from* it; ' *end* ' in that all radii from the circumference end in it.—C.]

[d] [*Cf.* 223 b 18, uniform rotation is the best measure, because the easiest to count.—C.]

265 b Ἔτι δὲ καὶ ὁμαλῆ ἐνδέχεται εἶναι τὴν κύκλῳ μόνην. τὰ γὰρ ἐπ᾽ εὐθείας ἀνωμάλως ἀπὸ τῆς ἀρχῆς φέρεται καὶ πρὸς τὸ τέλος· πάντα γὰρ ὅσωπερ ἂν ἀφίστηται πλεῖον τοῦ ἠρεμοῦντος, 15 φέρεται θᾶττον· τῆς δὲ κύκλῳ μόνης οὔτ᾽ ἀρχὴ οὔτε τέλος ἐν αὐτῇ πέφυκεν, ἀλλ᾽ ἐκτός.

Ὅτι δ᾽ ἡ κατὰ τόπον φορὰ πρώτη τῶν κινήσεων, μαρτυροῦσι πάντες ὅσοι περὶ κινήσεως πεποίηνται μνείαν· τὰς γὰρ ἀρχὰς αὐτῆς ἀποδιδόασι τοῖς κι- 20 νοῦσι τοιαύτην κίνησιν. διάκρισις γὰρ καὶ σύγ- κρισις κινήσεις κατὰ τόπον εἰσίν, οὕτω δὲ κινοῦσιν ἡ Φιλία καὶ τὸ Νεῖκος—τὸ μὲν γὰρ διακρίνει τὸ δὲ συγκρίνει αὐτῶν—καὶ τὸν Νοῦν δέ φησιν Ἀναξαγόρας διακρίνειν τὸν κινήσαντα πρῶτον. ὁμοίως δὲ καὶ ὅσοι τοιαύτην μὲν οὐδεμίαν αἰτίαν 25 λέγουσι, διὰ δὲ τὸ κενὸν κινεῖσθαί φασι· καὶ γὰρ οὗτοι τὴν κατὰ τόπον κίνησιν κινεῖσθαι τὴν φύσιν λέγουσιν· ἡ γὰρ διὰ τὸ κενὸν κίνησις φορὰ ἔστιν ὡς ἐν τόπῳ.[1] τῶν δ᾽ ἄλλων οὐδεμίαν ὑπάρχειν τοῖς πρώτοις ἀλλὰ τοῖς ἐκ τούτων οἴονται· αὐξά- νεσθαι γὰρ καὶ φθίνειν καὶ ἀλλοιοῦσθαι συγκρινο- μένων καὶ διακρινομένων τῶν ἀτόμων σωμάτων

---

[1] [φορὰ ἔστιν ὡς ἐν τόπῳ, '(is) in a sense motion in space' —'in a sense,' because Aristotle does not admit the exist- ence of empty space or of motion through it : φορά ἐστι ὡς ἐν τόπῳ ΕΚ : φορά ἐστι καὶ ὡς ἐν τόπῳ cett. Bekker (trans- lated by Dr. Wicksteed). (I assume that when ἐστι was understood as the copula with φορά, καί was inserted to help out—rather inadequately—the remaining ὡς ἐν τόπῳ): φορά ἐστιν ἐν τόπῳ Simplic. 1319. 7 (paraphr.).—C.]

---

[a] [In the case of natural (but not of ' violent ' or unnatural)

Again, it is rotation only that can be uniform ; for natural movements on the straight are never uniform as they pass from the beginning to the end, for in them the mobile moves more rapidly in proportion as it is further from the position of rest,[a] whereas in rotation, and in rotation alone, the beginning and end are not inherent in the path of motion but external to it.

That local movement in general takes precedence of other forms of change is testified by all who have treated of motion : they all assign as the principles of change just the very things that exemplify local motion. For 'resolution' and 'combination' are local movements ; and 'attraction' and 'repulsion'[b] likewise, inasmuch as the one severs and the other combines. Anaxagoras[c] too says that Intelligence, the first mover, severed things out. And it is the same with those[d] who allege no suchlike cause, but declare that things move because of the void ; for they too say that the movement or change of natural substance[e] is the local one, for the motion which the void makes possible is local, just as if it came about in a place ; whereas changes other than local are never regarded by these thinkers as affecting the primary substances but always as derivative ; for growth and qualitive change they consider as caused by the combination and resolution of the atoms. It

motion ; *cf.* 230 b 24. Hence, as the Oxf. Trans. notes, the middle ἀφίστηται, ' removes itself.'—C.]

[b] [The Love and Strife of Empedocles.—C.]

[c] [Frag. 13, καὶ ὅσον ἐκίνησεν ὁ Νοῦς, πᾶν τοῦτο διεκρίθη, and Frag. 12.—C.]

[d] [Leucippus and Democritus.—C.]

[e] [τὴν φύσιν, τουτέστι τὰ φυσικὰ καὶ πρῶτα καὶ ἄτομα σώματα, Simplic. 1318. 33.—C.]

ARISTOTLE

265 b 30 φασίν. τὸν αὐτὸν δὲ τρόπον καὶ ὅσοι διὰ πυκνότητα
ἢ μανότητα κατασκευάζουσι γένεσιν καὶ φθοράν·
συγκρίσει γὰρ καὶ διακρίσει ταῦτα διακοσμοῦσιν.
ἔτι δὲ παρὰ τούτους οἱ τὴν ψυχὴν αἰτίαν ποιοῦντες
κινήσεως· τὸ γὰρ αὐτὸ ἑαυτὸ κινοῦν ἀρχὴν εἶναί
φασι τῶν κινουμένων, κινεῖ δὲ τὸ ζῷον καὶ πᾶν
266 a τὸ ἔμψυχον τὴν κατὰ τόπον ἑαυτὸ κίνησιν. καὶ
κυρίως δὲ κινεῖσθαί φαμεν μόνον τὸ κινούμενον
κατὰ τόπον· ἂν δ' ἠρεμῇ μὲν ἐν τῷ αὐτῷ, αὐ-
ξάνηται δὲ ἢ φθίνῃ ἢ ἀλλοιούμενον τυγχάνῃ, πῇ
5 κινεῖσθαι, ἁπλῶς δὲ κινεῖσθαι οὔ φαμεν.

Ὅτι μὲν οὖν ἀεί τε κίνησις ἦν καὶ ἔσται τὸν ἅ-
παντα χρόνον, καὶ τίς ἀρχὴ τῆς ἀιδίου κινήσεως,
ἔτι δὲ τίς πρώτη κίνησις, καὶ τίνα κίνησιν ἀίδιον
ἐνδέχεται μόνην εἶναι, καὶ τὸ κινοῦν πρῶτον ὅτι
ἀκίνητον, εἴρηται.

---

[a] [Anaximenes, with whom Aristotle would group Thales
and Heracleitus. *Cf.* 187 a 12 ff.—C.]
[b] [Plato (*Phaedrus* 245 c) and his school.—C.]

CHAPTER X

ARGUMENT

[*The Prime Mover is without parts or magnitude. To prove
this, some premises must first be established* (266 a 10–12) :
   (1) *Nothing finite can cause a motion that will occupy an
unlimited time. This can be shown by considering the work
as done piecemeal by a fraction of the finite mover* (a 12–24).
   (2) *A finite magnitude cannot contain an infinite force ;
for it can be shown that otherwise a finite and an infinite
force would take the same time to effect the same movement*
(a 24–b 6).

is the same too with those ^{a} who get genesis and dissolution out of density and rarity, for it is by drawing together and separating apart that they get these dispositions. And yet again those ^{b} who think the soul is the cause of motion take their place in the same rank, for they declare that the self-moving is the principle and initiator of the movements of all things that move, and the movement which an animal or other living creature produces in itself is local movement. And in fact it is only what is moving in the sense of changing its place that we primarily and properly say is 'moving'; if it abides in the same place but grows or contracts or changes its qualities we say that it is moving 'in a way,' but not just that 'it is moving.'

We have now said what needed saying in demonstration of the fact that movement always was and always will be throughout time, and to show what is the principle of this everlasting motion, and what is the nature of the primary movement, and what is the only movement that can possibly be eternal, and that the prime mover is itself motionless.

CHAPTER X

ARGUMENT (*continued*)

(3) *A finite force cannot reside in an infinite magnitude. Proofs of this* (b 6–24).
  Summary of these results (b 25–27).
  Before proceeding to the conclusion, a problem of locomotion must be solved : How can a missile continue in motion after it has left the thrower's hand ? The original agent imparts to an intermediary (air or water) a motive force which is gradually exhausted. The theory that the effect is produced

ARGUMENT (*continued*)

by ' mutual replacement ' in the intermediary will not account for the observed fact (b 27–267 a 20).

To resume the main argument : The single continuous motion which we have seen must exist in the world can be caused only by a mover which is not moved or changed in any way. This mover must be felt at the circumference, rather

266 a 10

῾Ότι δὲ τοῦτ᾿ ἀμερὲς ἀναγκαῖον εἶναι καὶ μηδὲν
ἔχειν μέγεθος, νῦν λέγωμεν, πρῶτον περὶ τῶν
προτέρων αὐτοῦ διορίσαντες.

Τούτων δ᾿ ἓν μὲν ἔστιν ὅτι οὐχ οἷόν τε οὐδὲν

---

[a] [I have substituted for Dr. Wicksteed's rendering of this paragraph an interpretation published in the *Classical Quarterly*, xxvi. (1932) p. 52.—C.]

Dr. Wicksteed (supported, as he thought, by Aquinas) explained the use of the phrase ἐν πλείονι γὰρ τὸ μεῖζον here by supposing that Aristotle is thinking of the time it takes for a mobile to *pass a certain point*, or in other words, to *frank its boundary*, not of the time it takes to *advance a certain distance* for, if the whole and all its parts move with a uniform motion, it takes no longer for the whole to advance a certain distance

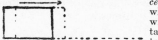

than for any part of it to do so, but it does take longer for the greater bulk of the whole to frank its boundary than for the lesser bulk of the part to do so.

Now in any time however short there can be movement, and whenever there is *any* movement *some* portion of the mobile will frank its boundary: in a longer time a greater portion, and in a shorter time a lesser portion. Thus the time during which a limited force causes uniform motion in a limited mobile is proportionate to (and can be measured by) the magnitude of that portion of the mobile that it causes to frank its boundary.

If the mobile, instead of being rectangular as in the first diagram, is circular or spherical, and the movement instead

PHYSICS, VIII. x.

than at the centre, of the spherical universe ; for there the
motion is quickest (a 20–b 9).

If the mover were itself in motion, the motion it caused
could not be continuous (b 9–17).

The Prime Mover cannot, then, be either a finite or an
infinite magnitude. Therefore it has no parts or magnitude
(b 17–26).—C.]

LET us now go on to show that the first mover
must necessarily be unsusceptible of partition, and
so not dimensional. This will involve the antecedent
establishment of certain theorems, the first of which
is as follows.

[a] It is impossible for a limited motor to cause a

of being rectilinear is rotatory, the same line of reasoning is
still applicable: the time occupied is then
measurable by the magnitude of the sector
to frank its boundary.

If this view is accepted, the passage
266 a 15–24 will be paraphrased as follows,
and its application to the subject in hand,
viz. the uniform rotation of the limited universe, and the agent which causes it, will be
obvious.

'Let A represent the limited motor (capable of causing)
B the limited mobile (to pass a point or to frank its bound-
ary) and C illimitable time. Now let D cause E, a part of
B (to frank its boundary).

[Note that this does not mean that the motion caused by
D is confined to the part E, but that it causes enough movement (in B) for E (and no more) to frank its boundary.]

'Then the time it takes (Z) cannot be as great as (the
illimitable time) C; for it will take a longer time for a
greater amount (of B) (to frank its boundary). Therefore
Z is not illimitable [see the note on this argument on p. 112].
So taking it in this way (that a part (D) of the motive power
(A) can move (B) during a definite stretch (Z) of time),
by adding one D to another I shall make up the (finite) A,

407

266 a πεπερασμένον κινεῖν ἄπειρον χρόνον. τρία γὰρ
ἔστι—τὸ κινοῦν, τὸ κινούμενον, τὸ ἐν ᾧ τρίτον
15 (ὁ χρόνος)· ταῦτα δὲ ἢ πάντα ἄπειρα ἢ πάντα
πεπερασμένα ἢ ἔνια, οἷον τὰ δύο ἢ τὸ ἕν. ἔστω
δὴ τὸ Α τὸ κινοῦν, τὸ δὲ κινούμενον Β, χρόνος
ἄπειρος ἐφ' οὗ Γ. τὸ δὴ Δ κινείτω τι μέρος τῆς
Β, τὸ ἐφ' οὗ Ε.   οὐ δὴ ἐν ἴσῳ τῷ Γ· ἐν πλείονι
γὰρ τὸ μεῖζον· ὥστ' οὐκ ἄπειρος ὁ χρόνος ὁ τὸ¹ Ζ.

---

¹ [τὸ Oxf. Trans. : τοῦ codd.—C.]

---

and by adding one E to another I shall make up the finite
B; but I shall not use up the time by deducting a corresponding length for each such addition, since it is illimitable.
Therefore the whole of A (the sum of all the D's) will take
only a finite period of the time C to move the whole of B
(the sum of all the E's, past the point, or to cause the whole
of B to frank its boundary).   So an illimitable motion can
not be imparted to anything by a finite mover.   Thus it is
clear that a finite mover cannot cause motion during illimitable time.'

To take the example of the ship-hauling.   Suppose the
point to be passed is represented by a post level with the
prow of the ship: if 50 men (D) can haul half the ship (E)
past the post in an hour (Z) but are then exhausted and can
do no more, 50 other men (another D) can haul the remaining half (another E) past the post in another hour (another
Z).   Therefore the whole gang of 100 men (A), i.e. both the
shifts of 50 men (both the D's), will take only a finite time
(two hours) to move the whole of the ship (B) past the post.
But it does not necessarily follow that if the whole gang
work together for an hour they will produce the same result
as if they work in shifts of 50 men, each shift working for
an hour.

ᵃ [The argument contemplates a finite mover and a finite
moved, each of which is not ἀμερὲς καὶ μηδὲν ἔχον μέγεθος
but can be considered as divided into parts operating separately.   The difficulties raised about the interpretation turn
on the apparent fallacy in the phrase ἐν πλείονι γὰρ τὸ μεῖζον,
which at first sight seems to mean that *the greater force* (A)

motion during an infinite time. For there are three
things to consider, the motor, the mobile, and thirdly
that in which the movement takes place, namely the
time. Now these must be either all of them without
limit, or else one, two, or all of them limited. Let
A, then, represent the motor, B the thing moved,
and C the unlimited time (supposed to be taken by
A to move B any given distance). Now let D (a
part of A) move E, a part of B (the same distance).
Then the time it takes (Z) cannot be as great as
(the unlimited time) C; for it will take D a longer
time to move the greater amount (any larger fraction
of B).[a] Therefore the time Z is not unlimited. So,

takes a longer time to move its load B than the fractional
force D takes to move its fractional load E. If, as it is
natural to suppose, D is the same fraction of A that E is of
B, this is false and contradicts 250 a 6. There is no fallacy
if we translate as above: 'for it will take D a longer time
to move the greater amount (i.e. any larger fraction of B).
Therefore the time Z is not unlimited.' The argument is:
If D takes a time Z to move its fractional load E, it will take
a time longer than Z to move two or more E's, one at a time,
the same distance (and it can move the load B fraction by
fraction in this way). But if there is a time longer than
Z, the time Z—and consequently any multiple of it—must
be finite. A's time is a multiple of Z and so finite.
In other words: If 10 colliers (A) carry 10 sacks of coal
(B) any distance you choose, they cannot take an unlimited
time about it. For each collier (D) can, and does, carry 1
sack (E) that distance in whatever time they all take (the
unit-time). Now if a single collier has to carry 2 (or 3,
etc.) sacks, he will have to make 2 (or 3, etc.) journeys
and take twice (or thrice, etc.) the unit-time: 'it will
take D a longer time to move the greater amount.' The
work can be done in this way, and it follows that the
unit-time is finite. Supposing one collier does the whole
work, I can add journey to journey and sack to sack up
to the total 10, and I shall deduct from the reserve of
time available 1 unit-time for each journey—10 unit-times

409

266 a οὕτω δὴ τῇ Δ προστιθεὶς καταναλώσω τὸ Α, καὶ
20 τῇ Ε τὸ Β· τὸν δὲ χρόνον οὐ καταναλώσω ἀεὶ
ἀφαιρῶν ἴσον (ἄπειρος γάρ)· ὥστε ἡ πᾶσα Α τὴν
ὅλην Β κινήσει ἐν πεπερασμένῳ χρόνῳ τοῦ Γ.
οὐκ ἄρα οἷόν τε ὑπὸ πεπερασμένου κινεῖσθαι οὐδὲν
25 ἄπειρον κίνησιν. ὅτι μὲν οὖν οὐκ ἐνδέχεται τὸ
πεπερασμένον ἄπειρον κινεῖν χρόνον, φανερόν.

Ὅτι δ' ὅλως οὐκ ἐνδέχεται ἐν πεπερασμένῳ
μεγέθει ἄπειρον εἶναι δύναμιν, ἐκ τῶνδε δῆλον.
ἔστω γὰρ ἀεὶ ἡ πλείων δύναμις ἡ τὸ ἴσον ἐν ἐλάττονι χρόνῳ ποιοῦσα, οἷον θερμαίνουσα ἢ γλυκαί-
νουσα ἢ ῥίπτουσα καὶ ὅλως κινοῦσα. ἀνάγκη ἄρα
καὶ ὑπὸ τοῦ πεπερασμένου μὲν ἄπειρον δ' ἔχοντος
30 δύναμιν πάσχειν τι τὸ πάσχον, καὶ πλείω ἢ ὑπ'
ἄλλου· πλείων γὰρ ἡ ἄπειρος δύναμις. ἀλλὰ μὴν
χρόνον γε οὐκ ἐνδέχεται εἶναι οὐδένα. εἰ γάρ ἐστιν
ὁ ἐφ' ᾧ Α χρόνος ἐν ᾧ ἡ ἄπειρος ἰσχὺς ἐθέρμηνεν
ἢ ἔωσεν, ἐν ᾧ δὲ πεπερασμένη τις ὁ ΑΒ,[1] πρὸς

---

[1] [ἐν ᾧ δὲ πεπερασμένη τις ὁ ΑΒ (sc. χρόνος, cf. τῷ Α χρόνῳ,
b 1): ἐν ᾧ δ' ὁ (ὁ om. ΕΚ) ΑΒ πεπερασμένη τις codd. Either
ἐν τῷ δ' ΑΒ πεπερασμένη τις (Oxf. Trans.), or ὁ δ' ΑΒ ἐν ᾧ
πεπερασμένη τις is possible. Simplic. 1324. 30 (paraphr.) τὸ
δὴ πεπερασμένην ἔχον δύναμιν τὸ αὐτὸ κινήσει ἐν πλείονι χρόνῳ
τῷ ΑΒ perhaps slightly favours the order of words I have
adopted.—C.]

---

in all. But 10-times a finite time is finite and will not exhaust the infinite reserve. Therefore the unit-time in which
the 10 colliers (the whole of A) move the 10 sacks (the whole
of B) is finite. The principle that the fractional force can
deal with a multiple of its proper load, if allowed to take
it piecemeal, was stated at 250 a 10 (see note there). So it
is not necessary to suppose that D must be a larger fraction
of A than E is of B (Simplic. 1322. 8).

taking it in this way (*i.e.* taking the work as done piecemeal, a fraction at a time), by adding one D to another I shall exhaust the (finite) A, and by adding one E to another I shall exhaust the (finite) B ; but I shall not use up the time by deducting from it a corresponding length for each such addition, since it is unlimited. Therefore the whole of A (the sum of all the D's) will take only a finite period of the time C to move the whole of B (the sum of all the E's). So an unlimited motion cannot be imparted to anything by a finite mover. Thus it is clear that a finite mover cannot cause a motion during unlimited time.

Proceeding next to the general proposition that an unlimited power cannot reside in a limited magnitude we take our line as follows. Let us define the greater power, in every case, as that which produces an equal effect in less time, whether it be heating or sweetening or hurling or, to put it universally, effecting any kind of change. If then a limited subject had unlimited power, the object on which it exercised that power would clearly experience some effect, and that more intense than would be produced by any other, for unlimited power must exceed all other. But it is impossible to assign any period of time that would correspond to this. For let A represent the time in which the unlimited force heats the object or thrusts it to a certain distance, and A + B the time in which a given limited force would produce the

Aristotle does not mention the factor of distance (or *extent* of any sort of change), but unless some finite distance is intended, it is nonsense to say that ‘ it takes longer to move the greater amount.’ I take him to have in view *any finite extent, however great.*—C.]

266 b ταύτην μείζω ἀεὶ λαμβάνων πεπερασμένην ἥξω
ποτὲ εἰς τὸ ἐν τῷ Α χρόνῳ κεκινηκέναι· πρὸς πεπερασμένον γὰρ ἀεὶ προστιθεὶς ὑπερβαλῶ παντὸς
ὡρισμένου, καὶ ἀφαιρῶν ἐλλείψω ὡσαύτως. ἐν ἴσῳ
5 ἄρα χρόνῳ κινήσει ἡ πεπερασμένη τῇ ἀπείρῳ· τοῦτο
δὲ ἀδύνατον. οὐδὲν ἄρα πεπερασμένον ἐνδέχεται
ἄπειρον δύναμιν ἔχειν.

Οὐ τοίνυν οὐδὲ ἐν ἀπείρῳ πεπερασμένην. καίτοι
ἐνδέχεται ἐν ἐλάττονι μεγέθει πλείω δύναμιν εἶναι·
ἀλλ᾽ ἔτι μᾶλλον ἐν μείζονι πλείω.[1] ἔστω δὴ τὸ
ἐφ᾽ οὗ ΑΒ ἄπειρον. τὸ δὴ ΒΓ ἔχει δύναμίν τινα,
10 ᾗ ἔν τινι χρόνῳ ἐκίνησε τὴν Δ—ἐν τῷ χρόνῳ ἐφ᾽
ᾧ ΕΖ. ἂν δὴ τῆς ΒΓ διπλασίαν λαμβάνω, ἐν
ἡμίσει κινήσει χρόνῳ τοῦ ΕΖ (ἔστω γὰρ αὕτη ἡ

---

[1] [πλείω : πλείων IH[1]. Simplicius 1341. 11 read πλείω, but
paraphrases πλείων (ἀλλ᾽ ἐν τῷ μείζονι τοῦ ἐλάττονος κατὰ τὸ
αὐτὸ εἶδος ἔτι πλείων ἔσται ἡ δύναμις). πλείω (ἐνδέχεται εἶναι)
can be defended as meaning ' It is possible for the power to
be greater (and therefore I am entitled to argue from the
case in which it is greater).'—C.]

---

[a] [A is supposed to be some period of time, however short,
and the limited force must, of course, take a *longer* time
(A + B). I can now reduce the excess of A + B over A to
nothing (or less than nothing) if I augment the limited
force by adding any constant amount as often as is required.
Each addition will subtract a corresponding fraction from
the time B and so I can cut down A + B to A (or to less
than A). But then a force that, however augmented, is still
limited will do the work in the time allowed for the unlimited
force, which is impossible. (This paragraph has been partly
re-written).—C.]

[b] [*Literally*, ' It is true that the greater power may reside
in the lesser body (a seed contains enough to produce a large
tree ; so why should not the converse be true, and the greatest
of all bodies—an infinite body—contain less than an infinite
power ? Simplicius) ; but still more is it possible that the
larger body should contain the greater power ' (or ' that the

412

same effect.[a] Then if I increase this given force by equal increments successively I shall sooner or later arrive at the point at which the effect will have been produced by the limited power in time A (for by successive additions I can make the power exceed any given limit, and by corresponding subtractions can make the time fall short of any). In this way the limited power will take the same time as the unlimited in effecting the movement. But this is impossible. Therefore no limited body can have unlimited power.

It follows also that the power of an unlimited body cannot be limited, although [b] there may be cases in which the smaller body has the greater power, as well as the more obvious cases in which the greater power accompanies the greater size. For let AB

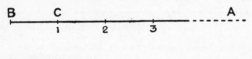

represent the unlimited body. Then the section BC will have a certain power, which would take a certain time to move D. Let EZ represent that time. Then, by the inverse ratio, twice BC will produce the same effect in half EZ [c] (ΘZ). So by continuing the

larger the body, the greater the power it contains,' if two bodies *of the same kind* are compared).—C.]

[c] [ἔστω γὰρ αὕτη ἡ ἀναλογία, 'for let us assume that proportion,' viz. 2 : 1, *doubling* the force and *halving* the time, for the sake of argument. Any other would do as well.—C.]

413

ARISTOTLE

266 b ἀναλογία), ὥστ' ἐν τῷ ΖΘ κινήσει. οὐκοῦν οὕτω λαμβάνων ἀεὶ τὴν μὲν ΑΒ οὐδέποτε διέξειμι,
τοῦ χρόνου δὲ τοῦ δοθέντος ἀεὶ ἐλάττω λήψομαι.
15 ἄπειρος ἄρα ἡ δύναμις ἔσται. πάσης γὰρ πεπερασμένης ὑπερβάλλει δυνάμεως· πάσης δὲ πεπερασμένης δυνάμεως ἀνάγκη πεπερασμένον εἶναι
καὶ τὸν χρόνον· εἰ γὰρ ἔν τινι ἡ τοσηδί, ἡ μείζων
ἐν ἐλάττονι μὲν ὡρισμένῳ δὲ κινήσει χρόνῳ, κατὰ
τὴν ἀντιστροφὴν τῆς ἀναλογίας. ἄπειρος δὲ πᾶσα
20 δύναμις, ὥσπερ καὶ πλῆθος καὶ μέγεθος τὸ ὑπε-
ρβάλλον παντὸς ὡρισμένου. ἔστι δὲ καὶ ὧδε δεῖξαι
τοῦτο· ληψόμεθα γὰρ δή τινα δύναμιν τὴν αὐτὴν
τῷ γένει τῇ ἐν τῷ ἀπείρῳ μεγέθει, ἐν πεπερασμένῳ μεγέθει οὖσαν, ἣ καταμετρήσει τὴν ἐν τῷ
ἀπείρῳ πεπερασμένην δύναμιν.

ᵃ [Or, ' but each time (I make such an addition) I shall
obtain a smaller fraction of the time allowed (*i.e.* the whole
time EZ); for as the additions to BC form the series 1, 2, 3,
4 . . . *n*, so the time-fractions form the series 1, $\frac{1}{2}$, $\frac{1}{3}$, $\frac{1}{4}$
. . . $\frac{1}{n}$, never reaching *o*). Hence the force (in the unlimited
body AB) must be unlimited. For it exceeds any limited
force ; and any limited force (BC or any multiple of BC in
the series) must correspond to a limited time (EZ or the
corresponding fraction of EZ in the series) ; for if a definite
force takes a definite time, a greater force must, according
to the inverse ratio, take a correspondingly smaller fraction
of time, but still a *definite* fraction (which will never dwindle
to *o*).   But (the time corresponding to AB must accordingly
be less than any finite amount, and the corresponding force
must exceed any definite amount ; and) any force—just as
any number or magnitude—that exceeds any definite amount
is unlimited.' The last sentence is ungrammatical, equivalent
to Simplicius's paraphrase (1342. 32) ἄπειρος δὲ πᾶσα δύναμις
ὑπερβάλλουσα παντὸς ὡρισμένου ὥσπερ καὶ πλῆθος καὶ μέγεθος.
—C.]
414

like additions I shall never come to the end of AB,
[a] but I shall sometime come to the multiple of BC
which will move D in less than any given period of
time. The motive power of AB then has no limit,
for it exceeds any limited power you may choose.
Again, the time taken by a limited force to effect
the movement must itself be limited, for if so much
force can effect it in so much time, then a greater
force will effect it in a less, but still definite, time,
in the inverse ratio; but an unlimited force (as
with an unlimited number or size) must exceed any
limited force.[b] An alternative proof is as follows.
We shall take a certain definite force of the same
kind as that supposed to be in the infinite body, and
let this force we take reside in a limited body and
be an exact measure of the force supposed to reside
in the unlimited body.[c]

[b] And unless the force could increase above any assignable limit the time could not decrease below any assignable
limit. Therefore the smallness of the time taken by a limited
force is itself limited.

[c] [This argument is left incomplete. Since the force (F)
supposed to be in the unlimited body AB is finite, we can take
a force (F′) which will be an *exact* measure (say one-third) of
F, and let it reside in a finite body (CD). The two forces are
to be ' of the same kind ' and will of course reside in bodies
of the same kind (*e.g.* the weights of two lumps of gold or of
any substance with a fixed specific gravity); accordingly the
forces will vary directly as the magnitudes of the bodies.
Therefore, since F′ is one-third of F, the magnitude of CD
is one-third (or in any case some definite fraction) of the
magnitude of AB. But that is impossible unless AB is of
limited size. Therefore AB—the body containing a limited
force—cannot be unlimited. Simplicius introduces a need-
less complication by not seeing that καταμετρεῖν means
' to be an *exact* measure of,' as at 233 b 3 and elsewhere.
—C.]

415

266 b 25 Ἲτι μὲν οὖν οὐκ ἐνδέχεται ἄπειρον εἶναι δύναμιν
ἐν πεπερασμένω μεγέθει, οὐδὲ πεπερασμένην ἐν
ἀπείρω, ἐκ τούτων δῆλον.

Περὶ δὲ τῶν φερομένων καλῶς ἔχει διαπορῆσαί
τινα ἀπορίαν πρῶτον. εἰ γὰρ πᾶν τὸ κινούμενον
κινεῖται ὑπό τινός, ὅσα μὴ αὐτὰ ἑαυτὰ κινεῖ, πῶς
80 κινεῖται ἔνια συνεχῶς μὴ ἀπτομένου τοῦ κινήσαντος,
οἶον τὰ ↥ιπτούμενα; εἰ δ’ ἁμα κινεῖ καὶ ἄλλο τι
Ὀ κινήσας, οἶον τὸν ἀέρα, ὃς κινούμενος κινεῖ,
ὁμοίως ἀδύνατον τοῦ πρώτου μὴ ἀπτομένου μηδὲ
κινοῦντος κινεῖσθαι, ἀλλ’ ἁμα πάντα καὶ κινεῖσθαι
267 a καὶ πεπαῦσθαι ὅταν τὸ πρῶτον κινοῦν παύσηται,
καὶ εἰ ποιεῖ, ὥσπερ ἡ λίθος, οἶον κινεῖν ὅ ἐκίνησεν.
ἀνάγκη δὴ τοῦτο μὲν λέγειν, ὅτι τὸ πρῶτον κινήσαν
ποιεῖ [οἶόν τε κινεῖν] ἢ τὸν ἀέρα τοιοῦτον[1] ἢ τὸ
5 ὖδωρ ἢ τι ἄλλο ὃ πέφυκε κινεῖν καὶ κινεῖσθαι̂ ἀλλ’

---

[1] [Either τοιοῦτον must be cut out (as by the Oxf. Trans.),
though it is in all MSS. and in Simplicius 1345. 28, or οἶόν τε
κινεῖν (οἶον καὶ κινεῖν E : οἶόν τι καὶ κινεῖν F) removed as a gloss
on τοιοῦτον : 'the first agent makes the air (an agent) of
the kind just described' (by οἶον κινεῖν in the previous
sentence). The intrusion of οἶόν τε κινεῖν is easily explained;
but why should τοιοῦτον be inserted ?—C.]

---

[a] Because if you break the contact of the original magnet
with the first bar of iron all the others instantly lose their
power; whereas in the case of missiles each successive
secondary agent becomes active as the previous one ceases
to be so. So the power is not exhausted all at once when
the first link in the chain ceases to exercise it, but is transmitted with gradually waning intensity to each successive
link. [Cf. Plato, Ion 533 D, where Socrates tells Ion the
rhapsode that when he recites there is a divine power of
inspiration moving his hearers through him, ' like the power
in the stone which Euripides calls the Magnesian stone

We have now proved that an unlimited force cannot reside in a limited magnitude, and also that the force residing in an unlimited magnitude cannot itself be limited.

But before discussing rotating bodies it will be well to examine a certain question concerning bodies in locomotion. If everything that is in motion is being moved by something, how comes it that certain things, missiles for example, that are not self-moving nevertheless continue their motion without a break when no longer in contact with the agent that gave them motion ? Even if that agent at the same time that he puts the missile in motion also sets something else (say air) in motion, which something when itself in motion has power to move other things, still when the prime agent has ceased to be in contact with this secondary agent and has therefore ceased to be moving it, it must be just as impossible for it as for the missile to be in motion : missile and secondary agent must all be in motion simultaneously, and must have ceased to be in motion the instant the prime mover ceases to move them ; and this holds good even if the prime agent is like the magnet, which has power to confer upon the iron bar it moves the power of moving another iron bar.[a] We are forced, therefore, to suppose that the prime mover conveys to the air (or water, or other such intermediary as is naturally capable both of moving and conveying motion) a power of conveying motion, but that this

though it is generally known as the stone of Heracles. This not only attracts rings that are made of iron, but puts into them the power of producing the same effect as the stone and attracting other rings in their turn. Sometimes there is quite a long chain of rings hanging from one another ; but all the power they have depends on the stone.'—C.]

ARISTOTLE

267 a οὐχ ἅμα παύεται κινοῦν καὶ κινούμενον, ἀλλὰ
κινούμενον μὲν ἅμα, ὅταν ὁ κινῶν παύσηται κινῶν,
κινοῦν δὲ ἔτι ἐστίν· διὸ κινεῖ τι ἄλλο ἐχόμενον. καὶ
ἐπὶ τούτου ὁ αὐτὸς λόγος· παύεται δὲ ὅταν ἀεὶ
ἐλάττων ἡ δύναμις τοῦ κινεῖν ἐγγίγνηται τῷ
10 ἐχομένῳ, τέλος δὲ παύεται ὅταν μηκέτι ποιήσῃ τὸ
πρότερον κινοῦν ἀλλὰ κινούμενον μόνον. ταῦτα
δ᾽ ἀνάγκη ἅμα παύεσθαι—τὸ μὲν κινοῦν τὸ δὲ
κινούμενον—καὶ τὴν ὅλην κίνησιν. αὕτη μὲν οὖν
ἐν τοῖς ἐνδεχομένοις ὁτὲ μὲν κινεῖσθαι ὁτὲ δ᾽
ἠρεμεῖν ἐγγίγνεται ἡ κίνησις· καὶ οὐ συνεχής,
ἀλλὰ φαίνεται· ἢ γὰρ ἐφεξῆς ὄντων ἢ ἁπτομένων
15 ἐστίν, οὐ γὰρ ἓν τὸ κινοῦν ἀλλ᾽ ἐχόμενα ἀλλήλων·
διὸ καὶ ἐν ἀέρι καὶ ἐν ὕδατι γίγνεται ἡ τοιαύτη
κίνησις, ἣν λέγουσί τινες ἀντιπερίστασιν εἶναι.
ἀδύνατον δὲ ἄλλως τὰ ἀπορηθέντα λύειν, εἰ μὴ
τὸν εἰρημένον τρόπον. ἡ δ᾽ ἀντιπερίστασις ἅμα
πάντα κινεῖσθαι ποιεῖ καὶ κινεῖν, ὥστε καὶ παύε-

ᵃ [*Literally,* ' And so it (the intermediary) moves something
else consecutive with it. And of this again the same thing
is true (that it ceases to be moved itself but moves the
next thing); παύεται δέ (sc. κινοῦν), but this imparting
of motion by the intermediary does come to an end in any
case in which the moving power gets continually less as it is
imparted to each successive member of the series.'—C.]

ᵇ ' Elasticity ' is the nearest equivalent. *Cf.* 215 a 15
[Vol. I. p. 350 note *a*, where Simplicius's definition of *anti-*
peristasis is quoted. The Oxford Trans. renders it by
' mutual replacement ' and refers to Plato, *Timaeus* 59 A,
79 B, C, E, 80 C. This last sentence and the following may be
more literally rendered : ' That is why movement of the kind
described occurs in air and water (their continuous structure
being suited to transmit motion in this way). Some describe

power is not exhausted when the intermediary ceases to be moved itself. Thus the intermediary will cease to be moved itself as soon as the prime mover ceases to move it, but will still be able to move something else. [a] Thus this something else will be put in motion after the prime mover's action has ceased, and will itself continue the series. The end of it all will approach as the motive power conveyed to each successive secondary agent wanes, till at last there comes one which can only move its neighbour without being able to convey motive force to it. At this point the last active intermediary will cease to convey motion, the passive intermediary that has no active power will cease to be in motion, and the missile will come to a stand, at the same instant. Now this movement occurs in things that are sometimes in motion and sometimes stationary, and it is not continuous, though it appears to be. For there is a succession of contiguous agents, since there is no one motor concerned but a series, one following upon another. And so there comes about both in air and water the kind of motion that some have called *antiperistasis*.[b] But whereas the only possible solution of the problem it suggests is that which has just been explained, the theory of those who call it *antiperistasis* would involve the simultaneity of the action of every motor and the passion of every mobile in the series, and the simultaneity of their cessation.

it as " mutual replacement," but (though mutual replacement may in fact occur) the difficulty under discussion cannot be solved otherwise than in the way described above. Moreover, the process of mutual replacement involves that all the members of the series receive motion and impart it simultaneously and consequently cease to do so simultaneously : whereas, etc.' (see next note).—C.]

267 a 20 σθαι· νῦν δὲ φαίνεταί τι ἓν κινούμενον συνεχῶς·
ὑπὸ τίνος οὖν; οὐ γὰρ ὑπὸ τοῦ αὐτοῦ.

Ἐπεὶ δ' ἐν τοῖς οὖσιν ἀνάγκη κίνησιν εἶναι
συνεχῆ, αὕτη δὲ μία ἐστίν, ἀνάγκη δὲ τὴν μίαν
μεγέθους τέ τινος εἶναι (οὐ γὰρ κινεῖται τὸ ἀμέγεθες)
καὶ ἑνὸς καὶ ὑφ' ἑνός (οὐ γὰρ ἔσται συνεχής, ἀλλ'
25 ἐχομένη ἑτέρα ἑτέρας καὶ διῃρημένη), τὸ δὲ κινοῦν
εἰ ἕν, ἢ κινούμενον κινεῖ ἢ ἀκίνητον ὄν· εἰ μὲν δὴ
κινούμενον, συνακολουθεῖν δεήσει καὶ μεταβάλλειν
267 b αὐτό, ἅμα δὲ κινεῖσθαι ὑπό τινος· ὥστε στήσεται
καὶ ἥξει εἰς τὸ κινεῖσθαι ὑπὸ ἀκινήτου. τοῦτο γὰρ
οὐκ ἀνάγκη συμμεταβάλλειν, ἀλλ' ἀεί τε δυνήσεται
κινεῖν (ἄπονον γὰρ καὶ τὸ οὕτω κινεῖν) καὶ ὁμαλὴς
αὕτη ἡ κίνησις ἢ μόνη ἢ μάλιστα· οὐ γὰρ ἔχει μετα-
5 βολὴν τὸ κινοῦν οὐδεμίαν. δεῖ δὲ οὐδὲ τὸ κινούμενον πρὸς ἐκεῖνο ἔχειν μεταβολήν, ἵνα ὁμοία ᾖ
ἡ κίνησις. ἀνάγκη δ' ἢ ἐν μέσῳ ἢ ἐν κύκλῳ εἶναι·
αὗται γὰρ αἱ ἀρχαί. ἀλλὰ τάχιστα κινεῖται τὰ

---

a [*Literally*, 'Whereas the appearance that is in fact
presented (and has to be explained) is that of a single thing
(the missile) kept in motion continuously (after the originator
of the movement, the thrower, has ceased to cause motion).
What then keeps it in motion ? Not the same agent (but
one or more intermediaries which do not simultaneously
cease to move and to be moved).'—C.]

b I take this qualification to refer to the heavenly spheres,
or the bodies they bear upon them, which being subject to
the influence of other immaterial beings (which the primum
mobile is not) change their relations to the prime motion and
are therefore uniform with reference to their own axes but
not with reference to the prime axis.

a Whereas the fact is that the supposed continuity of the movement of the single mobile which sets us inquiring after the motor is only apparent ; for in fact it is not impelled by one and the same motor throughout its course.

Now we have seen that there must be a continuous movement somewhere in the sum of things, and that it must be uniform, and that such uniform motion must be that of some dimensional magnitude (for that which is not dimensional cannot move), and that such magnitude must be unitary and must be kept in motion by a unitary motor (for otherwise the motion would not be continuous, but would be re-solved into a series of successive motions), and that this single motor must itself be either in motion or unmoving. Now if it is in motion (and is therefore a physical magnitude) it will have to follow up that which it is moving, and therefore be itself locally changing, and moreover must be referred back to some motor that causes its motion. This leaves us where we were, and the perpetual recession can only be arrested by supposing a motor that is not in motion. Such a motor need not undergo any change to preserve a constant relation with the mobile, but can exercise its kinetic power without ever being ex-hausted (for suchlike conveying of motion is not toil-some) ; and such motion or change as it directly causes must be uniform either uniquely or in the primary and supreme sense, for the motor is subject to no change. And for the motion to be uniform, the disposition of the mobile to the motor must also be without change.*b* Now the action of this unmoving cause must be felt either at the centre or the periphery, for these are the determining principles ; and since the swiftest

ARISTOTLE

267 b ἐγγύτατα τοῦ κινοῦντος, τοιαύτη δ' ἡ τοῦ κύκλου[1]
κίνησις· ἐκεῖ ἄρα τὸ κινοῦν.

10 Ἔχει δ' ἀπορίαν εἰ ἐνδέχεταί τι κινούμενον κινεῖν
συνεχῶς, ἀλλὰ μὴ—ὥσπερ τὸ ὠθοῦν πάλιν καὶ
πάλιν—τῷ ἐφεξῆς εἶναι συνεχῶς. ἢ γὰρ αὐτὸ δεῖ
ὠθεῖν ἢ ἕλκειν (ἢ ἄμφω), ἢ ἕτερόν τι ἐκδεχόμενον
ἄλλο παρ' ἄλλου, ὥσπερ πάλαι ἐλέχθη ἐπὶ τῶν
ῥιπτουμένων. εἰ δὲ διαιρετὸς ὢν ὁ ἀὴρ ἢ τὸ ὕδωρ
15 κινεῖ, ἀλλ' ὡς ⟨ἄλλος⟩[2] ἀεὶ κινούμενος· ἀμφοτέρως

---

[1] [κύκλου HK Simplic. 1354. 8 : ὅλου cett.—C.]
[2] [ἀλλ' ὡς ⟨ἄλλος⟩: ἄλλος F : ἄλλον E¹K : ἀλλ' ὡς cett. The
uncertainty of the readings in this sentence leaves it doubtful
how it is related to its neighbours. Simplicius 1356. 12
apparently read ὥσπερ πάλαι ἐλέχθη ἐπὶ τῶν ῥιπτουμένων, εἰ
διαιρετὸς (or διαιρετὸς γὰρ: E has γὰρ) ὢν ὁ ἀὴρ καὶ (sic) τὸ
ὕδωρ κινεῖ. ἀλλ' ὡς ἄλλος ἀεὶ κινούμενος· ἀμφοτέρως δ' κτλ., 'as
we said in the case of missiles, since the air or the water
causes the motion as being divisible into parts. But (it
causes the motion only) inasmuch as one part of it after
another is set in motion (and moves the next)'; for his
paraphrase εἴπερ διαιρετὸς ὢν ὁ ἀὴρ καὶ τὸ ὕδωρ, τούτεστιν
εὐδιαίρετα καὶ εὐκίνητα, κινεῖ· πῶς δὲ κινεῖ ὁ ἀήρ; ἄλλος ἀεὶ καὶ
ἄλλος κινούμενος καὶ οὕτως κινῶν seems explicable only if he
read (as the beginning of a new sentence) ἀλλ' ὡς ἄλλος (or,
less probably, ἀλλὰ πῶς; ὡς ἄλλος). It is another question
whether his reading is right. The reading attributed to
him by the Oxf. Trans. ἐπὶ τῶν ῥιπτουμένων, εἰ διαιρετὸς ὢν ὁ
ἀὴρ ἢ (sic) τὸ ὕδωρ κινεῖ ἄλλος ἀεὶ κινούμενος, may be preferred.
In printing εἰ δὲ διαιρετὸς κτλ. as a separate sentence I am
providing a text which suits Dr. Wicksteed's view of the
course of the argument.—C.]

---

[a] [Literally, ' circle,' i.e. circumference (ταχεῖα δὲ ἡ τοῦ
κύκλου κίνησις, τουτέστι τῆς περιφερείας, Simplic. 1354. 7).
In a revolving sphere the motion of a point on any circle
inscribed on its surface in a plane at right angles to its axis
is faster than that of any point in the same plane that is
nearer to the axis. And if the universe is conceived as a

movements must be those of the parts closest to the moving force, and the movement of the outermost sphere [a] is such, it is there that the motive influence is felt.

The question arises, however, whether it may not be possible for a motor which itself is in motion to cause a continuous movement in something else, not with the specious continuity of a succession of thrusts, but genuinely. Well, in such a case either (i.) the prime motor itself must all the time directly thrust or draw [b] the mobile (or both thrust and draw it),[c] or (ii.) there must be some continuous succession of intermediaries other than the prime motor, as we just now supposed to be the fact in the case of missiles, and if these intermediaries are constituted by an easily divisible substance, such as air or water, what is causing the movement at any time will be the particular division of that substance which at the time being is in motion. In both cases (i.) and (ii.), therefore, the movement is not one and unbroken,

nest of material spheres, each of a certain thickness, the motion will be quickest in the outermost sphere. Simplicius records a discussion as to what ' circle ' is here meant and where the Prime Mover can be. He ends with the suggestion μήποτε δὲ ἐν τῷ κύκλῳ λέγων ἐν τῷ ὅλῳ οὐρανῷ λέγει (1355. 38). This discussion may account for the variant ὅλου here. Cf. De gen. et corr. 336 b 3 ἡ τοῦ ὅλου (sc. οὐρανοῦ) φορά, meaning the motion of the First Heaven, as carrying with it the whole system of concentric spheres (Joachim, ad loc.). —C.]

[b] [Cf. 243 a 15 ff. where it was shown that all forms of locomotion of things that are moved by something else can be reduced to pushing or pulling. A twirling motion is a combination of pulling and pushing: the man turning a millstone is both thrusting away part of the stone and drawing towards himself another part.—C.]

[c] And this alternative (i.) has been shown to be impossible.

267 b δ' οὐχ οἷόν τε μίαν εἶναι, ἀλλ' ἐχομένην. μόνη ἄρα συνεχὴς ἦν κινεῖ τὸ ἀκίνητον· ἀεὶ γὰρ ὁμοίως ἔχον καὶ πρὸς τὸ κινούμενον ὁμοίως ἕξει καὶ συνεχῶς.

Διωρισμένων δὲ τούτων, φανερὸν ὅτι ἀδύνατον τὸ πρῶτον κινοῦν καὶ ἀκίνητον ἔχειν τι μέγεθος. 20 εἰ γὰρ μέγεθος ἔχει, ἀνάγκη ἤτοι πεπερασμένον αὐτὸ εἶναι ἢ ἄπειρον. ἄπειρον μὲν οὖν ὅτι οὐκ ἐνδέχεται μέγεθος εἶναι, δέδεικται πρότερον ἐν τοῖς Φυσικοῖς· ὅτι δὲ τὸ πεπερασμένον ἀδύνατον ἔχειν δύναμιν ἄπειρον, καὶ ὅτι ἀδύνατόν ὑπὸ πεπερασμένου κινεῖσθαί τι ἄπειρον χρόνον, δέδεικται 25 νῦν. τὸ δέ γε πρῶτον κινοῦν ἀΐδιον κινεῖ κίνησιν καὶ ἄπειρον χρόνον. φανερὸν τοίνυν ὅτι ἀδιαίρετόν ἐστι καὶ ἀμερὲς καὶ οὐδὲν ἔχον μέγεθος.

but successional. The only continuous movement, therefore, is that which is caused by the motionless motor, which ever maintains its own uniformity of disposition and will therefore maintain a uniform and continuous relation to the mobile.

All these points being established, it is clear that the prime and motionless motor cannot have magnitude. For if it had magnitude it must either be limited or unlimited. Now we have shown already, in our discourse on Physics,[a] that there cannot be an unlimited magnitude; and now we have further proved that a limited body cannot exert unlimited force and that nothing can be kept in motion for an unlimited time by a limited agent. But the prime motor causes an everlasting motion and maintains it through time without limit. It is manifest, therefore, that this prime motor is not divisible, has no parts, and is not dimensional.

[a] [Book III. chap. v., 205 a 7 ff.—C.]

INDEX

Note.—The references to Volume I. are in roman, those to Volume II. in italic.

ABOVE and BELOW, Relative, Supreme, i. 51, 243, 315
ABSTRACT : *see* Concrete
ABSTRACTION, i. 119, 121 ; *see also* i. 199, 229 ; ii. *337*
ACCIDENT, i. 141-163
ACCIDENTAL : *see* Incidental
ACHILLES, ii. *181, 183*
See also Bisection
ACTUALITY, ACTUALIZATION = Realization, i. 89, 193-197, 203-215, 227, 247, 249, 259, 261, 293, 369 ; ii. *53, 271-277, 297, 313, 315, 331, 337, 373-383*
ADDITION of terms, Limited and Illimitable, i. 247-251
AFTER : *see* Before
AGENT : *see* Mover
AIR—
    Relation to Water, i. 49, 327, 365-369 ; ii. *315*
    Substantiality of, i. 331, 361
AMBIGUOUS : *see* Verbal Ambiguity
ANAXAGORAS—
    on Origins, i. 41-49, 61, 221, 223 ; ii. *269, 281, 283, 339, 403*
    on the Unlimited, i. 221, 223, 241
    on the Void, i. 331
ANAXIMANDER on Unity and Multiplicity, i. 41
ANTIPERISTASIS, ii. *419*
ANTIPHON—
    on Squaring the circle, i. 19
    on Substantive existence, i. 111
ANTITHESIS—
    Nature of Primary Antithesis or Antitheses, i. 41, 51-67

Antithetical Principles need something to work on, i. 61, 63, 77-83
Antithetical Terms, ii. *221*
See also Extremes
APART, Definition of, ii. *35*
ARRIVAL('has arrived at'),Legitimate use of term, ii. *373-379*
ARROW, The Flying, ii. *181-185*
ART :
    Analogy with Nature, i. 125, 173
    of Making, i. 123, 125
    of Using, i. 123, 125
ARTIFICIAL PRODUCTS : *see* Natural Products
ASHES, Water poured on to, i. 333, 341, 343
ASTRONOMY, Relation to mathematics and physics, i. 119, 121
ATOMS—
    Combination and Resolution of ii. *403*
    of Matter, and Atomic Magnitudes, i. 37, 47, 49, 223, 247, 257, 395, 397 ; ii. *103, 115, 181-189, 297, 385, 387* ; *see also* Indivisible
ATTRACTION and REPULSION, ii. *269, 283, 403*
ATTRIBUTE :
    of the Part, of the Whole, i. 295 ; ii. *337*
    Potential and actual, i. 367-371 ; ii. *315*
AYTOMATON, Meaning and scope of, i. 157-163
AXIOM, Groundless assumption cannot be accepted as an, ii. *283*

INDEX

BECOMING : *see* Genesis

BEFORE and AFTER—

In Position, Movement, Time, i. 385, 387, 417, 419

See also Verbal Ambiguity, and Now

BEGINNING some-*When*, some-*Where*, i. 29 ; *see also* Origins

BEGINNINGS and ENDS, Actual and Potential, ii. *279, 373-383* ; *see also* ii. *363, 365*

BELOW : *see* Above

BETTER, BEST:

Meaning of, i. 123, 133, 169

The Better occurs in nature, ii. *359*

BETWEEN, defined, ii. *37*

BISECTION = Dichotomy:

Actual and Potential, bearing on continuity, i. 259 ; ii. *109, 183, 381*

See also Divisibility, Zeno

BOAT : Movement of boat and its contents, i. 313 ; ii. *193, 195* ; *see also* ii. *313*

BODY, Cannot be Illimitable, i. 233, 235, 243

BULK:

an inseparable attribute, i. 361

Variation in, i. 341, 369

CAUSE (αἰτία):

General discussion, i. 129-187 ; *cf.* i. 104

Classification of Causes, i. 129-139, 165-169

Efficient, i. 129-133, 167 ; *see also* Mover

Essential (direct, determinate), Incidental (indirect, indeterminate), i. 135-139, 149-163 ; ii. *337*

Formal, i. 129, 133, 165-169 ; *see also* Form

Final, i. 131, 133, 169-187 ; *see also* Goal

Material, i. 129, 133, 167 ; *see also* Subject

Purposeful Cause in art and in nature, i. 169-185

Relations between Causes, i. 165, 173, 185

CENTRE—

of Rotation compared with beginning, middle, end of recti. linear motion, ii. *401*

of Universe—

absolutely stable, i. 315

exerts active influence, i. 241, 243, 255, 345 ; ii. *399-403*

CHANCE (αὐτόματον): *see* Luck ; *see also* Incidental

CHANGE:

a wider term than movement, ii. *19, 67, 73, 343*

Agent and Patient of : essential, incidental, in virtue of a part, ii. *9-13, 333-339*

Whence and Whither of, ii. *11-15*

Different kinds of, i. 195 ; *see also* Growth, Locomotion, Modification

Incidental, i. 305, 307, 323 ; ii. *347, 351*

Potentiality of change inherent in matter, i. 341, 369

See also Genesis, Locomotion, Movement

CHAOS, i. 281

CIRCULAR MOTION : *see* Locomotion (circular)

COGNITION : *see* Understanding

COMING INTO BEING : *see* Genesis

COMING TO A STANDSTILL, TO REST, Meaning of, ii. *73-79*

COMPLETE : *see* Whole

COMPLETENESS—

incompatible with illimitability, i. 253, 255 ; ii. *399*

of Circumference, ii. *395*

COMPRESSION : *see* Condensation

CONCEIVABLE distinguished from possible, i. 263

CONCRETE and particular contrasted with abstract and general, i. 11, 12

CONDENSATION and RAREFACTION :

the Antithetical Principles of Modification, i. 41, 43, 367-371

Manifestations of—

Contraction and Expansion, i. 321, 341, 367-371

Combination and Resolution, ii. *357, 403*

involve locomotion, ii. *357, 403*

428

INDEX

CONSCIOUSNESS, relation to Time, i. 419

CONTIGUOUS = Touching = In contact :

Meaning and scope of, i. 307 ; ii. *39, 41, 93, 147, 155*

Agent and Patient must be, i. 205, 207

CONTINUITY, CONTINUOUS, CONTINUUM :

Characteristics and Meaning of, i. 23, 193, 259 ; ii. *37-41, 55, 93, 95, 107, 115, 117, 173, 345, 347*

inherent in Magnitude, Movement, Time, i. 259, 385, 389, 395, 399 ; ii. *109*

of Movement destroyed—

by discontinuity in—

the mobile, ii. *49-53, 57, 371, 381*

the time, ii. *49, 51, 57, 371-383*

the motor, ii. *55, 57, 419-425*

the track, ii. *49, 55, 57, 61*

by abrupt reversal of direction, ii. *369-373, 377, 379, 387-393, 399* ; see also ii. *363, 365*

but not by continuous change of direction, ii. *391-397*

Specious continuity of the successional, ii. *391, 421, 423*

No Continuum indivisible, i. 23, 397 ; ii. *107, 109, 115, 127-135, 329*

CONTRADICTORIES : see Opposites

CONTRARIES : see Extremes

CONTRAST, CONTRASTED TERMS or COUPLES : see Antithesis

CONVERGENT SERIES, Characteristics of, i. 247

COUNT, Distinction between the things we count, the numbers we count in, and the process of counting, i. 389, 397

CURRENTS in homogeneous mass, i. 29

CURVATURE, Change of, i. 369

DEFINITION, Nature and function of, i. 13, 35, 37

DEMOCRITUS :

Belief in void, i. 51, 331

First Principles, ii. *277, 283*

Theory of antithetical couples, i. 51

Theory of primary atoms, i. 15, 51, 221, 223

DENSITY and RARITY :

Nature of, i. 61, 363-371 ; ii. *357*

are affections of matter, i. 367-371

Bearing on theory of void, i. 363-367

of medium affects velocity, i. 351-355 ; see also Void

Variability of—

inherent in matter, i. 367-371 ; see also i. 341

Relation to movement, i. 365 367

See also Condensation

'DEPART FROM' and 'ARRIVE AT,' terms only applicable to an *actual* beginning and end, ii. *373-379*

DETERMINANTS : see Cause

DICHOTOMY : see Bisection

DIFFERENTIA—

not included in 'quality,' ii. *31*

See also Form

DIRECTIONS—

Cosmically-determined—

Influence of, i. 279, 281

Stability of, i. 279, 281

Physically-determined—

Relativity of, i. 279, 281

DISPLACEMENT, Bearing on hypothesis of the void, i. 359

DISTANCE :

Interdependence of distance, motion and time with respect to continuity (divisibility), ii. *97-101, 107-111*

with respect to limitability, ii. *109-113*

DIVERSITY : see Multiplicity

DIVISIBILITY :

Actual and conceptual, i. 229, 247, 249, 257, 373 ; ii. *93-101, 107-111, 115, 127-135, 141-147, 297, 329, 343, 381*

Correspondence between Divisibility of—

distance and time, ii. *107-111, 115, 117, 379* ; see also ii. *181-187*

of a movement and its constituents, ii. *127-135, 141-157*

429

INDEX

DIVISIBILITY (*contd.*)—
  In what sense an unlimited
      potentiality, i. 247, 249 ; ii.
      381, 383
  See also Continuity
DOWNWARD : *see* Upward
DUALITY implied in antithesis,
      i. 61

EARTH, at rest, i. 349
EFFECT : Relation to cause—
  normal, incidental, i. 149
  See also Cause
ELEATIC arguments given into
      by some thinkers, i. 37
ELEATICS : *see* Melissus, Parmen-
      ides, Zeno
ELEMENTS :
  Natural trend of physical, i. 279,
      303, 345, 349
  Nature and number of, i. 15, 41-
      49, 51-57, 59-67
  Plato's triad, Aristotle's triad,
      i. 93
EMBRACED IN, RESIDES IN :
  Meaning and scope of, i. 325, 405,
      407
EMPEDOCLES—
  on Attraction and Repulsion, ii.
      269, 281, 283
  on Chance, i. 143, 145, 171
  on Nature repeats itself, i. 43 ;
      ii. *269, 271, 281, 283*
  on Primal all-generative, i. 175
  on Primary substances, i. 41, 43,
      51, 61
  on Unity and Multiplicity, i. 41
EMPTY, Meaning of, i. 337
END :
  Meanings of, i. 123 ; ii. *55*
  a causal determinant in nature
      and art, i. 125, 131, 133, 165,
      175
  of Change—
    belongs to future, ii. *137-141,
        383, 385*
    indivisible, ii. *139, 141*
  Means of attaining, i. 167, 179,
      183, 185
  See also Beginnings
ENTITIES :
  Mathematical and Physical, i.
      119, 121
  Number of absolute, i. 15-37

'EQUALITY'—
  in Magnitudes analogous to 'like-
      ness' in Affections, ii. *253*
EQUIVOCAL: *see* Verbal Ambiguity
ERROR—
  in Assumption, in deduction, i.
      17 ; ii. *111, 181, 185*
ESSENCE : *see* Form
EXIST : Distinction between can
      be conceived and can exist,
      i. 263
EXISTS, IS : *see* Existence, Ex-
      istent, Verbal Ambiguity
EXISTENCE :
  Actual and Potential, ii. *17, 19,
      67, 73*
  Coming into : *see* Genesis
  Non-existence—absolute and in-
      cidental, the clue to problem
      of genesis, i. 85-89
  regarded as good, i. 93
  See also Realization, Matter
EXISTENT :
  One or more than one, i. 19-27
EXISTENTS and NON-EXIST-
      ENTS :
  Characteristics of natural, arti-
      ficial, i. 107
  Temporary, eternal, i. 405, 407
EXPANSION : *see* Condensation
EXTREMES,   CONTRARIES,
      POLES—
  constitute limits, maximum
      difference, i. 195, 237 ; ii. *287,
      363, 377, 379, 393, 395*

FAST : *see* Quick
FIRE identified with extreme
      heat, ii. *315*
FORM = IDENTIFYING   ES-
      SENCE = DISTINGUISH-
      ING CHARACTERISTICS :
  Meaning and function of, i. 117,
      119, 125, 167, 175
  and Shortage, opposite poles, i.
      195
  shortage and matter : factors of
      becoming, i. 77-97
  Relation to material, i. 113, 125,
      129, 257, 295, 327 ; ii. *231*
  See also i. 41
FORTUNE : *see* Luck
FREEZING, Instantaneous, ii. *297*
FUTURE : *see* Time

INDEX

GENERAL and ABSTRACT compared to particular and concrete, i. 11, 12

GENESIS:
Absolute = unqualified, Specific = qualified, i. 75, 77, 79, 89; ii. *15, 365*; *see also* i. 117
a Change, but not a movement, ii. *15-19, 67*; *see also* ii. *343*; *but see* i. 195; ii. *155, 157, 195*
not a modification, ii. *231*
not a subject of generation, ii. *23, 29*
dependent on Movement, Modification, ii. *231, 357, 359*; *see also* ii. *229*
Etymologically connected with nature, i. 115
Limiting terms of, ii. *363*
Natural and artificial process of, i. 77, 107, 115, 117; ii. *155, 157, 357, 359*
Prerequisites of, i. 49-59, 79, 83, 85; ii. *359*
Problem of, previous theories criticized, i. 43-51, 85-89;
Subject of, i. 71-79
See also Antithesis

GNOMONS, i. 217

GOAL:
Meaning of, i. 123
the main concern of the physicist, i. 127, 185
not subject to change, i. 11, 13
Relation to material, i. 179-187
Relation to process, i. 179-187

GROWTH and SHRINKAGE:
by Addition and Subtraction of like, unlike, by Expansion and Contraction, i. 195, 333, 341, 367, -369; ii. *227, 355*
involve local motion, ii. *357*

HABITS, not Modifications, may involve modifications, ii. *231-237*

HARMONICS: Relations between optics, harmonics, astronomy and geometry, i. 121

HEAT: Extreme heat identified with fire, ii. *315*

HEAVEN, HEAVENLY SPHERES, HEAVENLY BODIES:
Meaning of, i. 323, 325
Motion of, ii. *351, 421*
See also Locomotion (Circular), Movement (continuous)

HEAVY and LIGHT:
Meaning of, i. 195, 241, 243, 315; ii. *315*
The heavy potentially light, ii. *315*
Relation to Dense and Rare, i. 371; ii. *357*

HERACLITUS:
Paradox of, i. 17, 25
'All things become fire,' i. 237

HESIOD, on 'Chaos,' i. 281

HOMOGENEOUS:
Parts of Homogeneous substance have no distinguishing characteristics, i. 231, 237, 239, 323; ii. *311*
Universe not, i. 31, 237, 239

HOW and WHY—
imply different kinds of inquiry, i. 129, 167
See also Cause

IDENTICAL = 'One and the same'—
distinguished from 'the same, i. 213, 425, 427; ii. *45-61*

IDENTIFYING ESSENCE: *see* Form

IDENTITY, retained through changing relations, i. 389, 393

ILLIMITABLE, THE UN-LIMITED:
Problem of the, i. 215-265
additions, succession, i. 225, 227, 247-253, 259, 263, 265; ii. *211 411, 415*
analogous to material factor, i 255, 257, 261
cannot be exhausted, i. 225, 253, 259; ii. *383, 399*; *see also* i. 245-253
Concept of Illimitable, i. 45, 193, 223-227, 243-261
first encountered, i. 191, 193
inapplicable to experience. quality, substantive existence, point, i. 21, 217

431

INDEX

ILLIMITABLE, THE UN-
LIMITED (*contd.*)—
Concept of Illimitable (*contd.*)—
incompatible with whole, i. 255
of previous thinkers, i. 217-225,
241, 253
Relation to Continuous, i. 259
Under some Aspect, *e.g.*—
magnitude, i. 21, 45, 225, 227,
251, 259, 261; ii. *109, 111*
movement, i. 259, 411; ii. *399,
405*
number: *see* Illimitable Additions, Succession
time, i. 247-251, 259, 411, 413;
ii. *109, 111, 277, 279*
Considerations on which belief in
the unlimited rests, i. 225
Senses in which the illimitable can
and cannot exist, i. 229-265
See also Limit, Verbal Ambiguity, More
IMMOVABLE: *see* Motionless
'IN': *see* Verbal Ambiguity, Place
INCIDENTAL = Accidental:
attributes, characteristics, concomitance, i. 53, 109, 149;
ii. *383*
cause, effect, i. 149-155
change, i. 305, 307, 323; ii. *347,
351*
INDIVISIBLE:
End of change is, ii. *139, 141*
No continuum is, ii. *115*
qua entity, ii. *337*
See also Verbal Ambiguity
INDIVISIBLES:
cannot touch, ii. *93*
In what sense retain their identity
in changing relations, i. 389-
395, 409
Relation to continuity, i. 391,
393, 409; ii. *93, 95, 103*
to magnitude, i. 23
to motion, i. 393, 409; ii. *181-
187, 193-199*
See also Minimum, Now, Point
INFINITY: *see* Illimitable
INTELLIGENCE = Mind:
Anaxagoras's Prime Cause, i. 223;
ii. *269, 339, 403*
Free from admixture, ii. *339*
INTERMEDIARIES, Nature of motion conveyed by, ii. *417, 423*

INTERMEDIATES, function as
opposites, ii. *69*
INVESTIGATION, Method of, i.
11, 13
IS: *see* Existence, Existent, Verbal
Ambiguity

KNOWLEDGE: *see* Understanding

LEUCIPPUS, Belief in the void, i.
331
LIGHT: *see* Heavy
'LIKENESS,' 'EQUALITY,' ii.
253
LIMIT:
Distinguishable from the thing
it limits, i. 25, 387; *see also*
ii. *139, 141*
Distinction between being 'in
contact' and being 'limited,'
i. 25, 263
Indivisibility of Limit (*qua* limit),
i. 25; ii. *141*
See also Now
LIMITED: *see* Illimitable
LINE: *see* Distance, Magnitude
LINES and POINTS, Characteristics of, ii. *379-383*
LOCALITY: *see* Place (Cosmic)
LOCOMOTION = Change of Place:
affects no intimate characteristic
of subject, i. 389; ii. *361*
Change of proper place, of cosmic
place, i. 311, 313
Circular Motion, Rotation, Revolution—
Characteristics of, i. 321, 425;
ii. *47, 191, 195, 203, 241-245,
371, 391-403*
not comparable with rectilinear, ii. *245*
the only progression both continuous and everlasting, ii.
369-373, 379, 391-395, 399; *see
also* ii. *345, 363*
Uniform Rotation standard
measure of motion, i. 423,
425; ii. *401*
Centre of Rotation compared
with beginning, middle, end,
of rectilinear motion, ii. *401*
Rotating Sphere, in motion and
at rest, i 321, 323; ii. *191,
401*

INDEX

LOCOMOTION (*contd.*)—
Continuous Locomotion caused by motionless motor, ii. *425*
Direct, incidental, i. 323
divisible into species, ii. *217-221, 369, 371*
prior to all other change, i. 277; ii. *355-363, 397, 399, 403*
Rectilinear=Translation—
Characteristics of, ii. *201, 369, 371, 379, 387, 399, 401*
Relation to increase and decrease, to qualitive modification, i. 305; ii. *403*
LUCK, FORTUNE (τύχη, αὐτόματον), i. 141-163
Good and Bad, i. 155, 157
LYCOPHRON banned the word 'is,' i. 25

MAGNET, Power of, ii. *417*
MAGNITUDE, Continuity of: *see* Continuity
Concept necessary to definition of 'unlimited,' i. 21, 23, 231
Limits of actual, potential, conceptual, i. 225, 233, 257-263, 397; ii. *399, 425*; *see also* i. 387
No Minimum, i. 49, 397
not an essential attribute of moving cause, ii. *343*
not an attribute of Prime Motor, ii. *425*
Relation between magnitude of whole and of parts, i. 45
Relation to Movement, Time, i. 259, 385, 389, 399; ii. *103-117*
MATHEMATICAL ABSTRACTIONS, i. 119, 121
MATHEMATICS, Relation to Physics, Optics, Harmonics, Astronomy, i. 119, 121; *see also* i. 165, 281
MATTER:
Aristotelian, Platonic, i. 91-97
Inherent capacity of expanding and contracting, i. 341, 367-371
the Passive Principle of Nature, i. 63, 65, 77-83, 91-97; *see also* i. 55, 61

MEASUREMENT—
of Individuals by number, i. 387, 389, 395, 405, 425
of Motion by time, i. 387, 405, 423
of Time by motion, i. 423, 425
MEDIUM, Density of, effect on velocity, i. 351-359
MELISSUS:
False premises and unsound reasoning, i. 15, 21, 29
Argument against movement, i. 333, 341; ii. *301*
Conception of 'whole,' i. 255
MILLET SEED, ii. *261*
MIND : *see* Intelligence
MINIMUM, No Minimum component of a continuum, i. 23, 193, 259; ii. *107, 173, 181*
MISSILES=Projectiles, i. 349, 351 ; ii. *417-421*
MODIFICATION—
effected by sensible characteristics, ii. *225-229*
dependent on locomotion, ii. *355-361, 403*
experienced by the animate and inanimate, ii. *225*
occurs along specific lines, i. 53
presupposes substratum, i. 49
MODIFIER in contact with modified, ii. *227, 313, 319, 417-423*
MONAD=the irreducible Minimum, i. 253, 391, 401, 423; ii. *39, 41*
MORE, in addition, in succession, i. 247-253
MORE and LESS, i. 387
MOTIONLESS=Moveless=Immobile, Different meanings of, ii. *33*
MOVED=Mobile, PATIENT
Analysis of Patient, i. 71-83; ii. *9, 317*
Condition of Mobile in the act of moving, ii. *127*
Condition of Mobile at the end of the movement, ii. *137, 139*
Natural existents have inherent Principle of Movement, i. 107, 109
must have magnitude, ii. *343, 421*
must be divisible without limit, ii. *329*

433

MOVEMENT, MOTION, CHANGE
  Meaning and Nature of, i. 191-215, 341, 415 ; ii. *19, 73, 145, 197, 271, 341*
  Beginning of, ii. *141-145*
  End of, ii. *139, 141*
  Constituents (factors) of, i. 129, 131 ; ii. *49, 127-135, 145, 147*
  Changing relations between Constituents of, ii. *257-263*
  Contrary Movements defined, ii. *63-69, 393* ; *see also* i. 195
  Continuous, ii. *51-57, 61, 345-353, 359, 363, 365, 371-377, 381, 383, 387, 391-397*
  Dependent sequence of Magnitude, Motion, Time, i. 259, 385, 389, 399
  Discontinuous, ii. *55, 57, 349, 363, 365, 369-383, 387-397*
    Successive Movements discontinuous, ii. *345, 419-425*
    Interrupted Movement discontinuous, ii. *373, 381*ǀ
    Reversed Movement discontinuous, ii. *399*
    See also Constituents of movement
  distinguished from Change, and Genesis, ii. *17, 19, 67, 73, 343*
  Divisible, ii. *127-135, 149-157, 297*
  Indivisible, ii. *297*
  does not include Acquisition of habits, ii. *231-239*
  does not include Genesis and Extinction, ii. *15-19, 65, 67, 73* ; *but see* ii. *299, 301*
  does not pertain to Action and Passion, ii. *19-29*
  does not pertain to Conditions, Forms, Place, ii. *11, 19, 229*
  does not pertain to Relation, ii. *17, 19, 21, 233-239*
  does not pertain to Substantive Existence, ii. *19*
  Eternal—
    Conditions of, and Necessity for Eternal Movement, ii. *273-285, 341-345, 355, 359, 369, 379, 393-399, 411, 421-425*
    Involved in Eternity of Time, ii. *277*

Factors = Constituents of Movement, i. 129, 131 ; ii. *11, 127-135, 145*
  Their relation to the Movement, ii. *127-135, 145, 147, 257-263, 381*
  Their relation to each other, ii. *257-263, 409-415*
from one term to its opposite cannot be both continuous and everlasting, ii. *289, 295, 363, 365, 369, 371, 387, 389, 395, 399*
Goals of, ii. *11-15, 19*
Incidental Movement—
  caused by itself, ii. *317, 347-351*
  caused by something else, i. 305, 307 ; ii. *351*
Kinds of Motion :
  generically the same, ii. *211, 213*
  incomparable, ii. *241-255*
  Number of, i. 195 ; ii. *19, 29, 31, 217*
  which can, cannot co-exist in the same subject, ii. *365, 371, 389, 391*
  specifically different, ii. *371, 389*
  See also Condensation, Modification, Locomotion
Natural, unnatural, i. 345, 349 ; ii. *75-79, 307-317, 403*
Necessary conditions of, i. 129, 167 ; ii. *127, 149, 195, 197, 207, 217, 223, 273-277, 317*
Necessary conditions of Uniform, ii. *57, 59*
not itself a subject of Change, ii. *23*
occurs between Contraries or Contradictories, i. 53 ; ii. *13-17*
opposed to rest, to contrary motion, ii. *81, 365*
Opposite motions specifically different, ii. *371, 389*
Priority of locomotion : *see* Locomotion
Reality of, i. 17 ; ii. *269*
Relation to—
  Distance, ii. *97-101*
  Place, i. 305, 321, 323 ; ii. *77, 79, 403*

INDEX

MOVEMENT, MOTION, CHANGE
(contd.)—
Relation to (contd.)—
Time, i. 377, 379, 383-389, 399,
401, 405, 415-423 ; ii. *123*,
151-167, 173, 215, 385
Distance-Time, ii. 103-117
Void, i. 341, 345-359, 365, 367
and Rest ; see Rest
Reversing a movement involves
stopping it, ii. *371-379, 389,
391* ; see also ii. *363, 365, 369*
Self-movement, Intermittent, ii.
349
Subject of Movement also sub-
ject of contrary Movement
and of rest, ii. *27*
MOVER, EFFICIENT CAUSE,
FINAL CAUSE :
Different ways of classifying the,
i. 137
Need for and nature of Agent or
Agents, i. 167, 197, 205 ; ii.
*217, 287-291, 305-311, 315, 317,
321, 323, 329-333, 343, 351*
Intermediary, Primary and The
Prime Agent or Agents—
Relation to Motion, i. 167, 197 ;
ii. *345, 349, 353, 407-411, 419-
425*
True, Incidental, Intermediate
Agent or Agents, i. 85, 87 ;
ii. *9-13, 319-323, 351* ; see also
Self-mover
Prime Mover—
Action of Prime Mover not
Toilsome, ii. *421*
itself Motionless, ii. *337, 341-
347, 351, 405, 421*
itself Eternal, ii. *341, 343, 345*
itself not Dimensional, ii. *407,
425*
MOVER and MOVED :
Direct or Indirect, ii. *317*
Essential or Incidental, Integral or in virtue of a Part
or Factor, i. 71-79, 85, 307,
323 ; ii. *9-13, 305-309, 351*
How related, i. 193, 201, 205-215 ;
ii. *215-227, 273-279, 307, 313,
317-323, 329-333, 417-425*
Self-mover includes active and
passive factors, ii. *307-311,
317, 329, 333-337*

Active factor—
incidentally passive, ii. *347,
351*
not the Prime Agent, ii. *347-
351*
MULTIPLICITY = Plurality :
in Unity, actual and potential, i.
23-27 ; ii. *373, 375, 379-383*
involved in distinction between
subject and attribute, i. 31,
71, 73
of entities in Universe, i. 37-41

NAME, Relation to definition, i. 13
NATURAL :
and Artificial products, i. 17,
107-115, 173-179
and Forced movement and rest,
i. 345, 349 ; ii. *75-79, 83,
299, 307-317*
NATURE :
Chance results due to nature, to
art, i. 159-163
both Genesis and Goal, i. 115, 117,
123, 175
Principle of Movement and Rest,
i. 17, 107-111, 191 ; ii. *295*
Principles of : Previous specula-
tions on, i. 17, 41-59 ; Conclusions reached, i. 59-67, 79-83
purposeful, i. 123, 169-179
Study of, i. 11, 113, 117-127, 191,
223 ; ii. *269, 293*
Universal determinant of order,
ii. *281*
See also Movement
NECESSITY, Different kinds of,
(1) Inherent, Mechanical,
Unconditional ; (2) Hypo-
thetical, Logical, Condi-
tional, i. 169, 179-187
NEXT - IN - SUCCESSION, with
and without contact, ii. *39,
41, 55, 93*
NON-EXISTENCE :
Absolute, Incidental, i. 85-91
Eternal, Temporal, i. 405, 407
Platonic view of, i. 91-95
NON-EXISTENT (in the Absolute
Sense)—
cannot move, ii. *17* ; but not
therefore at rest, ii. *365*
cannot have position, ii. *19*

435

INDEX

NOW:
Problems concerning, i. 373-377
a numerator, i. 387-391, 421, 423 ; *see also* 259
cannot be arrested, i. 389-393
Functions of, i. 409-413, 417-421
indivisible, ii. *117-121*
Loose usage of the term, i. 411, 413
Relation to Motion and Rest, ii. *121, 123, 173, 175*
Relation to Time, i. 373, 375, 383, 387-393, 401, 409-413 ; ii. *117-121, 277, 279*
retains identity through changing relations, i. 375, 389-395, 409
the same everywhere, i. 389
NUMBER:
has lower but not upper limit, i. 257, 259
No definite number unlimited, i. 233, 259, 419
Two senses of, i. 387, 395-399
NUMERICAL REGISTER—
of Movement, i. 387-391, 421, 423
of Time, i. 259, 385-391, 423

OLYMPIC GAMES, i. 249
ONE : *see* Identical, Same, Unit, Unity; *also* Verbal Ambiguity
OPPOSITES—
Positive, Negative, Contrary, Contradictory, ii. *15, 17, 31, 33, 37, 71-85* ; *see also* Antithesis, Extremes, Intermediates
OPPOSITION—
involves two terms, i. 81
See also Opposites
OPTICS, Relation to geometry, i. 121
ORIGINS = Beginnings :
Views of previous thinkers on, i. 15, 41-45; *see also* i. 221, 223

PARMENIDES :
on Coming to be, i. 91
on One Being, i. 24, 25
on Principles of Nature, i. 15, 51
on the Whole, i. 255
Unsound assumptions and deductions of, i. 29-33

PARTS : Actual and Potential—
Relation to Whole, i. 23, 45, 133, 221, 231, 243, 249, 373 ; ii. *257, 297*
PASSING AWAY : *see* Perishing
PAST, PRESENT, FUTURE : *see* Now, Time
PERISHING :
Qualified and unqualified, ii. *17*
a change but not a movement, ii. *19* ; *but see* ii. *157*
See also Genesis
PHYSICS = Natural Philosophy = Study of Nature:
compared to Mathematics, Astronomy, i. 119
Scope of, i. 119-127, 185, 223, 227, 277 ; ii. *293, 295*
Views of previous thinkers, i. 15, 31, 41, 43, 65, 119, 121, 217, 221-225, 237, 239 ; ii. *295, 395*
PLACE, LOCALITY, POSITION, SITE :
General discussion of, i. 277-327
Absolute, Relative, i. 243, 279, 281, 303, 315
Change of; *see* Locomotion
compared to form, to matter, i. 287-293, 299, 309-313
to limit, i. 287, 325
to vessel, i. 291, 299, 313, 315
to room, i. 289
Conception of Place dependent on Movement, i. 305
Cosmic Place exerts active influence, i. 279, 281, 303, 325, 327, 345 ; ii. *403* ; *see also* ii. *79*
Positive and negative characteristics of, i. 279, 289, 291, 299, 303, 309, 313, 315; *see also* i. 345
Perplexities concerning place discussed and smoothed out, i. 281-293, 303-325
Relation to Movement, i. 419; ii. *19, 173*
Summary of Characteristics of, i. 303
What constitutes being in a, i. 305, 307, 313, 315, 321-325
PLATO :
Principles of nature, i. 41, 93
on Infinity, i. 217, 221, 253
on Place, i. 289, 291
on Time, ii. *277*

INDEX

PLURALITY : *see* Multiplicity
POINT, POINTS :
  cannot be continuous, contiguous, or next in succession, ii. *93, 95, 337*
  Double function of Point—
    actual and potential, ii. *373-379* at which Mobile pauses, ii. *373, 375, 381*; at which Mobile turns back, ii. *377, 379* which divides Time, ii. *383*
  Single function of Point which divides States, ii. *383-387*
  Illimitable Points traversable only in accidental sense, ii. *383*
  See also Now
POLES : *see* Extremes
POSITION : *see* Place
POTENTIALITY :
  essentially incomplete, i. 205; ii. *331*
  inherent in actuality, i. 193, 197
  distinguished from actuality, ii. *373, 377, 383*
  Meaning of, i. 195
  Process of actualizing, i. 195-199, 205-213
    capable and incapable of completion, i. 247, 249, 259; ii. *297, 313, 315, 331*
  Process of actualizing potentiality by stages, ii. *313, 315*
  Unactualized, i. 193, 197, 327
POWER :
  Greater Power defined, ii. *411*
  Seat of limited, unlimited, ii. *411-417*
PRINCIPLES :
  have no ulterior cause, ii. *285*
  not attributes of something else, i. 63
  of Movement and Rest—
    Number and nature of Principles of, i. 15, 17, 51-67, 77-83, 93, 167; ii. *341, 353, 421-425*
  inherent in natural existents, i. 107, 109
PRIORITY, Different meanings of, ii. *357*
PROJECTILES = Missiles, i. 349, 351; ii. *417-423*
PROPAGATION, Capacity of, i. 115

PROPORTION : *see* Ratio
PURPOSE—
  accidentally missed, attained, i. 149-163, 175, 177
  main concern of physicists, i. 125, 185
  manifested in nature and art, i. 169-179, 185
PYTHAGOREANS—
  on Nature of the unlimited, i. 217, 219, 231

QUA, Meaning and use of, i. 87, 121, on Nature of the void, i. 333, 335 199, 229; ii. *123, 333, 337*
QUALITY :
  cannot exist by itself, i. 21, 49; ii. *245, 247*
  Change with respect to, i. 195; ii. *29*
  incidentally a quantum, i. 21; ii. *127, 133, 135*
QUANTITY :
  cannot exist by itself, i. 21; ii. *245, 247*
  Change of, i. 195, 333, 341; ii. *29, 31, 227, 355*; *see also* i. 367, 369
QUANTUM : *see* Magnitude
QUICK = Swift, and SLOW :
  applicable to counting, i. 397
  inapplicable to that which is counted, i. 397
  inapplicable to counters (abstract numbers), i. 397
QUICKER and SLOWER MOTION—
  Meaning and Nature of, i. 379, 401, 417; ii. *103-107*

RAREFACTION : *see* Condensation
RARITY : *see* Density
RATIO, PROPORTION :
  Equal, unequal Ratios, i. 261, 353-357; ii. *257-263*
  when non-existent, i. 353-357; ii. *281*
REALIZATION : *see* Actuality
RELATION :
  Excellences, defects, habits, understanding, etc., determined by Relations, ii. *233 239*
  not a subject of change, ii. *17-21, 233*

437

INDEX

REPULSION : *see* Attraction
RESOLUTION : *see* Condensation
REST :
a Principle of nature, i. 107, 109
exists in, occupies time, i. 405 ;
ii. *123, 173, 175*
measured by time, i. 405
Natural, unnatural, ii. *79, 83, 299*
not identical with unchangingness, i. 205, 405 ; ii. *73, 75,
123, 173, 175*
opposed to Motion, ii. *71, 73*
opposed to Rest in opposite state,
ii. *71, 73*
Process of being brought to, ii.
73, 169, 171
Zeno's definition of, ii. *181*
and Motion—
Continuous, intermittent, ii.
293-303, 347-357 ; *see also* ii.
363, 365
See also Locomotion (circular)
RESULT :
Necessary presuppositions, i. 181-
187
Normal, accidental, i. 149, 177, 179
RIGIDITY, not involved in unity,
i. 29
ROCK, Splitting of, ii. *295, 297*
ROTATION : *see* Locomotion (Circular)

SAKE, Two senses of 'for the sake
of,' i. 123, 125
SAME, Qualified and unqualified
sense, i. 213, 425, 427 ; ii.
45-49, 383
SCALE OF MEASUREMENT, i.
387
SHIP, Hauling, ii. *259, 297* ; *see also*
ii. *407-415*
SHORTAGE, i. 87-95, 117, 205
SLOW : *see* Quick
SLOWER : *see* Quicker
SPHERE, Rotating Sphere at rest
and in motion, i. 321, 323 ;
ii. *191, 401*
SQUARING THE CIRCLE, i. 17, 19
STANDARD MEASURE, i. 399,
401, 423, 425
STONE, Wearing of, ii. *295*
SUBJECT = Substratum = Matter,
i. 31, 41, 43, 61-65, 73-83, 91-
95, 109-113, 235 ; ii. *11, 13*

SUBSTANCE : *see* Subject
SUBSTANTIVE EXISTENCE : i.
21, 23, 35, 37, 63, 77, 109-113,
193, 195
SUBSTRATUM : *see* Subject
SUBTRACTION, of terms, limited
and illimitable, i. 249, 251
SUCCESSION : Orderly succession
implies proportion, ii. *231*
SUCCESSIONAL, distinguished
from continuous, ii. *55, 345*
SURFACE :
Identity of Surface of content
and continent, i. 307, 325 ; *see
also* Together
of Rotating sphere is at rest, i.
325
See also Limit, Place

TENUOUS, TENUITY : *see* Density
TERMS :
Persistent and non persistent, i.
71-75
Simple and complex, i. 71-75
THRUST :
Problem of Thrusts in vacancy,
i. 351, 357
Problem of successional Thrusts,
ii. *417, 423*
TIME :
General discussion, i. 373, 427
Duration of, i. 411 ; ii. *277*
Interdependence of Distance,
Motion and Time—
with respect to divisibility,
continuity, i. 385, 389, 399,
419 ; ii. *97-101, 107-111*
with respect to limitability,
i 259, 411 ; ii. *109-113, 277,
279* ; *see also* i. 247-251
What constitutes being in, i.
401-407, 417-421
Meaning of 'proper,' ii. *149*
Numerical register of, i. 259, 385-
391, 423, 425
Properties of, i. 377, 379, 389,
397, 421, 423
Reality of, i. 373, 415
Relation to consciousness, i. 383,
385, 419, 421
Relation of motive force to
movement conditioned by,
ii. *415*

INDEX

TIME (contd.)—
Relation to Motion, ii. *121, 123*
Time an aspect of Motion, i.
391; ii. *279*
Time and Motion inseparable,
but not identical, i. 379, 383,
387, 405
Time the measure of Motion:
(with respect to duration), i.
399, 401, 405, 423; (with respect to velocity), i. 401, 405,
417, 423; ii. *103-109*
Time measured by uniform
Motion, i. 399, 423
Relation to Rest, ii. *121, 123*
Time the measure of Rest, i.
405
TOGETHER defined, ii. *35*; see
also i. 25-31, 359
TOUCHING: see Contiguous
TRANSLATION: see Locomotion
(Rectilinear)
TREND:
Natural Trends of elements, i.
279, 303
affect velocity, i. 357; ii. *79,
403*
differentiate subjects, i. 345,
349
not due to vacancy, i. 345, 365
TYXH: meaning and scope of τύχη
and αὐτόματον, i. 157-163

UNCHANGINGNESS, MOTION-
LESSNESS, not Synonymous
with Rest, i. 205, 405; ii.
73, 75, 123, 173, 175
UNDERSTANDING = Know-
ledge:
What constitutes, i. 11, 129; ii.
237
UNION: see Verbal Ambiguity
UNIT = One: Numerical, quantitive, substantival, i. 19-27,
257, 397, 399, 423; ii. *45-61*;
see also ii. *337*
UNITY:
Multiplicity in; see Multiplicity
What constitutes Unity of movement, ii. *49, 55, 61, 373, 379,
381*
UNIVERSE:
is not Homogeneous, i. 31, 37
Outside the, i. 217, 225, 251

rotates, i. 323
Supposed Origin of, i. 145; ii.
269, 277
is unmoved, i. 241, 323
is unplaced, i. 323
Views of previous thinkers on
the, i. 21, 29, 31
UNLIMITED: see Illimitable
'UNMOVED,' not identical with
'at rest,' i. 205, 405; ii. *73,
75, 123, 173, 175*
UPWARD, DOWNWARD—
Tendency, i. 315; ii. *315*

VACANCY: see Void
VACUITY: see Void
VELOCITY:
Bearing on theory of the void,
i. 351-357, 367
of parts of rotating sphere, ii.
195
measured by time, i. 401, 405,
417, 423; ii. *103-109*
VERBAL AMBIGUITY, AM-
BIGUOUS, EQUIVOCAL,
PRIMARY AND DERIVED
USE OF TERMS—
Affection (πάθος), ii. *11, 13*
After, i. 417-421
Before, i. 385, 417-421
Become, i. 85
Beginning, i. 29
Being, i. 25, 31-39
Cannot, ii. *201*
Coming to be, i. 75, 85, 87-91
Come out of, i. 49, 75, 85-89
Consists of, i. 49
Double, ii. *245, 247*
End, i. 123; ii. *55*
Equal, ii. *247, 253, 255*
Existent, i. 19-23
Exists in, i. 401-405
Form, i. 117
γίγνεσθαι, i. 75
Illimitable, no Limit, i. 227, 247-
251; ii. *111*
In, i. 293-299, 305, 307, 325, 401-
405, 417
Indivisible, i. 23, 229, 231; ii.
201, 337, 407, 425
Into (turn into), i. 85, 89
Is, Isn't, i. 25, 31, 33, 39, 247;
ii. *17*

INDEX

VERBAL AMBIGUITY, etc.
(*contd.*)—
Much, Little, i. 399; ii. *245, 247*
Nature, i. 117
Non-existent, i. 63, 87-91, 407
One, i. 19-27; ii. *45-61, 247*
Priority, ii. *357*
Quick, ii. *245*
Same, ii. *247, 251, 253*; *see also* Identical
Sharp, ii. *245*
Sweet, ii. *247, 251*
Turns into, i. 85, 89
Union, ii. *41*
Unity, i. 23; ii. *49, 61*
White, ii. *189, 247*
VESSEL, not part of its own content, i. 299
VOID = Vacancy :
Analogy with Place, i. 329, 339, 345, 347, 361, 365
Grounds for belief in, i. 329-335
shown to be invalid, i. 339-361, 367-371
Previous refutations inadequate, i. 329, 331
Meaning and nature of, i. 281, 331, 337, 339, 349
Problem of velocity and zero resistance, i. 351-357, 365, 367
Supposed function of, i. 333, 339, 365, 371

Supposed relation—
to Condensation and Expansion, i. 333, 341, 343, 363-369
to Displacement, i. 359, 361
to Locomotion, i. 341, 345-349; ii. *403*

WATER :
Clocks, i. 331
Relation to air, i. 327; ii. *315*
WHOLE :
Concrete, i. 11, 13
Continuous, discontinuous, i. 23-27
contrasted with unlimited, i. 253, 255
Relation to part, i. 23-27, 45, 133, 221, 231, 243, 249, 373; ii. *257, 297, 333, 337*

XUTHUS, i. 363

ZENO :
Refutations of Zeno's dilemmas, concerning—
Place, i. 299
Dichotomy, Achilles—
Preliminary, ii. *111, 181, 183*
Final, ii. *379-383*
Flying Arrow, ii. *181, 183, 185*
Stadium, ii. *185-189*
on Relation of Parts to Whole, ii. *261*